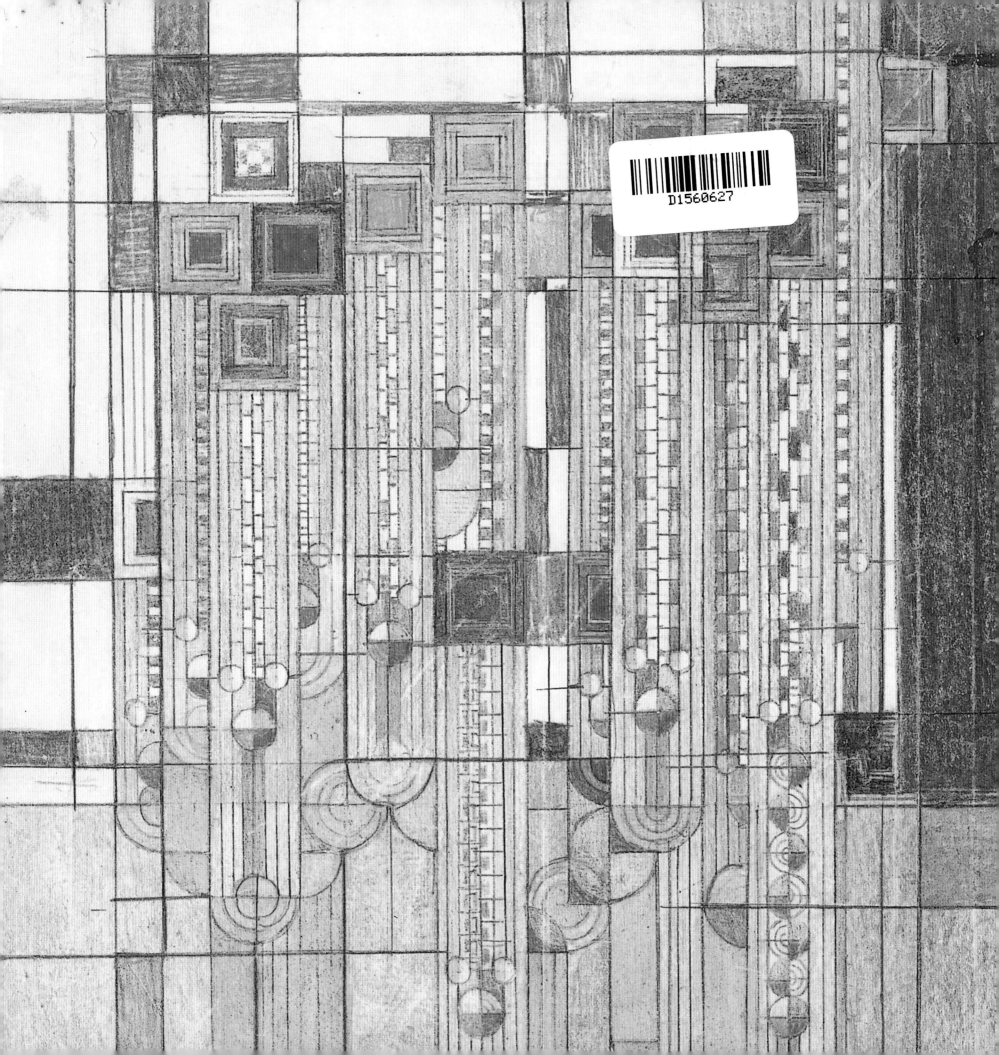

FRANK LLOYD WRIGHT DESIGNS

THE SKETCHES, PLANS AND DRAWINGS

NORTHEAST ELEVATION

TERRACE

NORTHWEST ELEVATION

FRANK LLOYD WRIGHT DESIGNS
THE SKETCHES, PLANS AND DRAWINGS

BRUCE BROOKS PFEIFFER

In association with the
FRANK LLOYD WRIGHT FOUNDATION

RIZZOLI
NEW YORK

New York · Paris · London · Milan

First published in the United States of America in 2011 by
RIZZOLI INTERNATIONAL PUBLICATIONS, INC.
300 Park Avenue South, New York, NY 10010
www.rizzoliusa.com

ISBN-13: 978-0-8478-3570-6
Library of Congress Control Number: 2011929620

© 2011 Rizzoli International Publications, Inc.
Text © 2011 Bruce Brooks Pfeiffer
Frank Lloyd Wright drawings © 2011
The Frank Lloyd Wright Foundation, Scottsdale, AZ.

Endpapers: Cover design for *Liberty*, "Saguaro Forms
and Cactus Flowers" (p.412). FLLW FDN #2604.010.
Page 1: Resort Inn and Tourist Facility. (See p.302.)
FLLW FDN # 4822.001.
Pages 2-3: Perspective for Raul Bailleres House.
(See p.136.) FLLW FDN # 5202.014.
Pages 4-5: Arizona State Capital (see p.354).
Perspective. FLLW FDN # 5732.006.

Designed by **ABIGAIL STURGES GRAPHIC DESIGN**

Distributed to the U. S. Trade by Random House, New York

Printed and bound in China

2011 2012 2013 2014 2015 2016/10 9 8 7 6 5 4 3 2 1

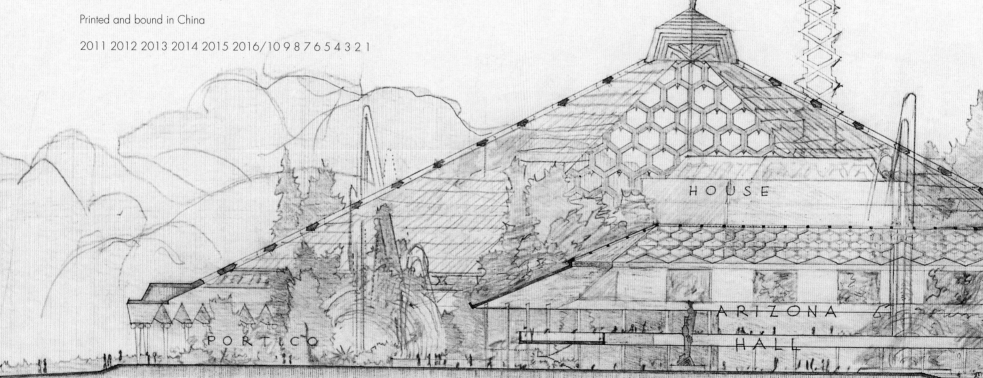

CARILLON &
TELEVISION

HOUSE

ARIZONA

HALL

PORTICO

PRO BONO PUBLICO ARIZONA
FRANK LLOYD WRIGHT ARCHITECT
LONGITUDINAL SECTION
SCALE : 1" = 16'-0"

CONTENTS

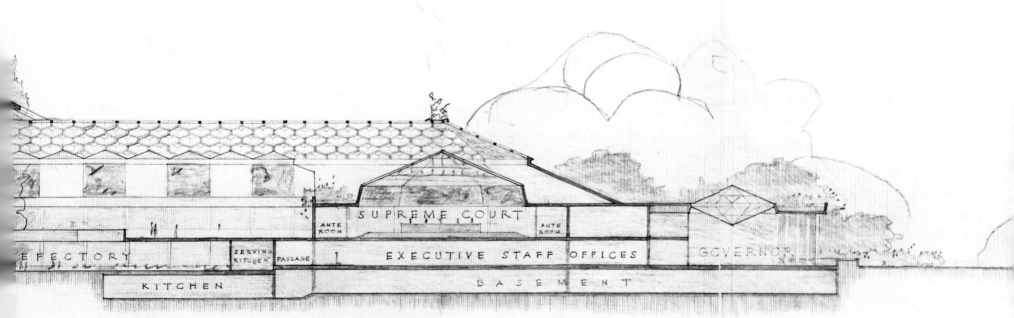

A NOTE ABOUT THE DRAWINGS

When a drawing or design for a building was made but not executed or constructed, the word project follows the title and date of a design throughout the headings in this volume. All other illustrations included in this book are designs for structures that were built, even if the buildings were subsequently demolished.

THE RED SQUARE

Frank Lloyd Wright chose the red square as his personal mark, or symbol, of approval. Rendered in red color pencil, the square appears on his drawings, both presentation drawings and construction documents. When signed and dated by him it signified his approval of the completed drawing. Later in life he sometimes placed the red square, initials, and date, on conceptual drawings. An event in his boyhood prompted this passion for the red square. In his autobiography he wrote:

"Always he was the one who knew where the tall, red lilies could be found afloat on tall meadow-grass. Where nuts and berries abounded, there he would be.

"The spot of red made by a lily on the green always gave him an emotion. Later, the red square as a spot of flame-red, became the crest with which he signed his drawings and marked his buildings."

—Frank Lloyd Wright

ACKNOWLEDGMENTS

William Blake once wrote "No man flies high on his own wings." For the work on this book I gratefully acknowledge my two editors at Rizzoli, David Morton and Douglas Curran, and my co-workers in the Frank Lloyd Wright Archives, Indira Berndtson, Oskar R. Munoz, and Margo L. Stipe. I am especially grateful to Oskar for his diligence and dedicated work in the preparation of the films of the Frank Lloyd Wright drawings in this book. Their assiduous work made this book possible.

A NOTE ABOUT THE NUMBERING OF THE DRAWINGS

Shortly after the death of Frank Lloyd Wright, some of his apprentices undertook the task of assigning file numbers to Wright's work. These are referred to as Project Record Numbers (PR#), referenced throughout in captions preceded by "FLLW FDN #"—for Frank Lloyd Wright Foundation number. The first two digits in a given number represent the year in which the work was begun (although recent research has often found the initial dating to be different from the actual year for which a work was begun; for convenience the original dating has been kept). The next two digits represent the sequence within that year, usually following an alphabetical order using the client(s) name. Following the decimal point, the three spaces represent the number (from 001 to 999) assigned for each drawing. If there are four spaces following the decimal point, they represent the number of the photograph assigned for that same work.

CARMEL
FOR MR AND MRS HALDORN
"THE WAVE" FRANK LLOYD WRIGHT

What is architecture anyway? Is it a vast collection of the various buildings which have been built to please the varying tastes of the various lords of mankind? No. I think not. I know that architecture is life; or at least it is life itself taking form and therefore is the truest record of life as it was lived in the world yesterday, as it is being lived today, or ever will be lived. So architecture I know to be a great spirit. No, it is not something which consists of the buildings which have been built by man on his earth. Architecture is that great living creative spirit which from generation to generation, from age to age, proceeds, persists, creates, according to the nature of man, and his circumstances as they both change. That really is architecture.[1]

Previous pages: Haldorn House. (See p.116.) Perspective. FLLW FDN # 4502.006.

Right: An early engineering drawing. FLLW FDN # 8501.001.

Frank Lloyd Wright's career in the art and craft of architecture endured for close to three-quarters of a century, from 1893 to 1959. In all of that work, be it large or small, he is well known today by those buildings which were built. For those projects which were never constructed, in recent years exhibitions and publications have brought a wider awareness of his designs for residences, commercial buildings, religious structures, hotels, resorts—all manner of buildings—which range across the whole gamut of building construction, and further to schemes that appear as out-of-this-world visionary concepts. In all, his aim was to create architecture for mankind as an inspiration, belonging to its time and place, and endowing beauty and repose along with respect for nature and the environment. He called architecture the mother art, and maintained that a nation without an architecture of its own was without a culture of its own. In this sense, he truly created an American architecture and gave to the nation a culture belonging to it rather than something adapted as an import from abroad.

His mother, always in love with architecture, was convinced, even before he was born, that her child would be a son, and grow up to become an architect who would build beautiful buildings. She nurtured this concept all throughout his childhood years. Later in life, when he was sometimes questioned as to why he chose to become an architect, he would reply, "I had nothing to do with the choice, it was my mother who decided it for me, even before I was born." It may appear to be a rather flippant answer, but it was the one he clung to all his life. And of course history has proven her correct, even to a degree that she could never have imagined.

At the age of 19, he enrolled in the University of Wisconsin, Madison. There was no College of

Architecture at that time, therefore he subscribed to a course of engineering under Professor Allan D. Conover. Besides being a member of the faculty, Conover was an engineer and Wright worked part-time in his office. In the classwork, he was assigned problems in engineering drawing. Three of them have survived, and they reveal him, even at that age, as a highly skilled draftsman. They also tell a rather personal story. Early in the school term, the first drawing is initialed F.Li.W., signifying the name Frank Lincoln Wright, which his father had given him. A later drawing (at right) is initialed, however, as F.LL.W. At this point in time, somewhere near the end of 1886 or beginning of 1887, Wright's father, William Carey Wright, had left the family, never to return. The young Wright then took on the name of his mother's family, Lloyd, in place of Lincoln. From then on he would be forever known as Frank Lloyd Wright.

Anxious to pursue a career in architecture, Wright found that Madison seemed to him to offer no future. Therefore in the spring of 1887, soon to turn 20, he left home and went to Chicago. The city was rebuilding after the disastrous fire of 1871. Here the American skyscraper was being born. Great architects were building great buildings, and Wright wanted to be a part of that energy. After a brief period of time working for different architects, he finally decided to try for a job at the firm of Adler and Sullivan. They were in the midst of producing drawings for the Chicago Auditorium. At his first meeting with Louis Sullivan, who was Dankmar Adler's designing partner, Sullivan advised Wright to prepare some drawings as an example of his skill. Wright went home and then returned with drawings. One has survived, an elevation of the house, at the bottom of which Wright later inscribed, "Drawing shown to Lieber Meister

when applying for a job." (Lieber Meister is the term he used, later in life, when speaking to, or writing of, Louis Sullivan.) If the engineering drawing shows his skill as a draftsman, here, a year later, he is shown as an architect, and one with great talent. Certain elements of this drawing prevail in all his subsequent residential work: the building lies comfortably on the land, belonging to it, not propped up as houses were at that time. The relationship between building and landscape is carefully balanced, the trees and foliage gracefully compliment the design, nature and architecture are well married to each other. The image, now over one hundred years old, lies almost precipitously on the paper. Olgivanna, Wright's third wife, who survived him for 28 years, wrote of this particular drawing, "It is like an exquisite poem. Its lines are so delicate, so tender that it looks as though the sheer transparent spirit of a building had settled lightly on the paper. One's breath is held lest it vanish. Such was the power of Frank Lloyd Wright's genius."[2]

Sullivan had no idea who this 20-year-old young man from Wisconsin was, but he instantly recognized a pronounced skill for design, and this was at a time when he urgently needed help for the interior decorative designs for the Chicago Auditorium. Wright was hired and soon elevated to the position of "Chief of Design," to the chagrin, and in some cases, jealousy, of other, older draftsmen in the Adler and Sullivan office.

Wright quickly caught on to the character of Sullivan's genius in creating decoration. Another drawing that illustrates this ability of his to make designs in the manner of Sullivan is a fragment that exists in Wright's hand for a decorative detail (following page), explained as "Fragment of bronze newel post head—Auditorium—Chicago."

Shade & Shadow of a Surface of Revolution
generated by the revolution of a Parabola about its axis. F.LL.W.

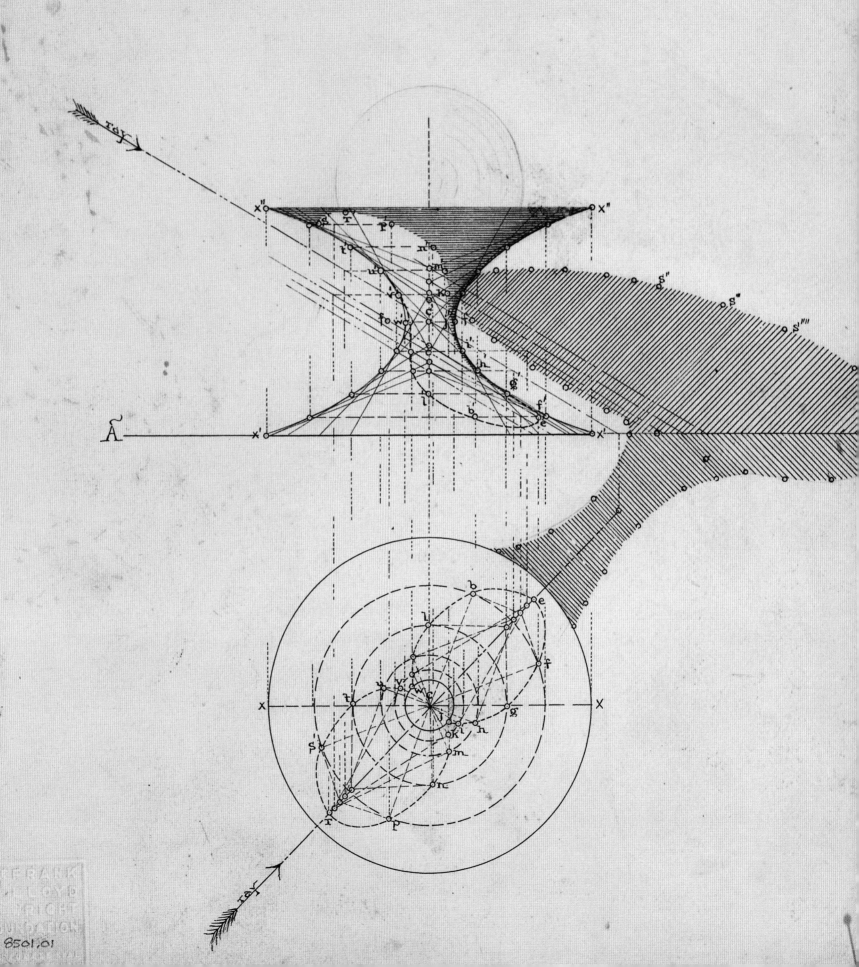

Above: Decorative detail.
FLLW FDN # 8801.001.
Right: Drawing prepared by Wright for
architect Louis Sullivan when applying
for a job with Adler & Sullivan in 1887.
FLLW FDN # 8701.001.

Wright was soon married and desired to build his own home in the Chicago suburb of Oak Park. Sullivan prepared a special contract to help the young man finance his home, and Wright's drawings for the house are titled "House to be Built at the Corner of Forest Avenue & Chicago Ave." It was a simple A-frame Shingle Style house, much in the manner of Shingle Style houses that were being constructed in the nation at that time. What is significant about the house, however, is that it does not hark back to any of the traditional or Victorian styles prevalent around Chicago and its suburbs. It also took great pains to use materials according to their nature: brick was treated as brick, wood as wood, shingles as shingles. No paint or wallpapering, the interiors were plain and simple by contrast to other homes, but rich in architectural details. His design for the dining room ceiling light grille was perhaps the first example of indirect lighting in a home anywhere. The design (following page, at left), made by him freehand with quill pen, is strongly Sullivanesque in character, as would be

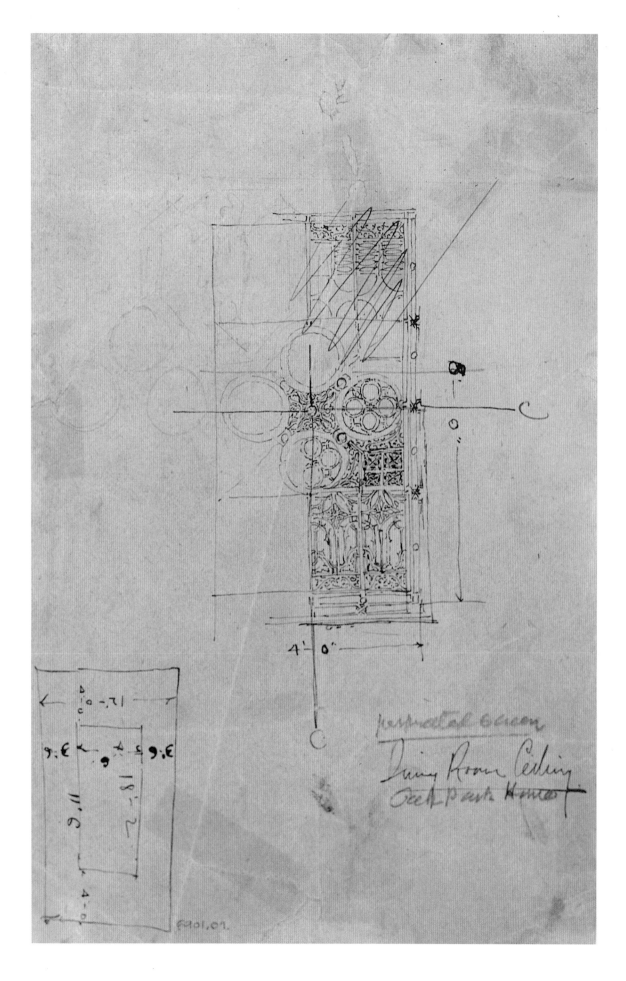

several of his decorative designs at the beginning of his career until he had mastered his own "vocabulary."

After spending close to seven years in the Adler and Sullivan firm, in 1893 Wright established his own architectural practice with offices in downtown Chicago, and in 1897 he added a studio to his home in Oak Park, known as the "Oak Park Workshop." By the end of the century, he had established his practice in the designs of what he called "The New Architecture of the Middle West." An important component of that was his residential work, in which he created an entirely new concept of what the American home should be. Those homes came to be called "Prairie Houses" because of the way in which they belonged on the prairie environment of the Chicago suburbs. The popular magazine *Ladies' Home Journal* commissioned him to make a design for "A Home in a Prairie Town." Two drawings reveal at this early stage his lucid ability to make a conceptual elevation of the house, with pencil on paper (following pages, bottom), and then follow it up with a formal presentation perspective with watercolor on art paper (following pages, top). Later in life he made it clear that the final rendering was his, when he inscribed along the bottom edge "FLLW del." (Frank Lloyd Wright delineator).

Of this ability to put down the idea for any building, he once explained to his apprentices: "I never sit down to a drawing board—and this has been a lifelong practice of mine—until I have the whole thing in my mind. I may alter it substantially, I may throw it away, I may find I'm up a blind alley, but unless I have the idea pretty well in shape, you won't see me at the drawing board with it."[3]

If his first idea set down on paper seemed the correct solution, it was then carried on to final

drawings. Those final drawings, the perspectives and plans that were made to show his clients, were mostly produced by his draftsmen in the early years, but after 1932 by the apprentices of the Taliesin Fellowship, those young men and women who gathered around him to learn the art and craft of architecture by working closely at his side. In many cases he carefully went over the final presentation drawings and added details to them to further embellish the images. The drawing for the Stuart Haldorn House (see pp. 8-9) is an example of this. Apprentice John deKoven Hill has made the perspective, Wright then added the foliage, the rocks at the shore, and the extended arcs over the view of the house. A large part of the great perspectives made after 1932 were drawn by apprentice John H. Howe, such as the Arizona State Capitol (above). Howe had the remarkable gift to quickly grasp the idea that Wright had conceptualized and then render it into a final perspective drawing. This gift of his, really sheer genius, produced drawings that Wright often simply initialed, signifying his approval, without adding to them or editing them.

The production of the working drawings, those documents prepared to explain the

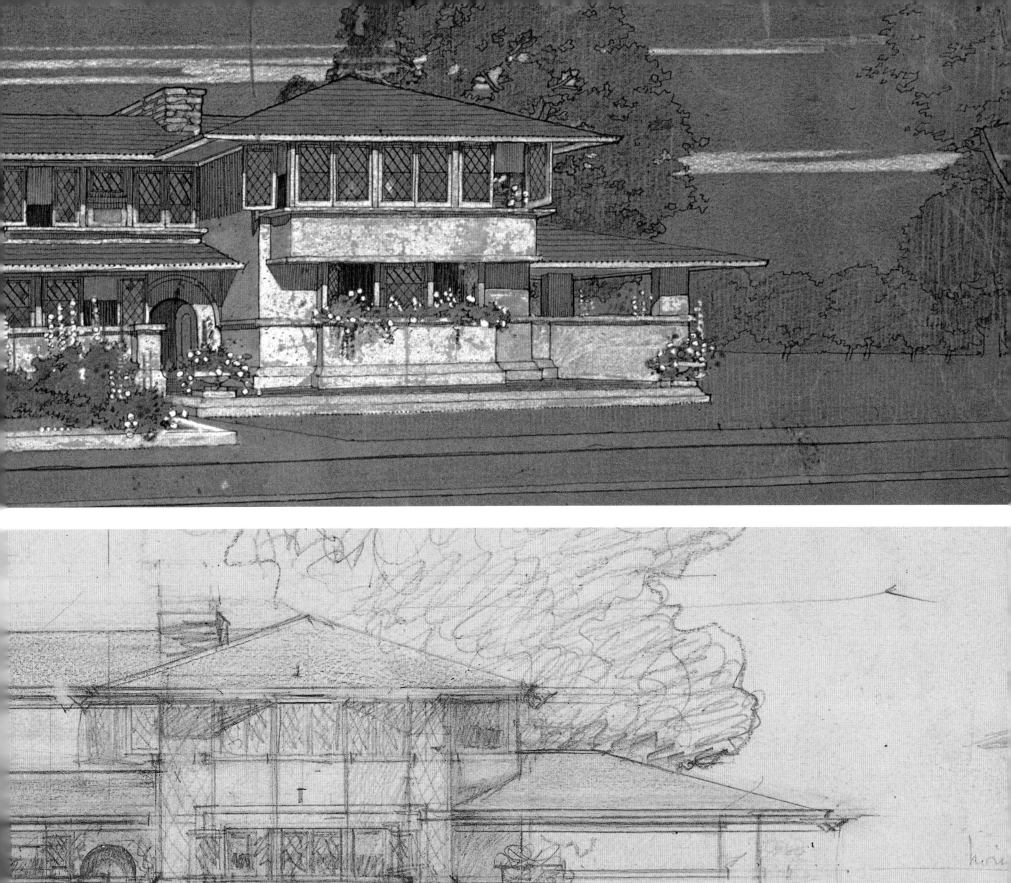

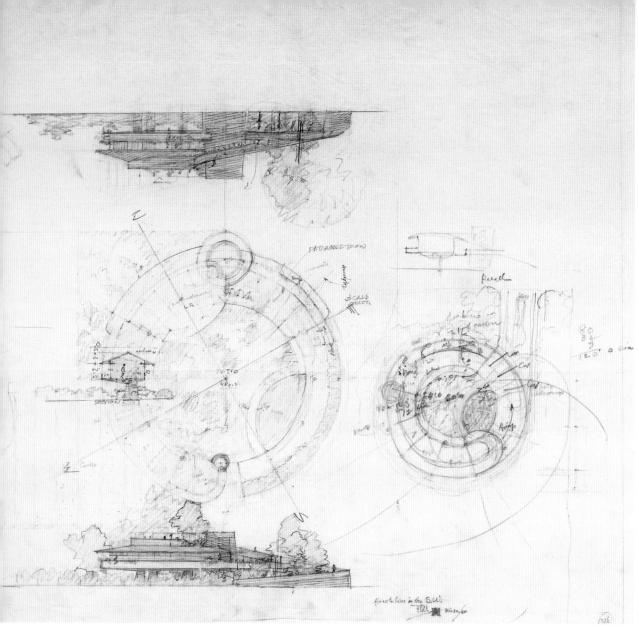

Early plan, section, and elevation. David Wright House. Phoenix, Arizona. 1950. FLLW FDN # 5011.001.

architectural and structural details necessary for the construction of the building, were prepared by draftsmen during the early years and by apprentices thereafter.

From the collection of drawings in the Frank Lloyd Wright Archives, several hundred have been published and exhibited. In general, those chosen were the dramatic and intriguing perspectives. They form a rich treasure of beautiful finished drawings. But to delve further, to study how those finished drawings originally came from the mind of the architect, reveals an equally rich treasure of first sketches.

Wright's conceptual drawings, those first sketches, are unique in that many of them convey

his ideas in minute detail. From those drawings, his draftsmen and apprentices were able to go further and develop the project. A remarkable example of this process is the drawing for the David Wright House (above), which Wright noted on the conceptual drawing as "How to live in the SW [Southwest]." From this drawing, with its careful notation of measurements, Howe was then able to translate that sketch into final drawings (above right).

At times his first sketch was indeed merely a sketch, which he later developed before turning it over to his apprentices. In 1958 he received the commission to design a chapel for the University of Oklahoma campus. When the idea was

fixed in his mind, he made a preliminary sketch on a piece of mail that was lying on his desk (p. 20, top left). He then made a more detailed plan (p. 20, bottom left), and followed that with a conceptual elevation (not shown). On the elevation he named the work "Trinity Chapel" and initialed the drawing. The comparison between the original sketch and this elevation is truly remarkable, and it fully illustrates Wright's ability to progress from a first sketch to a final solution—the idea was clearly consistent from beginning to end. Since the plan was based on the triangle, Wright named the chapel "Trinity." Because of the complex nature of the design, three preliminary perspectives were made

showing the chapel from different angles, after which apprentice Allen Lape Davison produced the final rendering (pp. 20-21, right). Unfortunately the clients were more disposed to a conventional solution, and the project was dropped. Realizing this, he wrote them, "My dear Mr. and Mrs. Jones: I have completely misunderstood the nature of the commission I was happy to receive . . . So I take it what I have done does not please you. Since I have no interest in a conventional chapel you may consider yourself entirely free to consider the episode closed. I will take my labor for my pains and hope to build the 'non-sectarian' elsewhere. Sometime. Sincerely yours and sorry. Frank Lloyd Wright."[4]

The question arises: are those great drawings that have become so well known his, or his draftsmen's and apprentices'? Quite truthfully they are mainly the work of those draftsmen and apprentices. Throughout his career, he was indeed fortunate to have highly skilled artists and draftsmen working alongside him as a fine production team. This team was not only capable of making elegant drawings, but also of producing what were then called the working drawings, those documents and specifications needed to build the building. After all, it was Wright's aim to design and build fine buildings, not draw beautiful drawings. He had, however, very pronounced ideas of what those drawings should

look like, at what angle the view should be made, how it should lay on the paper, the general tone of color, et cetera. Those instructions he conveyed to his draftsmen, and he carefully oversaw the work they produced as it went along. There are several examples where different perspectives, at different angles, were prepared to show him until he selected the one to be finally made. Be that as it may, those beautiful drawings were, for him, but a means to an end: to present the building to the client in order to get the building built. But where his genius in design is most apparent is in this far more unknown and often overlooked category: his original sketches, where his ideas first came onto paper.

19

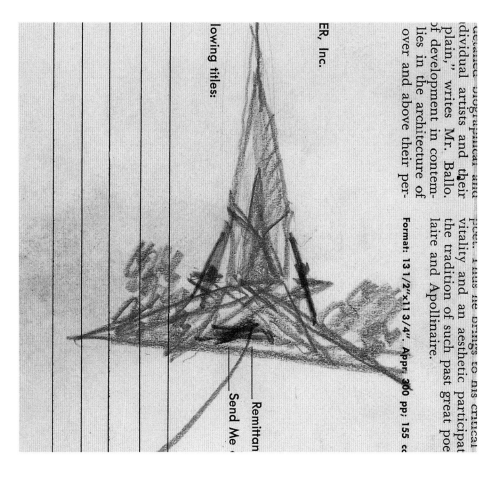

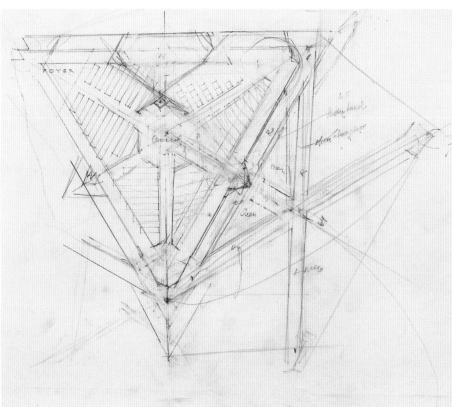

Trinity Chapel.
Norman,
Oklahoma.
1958, Project.
Top left: Preliminary
sketch. FLLW FDN
5810.002.
Left: Plan. FLLW FDN
5810.003. Right:
Perspective. FLLW
FDN # 5810.001.

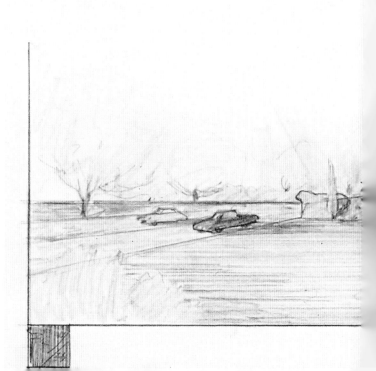

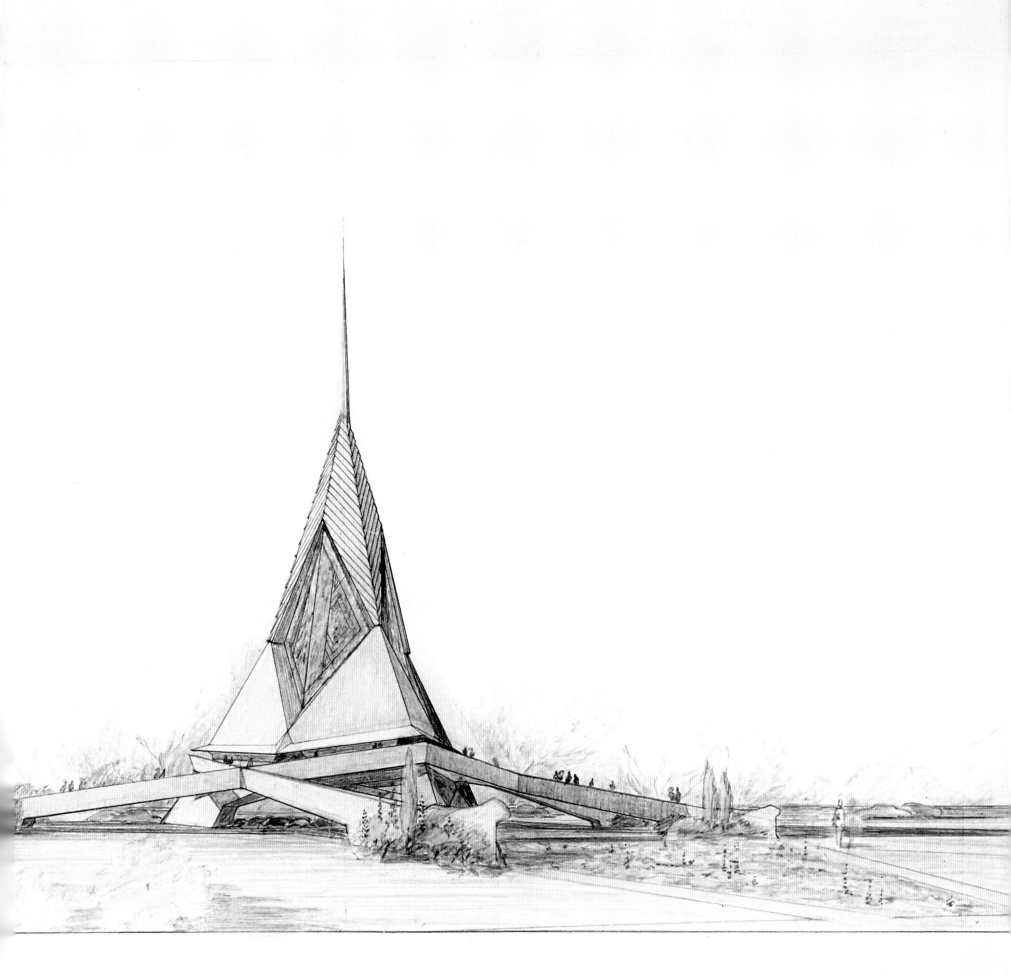

PART ONE

THE DWELLING PLACE

The greater part of Frank Lloyd Wright's architectural work was residential. From the very start of his career, clients came to him wishing for designs for their homes. While working in the office of Adler and Sullivan, he undertook residential work that came to that office. The firm preferred to build more commercial work, and if a friend or commercial client came to them for a house design, they turned it over to Wright. At the same time, he was married, building a home in the suburb of Oak Park, and raising a family. To help with the costs of these ventures, he undertook private residential work of his own, on his own time, and at home. The houses that he built during this period have come to be known as "the bootleg houses." When Sullivan learned about this, he confronted Wright with the fact that doing designs on his own was a breach of contract. Wright insisted that the work was done outside the offices of Adler and Sullivan, and on his own time. Sullivan did not accept this reasoning. The discussion between the two of them became vitriolic, and Wright quit.

In 1893 Wright opened his architectural practice in the Schiller Building, in Chicago, later known as the Garrick Theater, a building designed by Adler and Sullivan.

In his autobiography, Wright wrote: "W. H. Winslow of the Winslow Ornamental Iron Works had often been to Adler and Sullivan's to consult with me about the work at that office. W. H. turned up now to give me my first job. I was to be the architect of his new home at River Forest. I could hardly believe I really had a job. Difficult to believe the initiative I had taken was now a reality. But I soon enough found out that it was."[1]

It was a most remarkable design, and Wright later described it:

"The Winslow House had burst on the view of that provincial suburb like the Prima Vera in full bloom. It was new to Oak Park and River Forest. That house became an attraction, far and near. Incessantly it was courted and admired. Ridiculed, too, of course. Ridicule is always modeled on the opposite side of that shield."[2]

What prompted the design for the W. H. Winslow house? He explained:

"As I had regularly gone to and fro between Oak Park and my work with Adler and Sullivan in Chicago, here at hand was the typical American dwelling, the 'monogoria' of earlier days, standing about the Chicago prairie. That dwelling got there somehow and became typical. But by any faith in nature, implicit or explicit, it did not belong there. . . It has no sense of Unity at all nor any such sense of space as should belong to a free man among free people in a free country. It was stuck up and stuck on, however it might be done. Wherever it happened to be. To take one of those so-called 'homes' away would have improved the landscape and cleared the atmosphere. . . My first feeling therefore had been a yearning for simplicity. A new sense of simplicity as 'organic.' This had barely begun to take shape in my mind when the Winslow house was planned. But now it began in practice. Organic simplicity might be seen producing significant character in the harmonious order we call nature. Beauty in growing things. None were insignificant."[3]

The houses represented here begin with his own studio in Oak Park, Illinois. In 1889 he built his first home, a building in the Shingle Style prevalent at that region, but not related to any traditional or particular "style." The studio was later attached to it as he desired to have his place of work close to his home.

The range of houses spreads across the years of his career and also across the nation. The selection ends with a private residence he was drawing five days before his death on April 9, 1959.

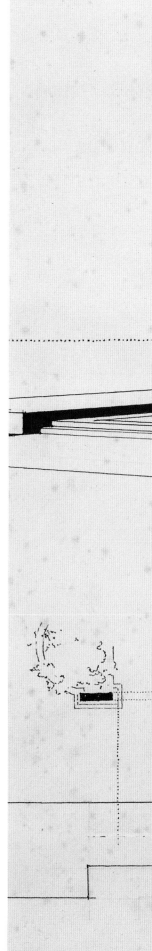

W. H. Winslow House. Oak Park, Illinois. 1893. Perspective and plan. FLLW FDN # 9305.001.

FRANK LLOYD WRIGHT HOME AND STUDIO

Oak Park, Illinois. 1889–1909

By 1897, he had undertaken the design of Luxfer prisms. The name Luxfer was derived from the Latin words "lux" (light) and "ferre" (to carry). The Luxfer Prism Company, headquartered in Chicago, manufactured four-inch squares of prismatic glass. These were installed in office windows, and they cast light further into the rooms, providing natural light in areas that before, far from the windows, were relatively dark. They were also embedded in sidewalks, to bring light into the basements of buildings where the lower levels reached out beneath the sidewalks.

The prisms were used widely throughout the Midwest. Wright's geometric designs for them were filed October 23, 1897, and patented in his name, "Frank L. Wright, Chicago," in the 1897 Official Gazette of the U. S. Patent Office.

Their successful use earned him such a substantial income that he was able to add a studio-workshop to his home in Oak Park, Illinois.

The building was in three main sections: reception, library, and drafting room, with a private office for Wright and a brick vault for drawings. The reception was in the center, with a

glorious stained-glass skylight, rich in autumnal colors. The octagonal library with high clerestory windows was the place where he met his clients and showed them the drawings. The drafting room was a unique space in which an octagonal balcony was hung by means of chains from the rafters in the ceiling, thus freeing the space below from what would have been necessary columns or piers. His first sketch presents not only the conceptual elevation, but also a drawing covered with details about construction and calculations, while the final drawing is a perspective (above).

Above: Perspective. FLLW FDN # 9506.001.
Right: Preliminary sketch. FLLW FDN # 9506.002.

The complex was adjacent to his home and connected by a passageway, in which an existing tree was allowed to grow through the area and out onto the roof above.

In time, the working element and residence of this complex came to be known as the "Frank Lloyd Wright Oak Park Home and Studio." But in Wright's time, he always referred to the work part as "The Oak Park Workshop," for in it there was both design work and the production of drawings and specifications needed to construct his buildings.

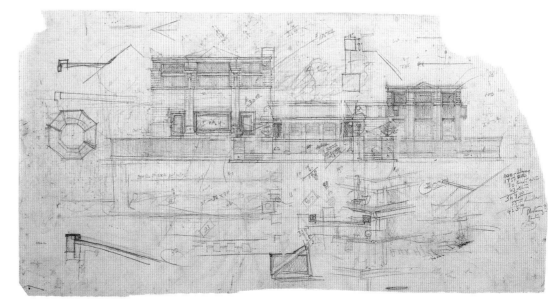

ISIDORE HELLER HOUSE

Chicago, Illinois. 1896

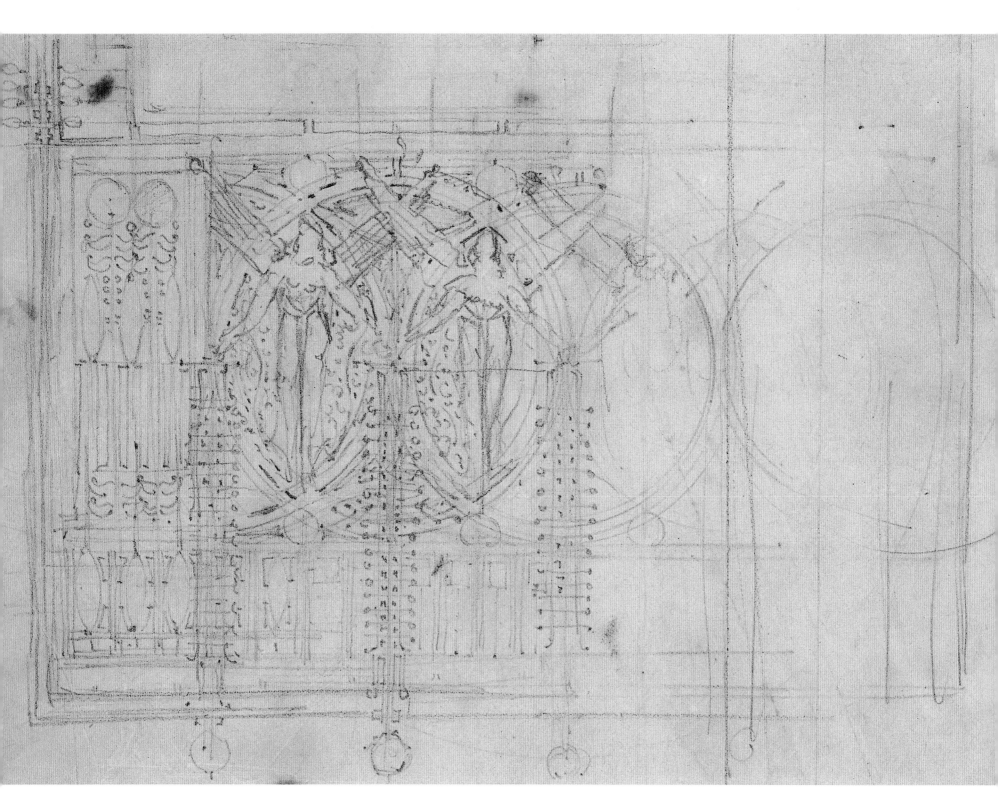

Left: Ornamental frieze detail. FLLW FDN # 9609.002.
Above: Elevation. FLLW FDN # 9606.001.

Following pages: Perspective. FllW FDN # 9606.005.

The long, narrow lot for the Isidore Heller house dictated a likewise long, narrow design, and the need for a third story to accommodate a playroom. This is not really a "prairie house" as such, but certain elements here foretell how those same elements would have strong significance in later works. One element is the line of continuing windows on the second story, or bedroom level. Up to that time, windows in houses were treated as holes punched in the walls. Wright was trying to get away from that tradition and bring more light into the rooms by means of extended windows grouped together (above). The ground-floor level is rather monumental in character, with a doorway framed in white stone set in relief against the gray Roman brick. The windows on this level reiterate this detail, framed in stone, but this time simpler, without the sculptural details of the entry (following page). A frieze runs along the exterior of the third level, its design still much in the idiom of Louis Sullivan (left).

In general, Wright's careful treatment of material is strongly evident in this house, as is also the manner in which the house is placed on the ground. This was in the era where the first floor was propped up aboveground so that the basement windows could receive daylight, a detail offensive to Wright, like some sort of "eyes" blinking at you through the shrubbery planted against them to somewhat conceal them. "So the universal 'cellar' showed itself above ground as a bank of some kind of masonry running around the whole, for the house to sit up on—like a chair."[4] However, in order to provide the necessary daylight for the basement, he created "wells" at ground level, out from the building but with walls of the same material as the building.

Along with the Winslow House, the Heller House reveals Wright's sense of scale, fine proportions, and an elegant use of materials.

RIOR WALLS FACED WITH VITRIFIED BUFF
RSE GREY BRICK ALTERNATE WITH BUFF AT
PERFORATED APRON DROPPED INSIDE OUT
ED TILES ALL HORIZONTAL JOINTS WHITE

OMAN BRICK ✦ BETWEEN SECOND AND THIRD STO

C STORY TREATED IN HIGH RELIEF SOFFITS P

R BAND ✦ TRIMMINGS GREY STONE ✦ ROOF COV

TICAL JOINTS COLOR OF BRICK ✦ ✦ ✦ ✦ ✦

JOSEPH HUSSER HOUSE

Chicago, Illinois. 1899, Demolished

Although few early sketches of the Joseph Husser House remain, Wright's final rendering is here included because of the significance of this design. Tragically, the house was demolished, and the final set of working drawings underwent severe water damage at one time. Conservation on the drawings was tedious and difficult, however it stabilized them; but still they remain faded and difficult to read. Why then this house, for which there is even less photography than for most of Wright's early work?

The Husser House can arguably be considered his first "Prairie house," built on what was then Chicago's elegant and highly fashionable South Side. The plan reveals that here Wright is opening interior space, what would later be called "the open plan." The main floor, containing entrance hall, living room, porch, dining room, kitchen, and servants' quarters, is raised to a second level, with heater, laundry, and storage on the ground level. Thus raised, the rooms command a greater view of the flat prairie and distant Lake Michigan. He would employ this same idea of raising the main level above a ground-floor level in other subsequent Prairie houses, among them the Thomas, Heurtley, Coonley, Tomek, and Robie houses to site a few that were built and remain today.

Another important detail in the Husser House that would become a steady application in most of Wright's residential work is the treatment of the extended soffit, or edge of the roof, projecting out over the windows. The decorative elements and the arches on the top level are examples of the influence, at this time in his work, of Louis Sullivan.

The house also reveals his careful treatment of materials, in which each is handled in accordance with its own nature. On the presentation drawing, for example, is carefully inscribed the use of materials. This is a rare instance where such detailed specifications appear carefully lettered on the lower edge of the drawing as presented to the clients.

"Exterior walls faced with dry yellow Roman brick. Horizontal joints wide and raked out to emphasize horizontal grain. Vertical joints stopped flush with mortar the color of the bricks.

Stone trimmings. Terra cotta capitals. Frieze in stucco relief. Soffits plain in plaster. Roof covering of light red flat tiles without modeled trimmings. Hips and ridges clean. Interior walls of lower entrance and principal rooms lined with a slender Roman brick light tan in color carrying gold insertion. And inlaid bans of olive oak. Plaster dead gold."

This treatment of raking the horizontal joints of the brickwork proved to be a detail he would employ throughout his career.

Right up to the end of his life, Frank Lloyd Wright was keenly aware of his work from the beginning to the end. His drawings were always available to him, in cabinets near where he worked. He occasionally would take out a draw-

ing, study it, and then add some inscription concerning it. Despite the importance of the Husser work in relation to the prairie houses, he claimed that the Ward Willits House (above), Highland Park, Illinois, was his first great Prairie house. Perhaps that was because in the Willits house there is no longer any element of Sullivan. He now has his own "vocabulary," and he is, in 1902, a master of residential designs appropriate to time, place, and man.

"Certainly the Willits House was the first great Prairie House. Here you will find the first statement in Modern Architecture from grade to coping, and where you will find the windows not holes cut in the building, but features planted against the building. . . And when you get into

this idea of eliminating the containment which is the box, and freeing architecture—setting the walls free and putting to work the screens and the big overhang, reaching out and amplifying space and dragging things in from the outside, you really have entered a new world of architecture which has never existed before."[5]

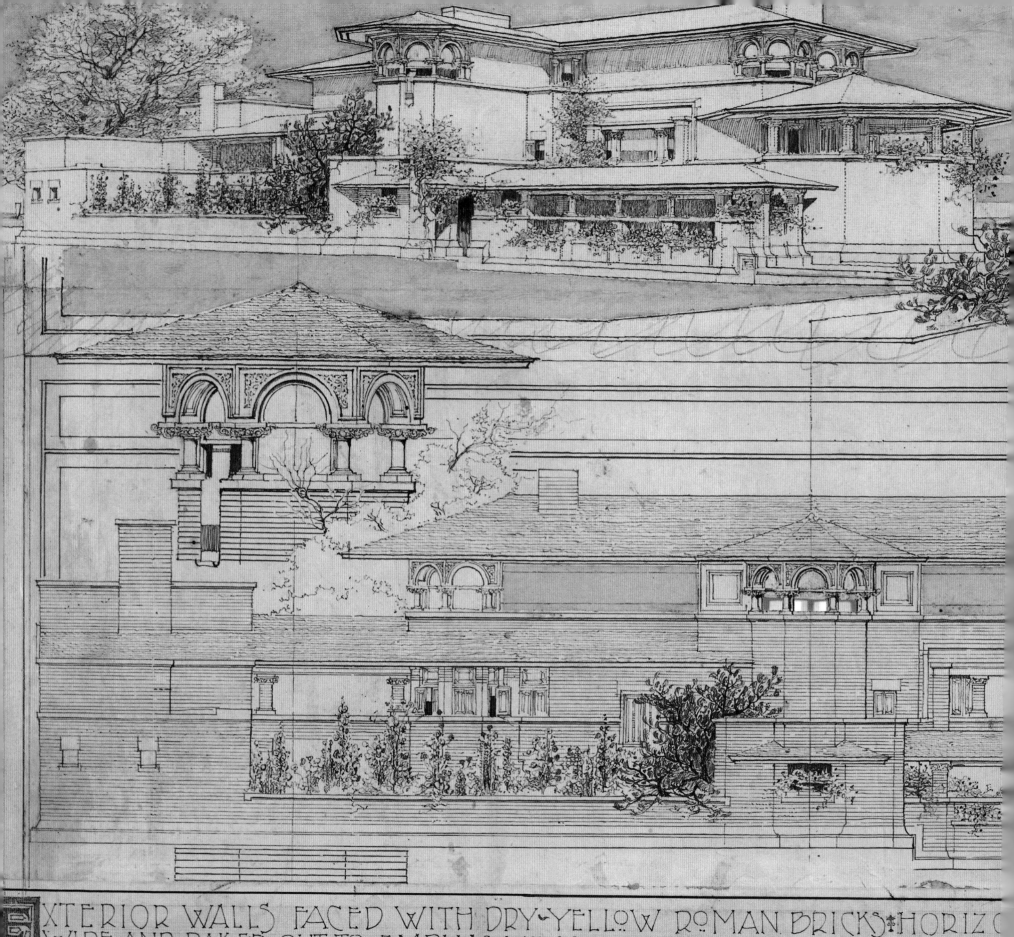

EXTERIOR WALLS FACED WITH DRY·YELLOW·ROMAN·BRICKS·HORIZ
WIDE AND RAKED OUT TO EMPHASIZE HORIZONTAL GRAIN·VERTICAL
STOPPED FLUSH WITH MORTAR THE COLOR OF THE BRICKS·STONE·TRIMMING·
CAPITALS·FRIEZE IN STUCCO RELIEF·SOFFITS PLAIN·IN PLASTER·ROOF·COVER
RED FLAT·TILES WITHOUT MODELED TRIMMINGS·HIPS AND RIDGES·CLEAN

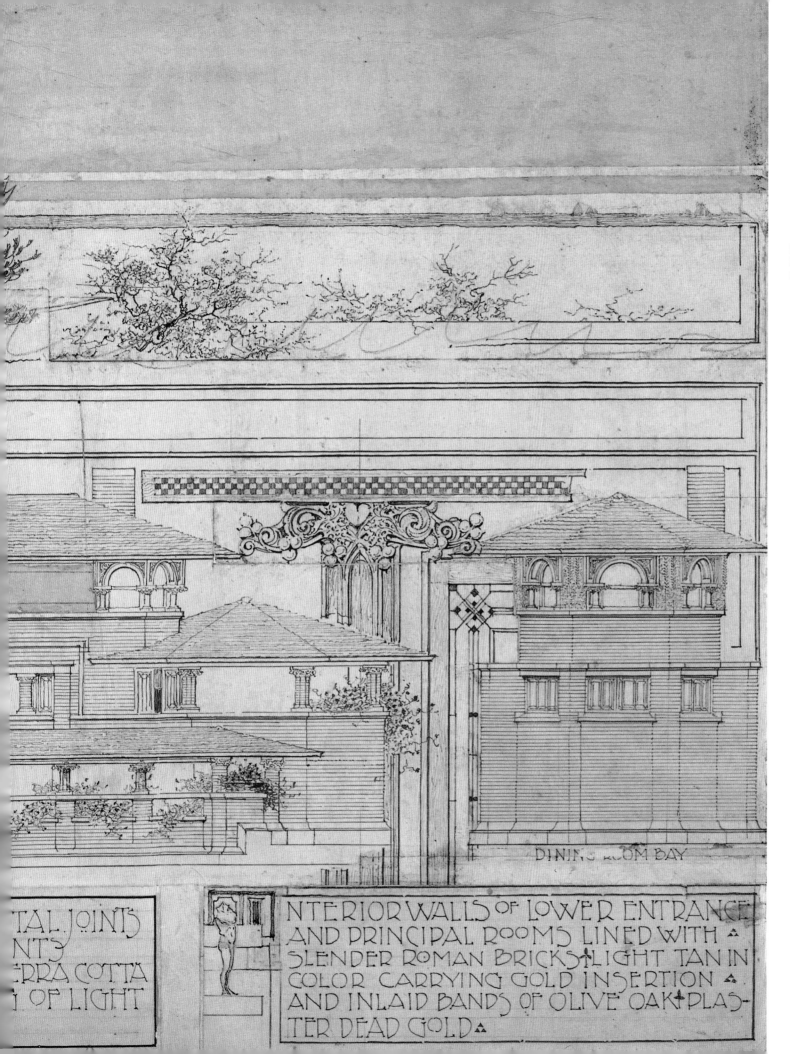

Husser House.
Perspective and Elevation.
FLLW FDN # 9901.002.

DINING ROOM BAY

TAL JOINTS
NTS
RRA COTTA
OF LIGHT

NTERIOR WALLS OF LOWER ENTRANCE
AND PRINCIPAL ROOMS LINED WITH ⧖
SLENDER ROMAN BRICKS LIGHT TAN IN
COLOR CARRYING GOLD INSERTION ⧖
AND INLAID BANDS OF OLIVE OAK PLAS-
TER DEAD GOLD ⧖

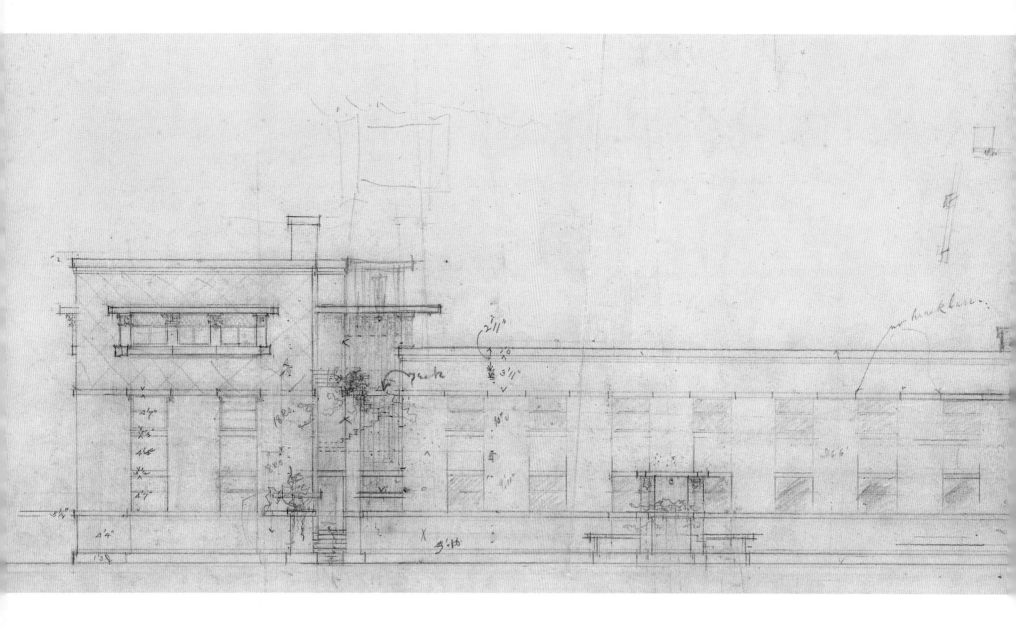

LEXINGTON TERRACE APARTMENTS

Chicago, Illinois. 1901, Project [6]

Edward C. Waller and Oscar J. Friedman were the clients for Lexington Terrace Apartments. (Waller's son would be the client for the famous but ill-fated Midway Gardens twelve years later.)

The program for Lexington Terrace called for apartments for low-income families. The apartments ranged from those with a single bedroom, living room, buffet (dining and kitchen), and bath, to those with two bedrooms, living room, separate kitchen and separate dining room, and bath. In some cases, the larger apartments were

provided with fireplaces. The scheme was necessarily compact, but Wright planned for a large courtyard in the center for a grass lawn, flowers, shrubs, and a fountain pool. A set of drawings was prepared showing two identical blocks of apartments with an ornamental entry in between the two. This scheme was dated 1901, though revisions to the plans in 1909 simplified the arched entry but kept the same configuration of the plan for apartments. The project, however, was never built.

Above: Elevation. FLLW FDN # 0111.005.
Right: Perspective. FLLW FDN # 011.028.

Following pages: Perspective. FLLW FDN # 011.002.

SPRINGFIELD 1899 SHUMAC

SUSAN LAWRENCE DANA HOUSE

Springfield, Illinois. 1902

Susan Lawrence Dana was descended from a family notably prominent in the political and social life of Springfield, the capital of Illinois. When she retained Frank Lloyd Wright, among her requirements were a dining room that would accommodate a sit-down dinner of forty and a special separate gallery for social events related to the arts and exhibitions (right and following pages). She also required a bowling alley and billiard room. The drawings Wright prepared for her bore the title "Alterations and Additions Residence of Mrs. R. D. Lawrence," Mrs. Dana's mother. Her house was a Victorian mansion rich in history, and the new house was intended to be constructed around it. As it happened, the new house totally enveloped the old one, with only one room remaining, the family's private sitting room. Wright took pains to keep this room intact, situated between the new large dining room and a new family living room. Yet he also made a new space for Mrs. Lawrence on the main level where she would be close to the social events, but also have a secluded private area in her old Victorian room. Concerning that old room, he wrote:

"Mrs. Dana was very beautiful and willful, and admirable in many ways. She came to me and wanted me to alter the old house. As the alteration proceeded, the old house began to disappear, until it was a little nucleus in the center of the new house. It was quite independent and I didn't want to alter it because they had a sentiment concerning it. The father was dead, the mother still living and they wanted to preserve the old house as a kind of memento to father, a place where she could go, sit, read, and knit. At first mother used to go in there but as she saw the new house, it became more and more manifest that the old stuff was pretty bad. Mother gradually wouldn't go in there anymore. She went into the new parts, and became more and more delighted with them. Finally the doors to the old house were closed.

"I often think of Mother Lawrence, she used to call me 'that boy' and she was very fond of me. I did my best by Mother Lawrence, I really thought I was doing something to preserve the memory of the old family life. But you see the old family life was dis-spirited by the new. If you are honoring your father and mother, take what was best in them, just not continue with what they had on them."[7]

The Dana House was the largest and most complete in every detail, from the architecture to the furnishings, that Wright had done up to that time. The gray Roman brickwork throughout was constructed from bricks especially imported for the house. The upper story exterior was sheathed in a frieze of reinforced stucco; the gently sloping roofs of red tile had fascias of stamped copper. When entering the house through an archway, with the transom composed of stained glass in the famous butterfly motif (p. 41), the vertical space around the stairway soars up three stories from the ground level to the bedroom level, lit by tall stained glass windows. In the dining room, along with the long table and chairs to seat forty, there was a small semicircular breakfast nook, with a stained glass abstraction of sumacs (left). In the gallery, Wright devised a different use of stained glass: against a plate glass window, the stained glass is hung like a tapestry. Indeed, the Dana House is world-famous for its glass. Wright considered it the finest of all his designs, along with the glass he did for Midway Gardens. "The glass in that house cost a fortune; today it would cost a hundred thousand dollars. I used to sit down and design glass, shake it out my sleeve, just like nobody's business, and loved doing it."[8]

Sketch for Dance Studio
1900

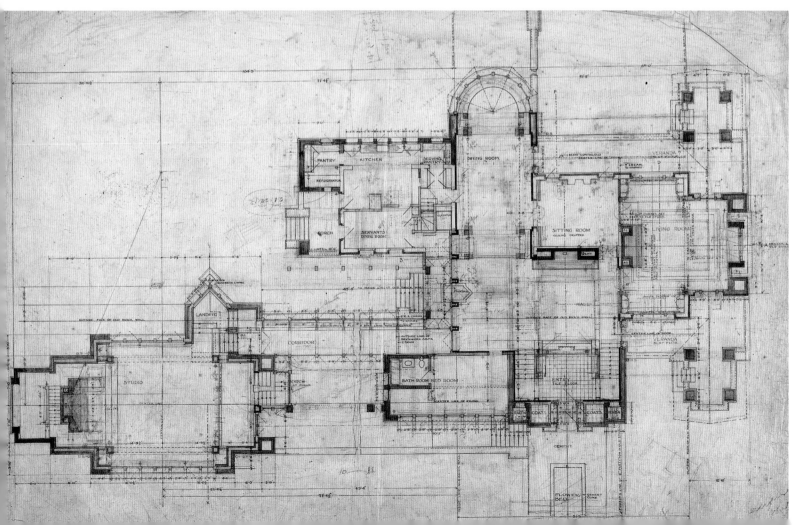

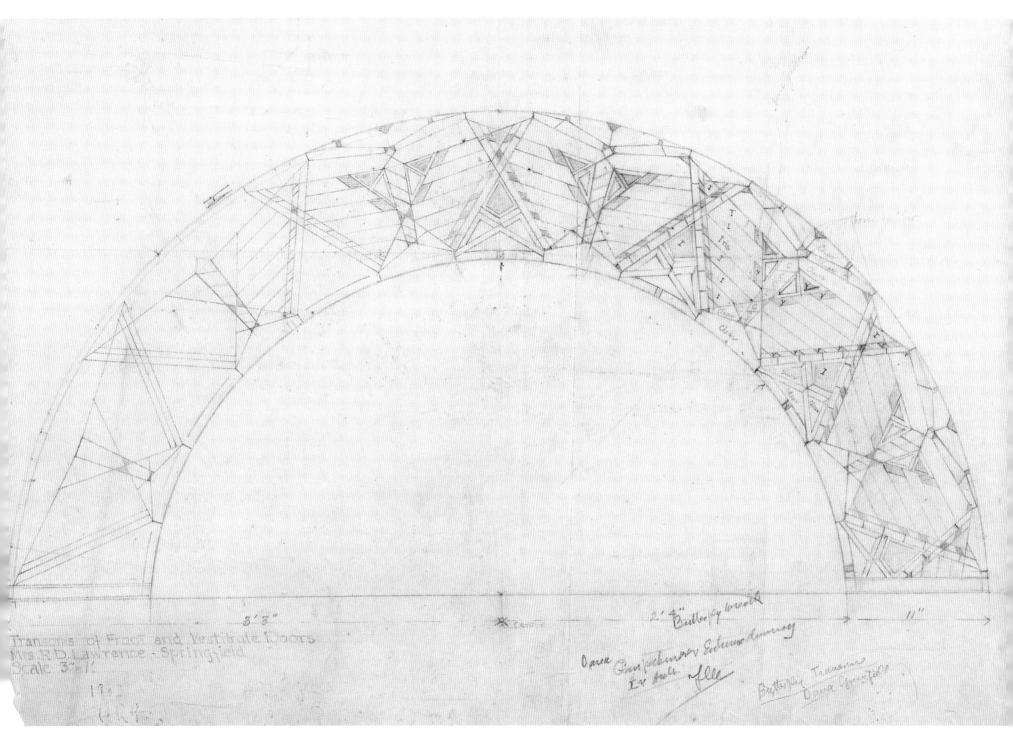

Transoms of Front and Vestibule Doors
Mrs. R.D. Lawrence - Springfield
Scale 3"=1'

Left, top: Sketch for studio.
FLLW FDN # 9905.002.
Left, bottom: Plan for alterations and additions
to the house. FLLW FDN # 9905.025.
Above: Design for stained glass transom in
butterfly motif. FLLW FDN # 9905.010.

EDWIN H. CHENEY HOUSE

Oak Park, Illinois. 1903

The residences that Wright was building in and around the suburbs of Chicago at the beginning of the twentieth century are generally classified as "the Prairie Houses." It was not necessarily a term that he himself coined, preferring to call his work at that time "The New Architecture of the Middle West." But the prairie was indeed a most important element of that work. Born and raised in the pastoral environment of southern Wisconsin, he came upon the Midwest prairie later, when he left Wisconsin and took up work and life on the prairies extending out from Chicago. The location became an instant inspiration to him.

"I loved the prairie by instinct as a great simplicity—the trees, flowers, sky itself, thrilling by contrast. I saw that a little height on the prairie was enough to look like much more—every detail as to height becoming intensely significant, breadths all falling short. Here was tremendous spaciousness."[9]

In response to this environment, he began to make the home more compatible with it, reducing the needless height of the attic, taking the damp cellar out of the ground and placing it on ground level. Above was the general living element of the home—the living room, dining room, library, kitchen, servants' rooms, and the generous roofed porches and terraces that extended out to embrace the land.

"I had an idea that the horizontal planes in buildings—those planes parallel to earth, identified themselves with the ground—make the building belong to the ground."[10]

In plan, those early homes he designed employed what has been identified as "the open plan." Living room, dining room, library were not planned as separate boxes within a larger box, but were opened up to one another producing a spatial flow that did away with useless partitions and doors.

"Taking the human being for my scale, I brought the whole house down in height to fit a normal one. Believing in no other scale that the human being, I broadened the mass out all I possibly could to bring it down into spaciousness. . . And at this time I saw a house, primarily, as livable interior space under ample shelter. I liked the sense of shelter in the look of the building. I still like it. The house began to associate with the ground and become natural to its prairie site."[11]

The sense of shelter was emphasized by the broad, low pitched roofs that extended generously out over the porches on the main floor and the second story windows. The windows were another innovation: in place of the customary double-hung, or guillotine, windows, he designed windows that swung open, thus allowing the entire window frame to open, rather than just half. Such windows were common in Europe, but they swung inward. To provide for open swinging sash, it was necessary for Wright to have special hardware manufactured. He liked the sense of the window fully opened, catching

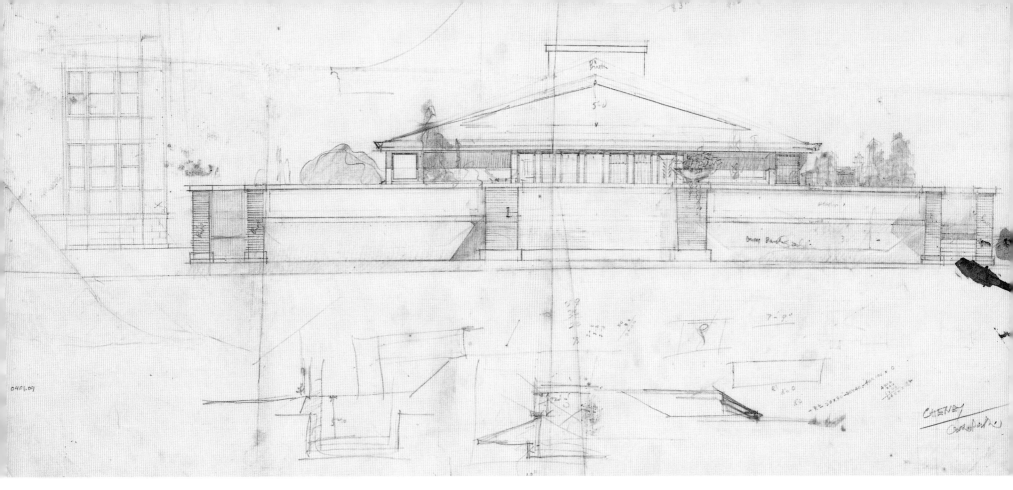

Left: Early conceptual sketch perspective.
FLLW FDN # 0401.012.
Above: Street-side elevation. FLLW FDN # 0401.009.

Following pages: Perspective. FLLW FDN # 0401.017.

the summer breezes or the sweet smell of nature immersed in moisture during rains, but amply protected by the extended overhanging roofs.

What was Wright's response to the use of building materials? Here he again was venturing into a new world of house construction. He used each material according to its inherent nature: stone as stone, brick as brick, wood as wood, no painting or papering, everything as natural as possible. This was indeed a startling use of materials, especially in the prevailing Victorian era.

Many of those early prairie houses were planned on three levels, the ground floor taking the place of the former cellar, with heating, laundry, and storage; above, the main floor, with living room, etc., and the second floor for the bedrooms and bathrooms.

The Edwin H. Cheney House, however, is a rare example where all the major rooms, living room, dining room, kitchen, bedrooms, and bathrooms, are on one level. The earliest date on the working drawings for the Cheney house is

October 31, 1903. However, three revision dates, on the same drawings, ranging from December 17, 1903, to March 3, 1904, as well as several other sketches, suggest Wright continued to develop his first scheme over a period of months. The house is actually a two-story structure, but Wright has cleverly provided a wall on the street side that conceals the ground floor and produces the effect of a single story house (above). On the ground floor, besides the usual heating, laundry, and storage, there are two bedrooms at the back, separated by an "Automobile Room." The "Automobile Room" was later changed to an apartment to eliminate the potential fire hazard presented by such close proximity to gasoline fumes. One of the bedrooms is designated as a servants' room, with a bathroom adjacent. The plan of the main floor is square with slight modifications at the rear, which provide corner windows for two of the four bedrooms, but all four bedrooms open onto an outdoor loggia, under the protecting roof. The

living room, dining room, and library extend in one unbroken space across the front of the house with a centrally located fireplace. A kitchen and two bathrooms complete the plan on this level. Casement windows extend around most of the house, while glass doors lead from the living room onto a paved terrace on the street side. This terrace serves as a bridge, on either side of which garden courts run along the sides of the building to the back of the house. At the front they join under the terrace above. A large, low-pitched hip roof protects the structure. An early conceptual plan for the Cheney House shows, in the upper right hand corner, a thumbnail sketch perspective (above left), a device Wright used from time to time to explain, presumably, to his draftsmen, what view he wanted prepared to present to the clients. A perspective (on following page) was rendered by Marian Mahony, one of Wright's most skilled draftsmen in his Oak Park workshop.

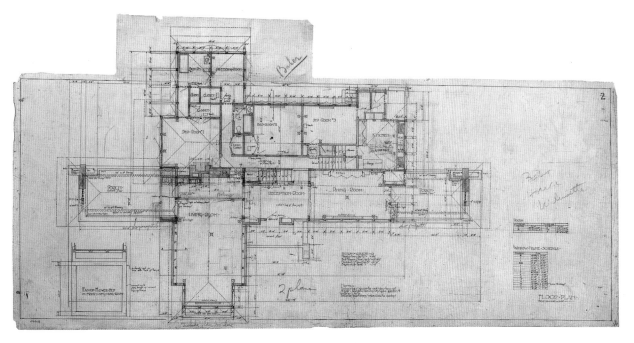

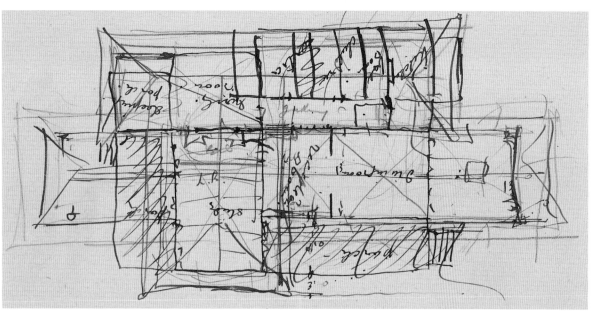

FRANK BAKER HOUSE

Wilmette, Illinois. 1909

Wright's first proposal for the Frank Baker House was somehow rejected by the clients, and he set to work on a second scheme. The first one, however, is represented by a fine perspective drawing, possibly drawn by Marian Mahony, whose work always featured trees and plants in her own inimitable way of representing them. Also, the perspective reveals a special "trick" that Wright instigated

and asked for from his draftsmen when preparing perspective drawings: the line framing the drawing is interrupted by the branches of a pronounced tree in front of the house (following pages). It might be said that this sort of detail, however small, was something he learned from his careful study of Japanese woodblock prints, mainly those of Hiroshige.

His initial sketch for the second Baker House was roughly made with pen and ink (above, bottom), and then followed with a more detailed plan (not shown). The final product provided the clients with a reception room in the center of the elongated plan, a two-story living room with its porch and the dining room with its porch, as well. The kitchen is next to the dining room, with a rear entry for provisions. The bedrooms

SEWANEE
William Norman Guthri
Tennessee – 1908

Left, top: Plan.
FLLW FDN # 0901.013.
Left, bottom: Initial sketch, plan.
FLLW FDN # 0901.002.
Above: Final perspective
drawing of Guthrie House
(project), which, in plan, was
identical to the Baker House.
FLLW FDN # 0813.001.

Following pages:
Baker House perspective.
FLLW FDN # 0810.001.

have been placed on a higher level, not a second floor. The split-level element of the house is difficult to read on the plans, but quite clear on the sections (top, left). No final perspective of the Baker house exists, but the perspective of the William Norman Guthrie House (above) does. The plan is identical, although the Guthrie house of 1908 was never built. Guthrie would appear again in 1927 as a very special client for Wright's apartment building St. Mark's-on-the-Bouwerie in 1927.

The Baker House underwent some additions and revisions in later years but still remains one of the finest examples of Wright's prairie houses.

Early Study in the
Stewart House of 1909

10

MR. F. J. BAKER
DWELLING. WILMETTE. ILL
FRANK. LLOYD. WRIGHT. ARCH

HARRY ADAMS HOUSE

Oak Park, Illinois.1912

The Harry Adams House might resemble the work that Wright was doing on the so-called prairie houses, but indeed it is not of the same genre. It was a commission that extended from September 12, 1912, when the first scheme was developed with a complete set of working drawings, to May 13, 1913, with yet another set, and finally a third set, as built, signed on October 6, 1913. Why there were three complete sets is not on record.

In all three proposals, Wright planned a full basement, with the first floor set directly on the ground, a marked change from his usual approach to the Prairie house. In fact, perhaps for this reason, the Adams House might well be considered a break from the prairie house idiom, as Wright at this time is headed in a new direction in residential designs: he is associating the house directly with the landscape. This design was made at the time that he had left Oak Park and Chicago and built his own home Taliesin in Wisconsin. On the Wisconsin property, the main living portion of the house is no longer raised above the ground level as was typical in Prairie houses, but lies directly on the site, fully embracing the landscape.

Two versions of the Adams House are here illustrated: an early elevation skektch (right, top) along with a finished perspective (following pages); and a later conceptual elevation (right, bottom), which reveals a drastic change in the concept. Whereas the earlier drawings show a formality and balance that is definitely symmetrical, with the chimney mass in the center, equal wings on either side, on the revised elevation, Wright has thrown symmetry to the winds and come upon a freer scheme altogether. This is how the house was built.

Right, top: An early conceptual sketch elevation. FLLW FDN # 1105.004.
Right, bottom: A later sketch elevation, showing a drastic change in concept from earlier sketch. FLLW FDN # 1105.002

Following pages: Perspective based on early concept for house. FLLW FDN # 1105.006.

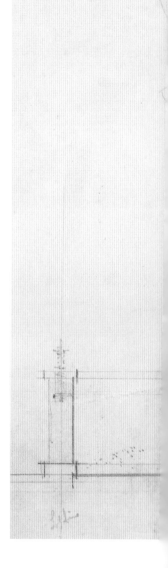

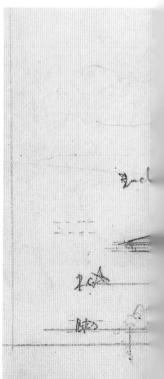

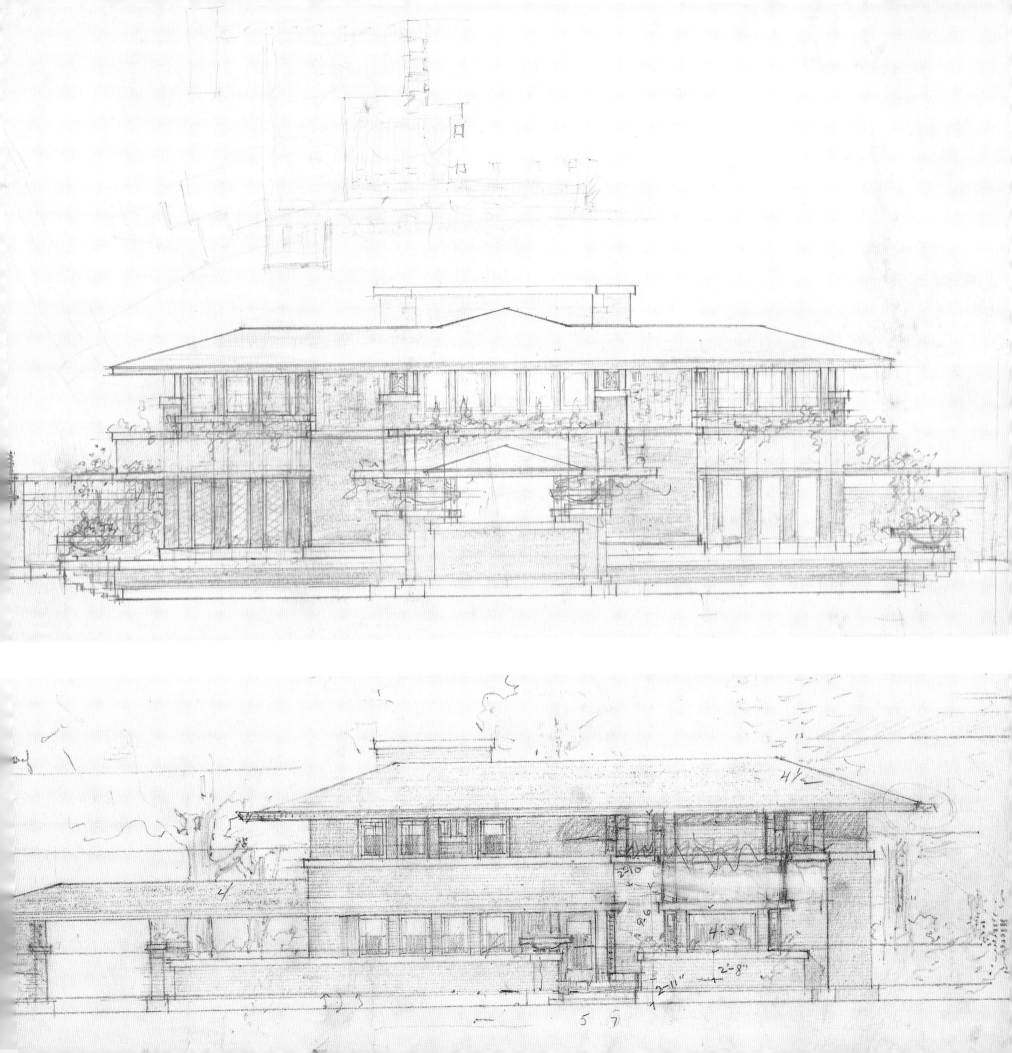

Study according to Adams
1911

F. C. BOGK HOUSE

Milwaukee, Wisconsin. 1916

In the early years when Wright was designing the prairie houses, to his dismay he often noticed that when a house was constructed, the client would invariably drag in his old Victorian furniture. To circumvent this, he began designing furniture as well, starting with built-in items such as seats and grilles by the fireplace, sideboards for the dining room, cabinets, and bookshelves. Then he went further and made designs for dining tables and chairs, hassocks, armchairs, beds, and light fixtures, as well. Large chairs, like recliners, he found rather irksome.

In some instances, he was asked to design rugs. For his client Frederick Bogk, for whom Wright designed a town house in Milwaukee, he also created designs for rugs in the living room and dining room which were woven in Czechoslovakia in 1916 (p. 56, top right).

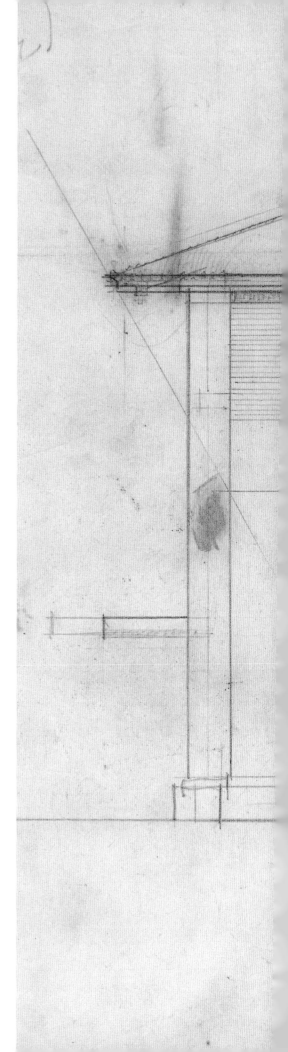

Elevation. FLLW FDN # 1602.011.

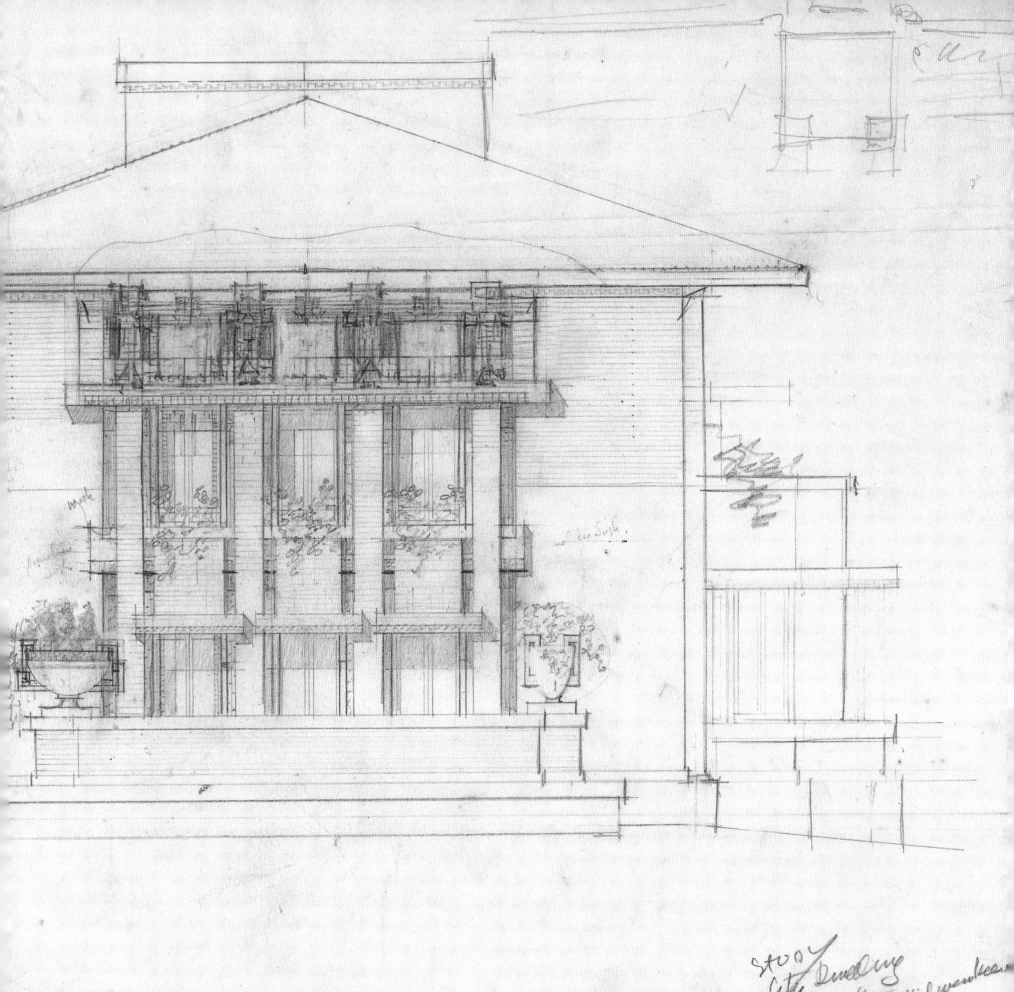

study
City Building
for Bogk — Milwaukee
1912

Designs for rugs, furniture, and fixtures.
Below: FLLW FDN # 7607.003.
Bottom: FLLW FDN # 7608.002.

Right: FLLW FDN # 1602.002.
Far right: FLLW FDN # 0803.001.

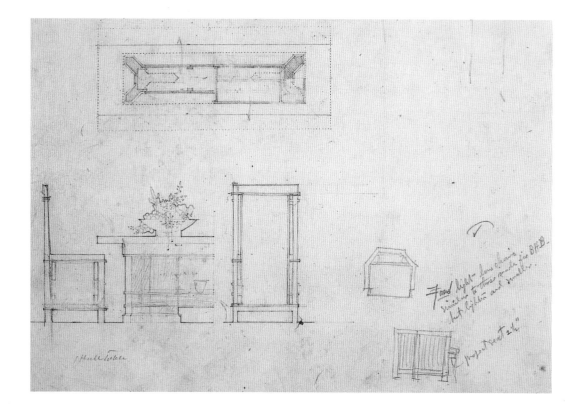

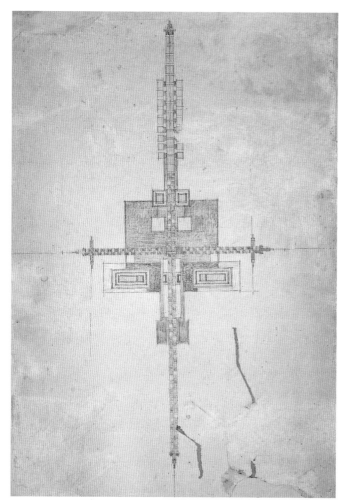

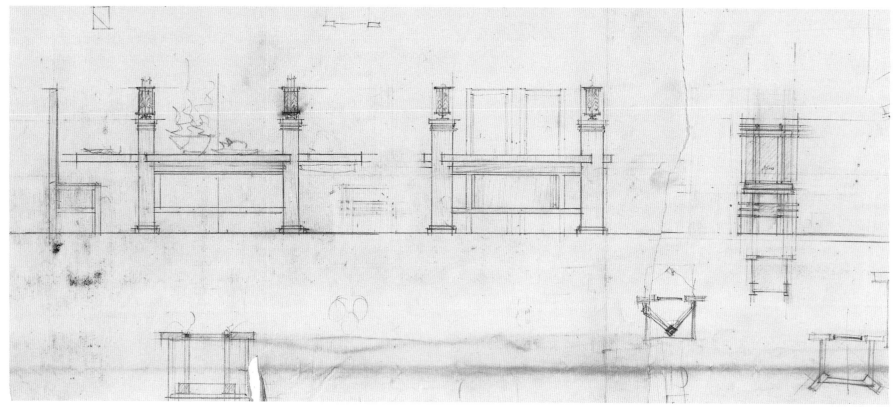

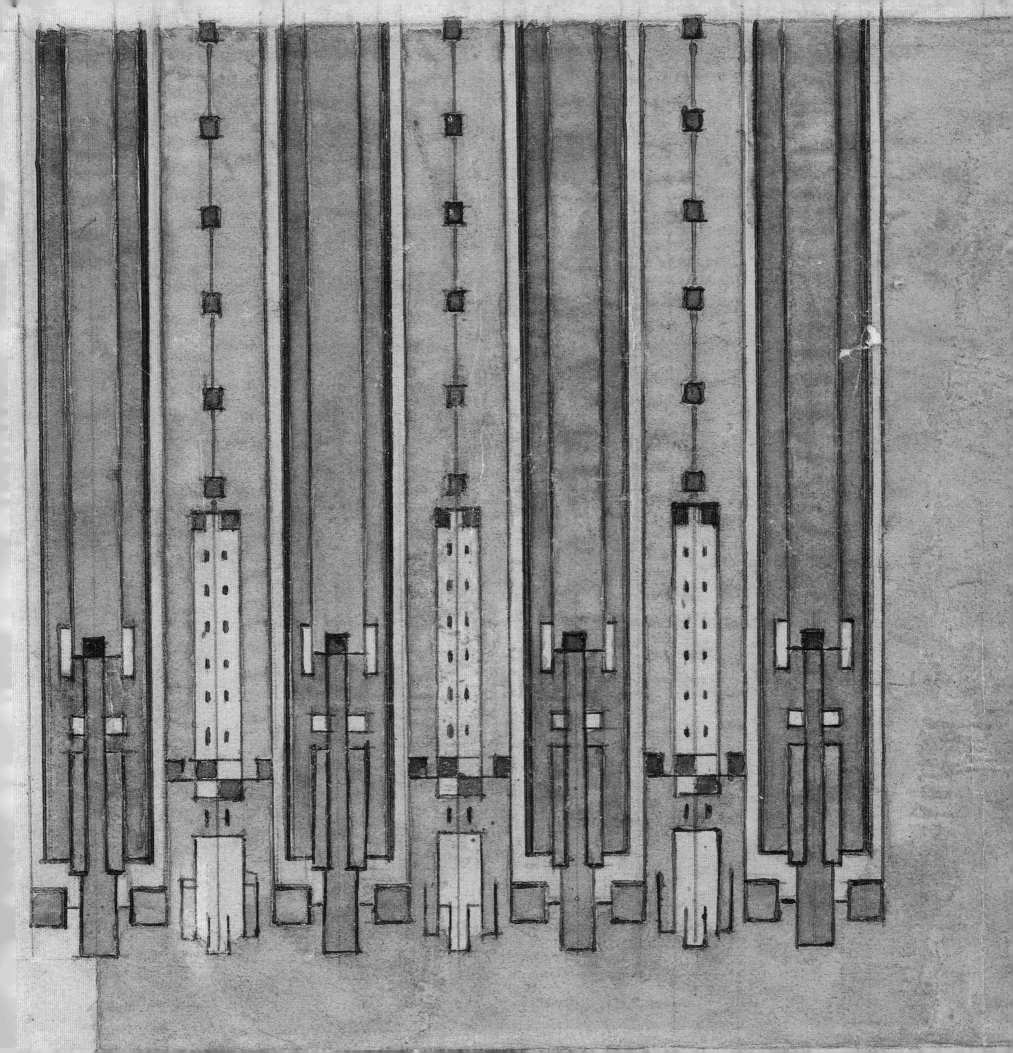

HENRY J. ALLEN HOUSE

Wichita, Kansas. 1917

Plan. FLLW FDN # 1701.001.

Henry J. Allen was the twenty-first governor of Kansas, as well as the editor of the leading newspaper, *The Wichita Beacon*. He was also a close personal friend of Wright's. At the time that Wright designed a home for him, the architect was deeply involved in his work on the Imperial Hotel in Japan. Some of the details in the Allen house appear in the Imperial Hotel, most notably the treatment of the interior brickwork, where the horizontal raked joints are pointed up with gold leaf. The overall brickwork is similar in both buildings. In brick construction, one particular detail that Wright generally specified was the raking of the horizontal joint, so as to emphasize a more sculptural aspect of the wall, and further, to point up, or fill in, the vertical joints, which even further accentuated this appearance.

The Allen House is situated on a corner lot, and for it Wright produced an L-shaped plan. The front part one story for the living room, the extended wing containing dining room, kitchen, and servants quarters on the ground floor, with bedrooms and bathrooms on the second story.

The house opens onto an enclosed garden with a decorative pool and lush planting, protected from the neighbors by the L-shaped plan and the garden wall that runs along the street side. At the far end of the garden there was originally a space planned for a garage. In the final plans a space for two cars was provided in the general house plan, next to the servants' quarters and kitchen. The space for the garage on the preliminary plan was then turned into a garden house, closed to the street, but open to the garden and with steps down to it. An interior perspective shows the entrance hall (p. 61) and some drawings were prepared for rugs, but these were never executed. A presentation drawing was prepared as an aerial view. Although not a "prairie house" per se, the Allen House has many of the features and characteristics of Wright's residential work

at that time. In some respects it closes an era in that genre, as Wright moves more out of the Midwest and into California, and he explores new forms and new materials.

However, as the plans were being developed into final form, Wright suggested that the living room, considering Allen's need for extensive entertaining, be widened more than originally planned. Allen objected to the additional cost, and the plan went ahead as originally laid out. Years later, on one of Wright's trips to the house en route from Wisconsin to his winter home, Taliesin West in Arizona, he stayed at the Allen house. During the visit, Allen admitted to him, "Frank, why didn't you insist that we make the living room wider? I sure could've used the space."

During the early years of the Taliesin Fellowship, the trip from Wisconsin to Arizona was really an exciting move—all the fellowship members along with Wright and his family making the trek in the form of a caravan. Often a site was found that seemed particularly appropriate for camping or enjoying a picnic lunch on the grass under some shade trees. Wright several times picked a graveyard, for its pastoral nature and abundant planting. When the fellowship arrived in Wichita, the Allens insisted on serving dinner to the Wrights and the entire fellowship, which—at that time—numbered about 32 apprentices. Mrs. Allen set the table with her finest linen and china and prepared a hardy feast. Among the guests one time was William Allen White, a crusading editor from Emporia, Kansas, and a friend of both the Wrights and the Allens. When White observed at dinner the robust manner in which the fellowship members were hungrily and quickly eating the spread that Mrs. Allen had set out for them, he turned to Wright and exclaimed, "Your Taliesin Fellowship, Frank, is the Great American Sponge!"

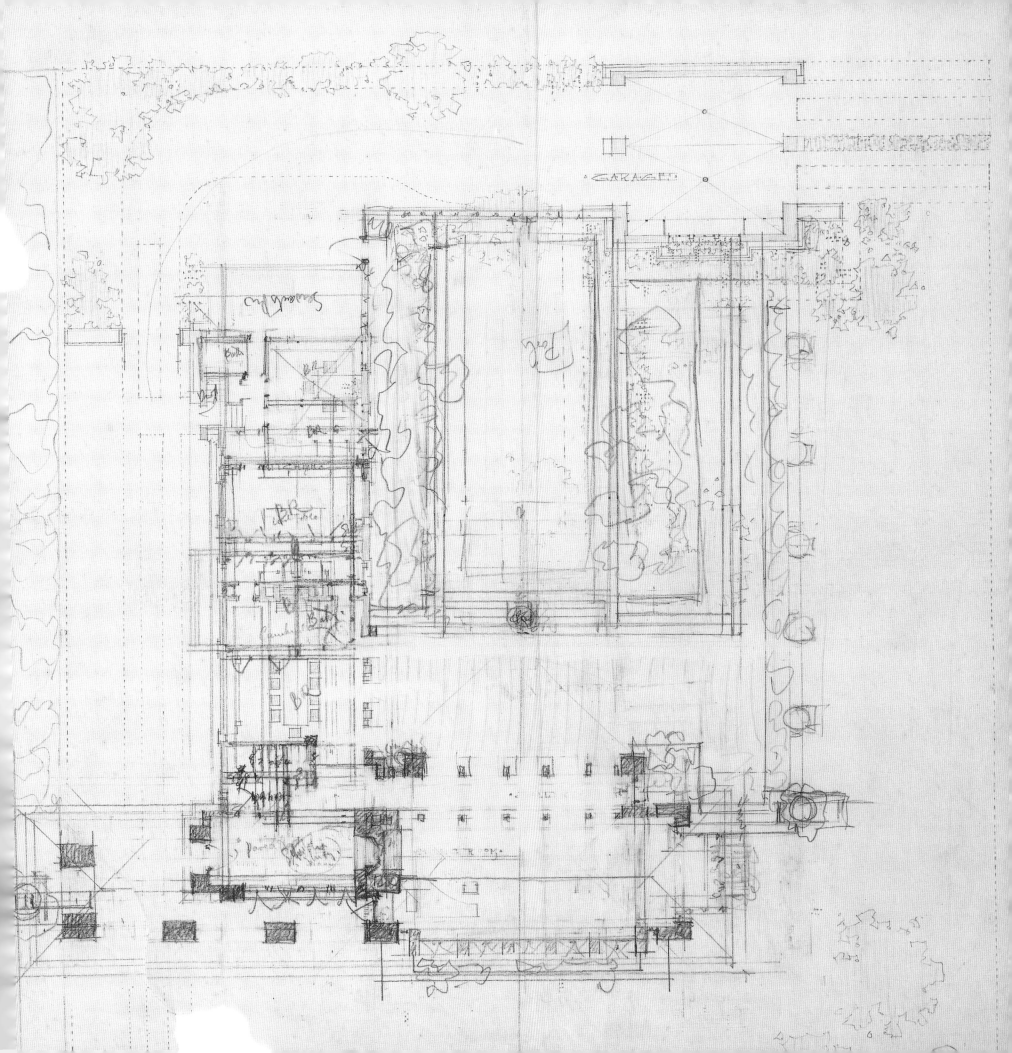

GARAGE

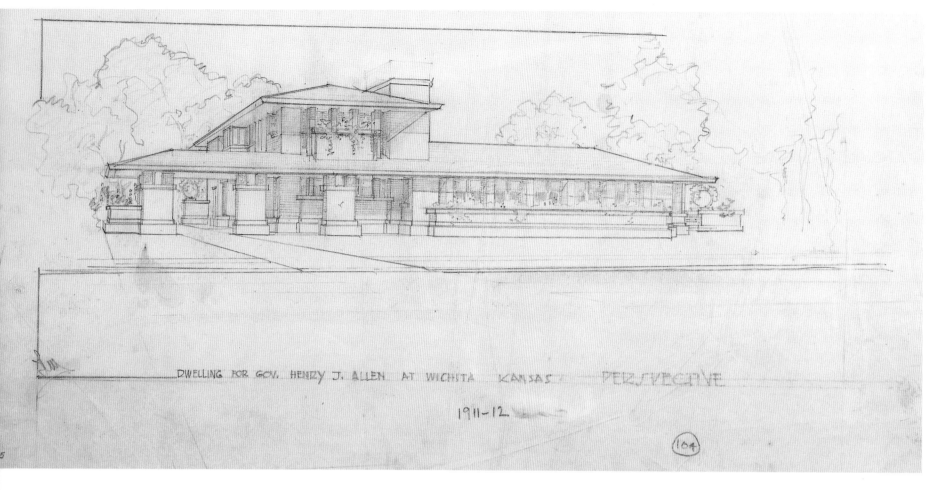

DWELLING FOR GOV. HENRY J. ALLEN AT WICHITA KANSAS — PERSPECTIVE

1911-12

104

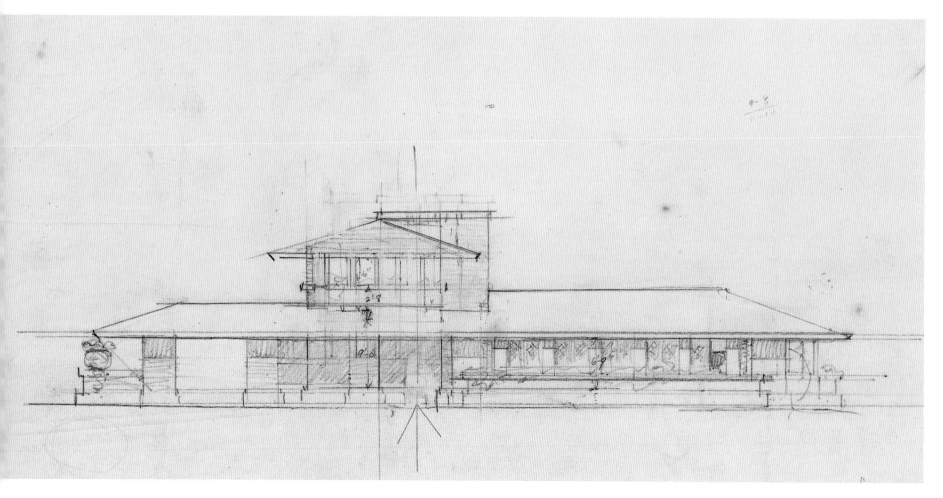

Left, top: Early perspective. FLLW FDN # 1701.005.
Left, bottom: Early conceptual sketch elevation.
FLLW FDN # 1701.002.
Above: Interior perspective of entry hall.
FLLW FDN # 1701.055.

DOHENY RANCH DEVELOPMENT

Beverly Hills, California. 1923, Project

Early in his life, in 1887 when he was 20, the lure of architecture and the excitement of building beautiful buildings drew him to Chicago. Now, in 1923, at the age of 56, that same excitement drew him to Los Angeles. But why Los Angeles? It was a booming town at that time and building was going on all over, most of it rather cheap and gaudy, if it was not the imitation of Spanish Colonial. He once made the remark that if the map of the United States was turned on end, anything that was loose would slide down to Los Angeles. Nonetheless, he was first drawn there for work for Aline Barnsdall, the oil heiress he had first met some years earlier in Chicago. Now settled in Hollywood, she asked Wright to design a home for her, a theater complex, and a community playhouse. Her home, the now famous Hollyhock House, was a work of great difficulty because its design and construction coincided with his work on the Imperial Hotel in Tokyo.

He strongly believed that Southern California needed an architecture that reflected its environment. Hollyhock House was just such a building, and for him a complete break with everything he had designed before, namely the prairie houses in the Midwest. He realized that the architectural grammar, appropriate to the prairie, was not for Los Angeles.

Other commissions were coming his way, and it appeared that Southern California was going to be a most lucrative area in which to design and build: a housing project in a Los Angeles canyon, a summer resort on Lake Tahoe, a merchandising building for Los Angeles, a concrete block house in Pasadena, and three others in Los Angeles. He wrote to Louis Sullivan, "Lieber Meister, Breakfast is ready. Sorry to come away without seeing you. Have pitched in here to locate. Perhaps you will come out later—to see this ice cream, cake, and soda water corner of the world. Affectionately, Frank (Los Angeles)."[12]

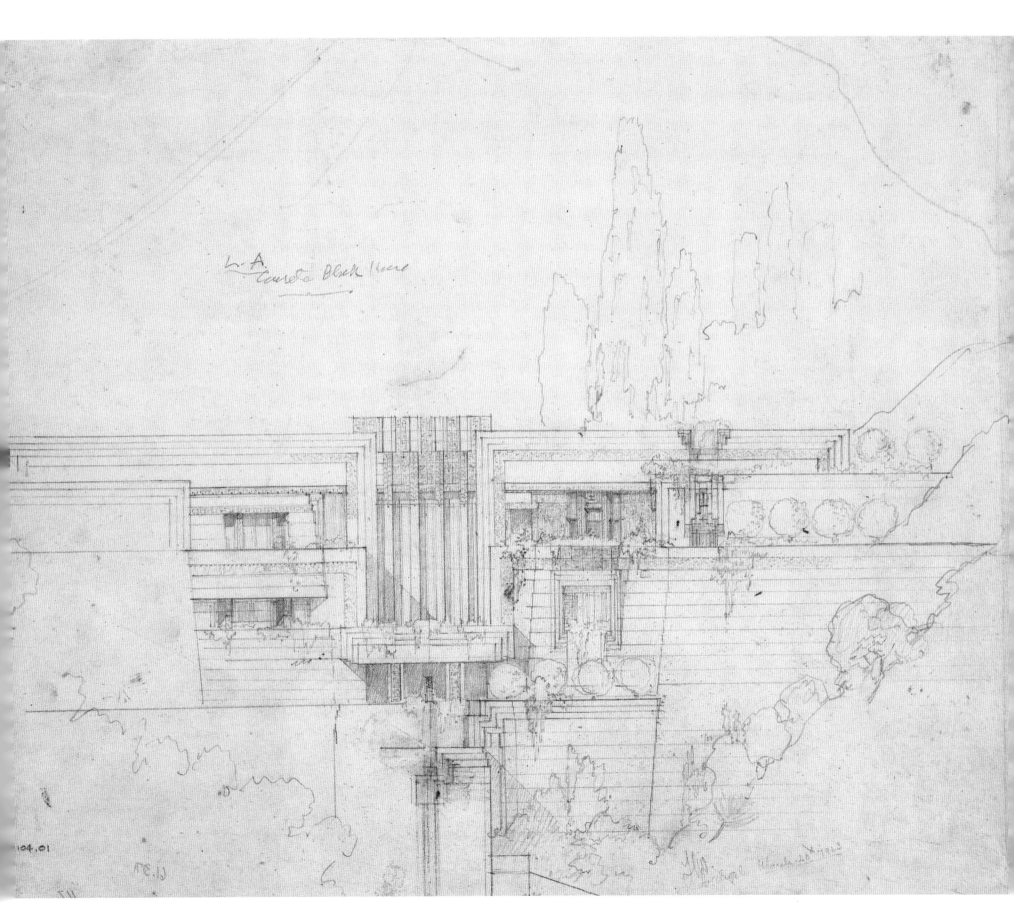

L. A.
Concrete Block House

104.01

The commission for a housing project was the Doheny Ranch Development, a work the origins of which are rather shrouded in mystery. Wright even misspelled the name of the client. He referred to him as Edward H. Doheny, whereas the client was actually Edward L. Doheny, an oil baron who owned a tract of land at the base of the Santa Monica Mountains. Wright misrepresented the site, referring to it as being in the San Gabriel Mountains. Such confusion is amplified by the lack of any correspondence on record between Wright and Doheny. Nonetheless, what Wright proposed was an entirely innovative way of building on hillside sites in a canyon.

Historically, such sites were bulldozed to make roads and house lots, literally destroying the terrain and creating a case for intense soil erosion. On the overall perspective (pp. 66-67), Wright inscribed, "Doheny Ranch Project—Hollywood Hills—Block houses—Roadway built with houses as architecture—contours of hills undisturbed." This was the key to the design, the roads are built as part of the houses, coming in either on the side or at the rear, leaving the house poised on the edge of the hill rather than set down on a lot with a road in front of it. Thus the roadways become as much architectural features as the houses themselves.

Wright prepared designs for three different house types, referred to as House A, House B, and House C. Although the houses themselves are not particularly large, the massive, exquisite, and decorative concrete block retaining walls that secure them to their hillside locations are prominent architectural features. There is a drama to them that all but takes one's breath away.

The overall perspectives, one looking at the ranch development, the other looking from within the development out, reveal this careful attention to preserving the natural contours of the site, and let architecture, retaining walls, and roadways become an integral part of it.

THE TEXTILE BLOCK HOUSES

Pasadena and Los Angeles, California. 1923–24

Below: Ennis House plan.
FLLW FDN # 2401.007
Right, top: Ennis House elevation.
FLLW FDN # 2401.001.
Right, bottom: Storer House perspective.
FLLW FDN # 2304.002.

Following pages: Ennis House perspective
and plan. FLLW FDN # 2401.003.

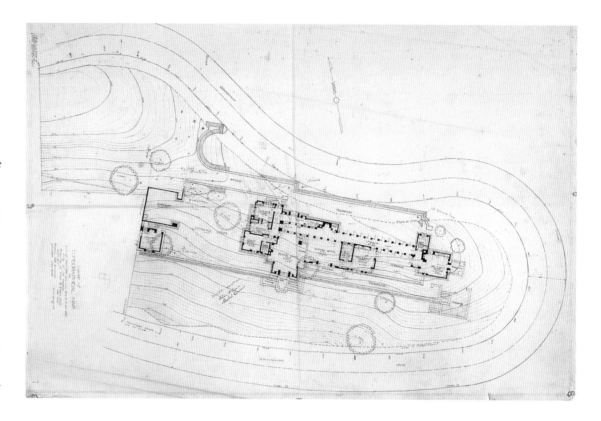

While in Los Angeles at work for Aline Barnsdall, Wright received requests to design homes for four clients, one in Pasadena for Alice Millard, the other three in Los Angeles, for Charles Ennis, John Storer, and Samuel Freeman. All of these were constructed with concrete blocks. Alice Millard, the first of this genre, was a "repeat" client; Wright had designed a house for her and her husband George Madison Millard.

"The Millards had lived in a little wooden dwelling I had built for them fifteen years ago at Highland Park, near Chicago. I was proud now to have a client survive the first house and ask me to build a second. . . So, gratefully, I determined she should have the best in my portfolio. That meant, to begin with, something that belonged to the ground on which it stood. Her house should be a sensible matter entirely—an interpretation of her needs in book-collecting for book-collectors. . . Gradually I unfolded to her the scheme of the textile block-slab house gradually forming in my mind since I got home from Japan. She wasn't frightened by the idea. Not at all. We would take that despised outcast of the building industry—the concrete block—out from underfoot in the gutter—find a hitherto unsuspected soul in it—make it live as a thing of beauty—textured like the trees."[13]

By textured, he was referring to the process of stamping designs in the concrete blocks and geometric patterns that were formed by blocks placed in the wooden forms in which the mixture of concrete was poured. Some blocks were perforated, to let light filter through, some were plain for interior walls, and other were stamped, but not perforated. The blocks were thin, with grooved edges on all four sides. This is how the term "textile" applied. The customary way for laying up block walls, as with as brick or stone walls, required skilled masons because of the mortar joints running horizontally and

vertically. In this new system of construction that Wright innovated here with the block houses, the blocks could be stacked, then thin steel rods, about the thickness of a pencil, were inserted into the grooves, thus weaving them together as the walls rose, and finally, at certain stages, concrete was poured into the grooves, a form of construction that could be achieved by unskilled labor. He named the Millard house "La Miniatura." The site was a narrow ravine, a piece of property that seemed unsuited for houses, and therefore was offered at a reasonably low price. Wright has situated the house in the ravine, to take advantage of a pond and surrounding banks with eucalyptus trees. Construction was difficult, since this was a prototype and required his constant supervision. But Alice

Millard was brave and weathered it all from beginning to end (pp. 72-73).

When he undertook the other block houses, the system was then fairly well perfected. Often the problem was the use of unskilled labor. Some cases of negligence, or perhaps ignorance in the process of construction, would give rise to serious structural problems that would develop in the future.

The houses in Los Angeles were built on hillside lots, which required, in the case of the Freeman and Ennis houses, retaining walls riding up the slopes to support the houses above. In the Ennis house, in particular, these walls form the greater part of the overall structure. The house is a three-bedroom dwelling, set upon a massive concrete block retaining wall relieved by their integral patterns to soften the entire dramatic

and somewhat overpowering expanse. For his conceptual plan he drew on the blueprint topographical survey, and then drew a concept elevation (above). A final plan is also drawn on a topo, to relate the house directly to the lay of the land (opposite page). The final rendering is also drawn in relation to the plan below it (following page).

The Storer (right) and Freeman (not shown) houses followed the same concrete-block construction, but on a much smaller scale than the Ennis. These four houses began and ended an era of Wright's architectural practice in the Los Angeles region. He had thought that he would be successful in his attempt to create an architecture indigenous to the region, but the desire for Californians to house themselves in Spanish Colonial prevailed.

1920-1 Perspective drawing of Barnsdall House, Hollywood, Los Angeles

Above: Millard House plan and elevation.
FLLW FDN # 2302.002.
Right: Milard House perspective.
FLLW FDN # 2302.001.

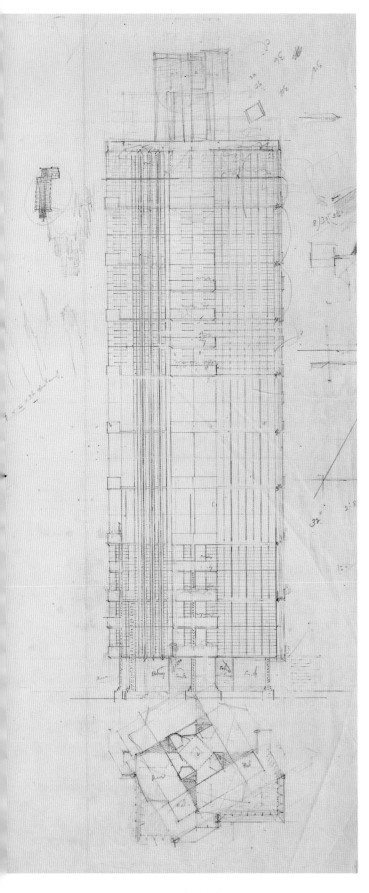

ST. MARK'S-IN-THE-BOUWERIE APARTMENT TOWER

New York, New York. 1929, Project

Frank Lloyd Wright and William Norman Guthrie met in the early years of the 1900s, when Guthrie was a frequent visitor to Chicago where he lectured in the Fine Arts Buildings. In that same building Wright had designed several shops and galleries. That certainly was the connection that brought the two men together. Guthrie was a strongly, if not strangely, impassioned person, a radical, a quixotic pastor whose far-advanced theories obviously attracted Wright. In 1908 the architect had designed a house for him in Sewanee, Tennessee. The house was not built, but the friendship between the two men prospered.

Years later, in 1927, Guthrie wrote an article about the perfect cathedral, and he asked Wright to make a design to illustrate it. The resulting design was the famous Steel Cathedral. Like the house, it was not built.

Guthrie had become the pastor of the small, historic church St. Mark's in the Bouwerie, located in Manhattan. Originally a church of that name had been built when New York was New Amsterdam, a Dutch colony of great importance due to the trade of New World products, mainly furs, shipped overseas to Holland. At that time, the church was located in fields of farming, 'bouwerie' being the Dutch word denoting farmlands.

The church is situated in a small park, and Guthrie desired to have Wright design an apartment tower adjacent to his church. The reason for such a building was to create revenue from rentals to help support the church. Although letters from Guthrie to Wright about the tower began in 1927, it was not until 1929 that Wright actually prepared his first sketches. The reason for the delay seems to have stemmed from the continual misunderstanding between architect and client. In order to be able to build such a building, Guthrie needed the approval of some of the key members in his congregation. He thus

proposed that Wright make a sketch of a design in order to sell the idea to others. He offered to pay Wright $150 for the sketch. This proposition was offensive to Wright, who felt that a client should have the conviction of employing him to make a definite design, not just a mere "sketch" as a sales tool. Wright responded to Guthrie's offer:

"There is no sacrifice I would not make to help you in your case forward—you know me well enough for that I hope. But when you talk of a $150 sketch, you show to what extent do you know nothing at all about the intensive organic effort in architecture, such as mine— and show with what sort of architects you have consorted in the past."[14]

Guthrie accused Wright of being egotistical and arrogant, and stated that any number of New York architects would be delighted to make a sketch to sell the project for $150. Wright stood his ground, and the letters between them, and very lengthy letters at that, went on for the rest of the year. One of the vestrymen, Horace Holly, intervened and assured Guthrie that Wright's typical fee schedule was indeed justified for a new building better than what any typical New York architect could ever design. With that issue settled, Wright set to work on the project.

By March 1929, Wright, his family, and a cadre of draftsmen, were fully installed in his desert camp "Ocotilla" near Chandler, Arizona. He was in the midst of preparing final working drawings for the hotel resort San Marcos-in-the-Desert. He wrote to Guthrie about the St. Mark's design:

"I am looking forward with pleasure to working out this problem with you. Have already made sketches and will bring them down with me sometime either in March or May. Tremendously busy here. Real opportunities opening on every side. I hope you are well. Would be nice if

ST. MARK'S TOWERS IN THE BOUWERIE NEW YORK CITY
FRANK LLOYD WRIGHT ARCHITECT

A final perspective rendering of tower.
FLLW FDN # 2905.006.

Right: Perspective drawing of a tower
building for the H. C. Price Company.
FLLW FDN # 5215.004.

you were out here in this desert instead of in the human desert. I suppose pouring water upon roots in sterile ground there is really your job." [15]

Among the draftsmen working with Wright on the drawings for San Marcos while living in camp-like conditions on the Arizona desert was Vladimir Karfik, from Czechoslovakia. He had previously worked for Le Corbusier, whom he found cold and disinterested in his draftsmen. Working with Wright, however, he found that he was often invited to take meals with Wright and Olgivanna, the atmosphere was always one of cordiality and mutual respect. It was Karfik who made the final color pencil renderings of St. Mark's tower.

In describing the tower when it was later published in *The Architectural Forum*, January 1938, Wright wrote:

"A shaft of concrete rises through the floors engaging each floor slab as one passes through the shaft at eighteen levels. Each floor proceeds outward as a cantilever slab extended from the shaft. The slab, thick at the shaft, grows thinner by way of an overlapping scale pattern as it goes outward until at the final leap to the rectangle it is no more than 3 inches thick. The outer enclosing shell of glass and copper is pendent from these cantilever slabs. The inner partitions rest upon the slab. Quadruple in plan (four double decked apartments to each floor, each apartment unaware of the other as all are looking outward), the structure eliminates entirely the weight and waste space of masonry walls. The central shaft, standing inside away from lighted space, carries the elevators and entrance hallway well within itself. Two of the exterior walls of every

apartment are entirely of glass set into sheet copper framing. But the building is so placed that the sun shines on only one wall at a time and the narrow upright blades, or mullions, project nine inches so that as the sun moves, shadows fall on the glass surfaces. The building increases substantially in area from floor to floor as the structure rises—in order that the glass frontage of each story may drip clear of the one below, the building, thus, cleaning itself. It is a logical development of the idea of a tall building in the age of glass and steel—as logical engineering as the Brooklyn Bridge or the ocean liner. But the benefits of modernity such as this are not merely economic. There is greater privacy, safety, and beauty for human lives within it than is possible in any other type of apartment building. Here again is the poise, balance, lightness and strength that may characterize the creations of this age instead of masonry mass which is an unsuitable, extravagant and unsafe hangover from feudal times."

Another drawing (p. 75) in the file shows four towers rather than one, but that proposal was obviously abandoned at an early stage. As time passed, indecision rose among the vestrymen and the go-ahead to prepare final drawings for the one tower was constantly postponed. About these delays, Wright wrote to Guthrie:

"I shall never be popular. I can't say I wish to be. But I can be faithful, efficient and valuable to anyone who sincerely wants to build a better building and get more out of it in every way than is common. I am not hard to work with because I never ask an unreasonable thing of anyone. If I can't show my client his best interest by educating him along one line—I try another. So it will be with you and your people. But so far you've been so afraid of committing yourself,— or something or other—the matter has never come squarely up to me in any way."[16]

Yet again Wright was loathe to lose a fine idea, and twenty-five years later, he took out the plans for St. Mark's and revised them for the H. C. Price Company office building in Bartlesville, Oklahoma. When the client, Hal Price, came to the Hillside drafting room following his first meeting with Wright, as he entered the room Wright exclaimed, "Mr. Price, I am going to give you a building I have been trying to build for 25 years."

Four years later, when the tower was completed, it was opened to the townspeople of Bartlesville and a lecture by Wright and Price was part of the occasion. When Wright's address was finished, a member of the audience rose and asked, "Mr. Wright, what is the first thing you consider when designing a building for a client?" To which he responded, "Well, I give the client what he wanted." Hal Price, at this point, interrupted and said, "Hold on now, Frank, when I came to you for a design for my company, all I wanted was a building of three stories with office space enough for our needs. And I got a nineteen-story tower, with ten rental duplex apartments as well as other office spaces for rent." Wright turned to Price, and with a great smile and a twinkle in his eyes, he said, "Hal, you didn't know what you wanted!"

VIEW FROM THE SOUTH
BUILDING FOR THE H.C. PRICE C

EDGAR J. KAUFMANN HOUSE, "FALLINGWATER"

Mill Run, Pennsylvania. 1934

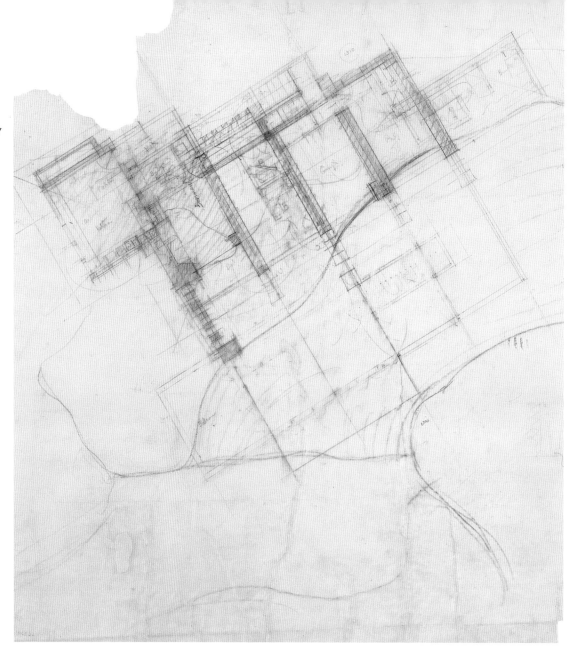

Preliminary plan. FLLW FDN # 3602.166.

When the Kaufmanns, Edgar and Liliane, first saw the preliminary studies that Wright had made for their country house (he himself coined the name "Fallingwater") they expressed surprise that the house was placed over the waterfalls. They had envisioned a location lower down the stream, looking up at the falls. Wright assured them that they would not just look at the falls, but live with them.

Their son, Edgar jr., was an apprentice to Wright in 1934. He had just returned from studies in painting and drawing in Vienna. America was in the throes of the Great Depression and he felt disconnected from the nation. A friend suggested he read Frank Lloyd Wright's *An Autobiography*. Reading it, he sensed that Wright had found what he himself was missing. He decided to become an apprentice, but not to become an architect. Indeed, his reason for coming to Taliesin was more to explore Wright's thought rather than preparing for a career in architecture. Soon his family came to meet the Wrights, and there was an immediate ambiance that formed from that first meeting. The Kaufmanns expressed a wish for a new country house on their property in Western Pennsylvania. The existing wood cottage seemed ill-placed, and not sufficient for their weekends in the country along with the various guests who accompanied them into this foray of woodland beauty. The principal feature of the property was a cascade of water pouring over the ledges of rock.

In December 1934, they invited Wright to come and see this location where they wanted a new house. On his return, Wright wrote to them, "The visit to the waterfall in the woods stays with me and a domicile has taken vague shape in my mind to the music of the stream."[17]

And thus Fallingwater was born. However, the design did not appear on Wright's drafting board for some time. In response to a letter from Kaufmann about the house design, he replied that the scheme was progressing, even though there was nothing down on paper. The apprentices grew anxious when Wright, upon receiving a phone call from Kaufmann who was in Milwaukee at the time, assured him there was something to show him, and invited him to drive over to Taliesin. At this invitation, the apprentices were horrified that still no design had been made. What they did not realize was that in his mind the design was percolating, and soon he sat down and let it out on paper. That initial conceptual elevation (p. 79) must surely have been what he presented to Kaufmann, and the final structure was little changed from this drawing, which shows how his first study is so complete in his mind that it foretells what the outcome will be. It is not known what other drawings he showed Kaufmann, but his conceptual plan reveals how he has positioned the house in relation to the stream, the waterfalls, and the rock ledge. On this drawing he has placed the house at an angle to the falls, with the massive supporting piers heavily drawn in graphite pencil at the basement level against the rock cliff and in the stream. The main floor level was drawn directly upon it in red, and in pencil, also denoting a special boulder that was intended to become the

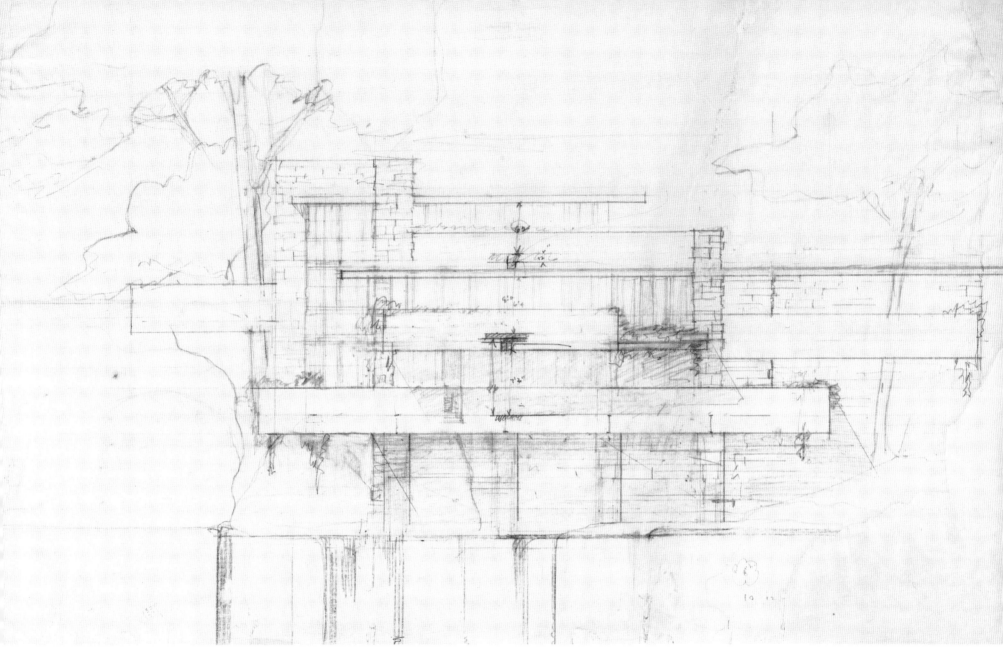

Preliminary elevation. FLLW FDN # 3602.049.

hearth for the fireplace. There are also indications of the second and third floors. Indeed, this one sheet is indicative of the almost three-dimensional vision that was Wright's special genius. Prior to the famous perspective of Fallingwater (pp. 84-85), three other views were proposed but later rejected (pp. 80-81, 83). Nonetheless, they represent different views of the house. The final ground-floor plan (p. 82) reveals the relationship of Fallingwater to the stream, the cliff, and the falls.

Fallingwater was Wright's first venture into the use of reinforced concrete for a residence. He realized that only with this material could he position the building with its cantilevered rooms and terraces over a waterfall.

During the construction, he sent an apprentice to help supervise and interpret the drawings which were made, revised, and made again as the building grew. From the time that the fellowship was opened in 1932, Wright so well-trained the young men and women at Taliesin that they were well-equipped to perform this task of superintendence. In the case of Fallingwater, it was essential, from the beginning, that the house be built in proper relation to the stream and the falls. This demanded a constant dialogue between Wright and the apprentice on location.

At first he assigned Robert Mosher, an apprentice who was called "Little Sunshine" because of his constant, beaming smile and his upbeat personality. He made some mistakes, which Kaufmann said cost him some money, but Wright prevailed:

"He may be, and is, costing us both a little money, but not much. Well, it's only fair that you pay your small share of the education of these young fellows—America's future architects. They are giving you and me, where your opus is concerned, something no money can buy; an alive and enthusiastic interest in our work and the eager cooperation that goes with it, too.

"On all the buildings I have built with the Fellowship alongside, from the very first I have found quicker comprehension and more intelligent faithful cooperation, counting in all the aggravating dropping of stitches from first to last, than I ever got out of 'experienced' professionals at any time."[18]

In one of the many letters between Wright and the supervising apprentice at Fallingwater, he made clear:

"In discussing matters with our client it is well to have in mind the motif of the building—that is say why it is as it is where it is. We got down into that glen to associate directly with the stream and planned the house for that association."[19]

Fallingwater was a difficult house to build because of several factors: its location above a stream of water that became a waterfall, the novel use of reinforced concrete for a residence, and the necessity of getting it built with a local contractor and workmen. Everything had to be done out there in the wilderness, far from urban civilization. In today's world, to order concrete is a simple matter of calling up a supplier, ordering a certain number of yards of concrete (as it is measured), and a huge truck arrives on site, the mix still churning in it so as not to set up, waiting to be funneled down into the forms. At Fallingwater, this was never the case. A small gasoline-operated concrete mixer prepared the concrete, then it was dumped into a wheelbarrow and brought up to the site and poured into the forms.

All during the construction, Wright was compelled to create drawing after drawing, send them on to his on-site apprentice, who was then able to explain them to the contractor and workmen. These included not only structural details but all interior drawings for all the rooms: shelves, bookcases, cabinets, lighting, etc. A skilled craftsman, Manuel Sandoval, made

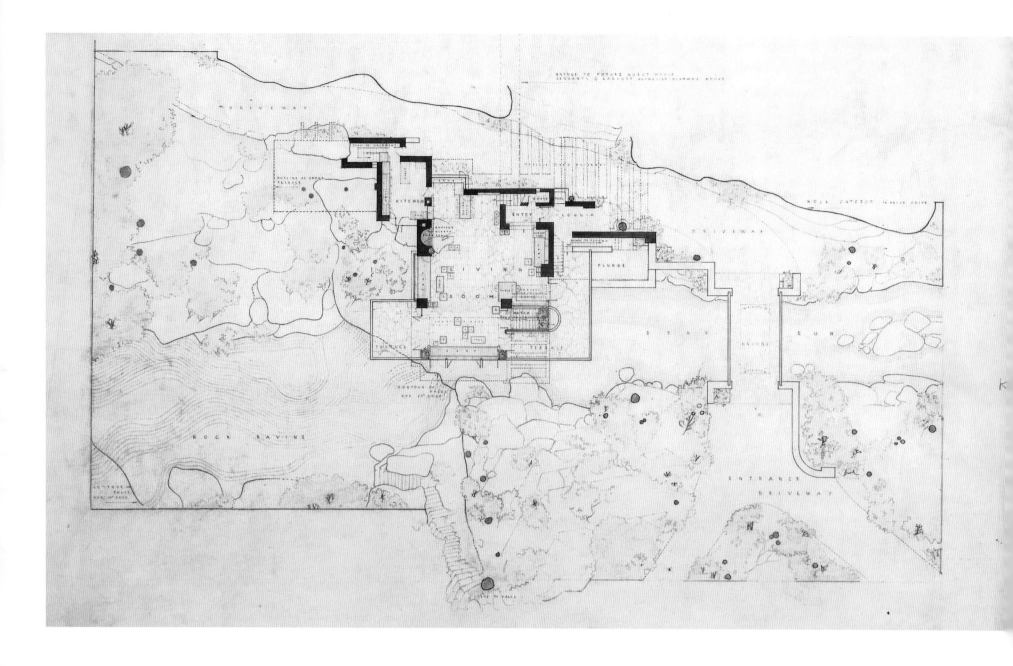

all the cabinetwork in the house out of black walnut, producing some of the finest cabinetwork ever achieved in a Frank Lloyd Wright house.

As the years went by, and after the deaths of Liliane and Edgar Sr., Edgar jr. was concerned with the fate of Fallingwater, and decided to provide that it be opened to the public and maintained by the Western Pennsylvania Conservancy. When asked why he chose a nature conservancy, he explained: for three good reasons—it was not a government agency, nor a university, nor a museum. He felt that any one of those three would not take proper care of the house and its surrounding environment—the natural world in which Fallingwater is a sympathetic and essential companion.

"Agelong upheavals of Earth formed the natural terrain, and the terrain nourished life. Humans came—aborigines, settlers, vacationers— among them my family. The family called on genius, and the terrain—barely altered— gained deep significance. . . . Thus it is clear that the dynamic process at the core of Fallingwater is a necessary unifying of humankind and the natural environment. When this is appreciated, Fallingwater is understood and will continue to be adaptive, opening the minds of human beings . . . to a sense of the marvelous."[20]

Above: Final plan. FLLW FDN # 3602.158.
Right, top: Early perspective.
FLLW FDN # 3602.002.
Right, bottom: Early perspective.
FLLW FDN # 3602.003.

Following pages: Perspective.
FLLW FDN #3602.004.

HERBERT F. JOHNSON HOUSE, "WINGSPREAD"

Wind Point, Wisconsin. 1937

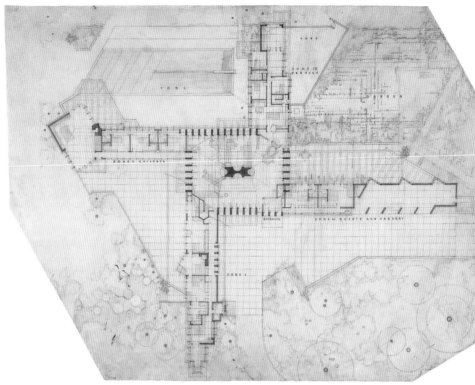

"Wingspread" is the name that Frank Lloyd Wright gave to the house he designed for Herbert Johnson, president of S. C. Johnson & Son, Co. The name derives from the plan in which four wings extend out from a central core, one for Mr. and Mrs. Johnson and their daughter, another for their three sons and a playroom, the third for guests and a carport, and finally one for the kitchen, service, and servants' quarters. His first sketch (above, left), which he carefully signed and dated January 15, 1936, clearly shows the plan with its central core and four wings. He referred to these wings as "zones" and considered the plan as an articulation that began with the Avery Coonley House, Riverside, Illinois, thirty years earlier. The central core is a three-story

great hall divided by a chimney stack with five fireplaces: the entrance hall, family living room, library, living room, and dining room. Above and running around the chimney is a cluster of skylights, while at ground level tall French doors open onto terraces and gardens. The house is oriented so that sunlight falls into each of the rooms.

During the construction of the house, a workman noticed that a white dove had flown into the belvedere of the building, then flown away and disappeared, never to return. He regarded this as a bad omen and told Wright that the young wife would never live in the house. Shortly after, Jane Johnson took sick and died. The bereaved husband lost all interest in completing the building. It took much persuasion on the part of Wright

(who now was friend as well as architect) to encourage him to continue.

"I felt sure she would want to see him finish what he had so happily begun with her; he needed, and now more than ever, a refuge such as that house would be for his children; he owed it, if not to himself, if not to her, then to Racine not to leave an empty shell of a house desecrated in desperation instead of nobly memorializing the memory of the wife he had lost. After a while I guess he began to see it something like that. Because we began to work on it again. We completed the house in every particular as planned for a wife and four children. He seemed to sigh with relief upon seeing actually realized the building—the house they had both worked on with me and of which he had fondly dreamed. It turned out a veritable thing of the

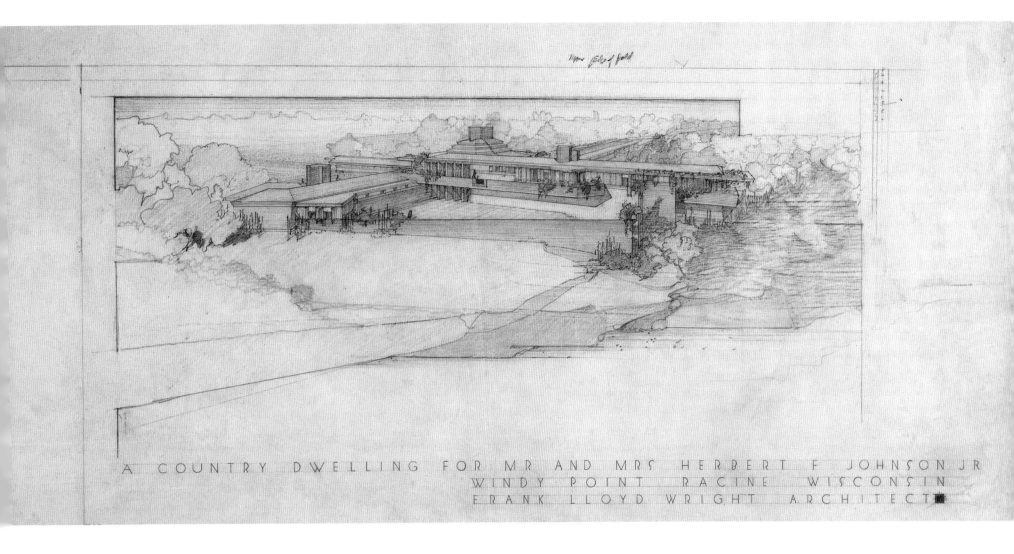

A COUNTRY DWELLING FOR MR AND MRS HERBERT F JOHNSON JR
WINDY POINT RACINE WISCONSIN
FRANK LLOYD WRIGHT ARCHITECT

Spirit: a true consort to the prairie. The 'last of the prairie houses' it shall be, so I thought, though I don't know why. Should you ever see it, observe this fact . . . the house did something remarkable to that site. The site was not stimulating before the house went up—but like developer poured over a negative, when you view the environment framed by the Architecture of the house from within, somehow, like magic—the charm appears in the landscape and will be there wherever you look. The site seems to come alive."[21]

Johnson flew his own plane, and the children, upon hearing the roaring motor, raced out to greet him. Wright observed this, and added a detail to the house that was not on the original plans: a glass enclosed observatory attached to the chimney-stack and reached by a spiral

staircase going from the family living room up and out onto the roof. Here the children—and the space is small, just big enough for the youngsters—could look out over the prairie and watch their father either take off or land his plane.

As to the quality of the building itself, it was constructed on a heavy footing course of white Kasota sandstone, and—what Wright considered—the best brickwork he had even seen in his life.

When the house was completed, Wright carefully undertook the planning for the landscaping. At the entrance court, he suggested a cluster of tall fir trees. When asked how they should be laid out, he asked for a sack of small potatoes. Standing at the edge of the area, one by one he tossed the potatoes out over the field, saying, "Plant a tree where each potato has landed."

Preliminary plans.
Far left: First sketch. FLLW FDN # 3703.004
Left: FLLW FDN # 3703.013.
Above: Perspective. FLLW FDN # 3703.001.

Following pages: Perspective.
FLLW FDN # 3703.002.

A COUNTRY DWELLING F

JR.

OR MR AND MRS HERBERT F JOHNSON

WINDY POINT RACINE WISCONSIN

FRANK LLOYD WRIGHT ARCHITECT

89

RALPH JESTER HOUSE

Palos Verdes, California. 1938, Project

One afternoon in the summer of 1938, Wright and Olgivanna were having tea in the Taliesin living room when Olgivanna asked, "Why is it, Frank, that you have never designed a home with rooms that are circular?" To which he countered, "Well, the forms of architecture, inspired by nature such as crystals and rock forms, employ the square, triangle, and hexagon." "But Frank," she continued, "In nature the circle is also prevalent, from the cosmos to a cross section of the human cell." And the conversation about circles in domiciles ended there.

Olgivanna maintained that a strong component of Wright's genius was his remarkable power of absorption. Regardless of where the idea came from, he took it and ran, so to speak. He himself once admitted, "I never turn my back on a good idea." Olgivanna, from her point, was well aware of this attribute of his psyche.

Several days after their conversation about circles, he came to her and said, "Olgivanna, look at this little 'abstraction' for a circular home." It was the plan, elevation, and perspective of the Ralph Jester House, in Palos Verdes, California. Subsequently he wrote to the client, "Have hit upon a nice scheme for you—a true abstraction. Where are you? When can I show it to you? I would like to show it to you myself." [22] The radical scheme of the house is why he wanted to show it to Jester in person. Usually when he came upon a scheme that was totally new in his work, he felt it important to explain the idea himself to the client.

The Jester House, with its group of circles facing onto a patio with a covered roof but open on the sides, was perfect for the California climate. The larger circle contained the living room, while smaller circles for the dining room and bedroom opened, as did the living room, onto the patio with full-length plate glass doors. The patio, in turn, opened onto a large circular swimming pool, the outer edge a negative one, so that the water would cascade over the edge and run down into a small ravine as the base of the wall. The circles and patio were six feet nine inches in height, while the living room, the more social element of the house, was twelve feet six inches high.

On the perspective and plan, he has inscribed: 'The plywood house—plywood back to back [...] and [...] applied to each other to form outside walls. The whole an open living room beside a pool. Hollywood Hills or Hawaiian Mountains. FLLW." (The house was also proposed for a client living in Hawaii.) Concerning his reference to plywood, he explained that plywood is strongest when bent in curvilinear shapes.

It seemed that the "abstraction" was more than Jester could absorb, and the project was abandoned. But Wright never lost sight of the plan, and over the next twenty-one years he proposed variations on this theme for other clients, in other locations. In a climate less conducive to the openness of the Jester House, he enclosed in the patio with floor-to-ceiling glass doors to form a central atrium.

Wright maintained that the circle allowed for even greater flexibility of movement within the room than either the square or the hexagon. But when each subsequent design went into the stage of working drawings, the clients were seized with apprehension and none of them were built. As to their surprise about living within a circular room, Wright once countered, "It is perfectly natural for human movement, after all, only the military walks square!"

Plan and perspective.
FLLW FDN # 3807.003.

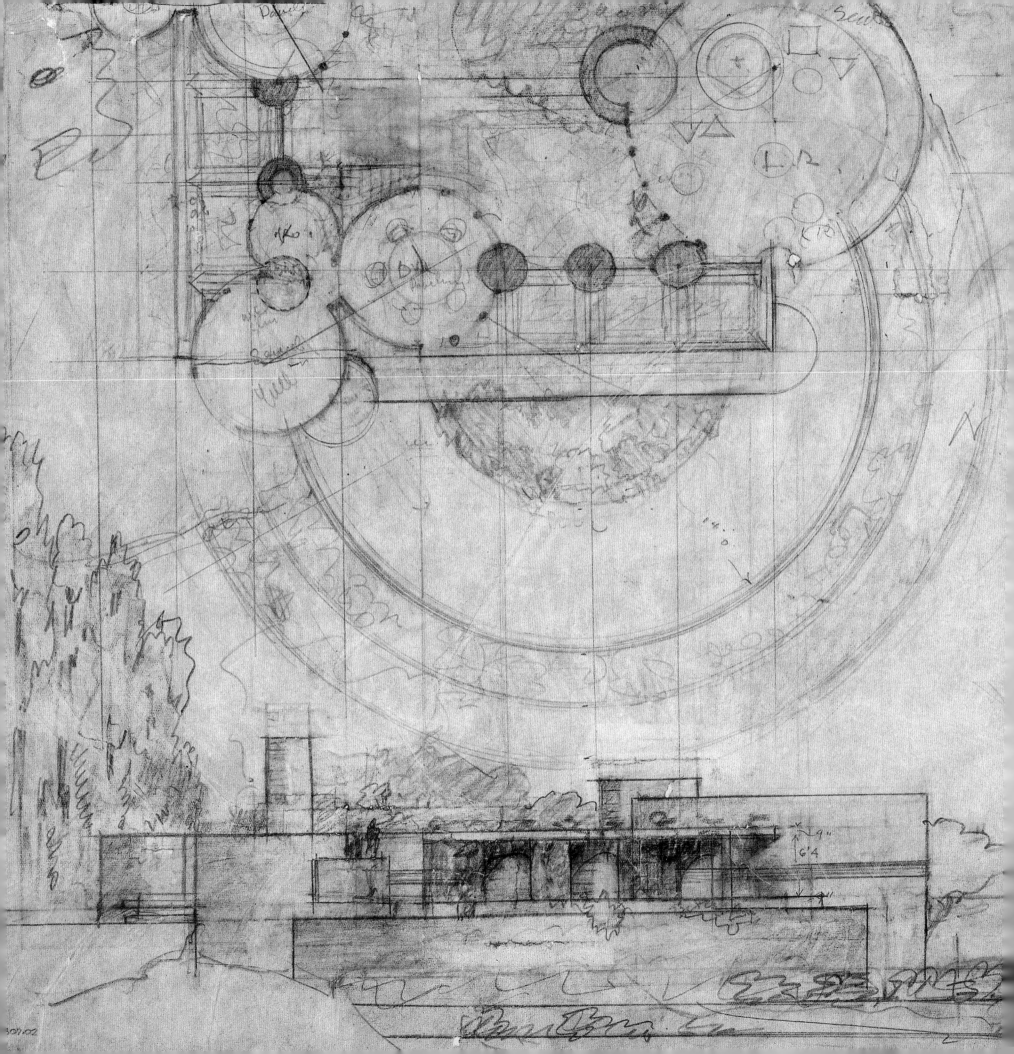

Plan and elevation.
FLLW FDN # 3807.002.

DR. LUDD M. SPIVEY HOUSE

Fort Lauderdale, Florida. 1939, Project

Dr. Ludd M. Spivey, President of Florida Southern College, was building a Frank Lloyd Wright campus in Lakeland, Florida, and at the same time desired to build a Wright house for himself in Fort Lauderdale. The site was a tract of land bordering a canal, and Wright produced a design that engaged it. In general, the plan is a group of circles, the main one being the two story living room. Adjacent to that is a circular kitchen, and two circular bedrooms with a connecting bathroom. The upper story of the living room is a circular balcony, projecting slightly over the living room lower walls. Windows look out onto the landscape under a flat, sheltering roof. The walls of the living room below are perforated concrete blocks, set with stained glass inserts, a detail that Wright also used for the Annie Pfeiffer Chapel at Florida Southern College. There are two entries to the house, one by the kitchen and passing the bedroom wing on the way to the living room. The other leads directly to stairs up to the living room balcony. The scheme is quintessentially "Floridian" in character, inviting cool breezes into the living room but providing more protection for the bedroom wing, an ideal dwelling for the tropics.

On this conceptual plan and elevation (opposite page, top), Wright has inscribed "Steamline Canal side cottage for Dr. Ludd M. Spivey, Lauderdale, Fla, April 4, '39. FLLW."

Although the doctor was an advocate of organic architecture, as his intense and dedicated campaign to build the Frank Lloyd Wright campus at Florida Southern College amply proves, when it came to building a Frank Lloyd Wright house for himself and his wife, that seemed to have been another case altogether. Questionably, perhaps it was Mrs. Spivey who was content living in more conventional surroundings and was hesitant to take a leap into the waters of modern architecture?

Some years later, another client, Dr. Alfred Bergman, commissioned Wright for a house in the same location as the Spivey opus, bordering a canal in Fort Lauderdale. Wright revised the Spivey plan for him, but that, too, was never built (p. 96-97).

Right, top: Early plan and elevation. FLLW FDN # 3911.004. Right, bottom: Perspective. FLLW FDN # 3911.003.

Following pages: Perspective of Bergman House. FLLW FDN # 4708.001

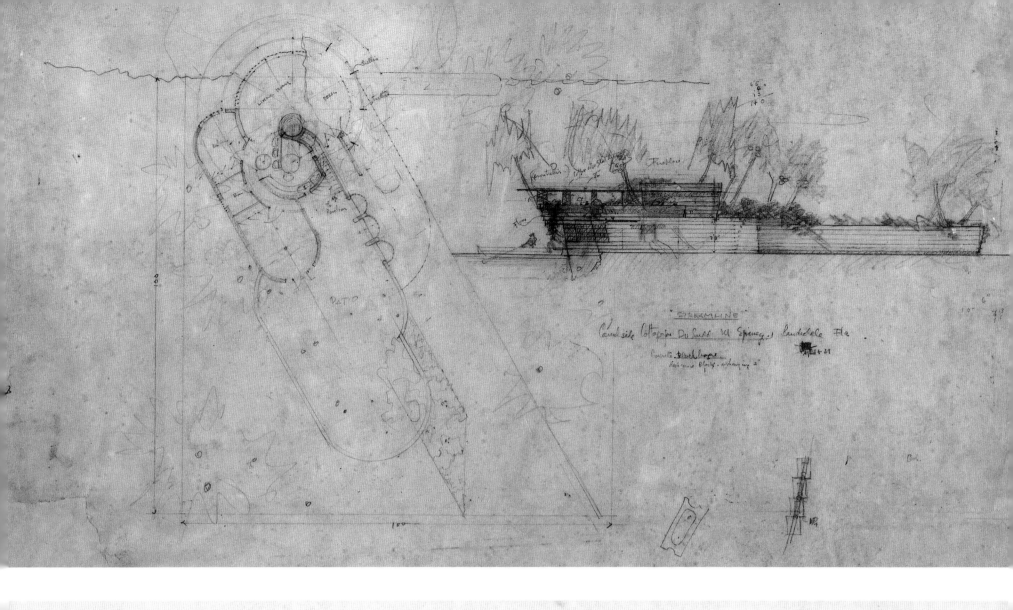

"STREAMLINE"

Canalside Cottage Dr Ludd M Spivey, Lauderdale Fla.

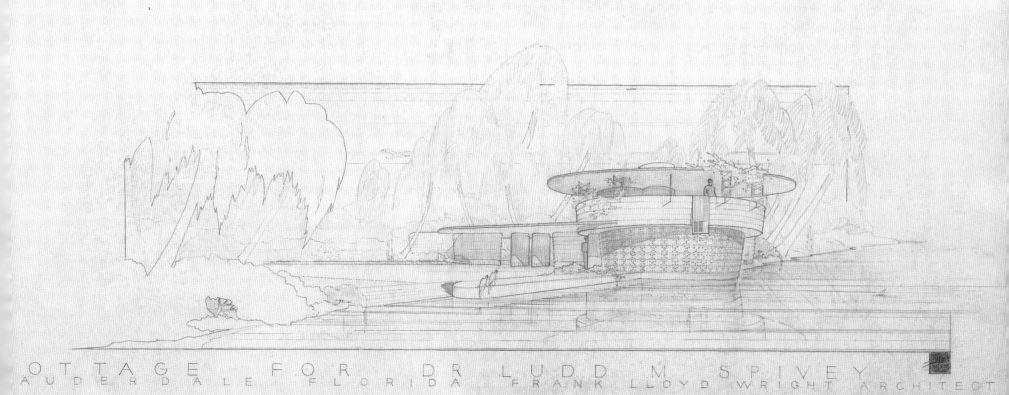

COTTAGE FOR DR LUDD M SPIVEY
LAUDERDALE FLORIDA   FRANK LLOYD WRIGHT ARCHITECT

HOUSE   FOR   MR.   AND   MRS.   ALFRED   C.

F R

ERGMAN   ST. PETERSBURG   FLORIDA

NK   LLOYD   WRIGHT   ARCHITECT

ROSE PAUSON HOUSE

Phoenix, Arizona. 1939, Destroyed

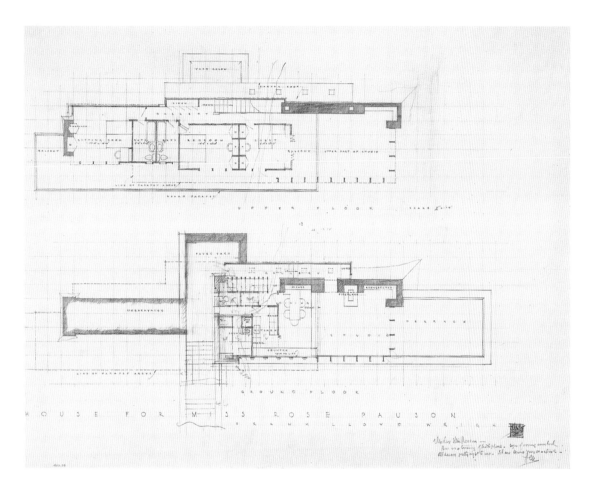

Frank Lloyd Wright enthusiasts have long admired the quiet strength and noble form of the Rose Pauson House. It is not a large work, but is beautifully beautifully in fine redwood contrasted with massive stone masonry. On two levels, the first contains the studio, dining area, kitchen, and servant's room. The first sketch (not shown) shows the plan and elevation, while a more detailed sketch elevation (top right) reveals another side, as seen from the entrance steps. The second level provides three bedrooms and two baths, with a balcony overlooking the studio. Her sister Gertrude Pauson occupied the house with her.

Rose Pauson was an artist, involved in painting, woodblock designs, and textiles. Accordingly, Wright has her studio-living room with tall glass doors facing north. As well as the north light being desirable for an artist, it also provides the finest view of the Phoenix Mountains. Although prolific in her output of landscapes and other works, created at her summer residence at 2510 Jackson Street in San Francisco, a house and studio in Los Altos, and her winter one on the desert, she never sold her work, instead giving it as gifts to her family and friends.

The entrance ascends from the roadway and carport up to the house via a long stretch of steps, almost as if approaching an Egyptian temple. To enter the house, a covered passageway, identified as the loggia, leads to a small outdoor stone balcony, and then, at a turn to the right, into the domicile itself. This type of entrance is typical for Wright: not going directly in, but reaching the interior by means of turns. Wright claimed that the Oriental mind thought in circular lines, while the Occidental thought in straight lines. He himself seemed a perfect combination of the two, and his work expressed that

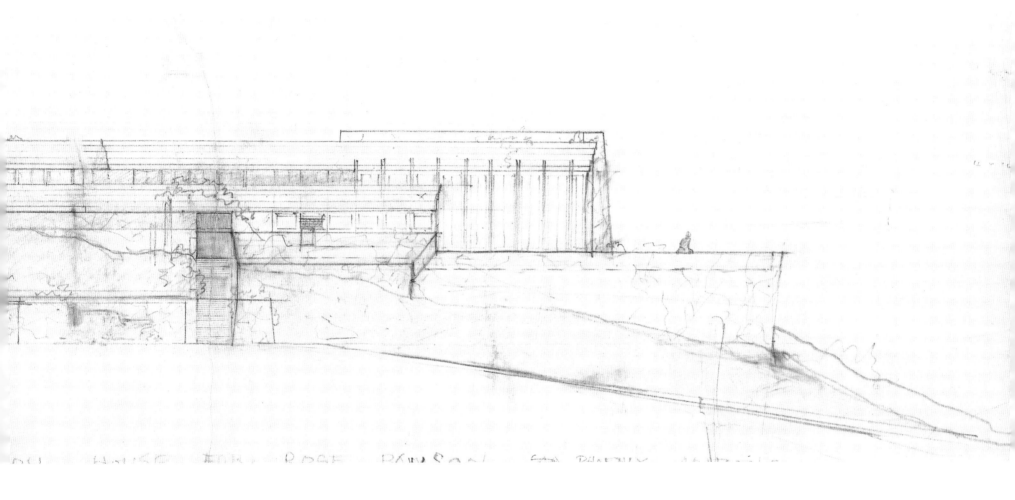

rare and wonderful grasp of the two worlds that Kipling, erroneously, claimed "shall never meet."

The Pauson House, whose construction began in 1940, cost $7,900 including the architect's fee. Yet a thorough study of the more than fifty sketches and working drawings that were prepared reveals such careful and intricate woodwork that it seems a cabinetmaker, not a carpenter, was required to execute it. The cost today for such work would be astronomical, to say the least. On the final perspective he has inscribed "Desert house just completed for the Pauson Sisters, Phoenix, Arizona."

Completed in 1942, the house was occupied by Rose and her sister for but one year. On their return to San Francisco following their first winter in their new house, the house was rented to other occupants. Fire broke out in April 1943, and the house was totally destroyed. Learning of this, Wright sent the following telegram to Rose:

"Shocked and mystified. Investigation should be thorough."[23] The loss of the Pauson House was a tragedy that resounded around the world. Its beauty now only captured in photography, it still remains "one of his best."

Left: Plan. FLLW FDN # 4011.008.
Above: Elevation. FLLW FDN # 4011.006.

Following pages: Final perspective. FLLW FDN # 4011.002.

A desert home just completed for the Pauson Sisters Phoenix Arizona

JOHN PEW HOUSE

Shorewood Hills, Wisconsin. 1939

The lot for the John Pew house is steeply sloped heavily wooded and descends down the hill to the shores of Lake Mendota. Since the lot was narrow, Wright conceived a plan that was raised off the ground, going vertical rather than horizontal. Yet the features of a long, wide balcony off the living room and the rooftop balcony over the living room lend a distinctly horizontal character to the building. The house was designed as a two-story structure, and its upper level is reserved for three bedrooms and a bath. Each bedroom has a corner window, but instead of the usual wide, long overhang, each room is provided with a projecting roof that shields each room's window, like the visor of a cap, rather than the wide brim of a hat.

As his career progressed, Wright invariably made the plan for the design before the elevation or any other details. "The plan is the thing. The thing comes to life in the plan. I think a plan is always beautiful—perhaps more beautiful than anything that ever comes after it. The idea is the plan; the plan contains the idea. The house is an idea, if it is a good house. That idea embraces all that composes or will compose the usefulness and beauty of that house. It is right there in the plan." [24]

A splendid example of this is seen on the sketch on the opposite page, where the plan was drawn first, immediately followed by the elevation which explains the exterior dimensions.

During the planning stages, Wright and Wes Peters, his son-in-law as well as apprentice and skilled engineer, went out to the site to mark the trees to be saved and those to be cut down: red strips of cloth for those to remove, white strips to save. A Norwegian woodsman was engaged to carry out the work of removing trees, and by mistake he took away those slated to be saved. Wes was distraught, and brought Wright to the site to see the damage. "That's alright," Wright replied, "we will adjust the location of the house, no problem."

When the bids came in to $6,900, the Pews were unable to procure a loan from their bank. The official remarked, "Kitchen open to the dining room without a door? All glass doors opening to the balcony? Floor heating? The house has no resale value." (No resale value? Years later the house was sold for close to $200,000. Pew was a forestry engineer at the University of Wisconsin, Madison, and he kept the cypress wood throughout the exterior and interior of the house in perfect condition.) As for the construction of house, Wes came to the rescue and undertook the contract himself.

When the house was newly completed, and it is one of Wright's finest and most romantic Usonian houses, Wes and Wright visited the Pews and saw that they were living graciously in their new domicile. Upon leaving, Wes turned to Wright and said, considering this was a work that combined generous balconies and a water feature (Lake Mendota), "Mr. Wright, we can call this house the poor man's Fallingwater." To which Wright countered, "No Wes, we will call Fallingwater the rich man's Pew house."

Elevation and plan. FLLW FDN # 4012.003.

Following pages: Final perspective. FLLW FDN # 4012.002.

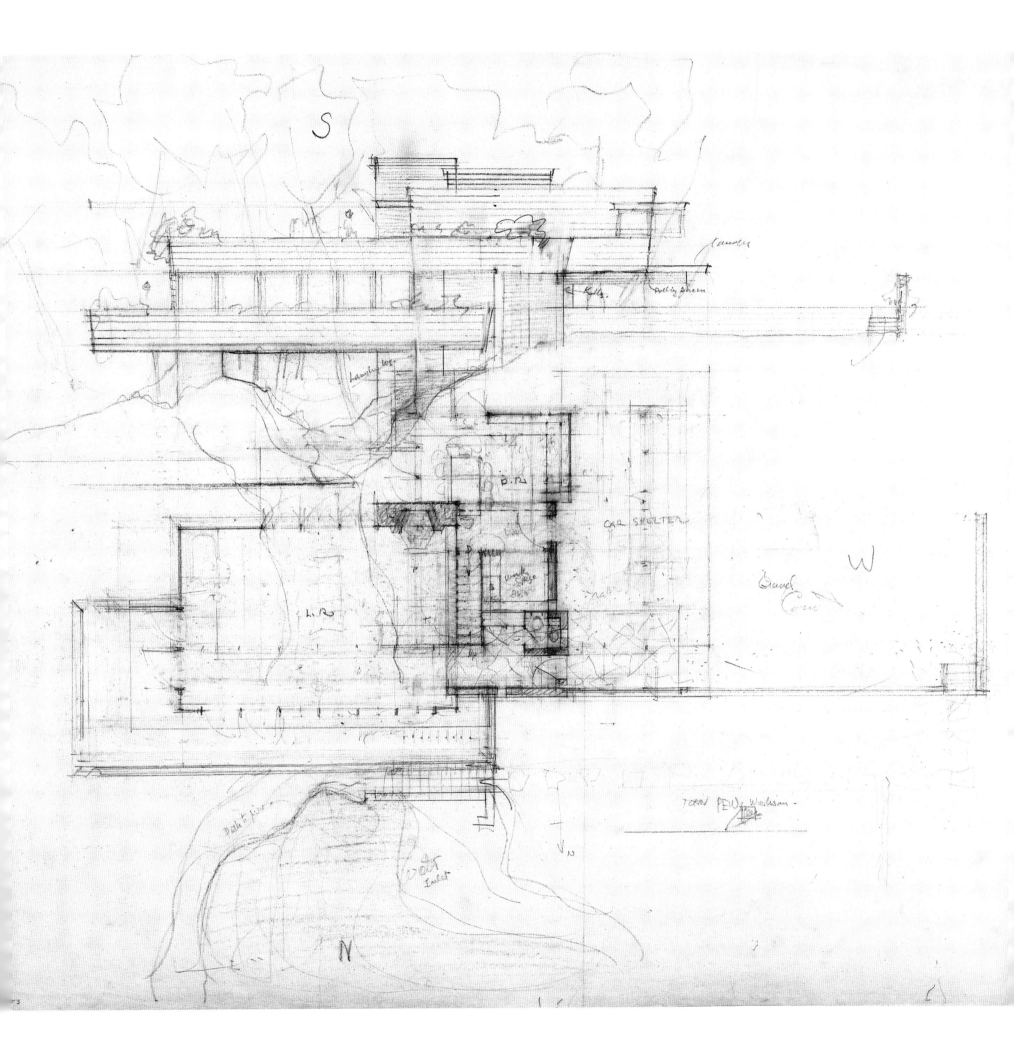

S

N

W

CAR SHELTER

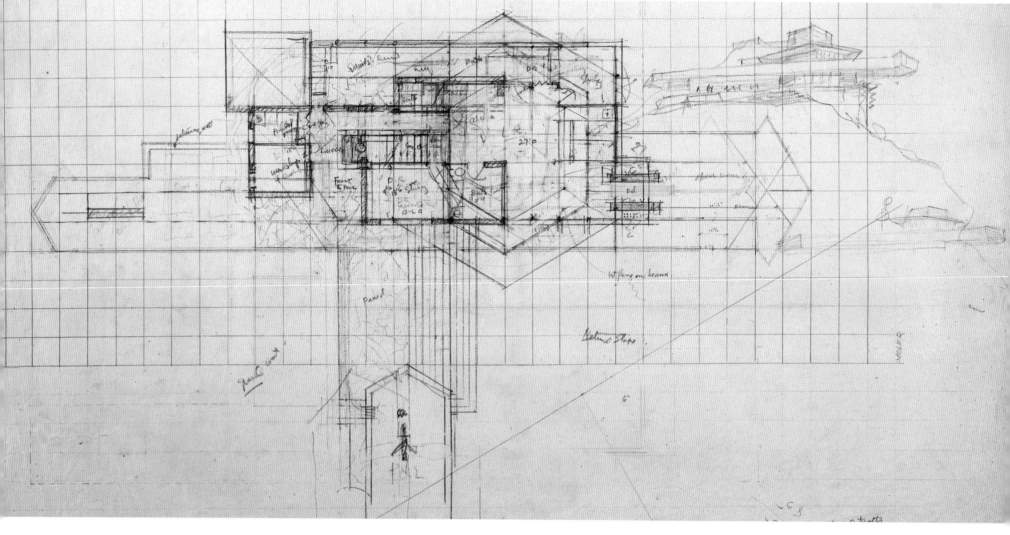

ARCH OBOLER HOUSE, "EAGLEFEATHER"

Malibu, California. 1940, Project

Above: Plans and thumbnail sketch.
FLLW FDN # 4018.009.
Right, top: Elevation. FLLW FDN # 4018.010.
Right, bottom: Section. FLLW FDN # 4018.031.

Following pages: Perspective. FLLW FDN # 4018.003.

Arch Oboler was a writer of radio plays and motion picture films, most of which were of a rather macabre nature. *Light Out* and *Inner Sanctum* were two of his famous radio plays during the 1940s. His property in Malibu, California, was on a tract of land with a pronounced hill, from which there was a distant view of the Pacific Ocean. Wright coined the phrase "Eaglefeather" for the home and studio he designed for Oboler. The conceptual sketch is a rare drawing where Wright has drawn the two floor plans, one above the other, the lower floor in red color pencil, the upper floor in blue, while on the side, in green, he made a thumbnail sketch view of the house (above).

The perspective (pp. 108-9) would indicate that the building sprung out from the top of the hill, but Wright was generally opposed to situating a home on a hill, believing that putting the house on the top of the hill it destroyed the hill. An elevation of Eaglefeather (oppoiste page, top) shows that the top of the hill does indeed rise above the house, and that the house engages the hillside. Inside, provisions were made for cinema projection, while at the lowest of three levels, a long, narrow room, walled in on all sides by stone walls, with a narrow slot window at the end was the studio, called Secret Retreat, where Oboler created his bizarre and often terrifying radio and film plots.

Eaglefeather was never built because Oboler's fortunes waxed and waned according to the income from his work, but on the flat ground of the site he did commission Wright for a studio and home, which was built. He later proposed an addition, which was called "Continuation," for more space to include a theater, but a family tragedy brought that work, already partially in construction, to an abrupt end.

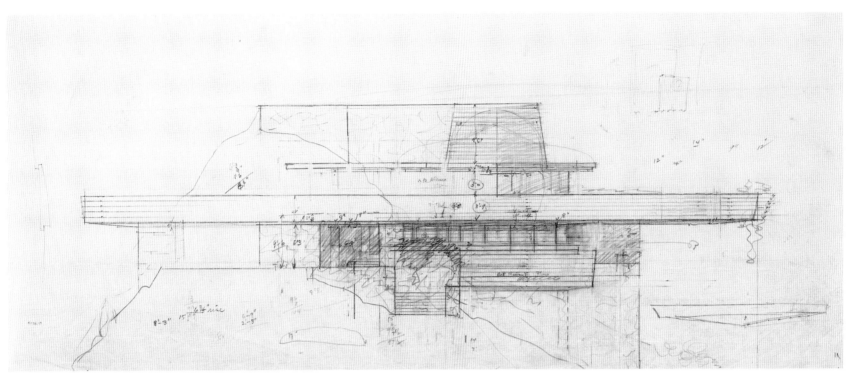

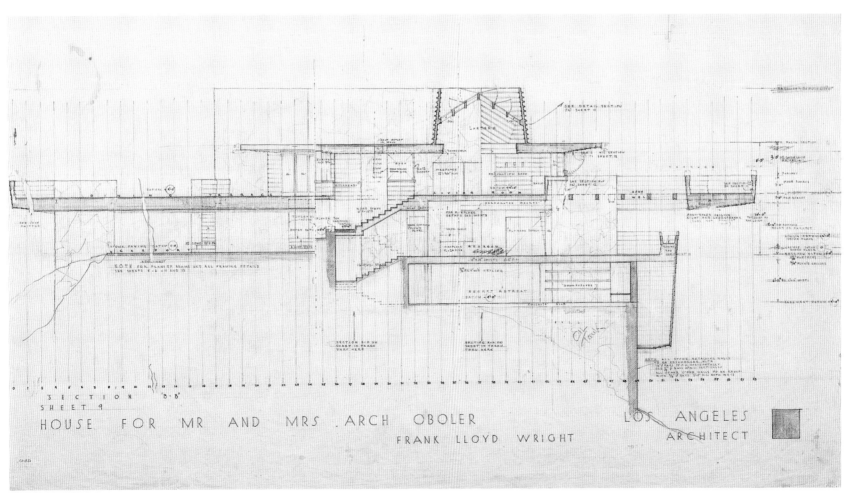

SECTION "B-B"
SHEET 9

HOUSE FOR MR AND MRS ARCH OBOLER   LOS ANGELES

FRANK LLOYD WRIGHT   ARCHITECT

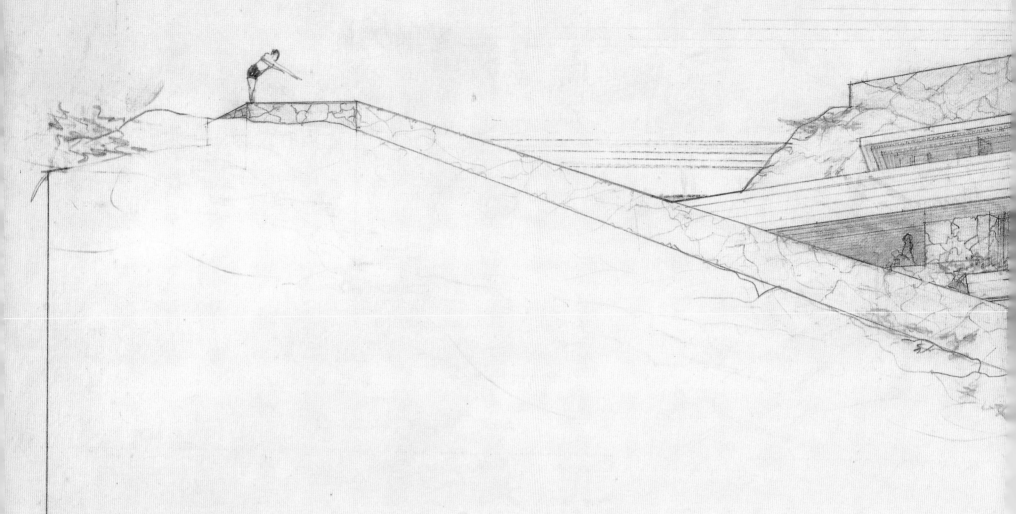

"EAGLEFEATHER"

FOR MR AND MRS ARCH O

FRANK LL

SOLER   LOS ANGELES
LOYD WRIGHT   ARCHITECT

LLOYD BURLINGHAM HOUSE, "POTTERY HOUSE"

El Paso, Texas. 1942, Project

When Wright published the Lloyd Burlingham House in his monograph issue of *The Architectural Forum*, January 1938, he described the project: "The Burlinghams have a place near El Paso piled with sweeping sands, continually drifting in swirling lines that suggest waves of the sea. This is a design for a pottery house, that is to say adobe. As contemplated here, the walls are molded accordingly. The general plan is a patio surrounded and protected by house and walls overlooking an immense valley."[25]

The nature of the site, along with the desire to use adobe in constructing the house, accord for the conceptual sketches, in plan, elevation, and thumbnail sketch wherein Wright has created a design that has no precedent. One drawing (not shown), drawn on the plot survey, indicates two arcs enclosing a central patio, one arc for the living room, and bedrooms, with glass doors opening onto the patio, while the opposite arc for the kitchen, laundry, servant's room, and storage has windows on the outside, but is closed to the patio. As well as facing into the patio, the living room also opens onto a semicircular outdoor terrace. This first sketch also contains an early version of the elevation along with a thumbnail sketch of the house. The drawing at the right, on the bottom, represens further developments of the plan, sections, and elevations.

The perspective (top right) reveals the pottery-like character of the house with adobe walls that have curved surfaces. There is an indication on some of the plans of a stairway between the dining room and kitchen that leads up to a studio on the roof above the dining room, but on the final perspective this has been eliminated. A unique feature of the house is the living room fireplace in which the hood is suspended from the ceiling above, the hearth open all around in a full circle. The domed structure on the far left of the perspective is a well and reservoir. Burlingham responded to the plan and perspective that he was enchanted with the house, and working drawings were begun but they were never completed.

Above: Perspective. FLLW FDN # 4202.001.
Right: Elevation. FLLW FDN # 4202.003.

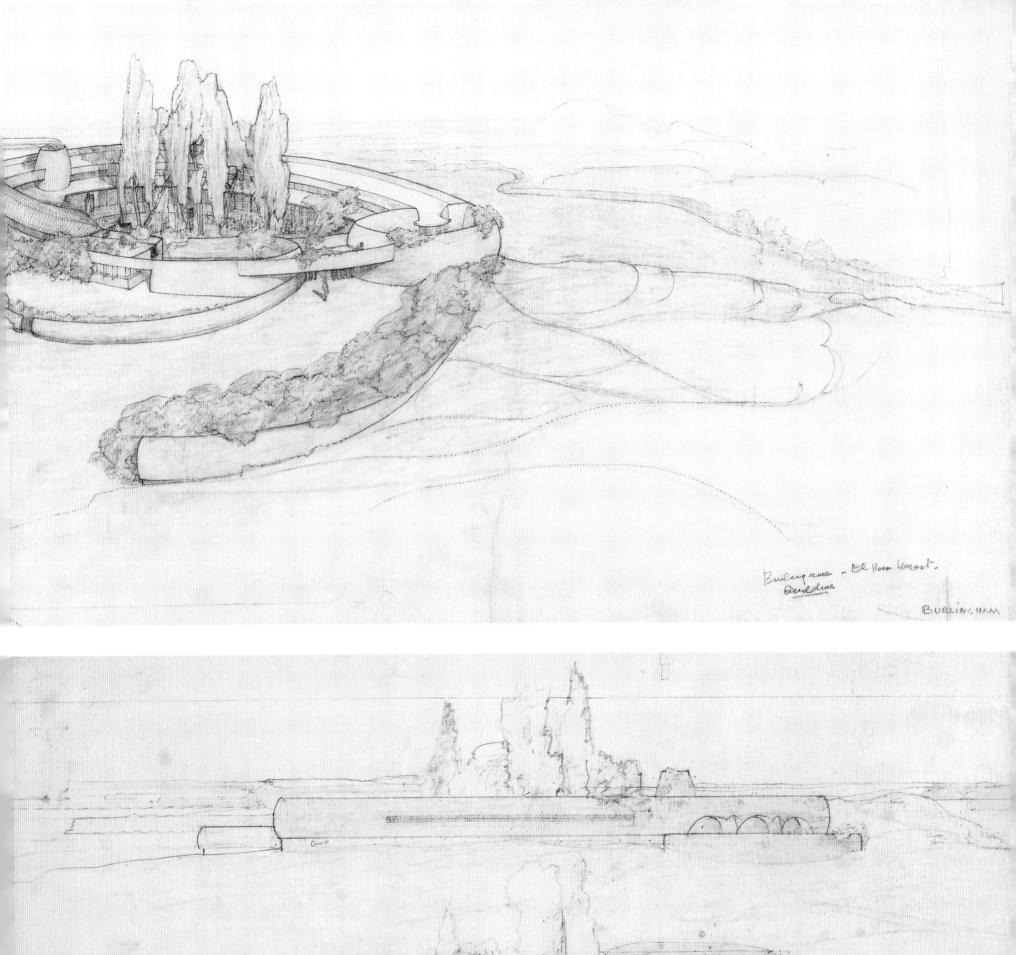

Burlingame - El Paso Robert.
Gardelene

BURLINGHAM

V. C. MORRIS HOUSE, "SEA CLIFF" SCHEME 1

San Francisco, California. 1943, Project

The first sketch (shown on p. 114) reveals the character of the house, a cliff-hanger with the top level extending with planting to the street level above.

The perspective of the V. C. Morris House looking up from the water's edge (p. 115) is one of the loveliest and most dramatic of all Wright's residential work. Wright's apprentice, John deKoven Hill, made the perspective and once remarked, "I especially made the waves at the foot of the hill inspired by Hokusai's famous print!" Seen from below, the house is the only cliff hanger Wright made of a house. The other famous cliff-hanger in the collection is the view from below of the Meteor Crater Resort in Arizona (see p. 302).

The Morris House clings to its 110-foot seaside cliff as a reinforced concrete tower of four levels, the top level being the living room, labeled as "lounge," followed by the breakfast room, kitchen, and entrance loggia. A small outdoor balcony from the breakfast room looks over the cliff and down to the ocean on the other side. Surrounding the lounge is another outdoor balcony, the parapet constructed with open metal railings so that from a seated position in the lounge, the view is still enjoyed. The next level down provides bedrooms for the owners and guests. Below is another level providing further guest rooms, this time with a square

Drawing of "pierade," planted with roof garden. FLLW FDN # 4303.001.

balcony. The lowest level is reserved for utilities and storage. All levels are connected by ramps, with an open well running down four levels with hanging plants from above. The house is connected to the cliff and the road on the street level by a covered "pierade," a term coined by Wright, which is planted as a roof garden (above). This arrangement prompted Wright to describe the opus "A house to the ocean, a garden to its neighbors." [26] Other roof slabs have turned up edges and are waterproof, covered with 16 inches of soil planted in grass, flowers, vines, and shrubs.

Drawings and specifications were made during the war years (Second World War), but construction had to be deferred at that time, since there was a ban on all construction materials that were needed for the war effort. Temporarily putting the project on hold, Mr. and Mrs. Morris, who ran a fine gift shop in San Francisco, then asked Wright to design a new shop for them (see p. 342). The construction of the shop became more costly than they had expected, but they went ahead with work just the same. It seemed that any concern about constructing the house was out of question. Wright once remarked about this as "The steamboat blew its whistle, and then had to return to shore for more firewood. . . ."

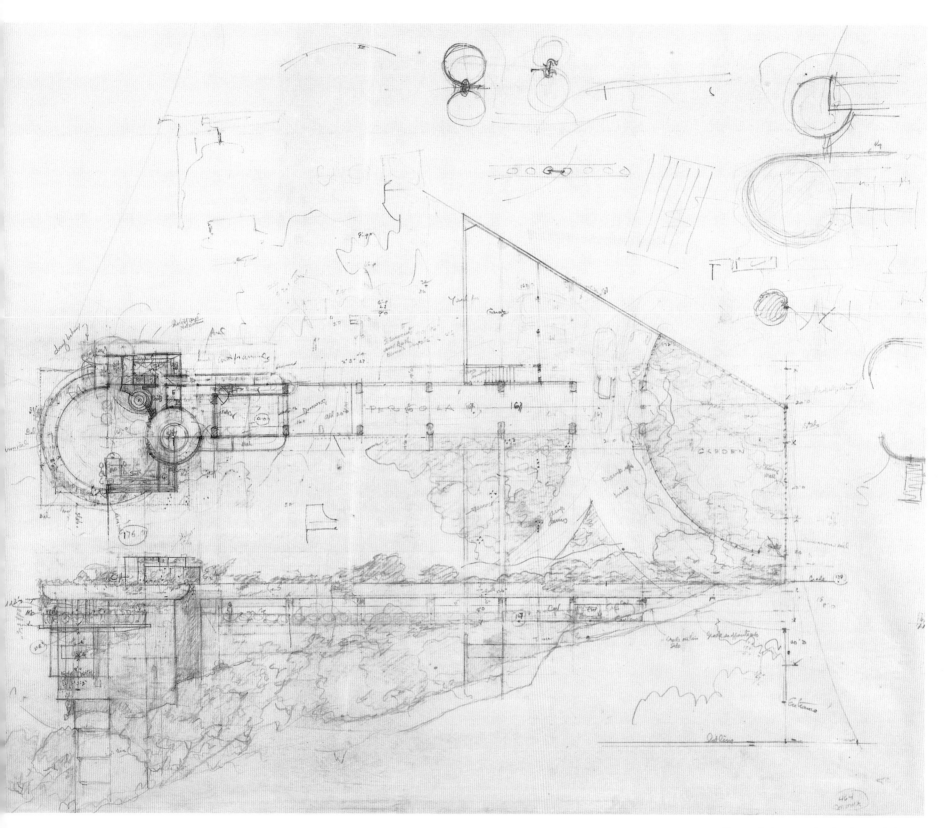

Above: Preliminary sketch, plan and elevation.
FLLW FDN # 4303.006
Right: Perspective. FLLW FDN # 4303.004.

STUART HALDORN HOUSE, "THE WAVE"

Carmel, California.1945, Project

The property for the Haldorn House had two pronounced circumstances. One, the property itself was of a most unusual configuration, and two, there were two roads on it, rather than the usual one. On the east side was the road to access the house itself, while along the south border of the site another road, also a public one, ran out to the west edge of the land and then further north along the seacoast. This prompted Wright to place the house far back from that seacoast drive as the plan reveals. Concerning the seaside road, Wright wrote, "The public road along the sea was a drawback hard to overcome." [27] His solution to this was to create a bridge over that seacoast drive so that under the bridge a wide, low tunnel was formed, providing the lower rooms of the house, on ground level, with a view toward the ocean, while the upper rooms, on a third level, looked over the bridge and to the ocean as well.

Wright often claimed that limitations were an artist's best friend. The peculiar configuration of the Haldorn property is a case in point: Wright has taken that peculiarity and made it a feature of his plan (seen at right and far right). The unusual shapes of the rooms respond also to the placing of the house at the extreme edge of the property. Considering that this residence was so close to the ocean with its waves breaking upon the rocky coast, Wright designed the fenestration so that windows were stacked in a stepped-out way, with the panes opening down to prevent the prevailing ocean spray from entering the rooms (p. 118). The reinforced concrete roof of the house was designed to be planted. As the perspective indicates (p. 119), Wright named his design "The Wave."

However, during the design stage, it was obvious that the construction of a bridge and the complicated plan of the house may have proved more than the budget would allow, and the project was abandoned. But it remains one of his most innovative designs, and the ingenious detail

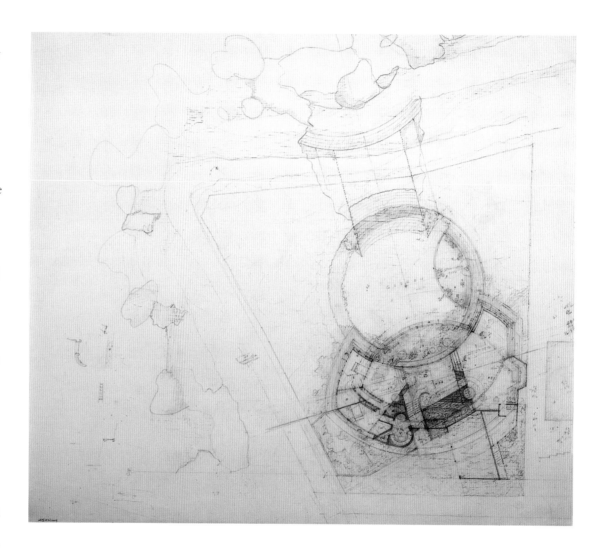

Above: Plan. FLLW FDN # 4502.004.
Right: Plan. FLLW FDN # 4502.002.

of the stepped-up fenestration facing the sea was eventually used for the Mrs. Clinton Walker House, later constructed in Carmel, California.

Wright rarely qualified the work that he had done in the past, but of the Haldorn House he did so, saying, "That was one the best houses I ever designed." [28]

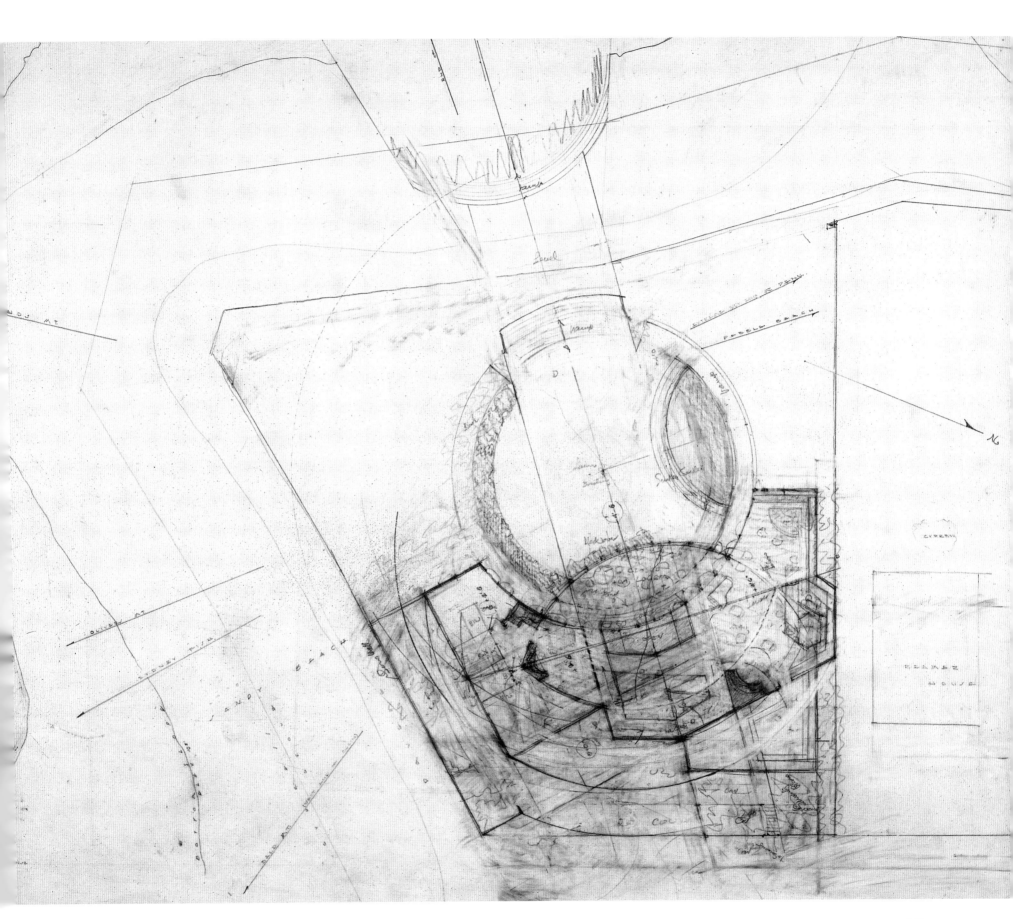

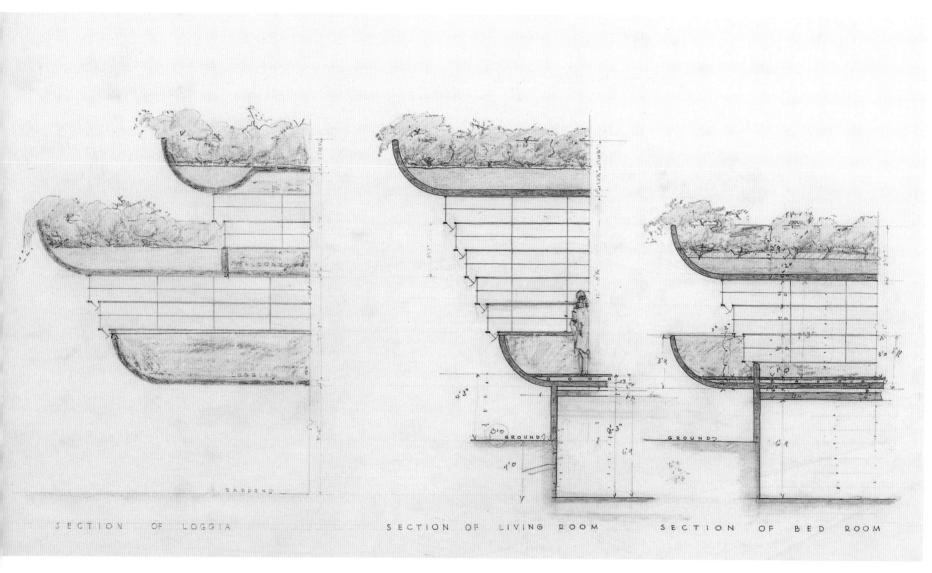

SECTION OF LOGGIA   SECTION OF LIVING ROOM   SECTION OF BED ROOM

Above: Section. FLLW FDN # 4502.009.
Right: Perspective. FLLW FDN # 4502.007.

DWELLING ON THE

MR AND MRS STUART HAL

FRANK LLOYD WRIGHT ARCH

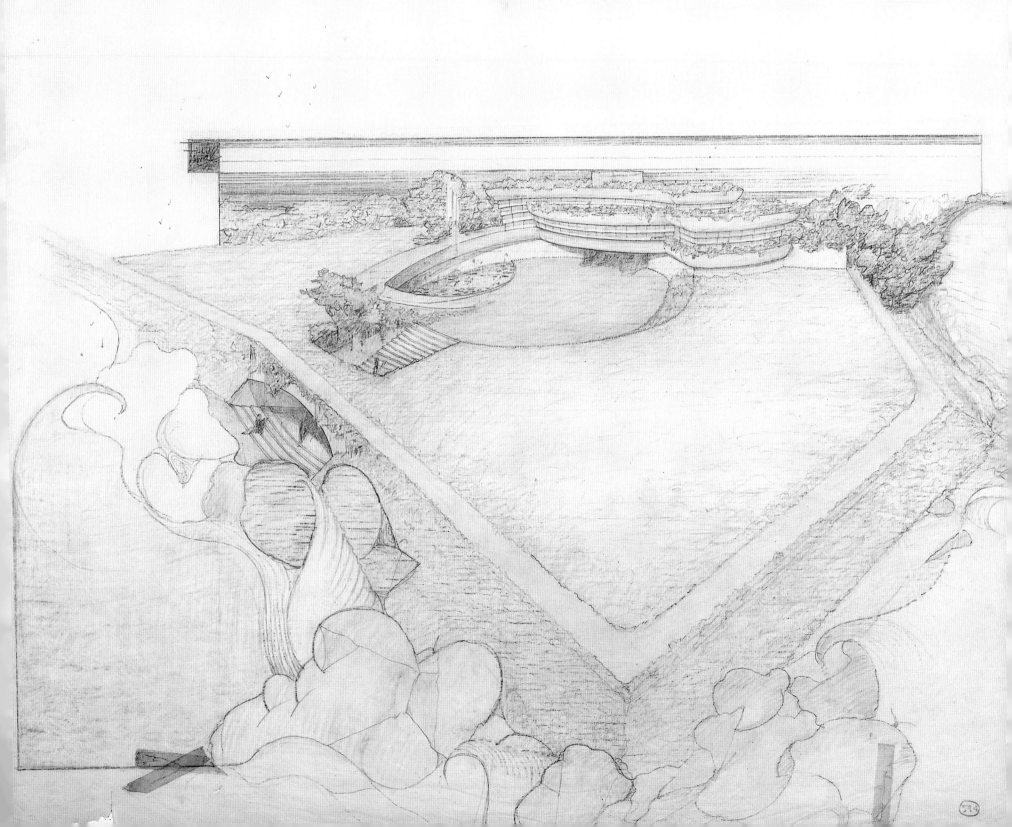

BENJAMIN ADELMAN HOUSE

Fox Point, Wisconsin. 1948, Project

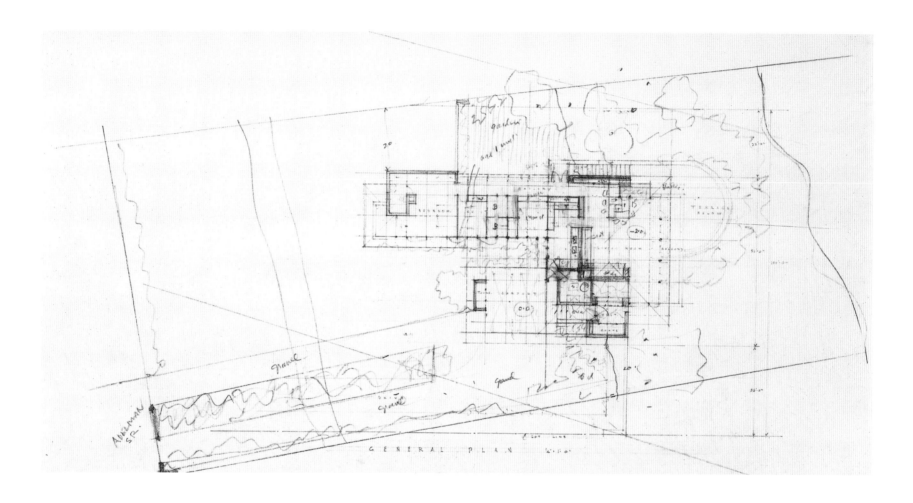

The property for the Benjamin Adelman house was a long, narrow lot that ended with a bluff overlooking Lake Michigan. The client called for a small, simple house with living room, kitchen, servant's room, den (or guest room), and master bedroom. Wright's first sketch plan provided for these requirements (above), but a revised first sketch (opposite page) shows how he suddenly altered the same plan, adding one more bedroom but making certain masonry elements, the fireplace mass, the north stone wall of the living room, and other masonry walls throughout the design conform to the irregular shape of the lot. It is curious how he decided to make this design change. A supreme example of this conforming to the irregularity of the site is his plan for the Stuart Haldorn House in Carmel, California.

In the plan for the house he had also taken into account the respect of the Jewish tradition concerning the Friday evening meal: the Shabbat evening home ritual. The workspace, or kitchen, in most small houses of this genre is open to the general living and dining area. Here, however, he realized that the Friday Home Ritual was a deeply religious and family-oriented moment, and the kitchen with the servant had to be closed off to the family at the dining table.

The masonry for the Adelman House, was designed to be constructed in the same manner as that of Wright's Taliesin West: stones cast into a form, the flat surface then exposed once the concrete is poured, cured, and then the formwork removed. This method of masonry is opposed, for example, to the stonework of Taliesin where the stones are laid up on their flat sides, with occasional stones sticking out slightly from the others, in reflection of the manner in which the stones are found in the quarry.

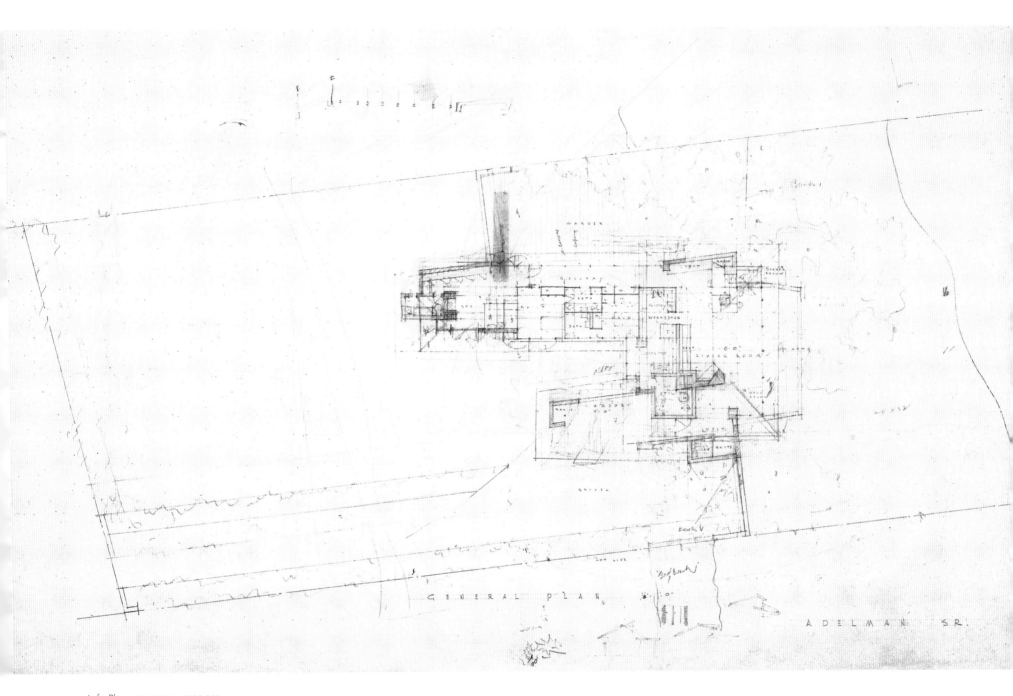

Left: Plan. FLLW FDN # 4802.001
Above: Plan. FLLW FDN # 4802.002

Following pages: Perspective.
FLLW FDN # 4802.007.

HERBERT JACOBS HOUSE #2, "SOLAR HEMICYCLE"

Middleton, Wisconsin. 1944

Plan, elevation, and section. FLLW FDN # 4812.001.

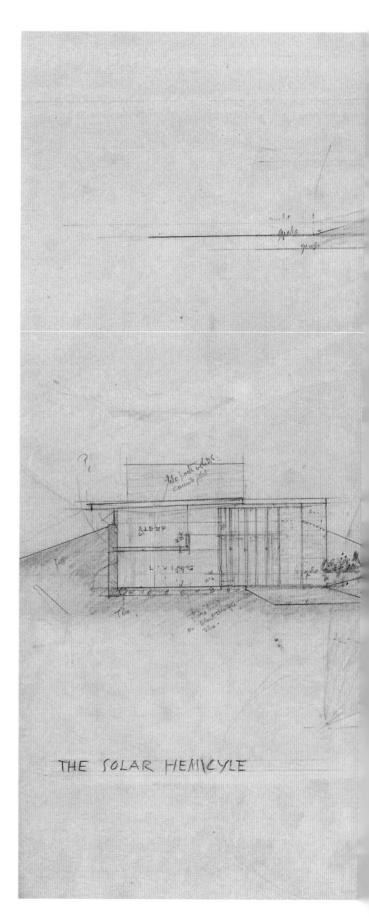

THE SOLAR HEMICYLE

When Katherine and Herbert Jacobs decided to sell their Frank Lloyd Wright house in the city suburbs and move to the country, they again asked Wright to design a home for them. Their first house, constructed in 1936, was the first built Usonian house (see pp. 128-9).[29] Two other Usonian houses had been designed the same year, but they were never constructed. In this, the first of a genre which Wright would design and build across the nation from the East Coast to the West, he revolutionized the home-building industry by establishing a totally new building system for the moderate-cost home.

"The house of moderate cost is not only America's major architectural problem but the problem most difficult for her major architects. As for me, I would rather solve it with satisfaction to myself and Usonia than build anything I can think of. . . . I am certain that any approach to the new house needed by indigenous culture—why worry about the house wanted by provincial ignorance—is fundamentally different. That house must be a pattern for more simple and, at the same time, more gracious living: new, but suitable to living conditions as they might so well be in the counrty we live in today."[30]

In preparing the ground for the first Jacobs House, known worldwide today as "Jacobs I," a small basement was excavated for a furnace, water heater, and laundry. Across the rest of the site a bed of crushed rock was laid, with heating pipes set upon it, a concrete slab then poured over the coils. Attached to the furnace, hot water would circulate through the pipes, and produce what Wright called "gravity heat," the warm air from the floor rising above, the cool air dropping to the slab to be heated, and so on. It would prove, in house after house, to be far more cost-effective in fuel than the traditional heating systems of that time. Masonry walls, either brick or stone, were then erected, and a three-ply wood roof set over the walls. Next came the wood wall construction, a series of panels composed of a plywood core, building paper adhered to each side, and finally boards and battens screwed onto each side. This sandwich wall became a unit that served for both exterior walls and interior walls, a great savings in labor and materials. Lastly came the glazing and appurtenance systems. In some cases the sandwich wall panels were constructed in a woodwork shop and then shipped to the site, as Wright described it, the factory comes to the building site. This was, of course, at a time when skilled masons and carpenters were not a relatively expensive labor force.

The construction of Jacobs I was so new to the trade that Wright himself, who lived only forty miles away, frequently came on site to supervise the work. In subsequent Usonian houses, the apprentice, who worked on the drawings and therefore was familiar with the building system, would be sent on-site to translate the drawings to the workmen while the house was in construction. In some cases, the apprentice acted as the general contractor and sublet contracts for other facets of the work such as masonry, carpentry, heating, plumbing, electrical, and so forth.

As Wright began designing the new house that the Jacobs requested, he wrote to them:

"Dear Herb Jacobs: We are about ready to make you the 'goat' for a fresh enterprise in architecture. If you don't get what is on the boards some other fellow will. So watch out! It's good. I think we have a real 'first' that you will like a lot. Only the 'picture' remains to be done—suppose you come out next Sunday . . .

Frank Lloyd Wright, February 8th, 1944."

Wright's design for the second Jacobs house was another innovation, this time in passive solar energy. Designed as a half circle two stories tall, the bedroom level was a balcony overlooking the tall living room, but in order to free the living room from posts and beams to carry this bed-

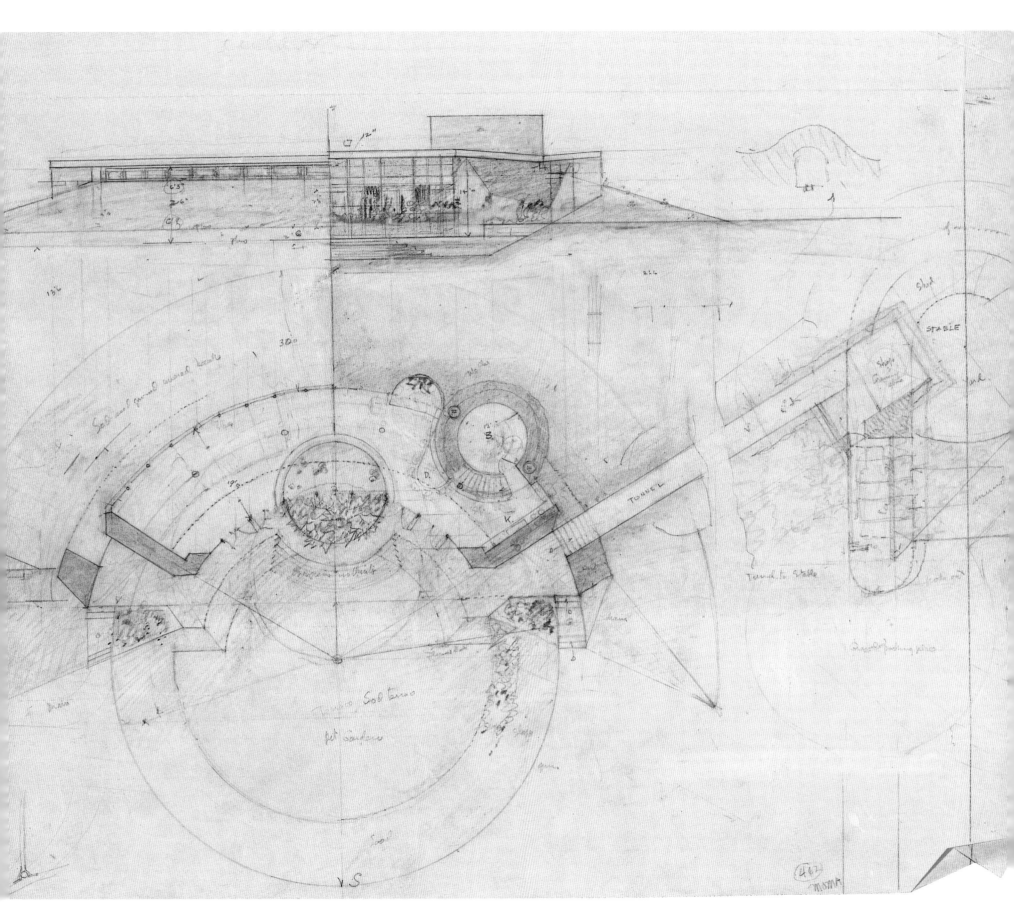

STABLE

TUNNEL

STABLE

Tunnel to Stable

S

125

SOLAR-HEMICYCLE FOR
FRANK LLOYD WRIGHT ARCHIT

room level, it was hung by steel rods from the ceiling rafters. The house faced the south, with a large overhanging roof projected out over the two-story glass windows. In winter, with the earth tilted back on its axis, the sunlight flooding the interior helped heat the house, along with the usual heating coils. In summer, as the earth tilted in the other direction, the overhanging roof shaded the tall windows. Imagine a hat with a wide brim: when the sun is high, the brim shades the eyes, but tilt one's head back a little and sunlight pours down one's face. This is how the Jacobs Solar Hemicycle, as it is known, used the sun during all the seasons. Added to this, an earth berm was banked up against on the north at the rear of the building, helping to keep it warm in the winter while cool in the summer. A tunnel through the berm, two stone planting

HERBERT JACOBS

CT

Perspective. FLLW FDN # 4812.002.

Following pages: Herbert Jacobs House #1. Madison, Wisconsin. Perspective. FLLW FDN # 3702.002-3.

boxes at the entrance, connects the house to the farm building at the rear. Herb Jacobs, a journalist for the Madison, Wisconsin, newspaper *Capital Times*, had become a farmer as well. Since the house was situated slightly below ground level, a circular sunken garden stretched out from the

half-circular house. On the outer edge of this circle, Wright provided for another, smaller berm, facing the prevailing winds, to act as a buffer and direct the winds up and over the house.

The first sketch of this house is another instance where Wright has drawn the plan, split

to show both ground and upper floor, at the same time as a split section and elevation directly above the plan. Off to the left side, a section (pp. 124-125) further illustrates the two-story living room and balcony bedrooms. This drawing was then followed by the "picture" made to show the Jacobs.

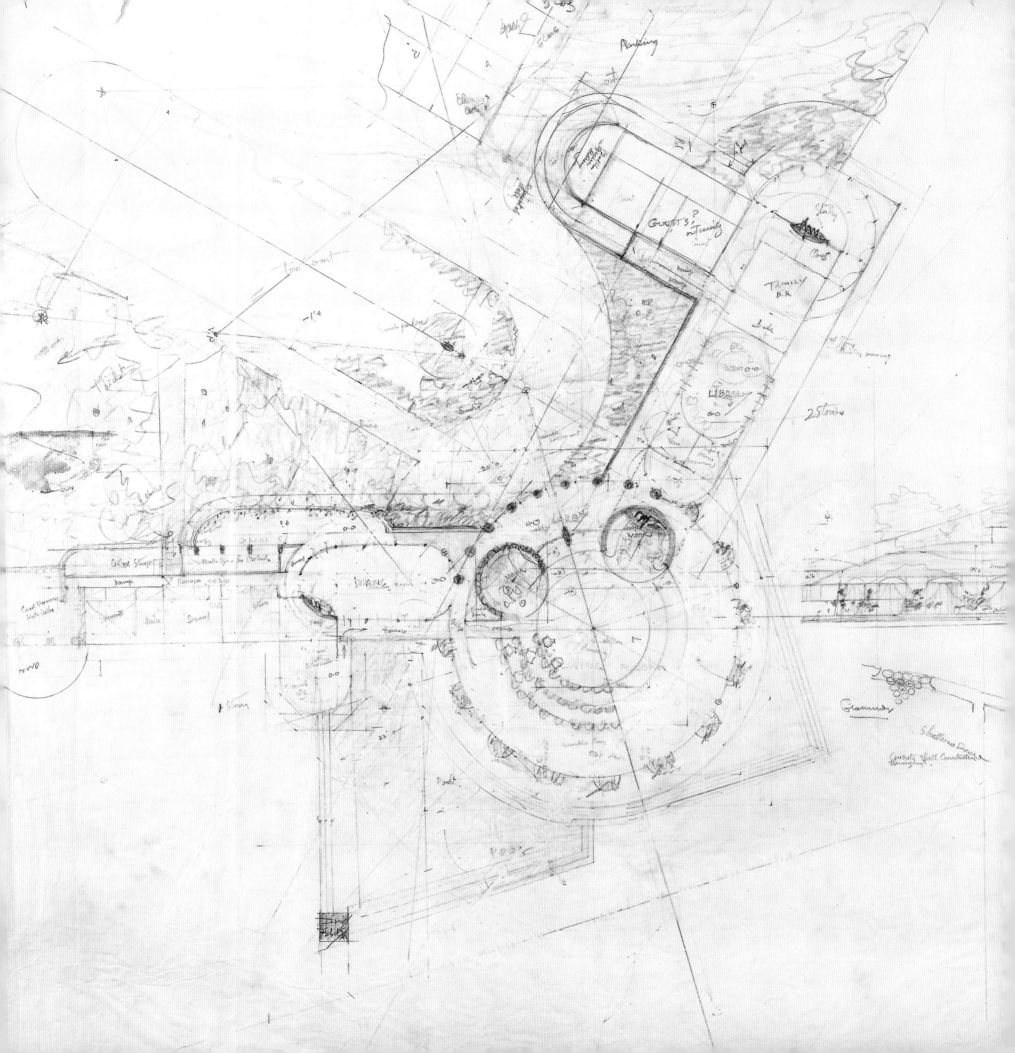

ROBERT F. WINDFOHR HOUSE, "CROWNFIELD"

Fort Worth, Texas. 1949, Project

Robert and Anne Windfohr arrived at Taliesin West on the morning of February 10, 1949, to consult with Wright about a large home they wanted to build in Fort Worth, Texas. Four days later Wright put his ideas for their home down on paper, with a plan and elevation drawn in graphite and color pencils, and signed by him on his customary red square logo, or "mon," at the lower left corner of the drawing (at left). In the center of the plan was a large circular living room with two half-circular "nooks," one for music, the other for a fireplace. On the periphery of the room glass doors opened onto steps, some down to a large swimming pool, others onto a grass lawn. Stretched out from the living room on one side, the plan provided for a large, long dining room, with a conservatory for orchids adjacent. This same wing also provided kitchen, servants' quarters, a projection out toward the pool for a card room, and dressing rooms on the lower level directly opening onto the pool. From the central living room, in the other direction was a lounge for men and for women, a two-story library, and guest accommodations. A second level above this provided the family rooms. All the roofs were dome-shaped, the one over the living room with a large circular skylight from which hung glass beads and spheres. A sectional sketch of this living room skylight was made by Wright on the conceptual plan (left), indicating the concrete roof and glass tubes. In consideration that the site was a vast flat plane, Wright chose the name "Crownfield" for the house. In every sense, Wright's design for the Windfohrs was a truly luxurious one, as well as one of his largest. On the perspective showing the entry (following page), he has inscribed "Note: Dear Anne—this is the original drawing of the entrance side of the house—not now much changed—kindly take good care of it and return—FLLW."

The Windfohrs, however, decided not to build. Their original request was for a house

costing $250,000—a handsome price at that time, 1949. It turned out that the property they planned for the house had not been purchased. They then asked Wright to reduce the size of the house to $150,000.00 and they would look for another tract of land. This never happened, and during a period of three years, they hesitated to make a payment on Wright's initial designs. He revised his fee to reflect the reduced cost of construction. But that proved to be the end of the commission. At one point he wrote them that the Windfohr House was the best thing on the boards at that time, meaning his work in his studio. The plans were returned to Wright's office. But they constituted an idea that Wright would not let lay idle.

On May 15, 1952, he received a letter from Raul Bailleres, president of the Credito Minero y Mercantil, S. A., a prominent banking and financial institution in Mexico. The letter requested that Wright design a country home on a steeply wooded and boulder-strewn tract of land at the edge of the bay in Acapulco. Wright replied:

"My dear Sir—I should like to build your house in Mexico as I feel Mexico is nearer the Architecture of the future than even here in the United States. So if you care to foot the expense of Mrs. Wright and myself on a week's trip to your Mexico City, we will come to talk with you and see the site at Acapulco."[31]

Wright and Olgivanna had a most delightful visit to Mexico and the site at Acapulco. She recalled that Senor Bailleres and his wife took them on a boat ride along the bay, looking up to the proposed site for the country home. The water in the bay was pleasingly cool on their visit in July, and the Wrights took off their shoes and stockings and waded in the shallow part of the bay next to the site.

In consideration of what design this project would be, the Windfohr plan seemed the perfect solution with respect to the Bailleres'

requirements. With the site, however, being a steep hill rather than a flat plane, he arranged the plan to conform to this limitation. Some of the boulders on the property were therefore incorporated in the design (see pp 2-3, 136-137). The location being a tropical one, the living room circle was roofed over but open to the terrace without glass doors. A curved ramp from the living room terrace proceeded down to a circular freshwater swimming pool, and another ramp, also circular, continued down to the edge of the bay. There was some consterna-

tion about the fireplace nook in the living room. Bailleres explained that in this tropical environment, a fireplace was unnecessary. Wright then proposed that a curtain of water could fall down the inside edge, or what would have been the rear wall of a fireplace, ending in a shallow pool at the base, where the hearth would nominally be. This would bring fresh breezes to people seated in the nook.

The hearth, as the heart of the home, thus transformed from fire to water, Wright explained.

As the commission progressed, Bailleres was having difficulties in procuring the property. Eventually it became impossible for him to do so, as the federal government was taking it over for projects of their own. Bailleres paid Wright his preliminary fee and returned the drawings.

In 1957, Marilyn Monroe came to Wright's suite at the Plaza Hotel and requested a home for herself and her husband, Arthur Miller. The site was as yet undetermined, but it was suggested it would be near New York, possibly in Connecticut. She envisioned a home that

NOTE

Dear Kim—

This is the original drawing of
the entrance side of the house—
not now much changed—
Kindly take good care of it and return

Frank

would eventually provide not only for the Millers but for their children as well.

Thus the Windfohr/Bailleres plan came to life once more, this time closer to the scheme as proposed for the former (p. 135, bottom). However, the Miller marriage proved difficult, the husband was not interested in starting a family, and they separated. The scheme for a house was abandoned. During the time that Marilyn Monroe and the Wrights met, the architect and his wife had great admiration for the actress. Olgivanna described her as intelligent, charming, and witty, with an effervescent

personality. The movies she played in were favorites with the Wrights, and despite the disappointment of not building this design, they maintained an affection as well as admiration for her. Her suicide in August 1962, was a deep blow to Olgivanna. (Wright had died some years prior to this tragedy.)

Thus his labor for Windfohr, Bailleres, and Monroe, who were involved in this rare and original Frank Lloyd Wright design, showed how he was determined to see this structure built and how the application of the same basic concept served graciously for the lifestyles of each.

Perspective showing entry. FLLW FDN # 4919.014.

Following pages:
Top: Perspective. FLLW FDN # 4919.015
Left, bottom: Perspective. FLLW FDN # 4919.016
Right, bottom: Perspective of house for Marilyn Monroe and Arthur Miller. 1957, project. FLLW FDN # 5719.001.

Pages 136-37: Perspective for Raul Baileres House. Acapulco, Mexico. 1952, project. FLLW FDN # 5202.013.

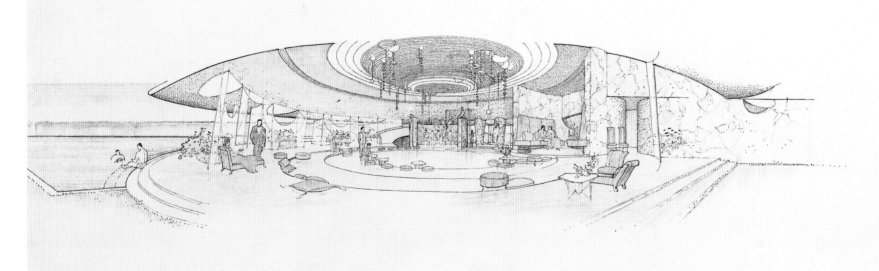

DWELLING FOR MR. and MRS. ROBERT F WINDFOHR   FORT WORT
FRANK LLOYD WRIGHT   ARCHITECT

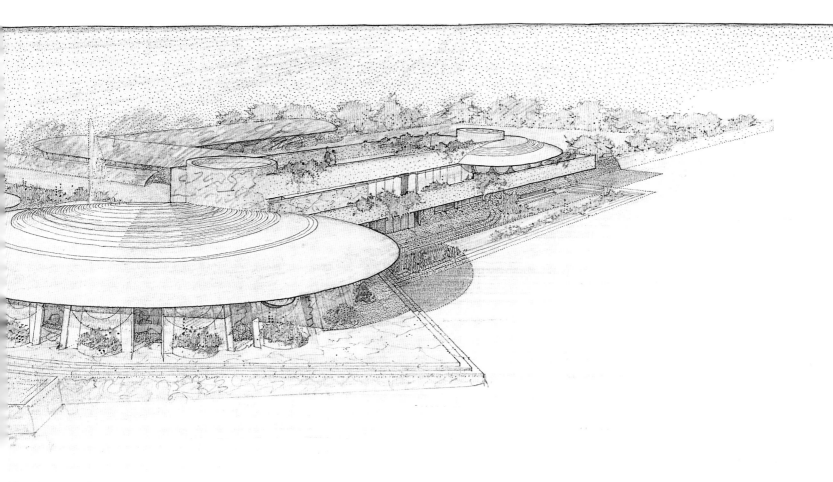

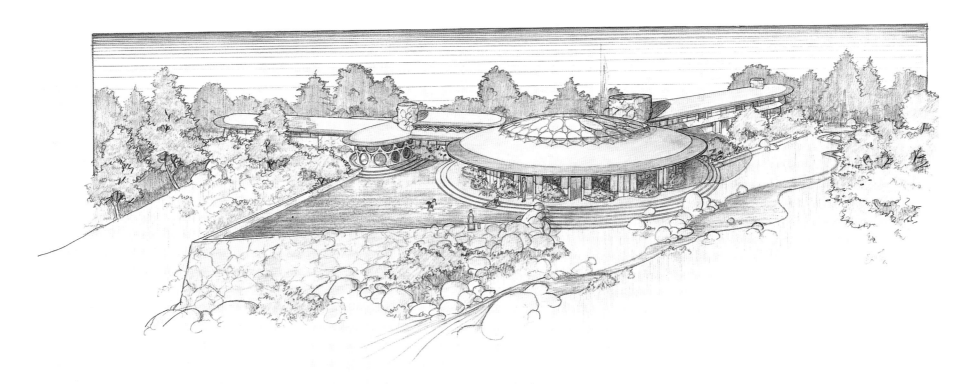

HOUSE FOR MR. AND MRS. ARTHUR MILLER

FRANK LLOYD WRIGHT ARCHITECT

BOULDER

STONE

AIR COOLED

VIEW OF PATIO

COUNTRY HOME IN ACAPUL

FRANK LLOYD W

INLET

STONE   SPRAY

STONE

O   FOR   SENOR   RAÚL   BAILLERE

IGHT   ARCHITECT

RAYMOND CARLSON HOUSE

Phoenix, Arizona. 1950

Left: Plan. FLLW FDN # 5004.004.
Right: Plan. FLLW FDN # 5004.002.

Following pages: Perspective.
FLLW FDN # 5004.016

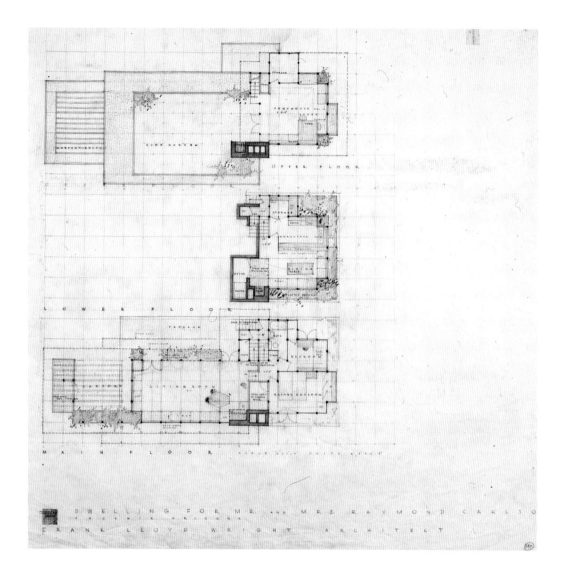

highlighted the recently constructed Taliesin West, Wright's winter home and workshop in Scottsdale, on a great mesa backed up along the McDowell Mountain Range.

Wright and Olgivanna were enthusiastic subscribers to *Arizona Highways* and would send the colorful Christmas issue to their friends, clients, and former apprentices. Carlson and Wright became fine friends, and in 1950, when Carlson wanted to build a home, he asked Wright to be his architect. The site was in a typical crowded subdivision, precisely the type of site Wright abhorred and advised his residential clients to avoid. But Carlson had acquired the property, and taking into account Wright's genuine affection for him, a plan was made. This became a one-of-a-kind house, standing by itself in the cadre of Wright's house designs. His first sketch again began with the plan, followed by an elevation. On the same sheet (shown at right), he has indicated some specific structural details, and signed the sheet "Mar 15—50." On the side of the drawing, Wright has made several sketches detailing the type of construction he envisioned, along with notes across most of the drawings further explaining certain details.

The materials were gray transite, an exterior wall-board type of panel, set between posts of redwood, lacquered turquoise blue so as to protect the wood against the strong Arizona sunshine. The house is on three levels. The main floor provides a living room and carport, but four steps down lead to a sunken level containing kitchen, dining, and utilities. Surrounding this lower level is an outdoor planting area, so that views from the kitchen or dining room look into flowers and shrubs rather than the next-door neighbors. A few steps up from the living room gains two bedrooms and bath, while the upper floor is a penthouse study over the bedrooms and a roof garden over the living room. The building is situated on the furthermost southern edge of the property so as to provide

Raymond Carlson was the editor of *Arizona Highways*, a monthly periodical that featured the deserts, canyons, mesas, mountains, and northern forests of the state. It also profiled the various pioneers of the region, as well as the Native Americans. Historic towns and cities were also featured. The arts and crafts of Hopi, Pima, and Navajo were illustrated from time to time. When color photography became prevalent, there were issues, especially in the spring, of the flowering cacti in brilliant, luscious tones of color. Carpets of wildflowers, purple, red, orange, and yellow wove around rocks and trees across the desert. The magazine's Christmas issue showed all these desert environs cloaked in snow. In May 1940, the magazine

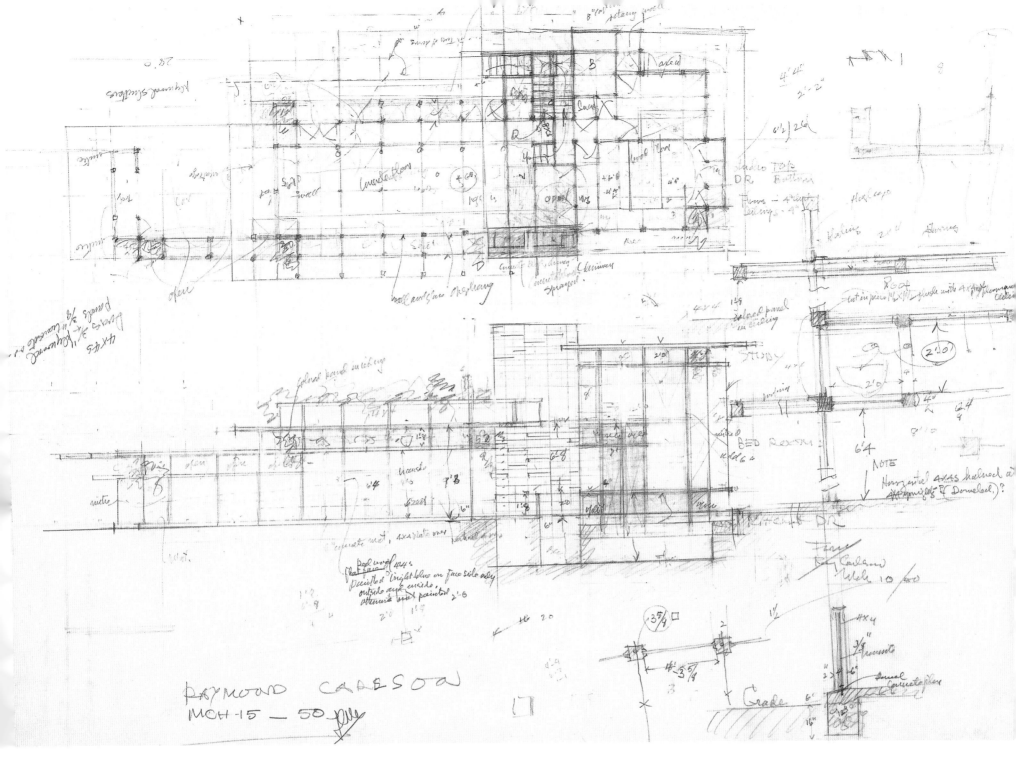

a spacious lawn in front. High oleander bushes shield the house from the street and other neighbors.

The total cost of construction was $15,000. (This was in 1950.) Wright was so pleased with the result that he gave half of his commission, ($1,500) back to Carlson and the other half to the contractor.

Later, when apprentice Richard Carney was driving Wright from Taliesin West to Sky Harbor, the Phoenix airport, as they approached the area near the Carlson house, Wright said, "Dick, let's stop by and see Ray's house." There was nobody home at the house, and Wright took out a ballpoint pen and on the front door wrote, "Hoorah for Ray. FLlW." When he finally

boarded the plane, Dick was afraid that Carlson would see the inscription and think it might be an act of vandalism. He called Carlson, and even before he could explain, Carlson exclaimed, "I know what it is, and I have already covered it with a coat of clear lacquer to protect it!"

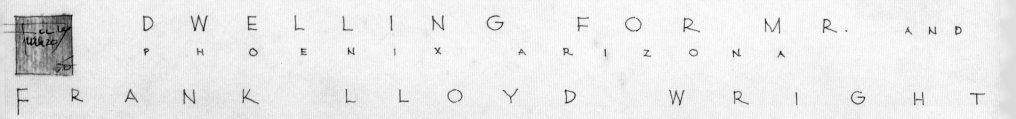

DWELLING FOR MR. AND
PHOENIX ARIZONA
FRANK LLOYD WRIGHT

MRS. RAYMOND CARLSON

ARCHITECT

LILIANE AND EDGAR J. KAUFMANN HOUSE, "BOULDER HOUSE"

Palm Springs, California. 1951, Project

When Wright discovered that Edgar Kaufmann had built a winter home in Palm Springs designed by Richard Neutra, he was extremely put out, and threatened to break off any association with Kaufmann. It took Edgar jr. much persuasion to smooth over the situation, and Kaufmann then purchased additional land and employed Wright to build a house there. From the letters, it became obvious that this house was designed with Liliane Kaufmann, in mind. "The house for the queen is designed. Boulder House it is. Feminine in essence; broad as the hills in feeling. I will get you out of the nasty little cliché with a fine sweep."[32] He is obviously referring to the Neutra house nearby.

The plan is a series of three lozenges. The larger one provides a living room and bedrooms for the Kaufmanns. A bridge spans over the pool to another lozenge for guest rooms, while another bridge spans over to the dining room. Kitchen, utilities, servants' quarters, and carport swing down in a long arc to the entrance road. Mrs. Kaufmann desired a swimming pool in which she could do laps, but said she was not content with the usual shape of swimming pools. To accommodate her, Wright designed a pool in the nature of a "moat" running all around the main lozenge. This is the reason for the two bridges in the plan. An Indian bath was proposed next to her bedroom, from which she could open a water gate and swim around the house, all the while enjoying the views of the surrounding mountains and desert foliage. The site was strewn with boulders, which Wright incorporated as integral elements in the walls of the house (as see in perspective drawing on p. 144). This unique detail prompted him to call the house "Boulder House," accordingly. Although Kaufmann had purchased the property explicitly for this house, it never materialized, most likely because of the death of Liliane in 1952.

The concept plan no longer exists, and the final presentation plan he made to show the Kaufman's is also lost. It was published in a French journal in 1952, but evidently never returned to Wright's office. The conceptual elevation, however, does exist (seen on following page, bottom), and it is one of the loveliest drawings in the Frank Lloyd Wright collection.

As an interesting footnote to the project, on the bird's-eye view (at right) far over on the right side can be seen the roof of the neighboring Neutra House.

Wright was loath to ever comment on which of his works was the "masterpiece," and whenever he was questioned, he invariably would reply "The next one." Yet somehow this design remained for him something very special, perhaps not only for its unique character, but also for the affection he felt for the Kaufmann family. A year after Liliane's death, he wrote to Kaufmann about the Boulder House, "It was a rare beautiful thing. One of my very best."[33]

Perspective.
FLLW FDN # 511.001.

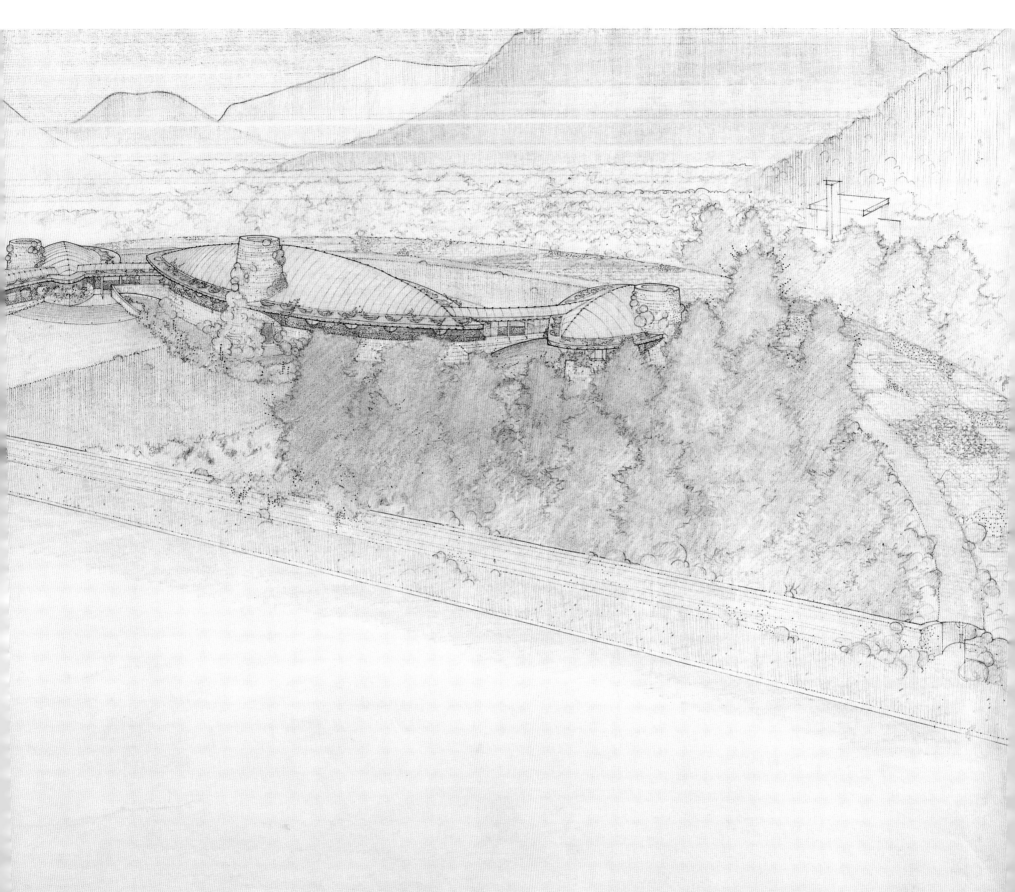

ER HOUSE" FOR LILIANE AND EJ KAUFMANN
PRINGS...CALIFORNIA...DESERT BOULDER FIELD
LLOYD WRIGHT ARCHITECT

Right: Perspective.
FLLW FDN # 5111.002.
Below: Early elevation.
FLLW FDN # 511.003.

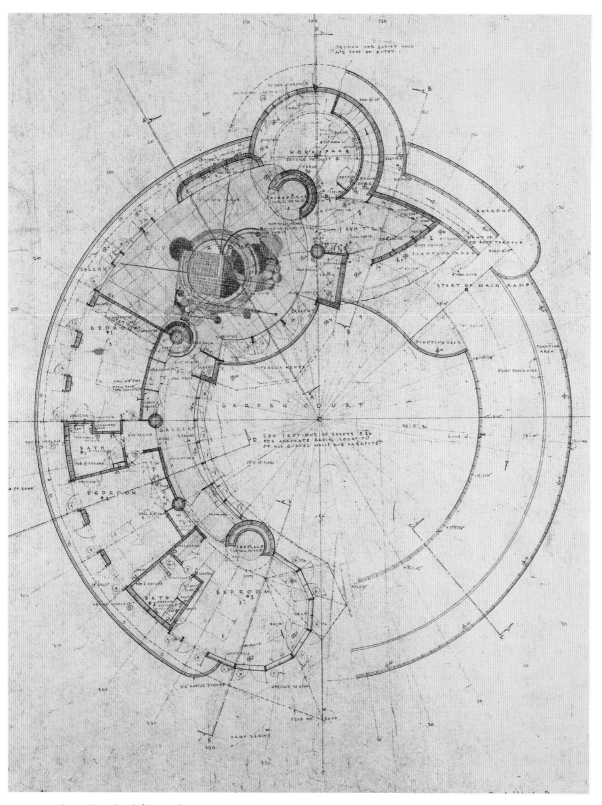

RUG FOR THE DAVID WRIGHT HOUSE

Phoenix, Arizona. 1951

When David Wright, son of Frank Lloyd Wright, moved into his house that Wright had designed for him in Phoenix, he asked his father to design a rug for their living room. In 1926 Wright had made designs for the covers for *Liberty Magazine*, but he was told that the designs were far too radical. He kept the file of drawings for other purposes, namely for textiles and carpet designs. For David's rug, he went through his *Liberty* covers file and selected the one called "March Balloons" as a starting point from which to make this design. It is composed of interlocking circles grouped around the rims of larger circles, some tangent to the rims, others detached from them. When installed, the rug, handwoven by V'Soske in Puerto Rico, became a strong feature in the living room. Concerning Wright designs for rugs, he once referred to them as "underfoot patterns." His first sketch for the rug was made on color pencils on a blueprint plan of the house (at left).

The final rendering for the rug (at right) was produced by Wright's apprentice Ling Po, who came from China in 1946 to join the Taliesin Fellowship. Ling was an extraordinary artist, and Wright relied upon his artistry over and over again. One day Ling was seated at his table in the drafting room with a large sheet of white paper spread out on his drafting board. With a brush and black ink he was tirelessly practicing Chinese calligraphy. When asked what he was doing, Ling replied, "In the Chinese family, the master of the house and his sons are constantly improving their skills in calligraphy, while the mistress and her daughters are constantly improving theirs in the art of embroidery."

Above: First sketch for rug drawn on a blueprint plan for David Wright House. FLLW FDN # 5121.001.

Right: Final rendering. FLLW FDN # 5121.003.

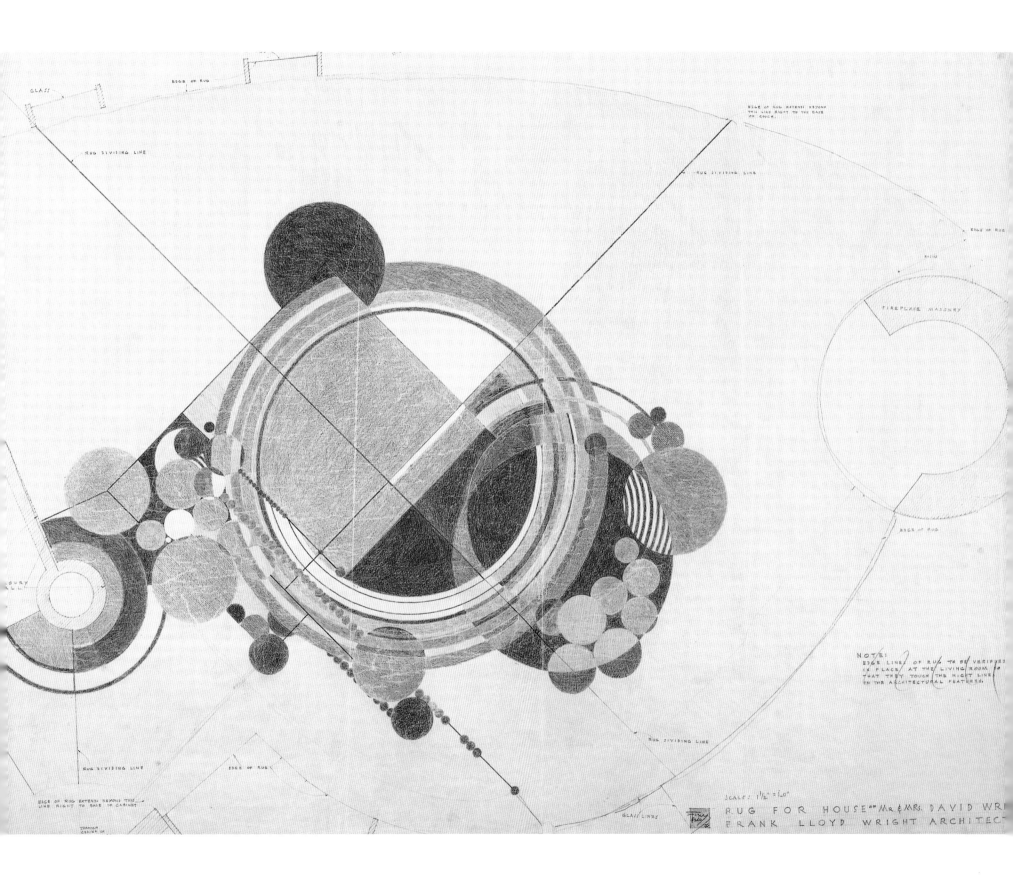

GLASS

EDGE OF RUG

RUG DIVIDING LINE

EDGE OF RUG EXTEND BEYOND
THIS LINE RIGHT TO THE BACK
OR COUCH.

RUG DIVIDING LINE

EDGE OF RUG

RUG DIVIDING LINE

FIREPLACE MASONRY

EDGE OF RUG

NOTE:
EDGE LINES OF RUG TO BE VERIFIED
IN PLACE AT THE LIVING ROOM SO
THAT THEY TOUCH THE RIGHT LINE OF
ON THE ARCHITECTURAL FEATURES.

RUG DIVIDING LINE

RUG DIVIDING LINE

EDGE OF RUG

EDGE OF RUG EXTEND BEYOND THIS
LINE RIGHT TO BASE OR CABINET

GLASS LINES

SCALE: 1½" = 1'0"

RUG FOR HOUSE OF Mr. & Mrs. DAVID WRI
FRANK LLOYD WRIGHT ARCHITECT

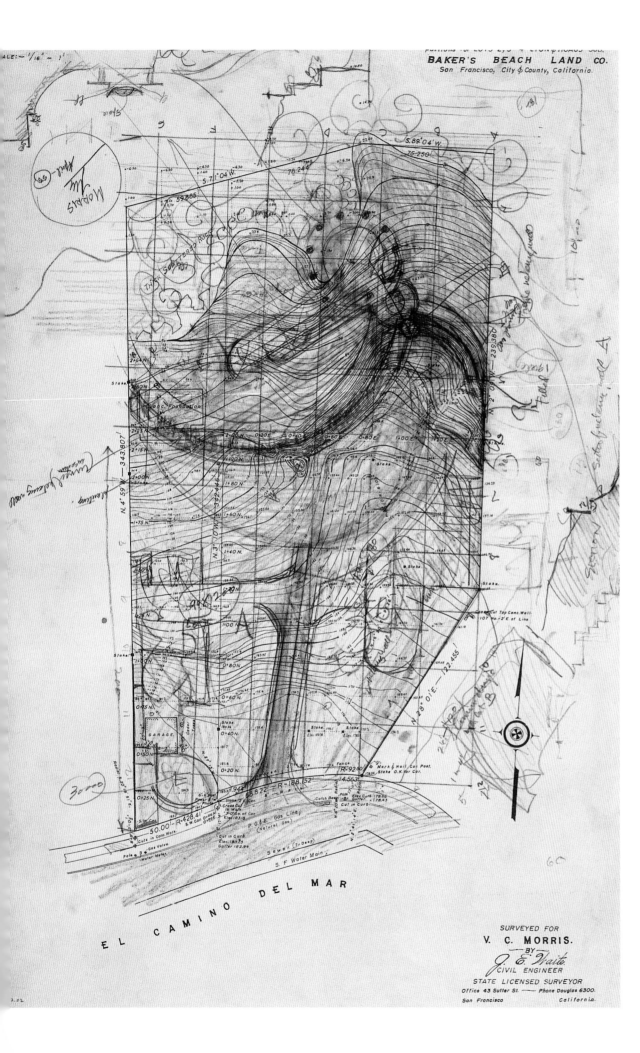

V. C. MORRIS HOUSE, SCHEME 2

San Francisco, California. 1954, Project

Once their gift shop was constructed up and running, by 1954 Mr. and Mrs. Morris asked Wright if he would make another design for their seaside property in San Francisco. The first design proved too extravagant and costly, and thus they now requested a simpler design. This time Wright placed the house lower down the slope, nearer to the ocean, and offered a more condensed plan. For his first sketch, he took the topographical survey, turned it around, and drew the plan as seen from the ocean side (left). On this plan, two large arcs above the house plan itself represent curved retaining walls. His note with an arrow explains this feature. The house is placed on one level, with a large circular living room supported on a pedestal of reinforced concrete. Tangent to this, but on the same level, are the bedrooms nestled into the cliff side. Above, at street level, the road leads to a carport and elevator as well as a stair tower. Wright believed that in making the new house less "extravagant" the scheme was feasible. On the perspective drawing (at right), Wright has added fir trees and a dramatic sweep of the ocean waves. His inscription has been smudged and is illegible, but segments of it refer to the pedestal and retaining walls in regards to the "quake."

However, the prospect of getting materials and workmen down that steep slope to form and pour the concrete pedestal and house, not to mention the stair tower and elevator, proved to be more than his clients were willing to gamble. Though less costly than the first proposal, it still was more than they would undertake. The work went no further than his preliminary sketches.

Elevator

HOUSE FOR MR. AND MRS. V. C. MORRIS
SAN FRANCISCO, CALIFORNIA

F R A N K   L L O Y D   W R I G H T   A R C H I T E C T

SEACLIFF

Left: Preliminary sketch with plan drawn atop
topographical survey. FLLW FDN # 5412.002.
Above: Perspective. FLLW FDN # 5412.001.

Following pages:
Left: Plan. FLLW FDN # 5417.005.
Right: Elevation. FLLW FDN # 5412.004

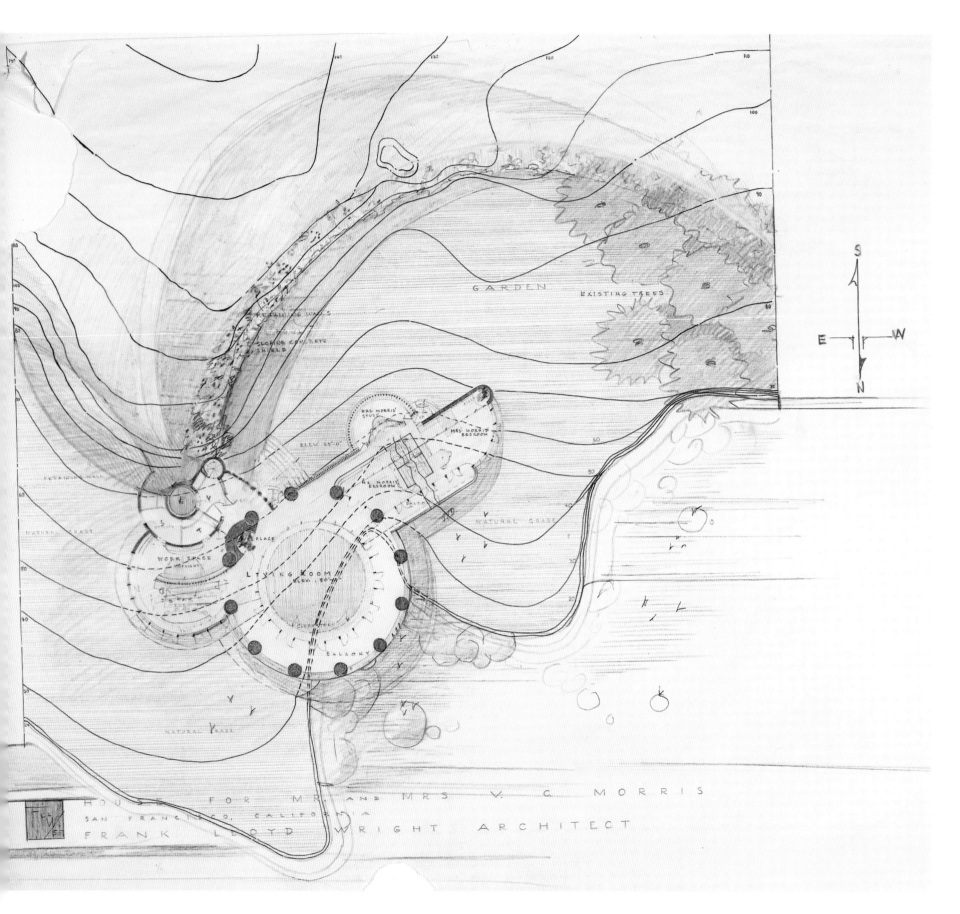

GARDEN   EXISTING TREES

MRS. MORRIS'
STUDY
MRS. MORRIS'
BEDROOM
ELEV. 55'-0"

MR. MORRIS'
BEDROOM

RETAINING WALL

NATURAL GRADE

NATURAL GRADE

WORK SPACE

LIVING ROOM
ELEV. 50'-0"

CLERESTORY

BALCONY

NATURAL GRADE

HOUSE FOR MR. AND MRS. V. C. MORRIS
SAN FRANCISCO, CALIFORNIA
FRANK LLOYD WRIGHT ARCHITECT

ROCK

ELEVATION   SCALE: 1/8" = 1'-0"

MAX HOFFMAN HOUSE, SCHEME 1

Rye, New York. 1954, Project

Vienna-born Max Hoffman was a race-car driver who came to the United States and acquired the dealership of Jaguar automobiles. He commissioned Wright to design a showroom for him in Manhattan. Constructed at 430 Park Avenue at the corner of 56th Street, it was a showroom of glass and mirrors, and was rich with planting: glass, mirror, verdant green, and shiny new automobiles, the very essence of elegance, all to tempt the customer. Partway through the development of the project, Hoffman lost his nationwide control of the Jaguar concession, and he took up with Mercedes-Benz instead.

At the same time that the showroom was on the boards at Taliesin, he asked Wright to design a home for him in Rye, New York, overlooking Long Island Sound. Wright's proposal, given Hoffman's stature in life, was a large L-shaped one-story structure of stone, with a tall cathedral-like roof of copper over the living room. When Hoffman saw the preliminary drawings, he expressed alarm, complaining that he was a small man (not tall at all) and he would feel lost inside such a tall living room. Wright then proposed a second scheme, based on the same footprint, but using a diamond-shaped grid. Again Hoffman expressed his displeasure with this design, and finally Wright made a third attempt, this time on the same footprint plan of the first one but simpler in geometry. This design Hoffman approved, and the house was constructed. Morton Delson, Wright's apprentice, supervised the construction along with the constant presence of Hoffman himself, meticulously anxious about every detail all along the way. Thus the workmanship throughout was excellent, and Hoffman was finally pleased.

Shown here is the design for the first proposal, the most romantic by far. Again, Wright has made his first sketch on the topographical survey in white chalk on the blueprint (right). Often his first plan is done on the topographical plans, so

as to relate the building to the lay of the land. In this case, a more detailed plan and elevations follow. A presentation plan and perspectives (following pages) were shown to Hoffman and obviously the detail view of the living room is what alarmed him with its the tall copper-clad living room roof.

Above: Plan on topographical survey. FLLW FDN # 5504.010.
Rght, top:: Plan and elevations. FLLW FDN # 5504.009.
Right, bottom: Elevation. FLLW FDN # 5504.002.

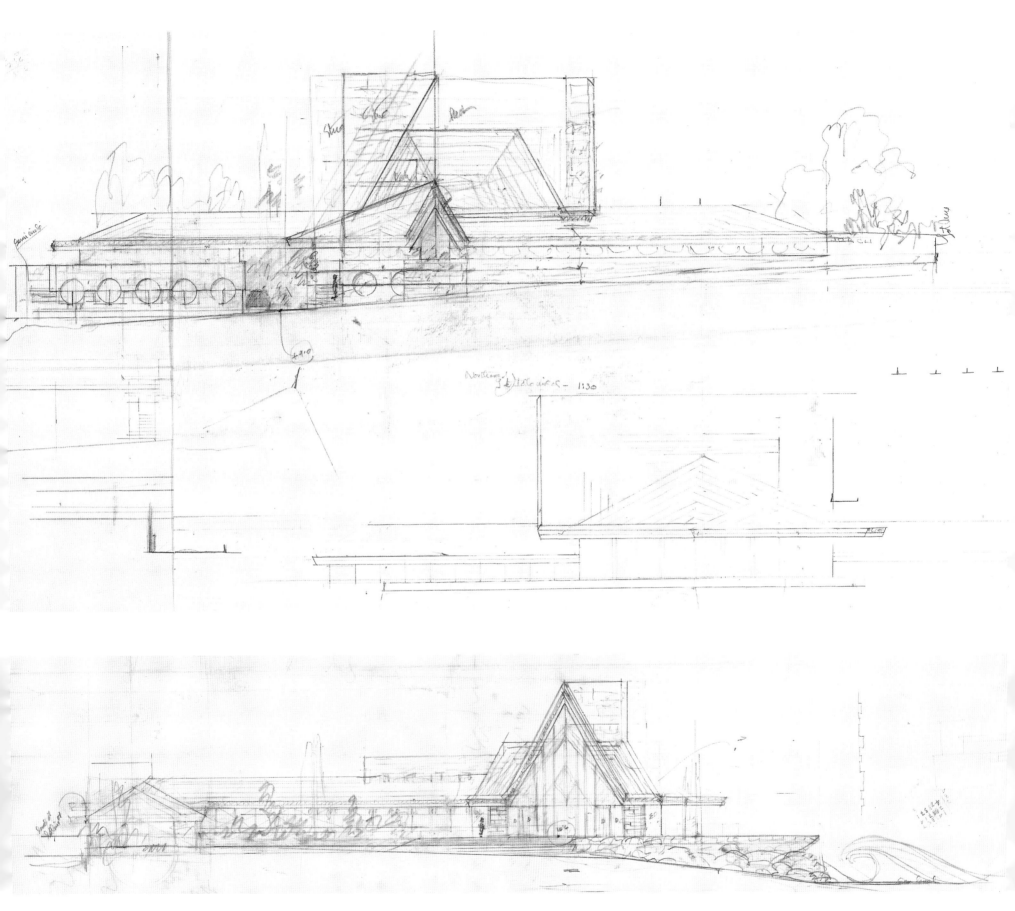

153

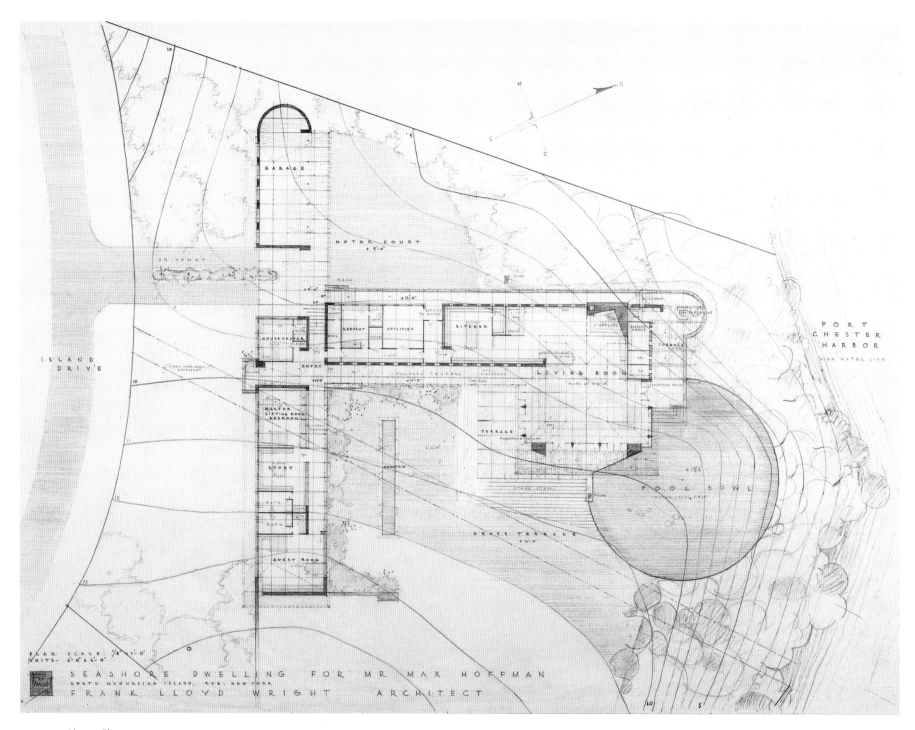

Above: Plan. FLLW FDN # 5504.004.
Right: Perspective. FLLW FDN # 5504.006.

RUG FOR MAX HOFFMAN

Rye, New York. 1957
Executed for Taliesin, Spring Green, Wisconsin. 1962

When the house was completed, Hoffman asked Wright to design a special rug for the living room. It seemed that, as before, he was a difficult client to please, and he rejected Wright's design.

In his home, Taliesin, Wright always placed a large Chinese rug in the living room. Over the years, it had to be replaced because of the wear and tear on a delicate rug in a room that was used not only by Wright and his family, but also by his apprentices and guests. When the fellowship numbered 65 apprentices, and considering that each week there was a dinner and concert in the living room, the Chinese rugs suffered even more.

Shortly before he died, Olgivanna asked Wright if he would design a special rug for the living room, thus sparing the Oriental ones. He thought that was indeed a good idea, and he would get to it someday. Unfortunately, he died before making a design. Olgivanna then thought that since Hoffman had refused Wright's design for his rug, and since the Hoffman design, along with runners, was exactly the same dimension as the Taliesin living room and the long corridor stretching from the room to Wright's bedroom at the far end, it seemed truly providential that it should be made for Taliesin. Accordingly, the design was sent to V'Soske, in Puerto Rico, who had woven the David Wright rug. Once woven, both the large rug and the long runner were installed at Taliesin, where they remain to this day.

Above: Perspective of Max Hoffman House, Scheme 1.
FLLW FDN # 5504.007.
Right: Rug for Hoffman House.
FLLW FDN # 5707.002.

CUT RUG TO
FIT FIXTURES

BOOK CASE   BOOK CASE

LIVING ROOM OF HOUSE FOR MR. MAX. HOFFMAN

HELEN DONAHOE HOUSE, "THE DONAHOE TRIPTYCH"

Scottsdale, Arizona. 1959, Project

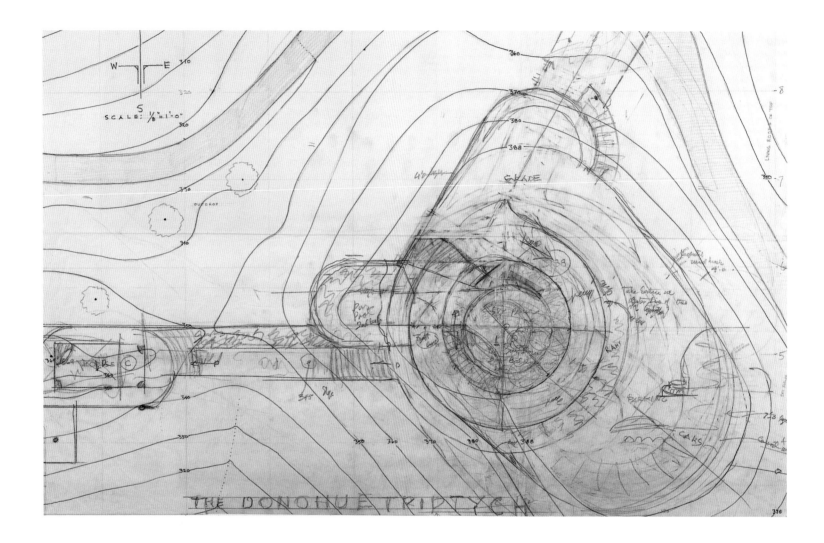

Helen Donahoe desired a winter home in Arizona so that she could escape the snow and ice of Oklahoma and bask in the clear, warm sunshine of the desert. When she approached Wright with her desire, she mentioned that she would also like homes for her two sons and their families so that they could be a family all together in Arizona. Her property presented a problem: it was a hilltop location upon which a previous owner had sheared off the top of the hill, making it flat.

Again, as Wright so often explained, limitations are an artist's best friend. Usually loathe to put any building on the top of a hill, believing that in so doing, he was destroying the hill, in this case, it seemed that the hill had already been destroyed, and what he designed for the site would indeed put the top back on the mountain, so to speak. The program called for a house for Mrs. Donahoe, but rather than making it large enough to accommodate her sons and their families, he conceived of a group of three houses,

thus the name he coined for "The Donahoe Triptych."

His first sketch (above) illustrates how the main house for Mrs. Donahoe would be connected via bridges to the two other, but smaller, homes for her sons.

Her house was at the apex, a three-story structure mainly circular in form, with an outside ramp rising to the third level and arriving at the main living room, called the "Sky Parlor," with a glass-domed roof (double layer for insulation)

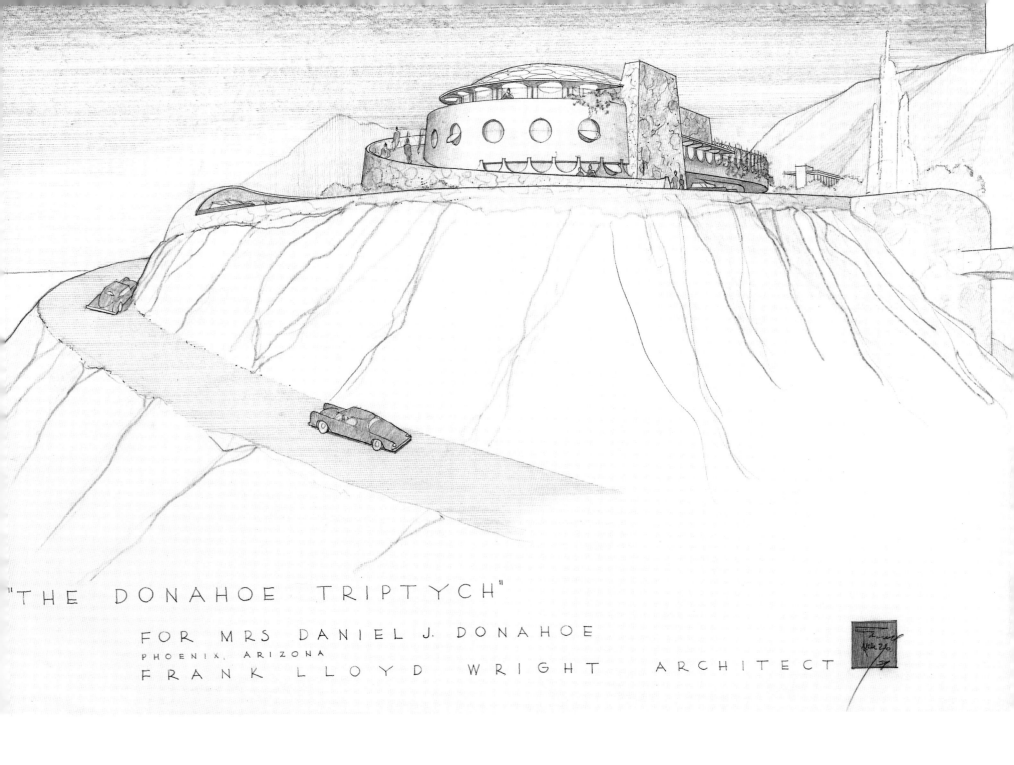

"THE DONAHOE TRIPTYCH"

FOR MRS DANIEL J. DONAHOE
PHOENIX, ARIZONA
FRANK LLOYD WRIGHT ARCHITECT

and an outdoor balcony with views of the distant desert mountains in all directions. Below, the other levels provided a special suite of rooms with an outdoor terrace and pool for Mrs. Donahoe, along with rooms for guests, the main dining room, kitchen facilities, and servants' quarters.

For her two sons, bridges connected to the main residence spanned over the approach road and arrived at each of the two-story houses. The carport at her house is a specially concealed wall

of reinforced concrete and desert masonry that curves up and over as though fashioned out of the very mountain itself, barely discernible until it is actually approached: a unique type of carport never before designed by Wright.

The final presentation perspectives were approved and signed by Wright on March 26, 1959. Two weeks later, he was dead. Mrs. Donahoe declined to go forward with the project.

Left; Plan. FLLW FDN # 5901.007.
Above: Perspective. FLLW FDN # 5901.022.

Following pages: Perspective. FLLW FDN # 5901.021.

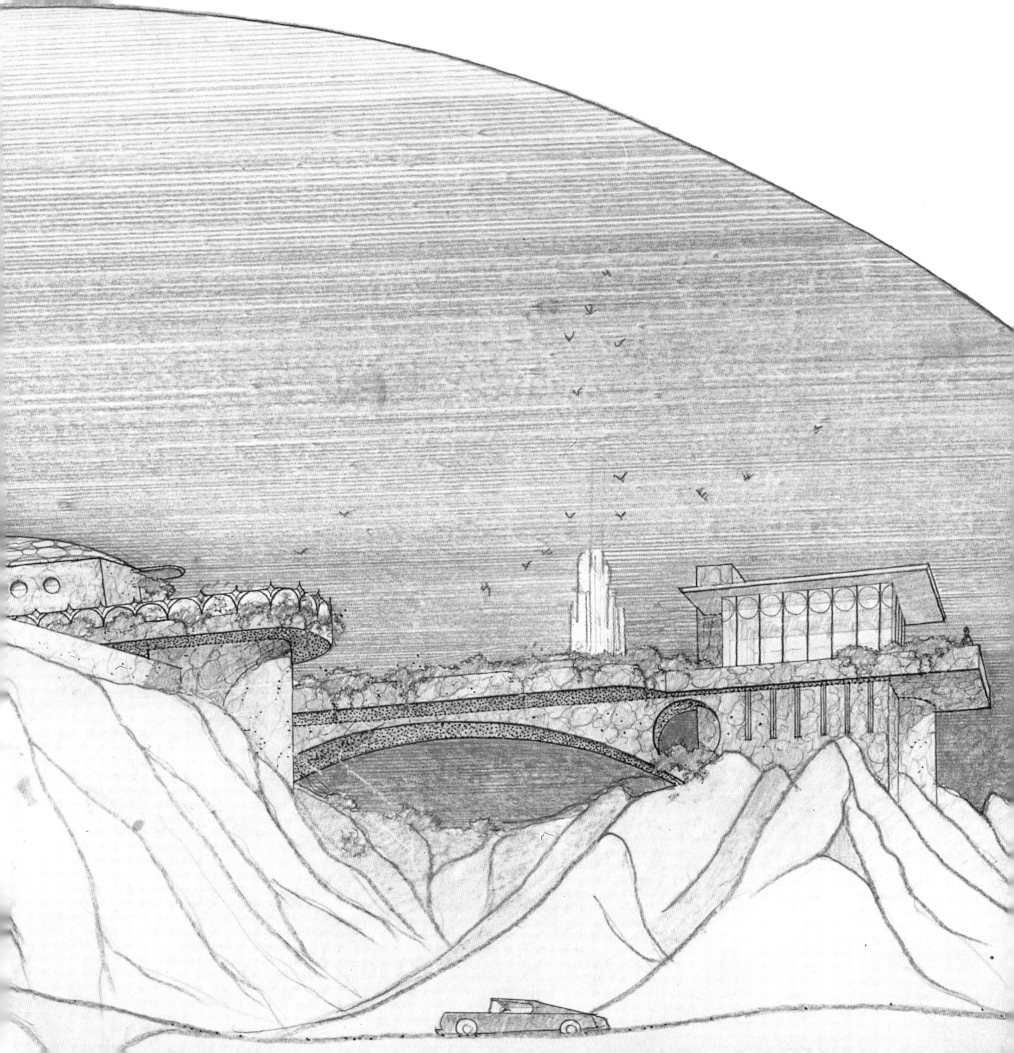

PART TWO

BUILDINGS FOR WORSHIP

When Frank Lloyd Wright spoke to his apprentices or gave public lectures, he often brought up the subject of nature, and would advise, "Study Nature." He always spelled *Nature* with a capital "N," explaining that Nature was the only body of God we would ever see, and further explaining that as one spells *God* with a capital "G" he chose to spell *Nature* with a capital "N." Given his strong transcendental background combined with his Unitarian upbringing, he was a dedicated advocate of the beauty and sanctity of all things in the natural world. When he was asked if being inside a great space such as St. Patrick's Cathedral in New York was an inspiration to him, he replied that he would gain more inspiration from being in deep forest.

Yet by the study of nature he meant more than simply the trees, flowers, meadows, oceans, and mountains. He meant the study of the nature of whatever might be: the nature of a client, of a site for a building, or of a structure for reverence and prayer. Therefore it was this ability of his to look into the nature of whatever it is that resulted in the variety of significant forms that he chose when designing buildings for worship.

Design for wedding chapel for the Claremont Hotel. Berkeley, California. (See p.182.) FLLW FDN # 5731.001.

WEDDING
BERKELEY, CALIFO
FRANKL

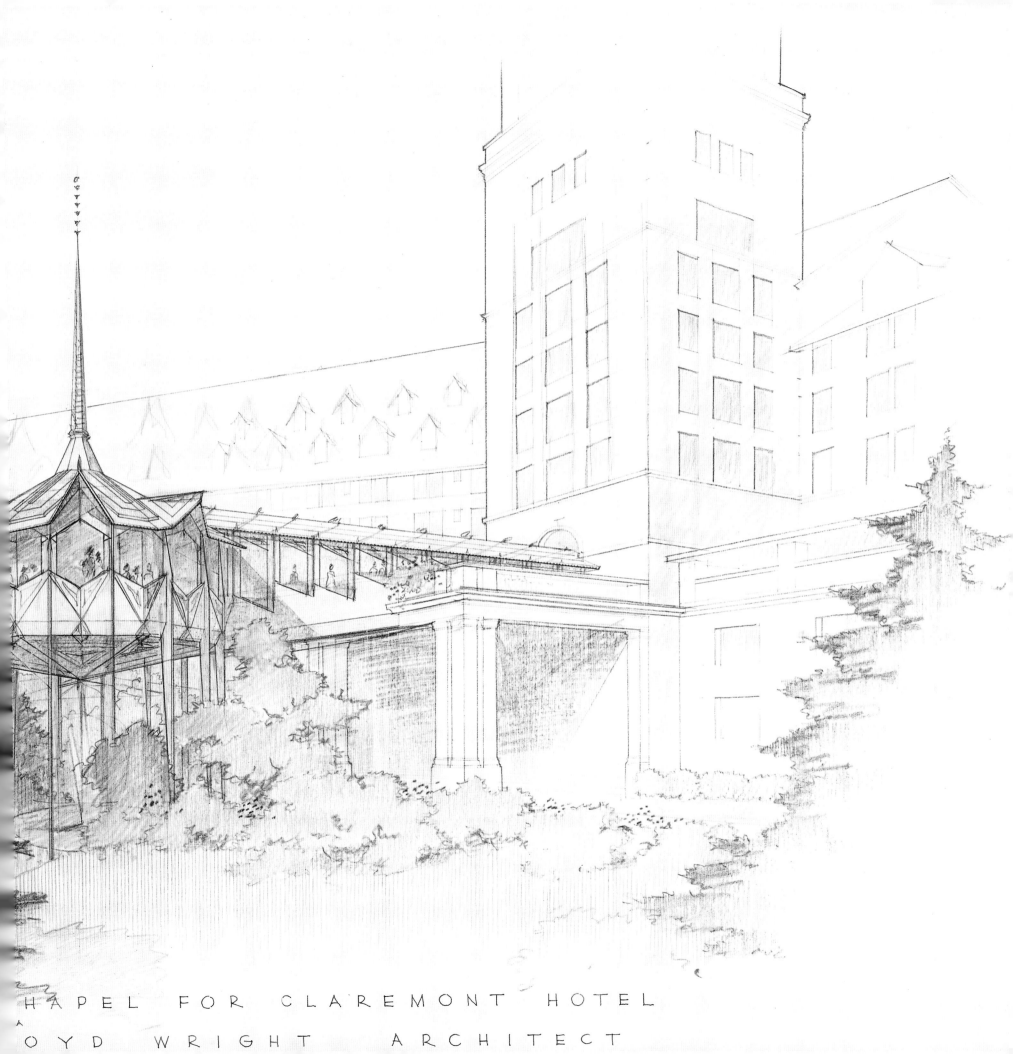

HAPEL FOR CLAREMONT HOTEL

OYD WRIGHT ARCHITECT

UNITY TEMPLE

Oak Park, Illinois. 1905

On June 6, 1905, Unity Church in Oak Park, Illinois, caught fire and burned to the ground. A committee was set up to find an architect in order to rebuild. Fortunately for Frank Lloyd Wright, Charles E. Roberts was on that committee. Roberts, as well as being a client of Wright's, was also a close personal friend. Among his many extraordinary attributes, he was what was considered in those days, a Progressive Republican (what would be considered today a liberal Democrat). Through his force and determination, Wright was chosen to be the architect for what would forever be known as "Unity Temple."

Wright was descended from a long line of Unitarian preachers on his mother's side of the family. Unity was an ultimate factor in Unitarian belief, and he felt that the square form was the perfect expression of that sense of unity, all sides being equal, all combining in perfect unity. That became the architectural form that Wright chose for this work.

The site for the new building was a long, rather narrow lot, with the narrow side facing the main street. Ordinarily a church design would be composed of a long, narrow building, as most conventional churches and cathedrals were. That would place the front door at the main street. However Wright chose to put the main entrance on the long side, with a foyer providing access to the religious part, Unity Temple, on one side in a square plan, while the secular part, Unity House, reserved for classroom and social functions and rectangular in plan, was on the other side (pp. 166-167).

There was a limited budget to construct a church for a congregation of four hundred. Wright chose the cheapest material—concrete—and by keeping the main plan as square, formwork for one side would be useful for the other three. The decorative elements in the columns were achieved by attaching wood blocks of varying sizes inside the wood forms before the concrete was poured. The result was a concrete column with integral ornament, capable of being produced in multiple examples by what Wright often called "machine technique." Here was a fine example of what he meant when he said that the machine can be a tool in the hands of the artist.

He wrote in his autobiography that when he set to work on the scheme, he made forty preliminary studies but saved none of them. What has been saved are some of his preliminary studies for details: the column shafts (above), the pulpit (opposite page, top), the lighting features, and the outdoor bronze lanterns and planting boxes.

Left: Designs for columns.
FLLW FDN # 061.008.
Right, top: Design for pulpit.
FLLW FDN # 0611.023.
Right, bottom: Interior view.
FLLW FDN # 0611.009.

Following pages: Perspective.
FLLW FDN # 0611.003.

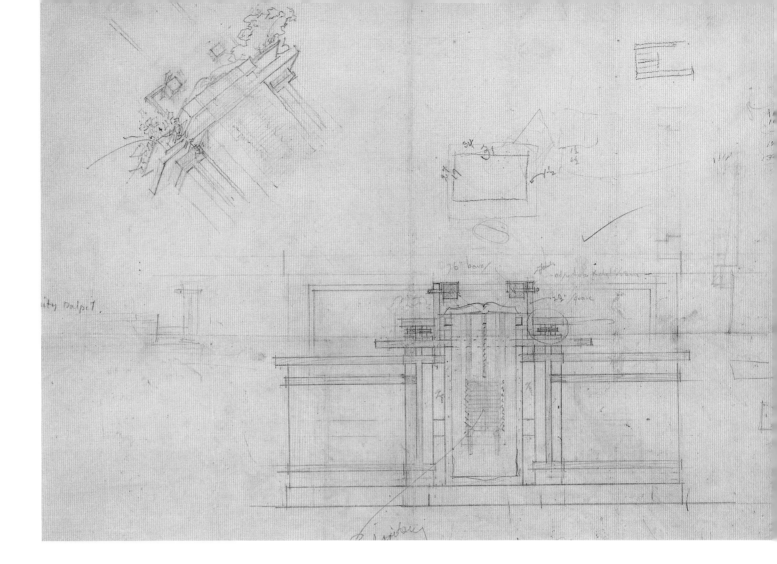

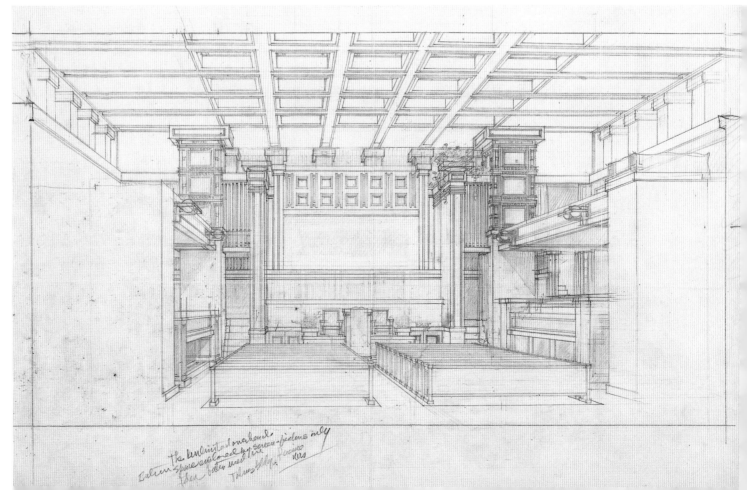

Wright prepared a preliminary sketch of an interior view (previous page, bottom) Years later, when coming upon this drawing, Wright inscribed, "The unlimited overhead—interior space enclosed by screen-features only. Idea later used in Johnson bldg Racine. FLlW."

Of course, in building for a building committee, there was always some dissension among certain members. Such a person was Mr. Skillin, who was sure the room would be too dark and the acoustics would be poor. Wright had placed the pastor in such a way that all parishioners were in view from the pulpit. The overhead skylight reached across the entire interior with stained glass in shades of amber and yellow. Even on cloudy or rainy days, the room was bathed in an atmosphere of sunlight. During the design stages and even during construction, none of this convinced Mr. Skillin. Wright wrote of the opening ceremonies:

"This building, however, is finished and the Sunday for dedication arrives. I do not want to go. Stay at home. When the church was opened the phone began to ring. Happy contented voices are heard in the congregation. Finally weary, I take little Francie by the hand to go out into the air to get away from it all. Enough. But just as the hat goes on my head, another ring, a prosaic voice, Mr. Skillin's: 'Take back all I said . . . light everywhere—all pleased.' Hear well? 'Yes, see and hear fine—see it all now.'

"'I'm glad. Goodbye.' At last the doubting member, sincere in praise, a good sport besides. Francie got tossed in the air. She came down with a squeal of delight. And that is how it was and is and will be as often as a building is born." [1]

The famous perspective, made by Wright's assistant Marian Mahony (right), was later redrawn and published in Germany, along with the plans. Photographs of the complete structure were also published by the same Berlin publisher, Ernst Wasmuth. When the portfolio of his work was released in Germany in 1910, and then the photographic edition of the same work, in 1911, Unity Temple became one of the most seminal works of architecture that broke with past traditional forms and ushered in an entirely new epoch in building—modern architecture.

FOR THE WORSHIP OF GOD
AND THE SERVICE OF MAN

STEEL CATHEDRAL

For William Norman Guthrie
New York, New York. 1927, Project

Below: Plan. FLLW FDN # 2602.002.
Right: Elevation. FLLW FDN # 2602.003.

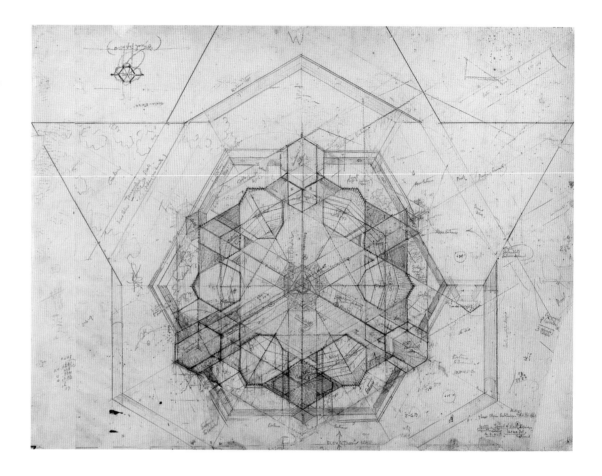

Wright's design for a massive religious structure that has become known as "The Steel Cathedral" came as the result of an article that William Norman Guthrie was writing about a great church design. Guthrie and Wright had known each other since 1908 when the architect designed a prairie house for him. It was never built, but the friendship between the two men prospered. Guthrie was the pastor of the New York Episcopalian church St. Mark's-in-the-Bouwerie. He was a quixotic, enigmatic person, with radical ideas not only about church design but about church ritual as well. His sermons included dance and song along with the religious texts usually required. Often these rather unconventional ceremonies brought criticism down upon his head, but he adhered to his ideas regardless of popular opinion. He was just the sort of person Wright found himself drawn to, a man dedicated to ideas and dedicated to reform. He wanted Wright to illustrate the article he was writing about his "dream" cathedral, one that would hold one million people with major cathedrals and related chapels all within one mammoth structure. Obviously the idea had great appeal for Wright. Following Guthrie's letter asking about the illustrations for his article, Wright replied, "I believe in the 'Cathedral' idea, there would be some good effects as the result of broadcasting it. And we might build it before we died—Who knows? I have already got it born."[2]

Wright's plan was a large hexagon in which around the periphery there were six large polygonal cathedrals, with twelve smaller chapels, two on each side of each cathedral (shown here). These are all enclosed in a vast pyramid of steel and glass rising almost twice the height of the Eiffel Tower. Wright described this great glass-enclosed-void as "The Hall of the Elements," and the various sects of the cathedrals and chapels are united within it.

The plan and its first elevation (first elevation not shown) appear to be Wright's answer to Guthrie's proposal. However, a second elevation (opposite page) in which the former cathedral shapes are rendering in more abstract, solid, geometric shapes, bears an interesting series of Wright's inscriptions such as "Commercial Arts Festival" and, later, "Broadacres Cathedral." He has indicated "Spiral roadway to garden at top—outside and inside—descending beneath ascent." This would seem to be a further development of the Gordon Strong Automobile Objective and Planetarium that he had designed two years earlier. The "Broadacres Cathedral" obviously refers to the model he made in 1934 of Broadacre City, where the footprint plan of a cathedral is identical to the plan of this project.

It goes without saying that the Steel Cathedral was far too ambitious, even far too fantastic, to ever be built. Yet it reveals Wright's mind at work on a project with no limitations as to cost or possible construction. His three drawings are among the most intriguing in the entire collection.

The Steel Cathedral did provide some seeds for a later work, namely the Beth Sholom Synagogue, 1954, Elkins Park, Pennsylvania. Here again, the main feature of the building is a glass pyramid embracing the entire space within the building, but on a much more modified scale.

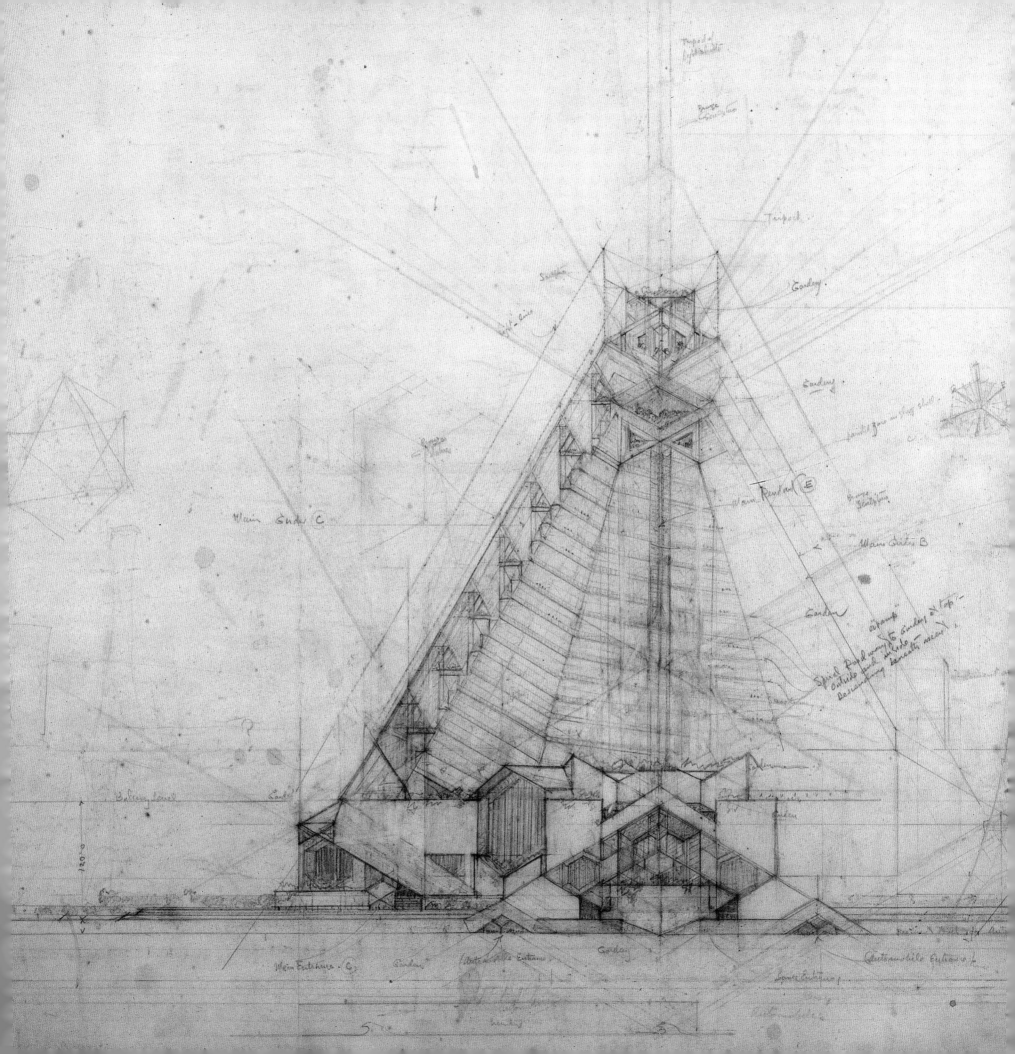

FACADE

END

RHODODENDRON CHAPEL
"PRIVATE TO THE BEAUTY OF THOUGHT"
(TEMPLE TO POETRY)
FOR E J KAUFMANN

PLAN

RHODODENDRON CHAPEL

For Edgar J. Kaufmann
Mill Run, Pennsylvania. 1952, Project

Liliane, Edgar Kaufmann Sr., and Edgar Kaufmann jr. shared a profound love for nature and the belief in its sanctity and even healing power. The home that Frank Lloyd Wright gave them in their woodland setting was certainly a vehicle for these feelings. "Fallingwater is a great blessing, one the great blessings to be experienced here on earth. I think nothing yet ever equaled the coordination and sympathetic expression of the great principle of repose where forest and stream and rock and all the elements of structure are combined so quietly that you listen not to any noise whatsoever although the music of the stream is there."[3]

Over the years since Fallingwater was first built, the Kaufmanns underwent several turbulent episodes and personal tragedies. Realizing this, Edgar jr. wrote a letter to Wright asking him to design a special chapel on the grounds near Fallingwater.

"Dear Mr. Wright: Will you build a place of prayer at Bear Run? All three of us would like a focus of attention for the spiritual reality which we know underlies life and work and the joys we share.

"Nature is the great restorer, concentrated here to balance our city living. Mother brings a choice of flowers and foods and comforts, Father brings broad scope of action and actualities, and I some ideas and music, all this combines into a rich life for which we are grateful and humbly so.

"Yet black storm clouds clash around us, often within us, born of wrongs, blindness and sin that bind the world and with which we bind ourselves. We know that only by special efforts of will can we be restored from these stormy depths to peace and well-being, even here among many blessings. For this we would like a spot set aside."[4]

No particular site was selected and presented to Wright in order that he may begin his designs. Edgar jr. and his mother, who were the two who formally commissioned Wright for a

chapel design, had themselves not chosen a site, but it is assumed it would have been on an area upstream from Fallingwater. Wright's conceptual sketch, showing plan and elevations, is one of the loveliest in the entire collection of Frank Lloyd Wright drawings. His thoughtful inscription reads, "Rhododendron Chapel, 'Private to the Beauty of Thought' (Temple to Poetry) for E. J. Kaufmann." The drawing (opposite page, top) was signed "FLlW April 28/ 52."

He named it Rhododendron Chapel after the shrub that was prevalent in the region. The stonework would have been similar to that of the main house. A gabled roof rising out of the stonework below was all glass in two layers so as to provide insulation. Here was a detail that harked back to the glass rising overhead in the Steel Cathedral and would find yet another application in the Beth Sholom Synagogue two years later.

Six months after Wright presented these drawings, Liliane Kaufmann committed suicide at Fallingwater. Despite Wright's urging that father and son go forward with the chapel as a memorial to mother, the project was dropped.

Left, top: Preliminary plan and elevations. FLLW FDN # 5308.014.
Left, bottom: Perspective sketch. FLLW FDN # 5308.001.
Above: Perspective. FLLW FDN # 5308.017.

BETH SHOLOM SYNAGOGUE

Elkins Park, Pennsylvania. 1954

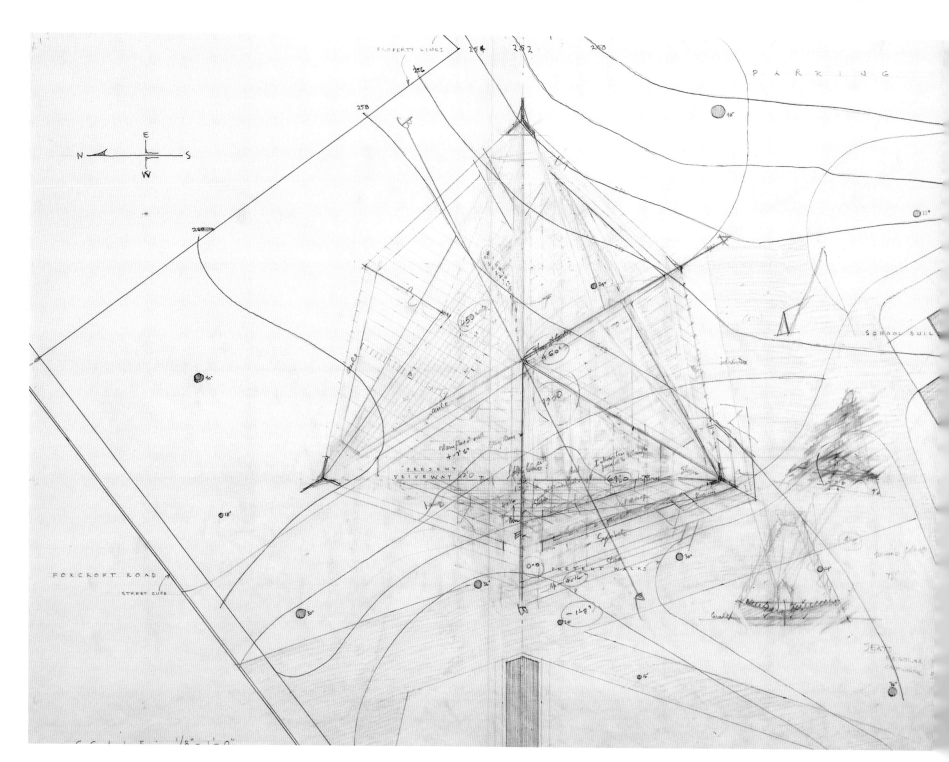

Left: Preliminary plan with section sketches. FLLW FDN # 5313.004.

Below: Plan. FLLW FDN # 5313.024.

Obviously the concept of a religious edifice, such as he had designed for the Steel Cathedral, never left him. A place wherein light descends from above into the entire building, light as a great benefactor, during the daytime, a constant beneficent source consistently abnegating darkness, while at night light pours forth from the entire structure, a constant beacon of faith and endurance. These attributes he envisioned in 1927, and now again, but on a smaller scale, yet just as powerful and meaningful; he brought this idea to fruition in his design for the Beth Sholom Synagogue. Prior to his initial sketches, the client, Rabbi Mortimer Cohen, was anxious that his architect be familiar with Jewish symbolism and details of features pertinent to Judaism. Over and over again he sent Wright material and photographs of other synagogues, all in an honest effort to help educate his architect.

Wright's first plan placed the structure inside a six sided hexagon (opposite page) and on the plan he has sketched some sections, which he further developed on another sheet (not shown). A rudimentary perspective was then made, with some notations by the architect.

As Wright set to work on the plan (right) the gently sloping facets of the main floor of the temple itself were intended, as Wright explained, to create a kind of edifice so people, on entering, would feel that they were resting in the very hands of God. The large tripod beams, from which are suspended the glass walls and roof (one and the same thing in this building), are marked with designs stamped in metal which become large sculptural lamps running on up the exterior of the beams to represent the menorah—the seven branched candles of light. Inside, the holy arc, the wings of the seraphim, and the sacred inscriptions are there in the synagogue as features of the architecture, related to the building as a whole. Mt. Sinai traditionally denotes revelation;

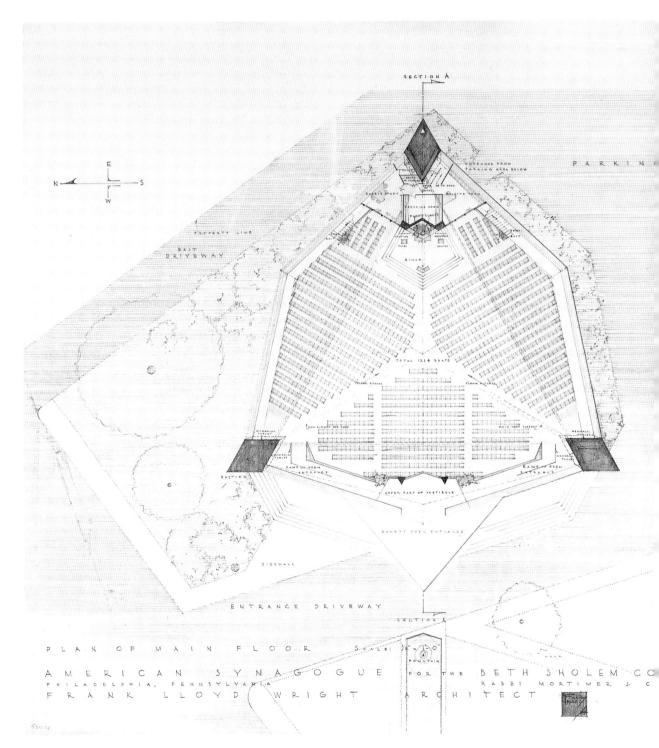

Scheme I American Synagogue for Beth Sholom Hebrew Church
may be increased up to 10000 seats
or diminished to 500.
Various forms by Modification of plane — infinite

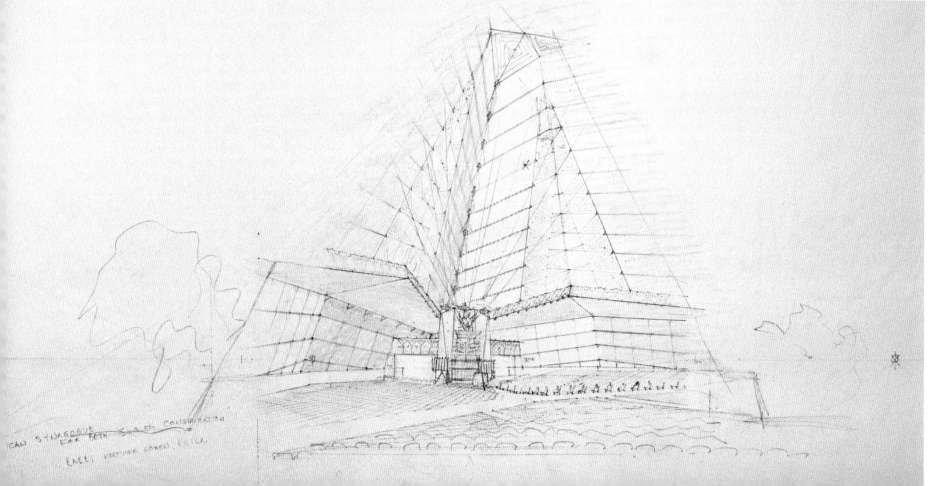

AMERICAN SYNAGOGUE FOR BETH SHALOM CONGREGATION
ELKINS PARK, PENNSYLVANIA

revelation is synonymous with light; light is the essence of this temple.

When the final preliminary designs were ready to be sent to the rabbi, Wright included this letter of explanation:

"Dear Rabbi:

"Herewith the promised 'hosanna'—a temple that is truly a religious tribute to the living God. Judaism needs one in America. To do it for you has pleased me. The scheme or plan is capable of infinite variation, and could be expanded or diminished and made into different shapes as might be desired.

"The scheme is truly simple. Construction is modern as can be. Stamped copper shells erected for structural members are filled with concrete in which the necessary steel rods are embedded for stresses: the tops of the shells removable for this purpose—thus no forming is necessary.

"The building is set up on an interior temporary scaffold. The outer walls are double-wired glass—a blue tinted plastic inside—about an inch of air space between. Heat rises at the walls from the floor. The stained glass windows could be composed from scenes from the Bible?

"Here you have a coherent statement of worship. I hope it pleases you and your people.

"Faithfully, Frank Lloyd Wright, March 15, 1954."

Four days later came the rabbi's reaction to the design:

"You have taken the supreme moment of Jewish history and experience—the revelation of God to Israel through Moses at Mt. Sinai, and you have translated that moment with all it signifies into a design of beauty and reverence. In a word, your building is Mt. Sinai."[5]

CHRISTIAN SCIENCE CHURCH

Bolinas, California. 1956, Project

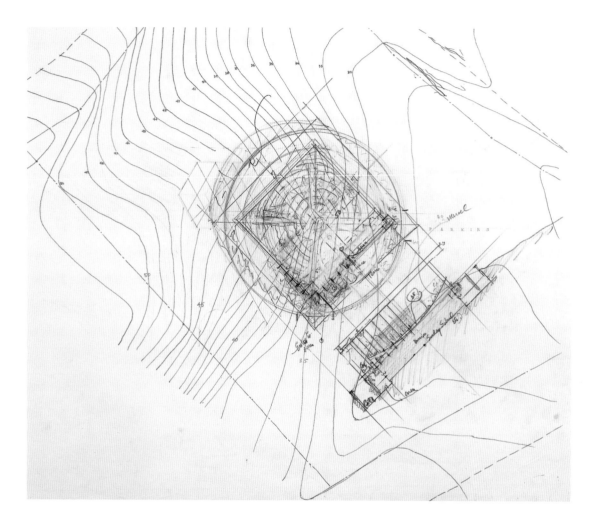

Several of Wright's early clients were Christian Scientists, most notable among them was Mrs. Avery Coonley. It has long been a mystery why Wright, in designing the Coonley House in Riverside, Illinois, placed two identical stairways, one on each side of the fireplace in the living room. Recently, a grandson of Mrs. Coonley explained that his grandmother was a Christian Scientist practitioner, that is, she counseled other Christian Scientists who needed her help for healing. He claimed that she had close to five hundred patients. So that a patient, when leaving, would not encounter the next one arriving, the staircases were arranged so that a person going down would not meet another person coming up. On the ground level, a corridor with a closed door provided further privacy for the one who was leaving. This fully explained the reason for the two stairways, when one would have been sufficient.

Wright was certainly familiar with the precepts of the Christian Science faith. When he had made his design for this Christian Scientist Church, he prepared a caption for its exhibition:

"Temple of the Mind. The Mind taking precedence of Spirit. Intelligence above feeling. Putting Mind above Spirit by calling Spirit Mind."

In his plan (above, left), a large circle embraces a square, the actual building itself, while the square embraces circular seating.

S T I A N   S C I E N C E   C H U R C H
S,   M A R I N   C O U N T Y ,   C A L I F O R N I A
K   L   L O Y D   W R I G H T   A R C H I T E C T

All four sides of the building are glass, one side a bank of tall glass doors, the other three stationary glass windows rising from the masonry walls. Everything about the auditorium speaks of clarity, light, openness, and a connection to the natural world outside, the trees in the forest at the rear, and the broad grassy stretch in front. A lower level provides space for a Sunday school with a deep well on three sides so as to allow natural light to enter the room.

Left: Plan. FLLW FDN # 5527.001.
Above: Perspective. FLLW FDN # 5527.009.

177

ANNUNCIATION GREEK ORTHODOX CHURCH

For the Milwaukee Hellenic Community
Wauwatosa, Wisconsin. 1956

Because Frank Lloyd Wright had the ability to look into things rather than at them, he was well qualified to design a variety of religious structures—seeking to find the form that would best symbolize and express the essential nature of each particular denomination. For the Unity Temple in Oak Park, he chose the square as a symbol of unity, each side unified with the other. For the Unitarian meeting house he designed for Madison, Wisconsin, he chose the triangle as the symbol of aspiration.

When the commission came to him from the Milwaukee Hellenic Community to design a church for them, he asked his wife, Olgivanna, who was brought up in the Greek Orthodox faith, what were the key symbolic forms. She replied that historically they were the Greek cross and the dome. His first sketch is a perfect marriage of those two forms as he put them down on paper, and that concept remained constant through all of the stages of developing the design, from first sketches to final working drawings and construction documents.

The cross is evident in the plan as it reaches the outer line of the circle, and the dome is apparent in the graceful covering of the structure as well as the inverted dome which forms the floor of the balcony, while the arms of the cross also rise to support the balcony. The main floor is planned so that the lectern is in the center, visible to all. At three points, spiral stairs ascend to the balcony where an organ and chorus is stationed as well as seating for more members of the congregation. On the exterior walls of the balcony, gentle arches provide fenestration for the church. The domed ceiling is covered in gold leaf.

The construction of this dome is most innovative: it is a reinforced concrete shell that rests on a steel track containing thousands of very small ball bearings set in grease—to allow for the

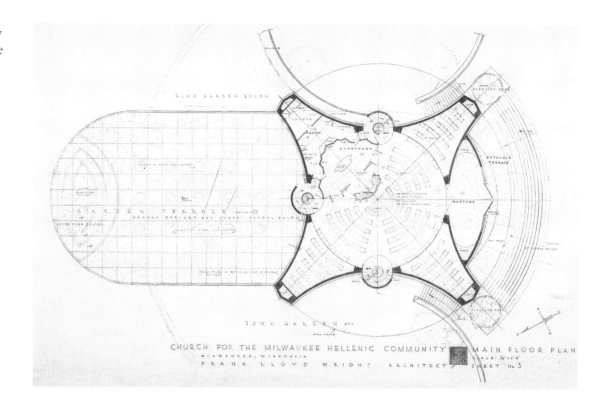

CHURCH FOR THE MILWAUKEE HELLENIC COMMUNITY MAIN FLOOR PLAN
FRANK LLOYD WRIGHT ARCHITECT

necessary expansion and contraction. The dome thus can move in response to temperature changes without exerting force on the exterior walls. At the point where the dome meets the wall, a ring of glass spheres is set between the concrete supports. The effect is astounding: where one expects to find heavy support, one sees light, through a thin chain of glistening glass spheres.

In preparing material for an exhibition of his recent work, Wright composed the following caption about the Annunciation Greek Orthodox Church:

"The domed religion of antiquity at home in modern times. The romance of the past distinguished."

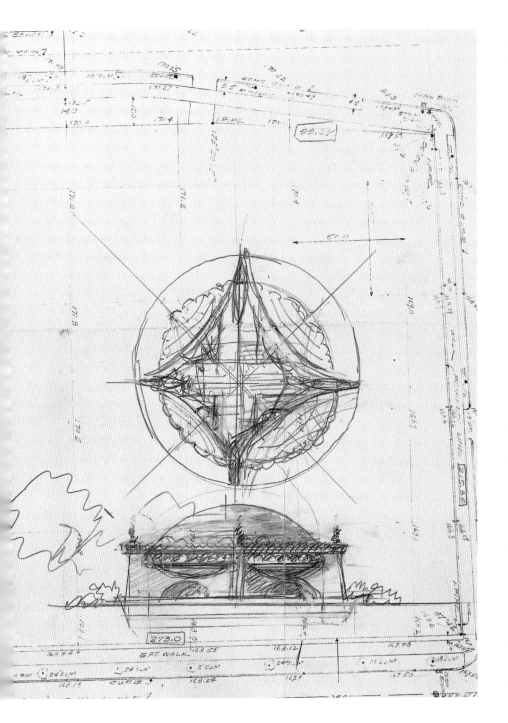

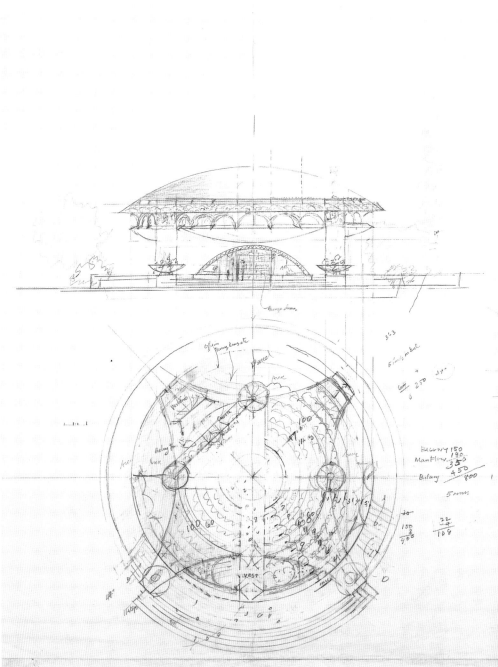

Left: Plan. FLLW FDN # 5611.030.
Below, left: Plan and elevation.
FLLW FDN # 5611.003.
Below, right: Plan and elevation.
FLLW FDN # 5611.001.

CHURCH FOR THE MILWAUKEE HELLENIC
MILWAUKEE, WISCONSIN
FRANK LLOYD WRIGHT, ARCHITECT

Perspective. FLLW FDN # 5611.002.

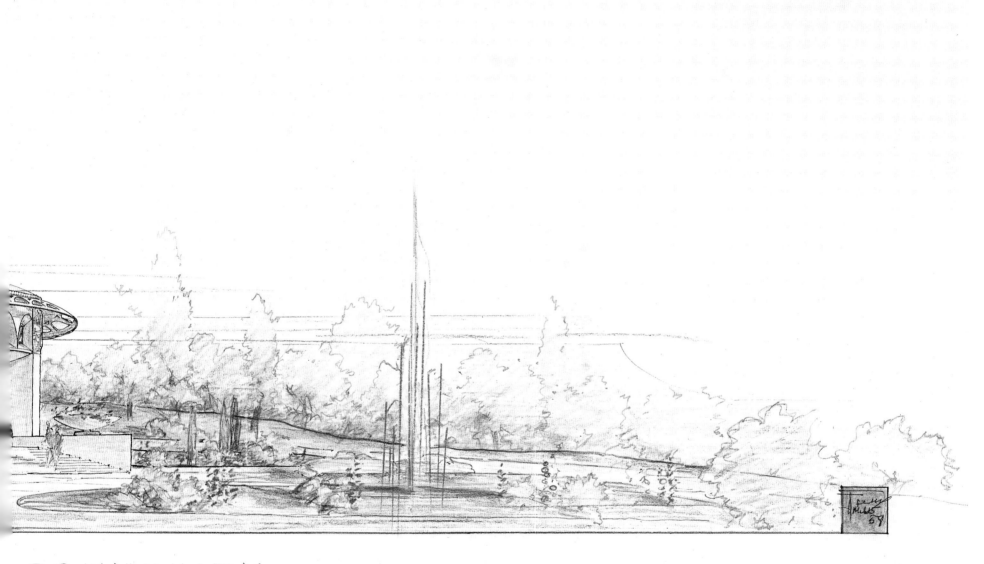

COMMUNITY

WEDDING CHAPEL

For the Hotel Claremont
Berkeley, California. 1957, Project

Below: Preliminary plan and elevation. FLLW FDN # 5709.001.
Bottom: Preliminary plan and elevation. FLLW FDN # 5709.007.
Right: Plans. FLLW FDN # 5731.007.

The Hotel Claremont in Berkeley was desirous of adding a special wedding chapel to their existing building. Wright's first design was this rather whimsical plan and elevation (right, top) of a chapel leading out from the main building onto a grassy lawn with fir trees. He rather mischievously, with tongue in cheek, labeled it "Rococo Wedding Chapel." Early in the commission, he was apprised of the fact that the chapel could not be attached to the hotel on ground level, but had to join the building on the second floor and be situated out over the front lawn and fir trees.

During the late fifties, when the International Style was tragically in vogue (Wright claimed it had neither style nor was international), placing buildings up on poles, or piloti, was then a rather popular architectural device. Wright declared that as such, the building was removed from the ground. This was, to him, a reprehensible act. Now in the case with this wedding chapel, the situation dictated that it be up off the ground. As with his dictum about limitations being an artist's best friend, again it can be seen how he solved this problem by making an artistic feature of the piloti, a slender series of metal "legs," graceful and delicate, upon which the building rests, like a ballerina poised and made ready for the next leap. The chapel is gained by a descending covered corridor from the hotel.

The chapel itself is eight-sided in plan, with hexagonal windows shielded by elaborate copper dormers, lending a festive element for special occasions. Rising above the copper roof is a spire with lights, reiterating the delicate piloti below.

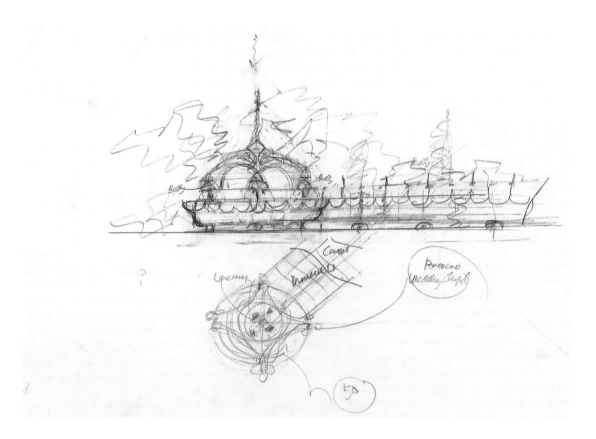

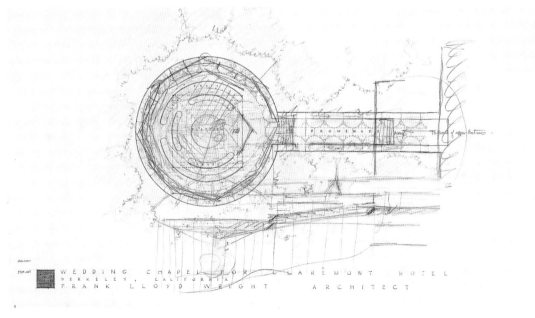

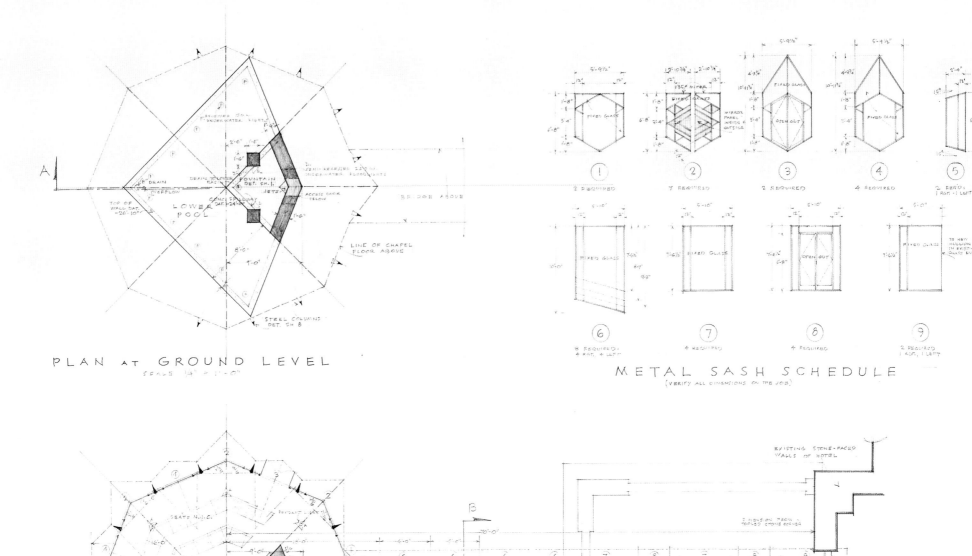

PLAN at GROUND LEVEL
SCALE 1/4" = 1'-0"

METAL SASH SCHEDULE
(VERIFY ALL DIMENSIONS ON THE JOB)

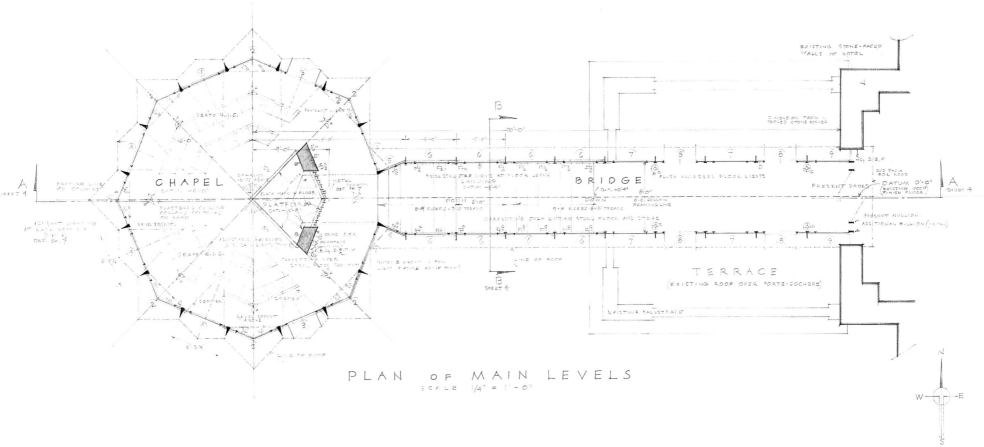

PLAN of MAIN LEVELS
SCALE 1/4" = 1'-0"

WEDDING CHAPEL FOR HOTEL CLAREMONT GENERAL PLANS
BERKELEY CALIFORNIA SCALE 1/4" = 1'-0"
FRANK LLOYD WRIGHT ARCHITECT SHEET NO. 2

PART THREE

BUILDINGS FOR CULTURE
AND EDUCATION

Frank Lloyd Wright's designs for buildings for culture and education began in 1915 when he was called upon to design a theater in Chicago. Although the theater certainly represented entertainment, in Wright's way of thinking it was also a strong cultural institution. His theater designs spanned forty years, with none of them constructed until the Dallas Theater Center was built in 1955.

In the realm of education, his most prestigious design was without doubt the campus he created for Florida Southern College, in Lakeland, Florida. This was a work that went on from 1938 to 1957, and several buildings were built, with others remaining as projects only.

The civic center he designed for Madison, Wisconsin, the Monona Terrace Civic Center, was another project that lingered on from 1938 to 1955. The first scheme was later revised, but that was defeated as well as the first one, this time through the manipulation of politics.

Certainly his museum for the Solomon R. Guggenheim Foundation stands as one of the most remarkable and famous buildings of the twentieth century, if not of all time. This was another one of the commissions that went on from 1943 until construction was begun in 1956. No other project in his long career of nearly seven decades exacted such a toll upon through changes of the museum's needs to strong popular opinion that the building was unfit as a place to exhibit fine art. His designs for the two Pittsburgh Point Park Civic Centers show Wright extending the envelope of modern technology and advanced engineering into realms hitherto never imagined. They two, like the Monona projects, were doomed to a life on paper, only.

With his love for the city of Venice, he was given the chance to design a student library and domicile on its historic Grand Canal. This design ranks among one of the most charming, one

might even say endearing, works of architecture he ever created. Its charm is pure Venetian, rendered with deep respect for that city's traditions. It failed, due to popular pressure fearing "a modern building on such a historic location" would injure tourist trade.

In Baghdad, Wright found himself, as he expressed it, "captured by his boyhood"—meaning his youthful love for the *One Thousand and One Nights*, and now, nearly 60 years later, able to design buildings for a part of the world for which he held deep respect.

Perspective for Pittsburgh
Point Park Civic Center and
Twin Suspension Bridges,
Scheme 2. (See p.226.)
FLLW FDN # 4836.009.

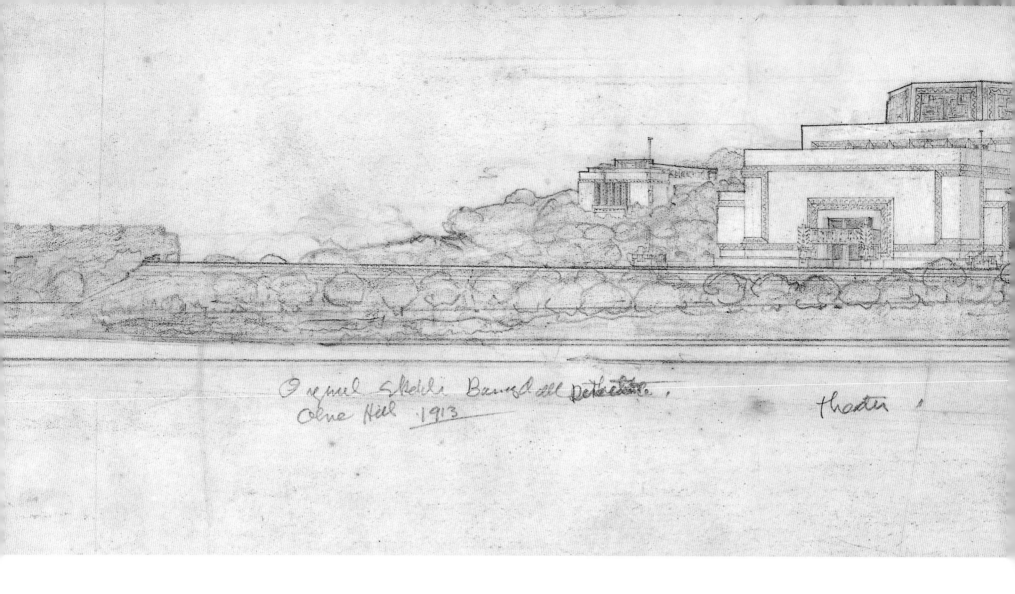

O riginal Sketch Barnsdall residence.
Olive Hill 1913

theater

OLIVE HILL THEATER

For Aline Barnsdall
Los Angeles, California. 1918–1920, Project

Aline Barnsdall's passion was drama—the theater—and she was a pioneer in her concepts of what a theater design should be. Her father, Theodore Barnsdall, was an oil baron in Pennsylvania, at a time when that state was the predominant supplier of crude oil. The money she inherited from him allowed her to pursue her interest in drama, and it took her to Chicago where she first met Frank Lloyd Wright in 1915. Recognizing his own pioneering work in residential design, she believed he would be the perfect architect to design a special theater for her. Wright wrote, "I met Miss Barnsdall shortly after the tragedy at Taliesin, while I was still in

Chicago at the Cedar Street house. Henry Sell brought her to see me in connection with a project for a theater in which she was interested. . . Her very large, wide-open eyes gave her a disingenuous expression not connected with the theater and her extremely small hands and feet somehow not connected with such ambition as hers." [1]

His sketches for a theater in Chicago (p. 188, top and bottom) revealed a new approach to theater design—the elimination of the customary proscenium wherein the audience was in one box, as Wright put it, and the performers in another. However, no final drawings were prepared; she left Chicago and eventually settled in Los Angeles.

There she purchased a large tract of land, called Olive Hill, and commissioned Wright to design her home, the famous Hollyhock House named after her favorite flower. Never losing interest in her passion, the theater, she then proposed to Wright the design of a most ambitious project that would include a drama theater, a motion picture theater, a residence for the director, and a special abode for the actors, while at the base of the property there would be a long series of shops and rental houses (above).

Wright set to work on these schemes, but nothing materialized except two other residences, called Residence A and Residence B,

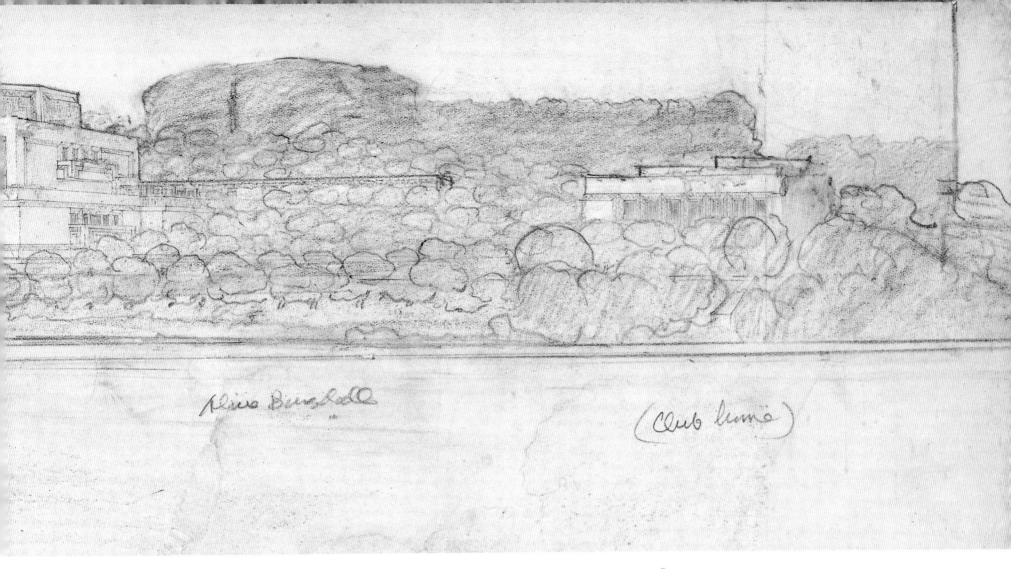

Aline Barnsdall

(Club house)

Perspective. FLLW FDN # 2005.003.

Following pages
Left, top: Section sketch for a theater in Chicago for
Aline Barnsdall. 1915, project. FLLW FDN # 1517.005
Left, bottom: Elevation sketches for a theater in Chicago
for Aline Barnsdall. FLLW FDN # 1517.003
Right: Perspective of Olive Hill Theater. FLLW FDN # 2005.001.

constructed near the top of the hill in relation to Hollyhock House. He soon discovered the peripatetic nature of Miss Barnsdall. Whenever a problem faced her, she would book passage on a streamship and travel. She claimed it cleared her mind, but it made for a difficult situation between architect and client. This changeable nature of hers, and her inability to settle down or see many things through to completion, may account for the demise of this ambitious project.

"A restless spirit, disinclined to stay long at any time in any one place as she traveled over the face of the globe, she would drop suggestions as a war-plane drops bombs and sails away into the blue. Now to add to this discomfort, the fates picked me up and were dragging me to and fro over the Pacific, for four or five years, to build the Imperial Hotel at Tokio[sic]."[2]

Wright himself enjoyed theatrical performances, and in whichever city he happened to be—Chicago, New York, San Francisco, Los Angeles—he would invariably seek out the theater. His son John recollected when he was with his father at a Vaudeville performance in Chicago: "When in the theater, tan, stick, and all, he would parade down the aisle to his seat, pause—swing about toward the audience, remove his cape—look right, left, up into the balconies like a Caesar about to make an oration—then he would sit down. His laugh was so contagious it sent the audience into spasms. One night the comedian, laughing all the while himself, looked directly at him and bowed in tribute.[3]

"Dad would sit in quiet ecstasy when we would go to the great Auditorium Theatre, the work of his master, Louis Sullivan. He told me, then, that the auditorium was acknowledged to be the greatest building achievement of the period, and to this day, all things considered, it is probably the best room for opera yet built in the world. He would point out where his own feeling for flatter planes crept into the detail, eliminating much of the free-flowing efflorescence of Sullivan's leaf ornament. This was conspicuously apparent on the gilded reliefs of the

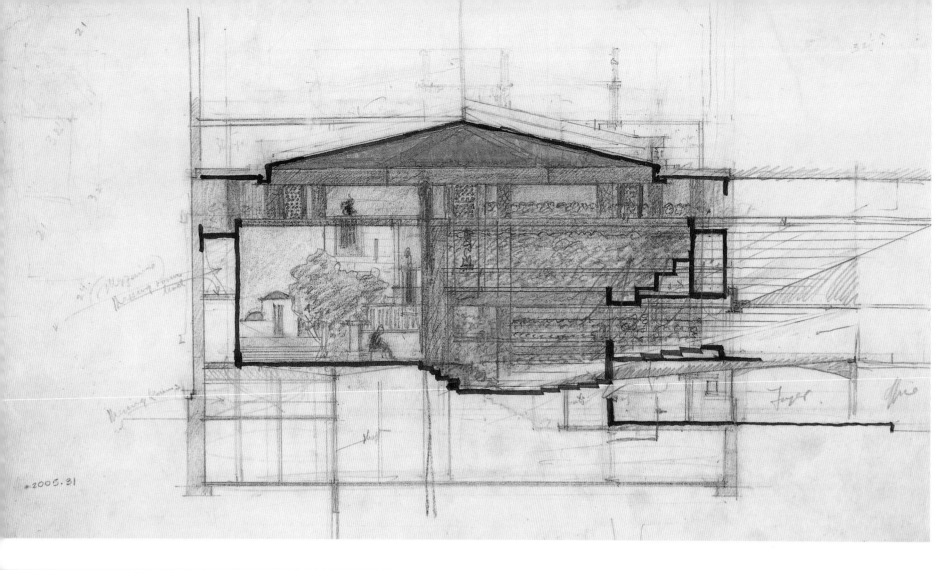

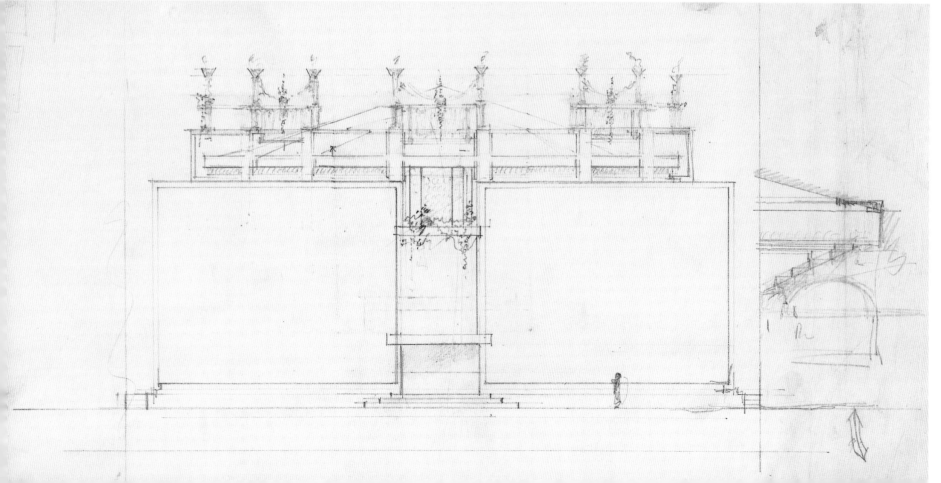

proscenium, inscribed with the names of great composers. He called my attention to Beethoven, 'Beethoven is not for the shallow,' he said. 'Beethoven believed that the barriers are not yet erected which can say to aspiring genius, 'Thus far and no further.'"[4]

In designing the theater for Aline Barnsdall, the difficulty lay in her indecision about how large or how small she wanted the theater in the first place. Added to her wish for a theater, she also proposed a major investment of development—the rental shops and stores Wright designed for her bordering on one side of her property. "My client, I soon found, had ideas and wanted yours but never worked much nor for long at a time, being possessed by incorrigible wanderlust that made me wonder, sometimes, what she wanted . . ."[5]

Despite how difficult a client Miss Barnsdall could be—and she was definitely the most diffi-cult he ever had up to that time—he persevered on the theater project, creating a file of sketches and studies numbering close to one hundred drawings. Perhaps it was his love for the theater that sustained him throughout this endeavor despite the differences, disagreements, and disappointments that went hand in hand along the way.

COMMUNITY PLAYHOUSE, "THE LITTLE DIPPER"

For Aline Barnsdall
Los Angeles, California. 1923, Project

Aline Barnsdall never married, but she did bear a child, a daughter named Betty Barnsdall, affectionately called "Sugar Top" by her mother. Barnsdall's interest in the theater found another avenue of expression, perhaps in connection with the education of her daughter, namely a building devoted to children's theatrical productions and progressive education. This was her dream of a community playhouse focusing on children, and she asked Wright to design just such a building on her Olive Hill property, close to Hollyhock House.

The project was named "The Little Dipper" because of the similarity of the plan to the constellation Ursa Minor, a group of seven stars colloquially known as The Little Dipper because of the bowl and handle. In this project, the bowl is an outdoor area arranged as seating, while the handle is the long structure of the building itself, the portion adjacent to the bowl opening by means of sliding glass to provide a stage.

At the time of this project, Wright was innovating the use of concrete block as a beautiful product with which to build, rather than the usual gutter to which it had been confined. His first work in this was the house for Alice Millard, La Miniatura. Here the blocks were laid up in the conventional method with mortar joints. In The Little Dipper the next year, he perfected a novel system of construction no longer utilizing the mortar joint—which required skilled masons—by stacking the blocks without mortar but with reinforcing rods of steel embedded in the blocks by pouring a liquid mixture of concrete, thus a system of building that could be achieved with unskilled labor (see pp. 192-193).

The Little Dipper was begun in construction but halted abruptly. Barnsdall was giving Hollyhock House and Residence A to the City of Los Angeles for the California Art Club, and there arose some concern on the part of the City about the construction costs of The Little Dipper. Only

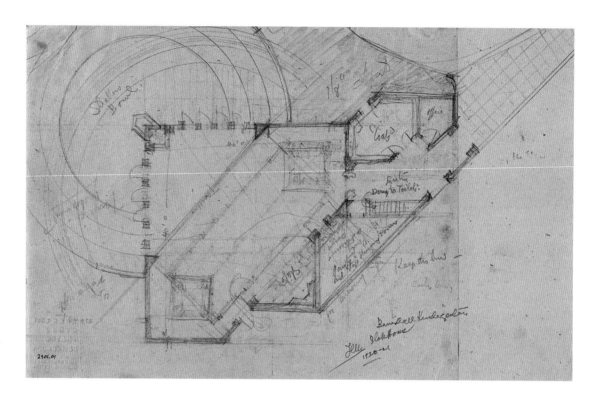

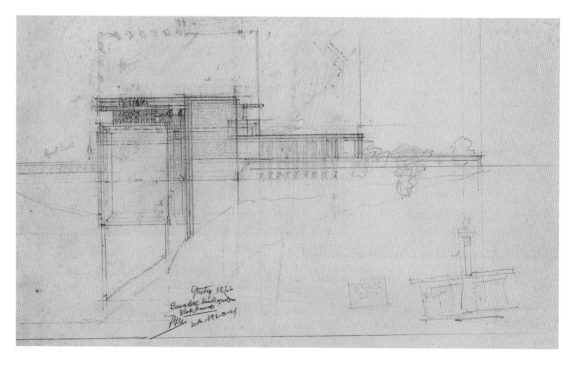

Perspective. FLLW FDN # 2301.008.

a few retaining walls were actually built, and these were later converted into a park as a memorial to Barnsdall's father.

Again not one to let a fine project become abandoned when he found another use for it, Wright proposed The Little Dipper be constructed as a children's building at Florida Southern College in 1949 (see p. 191). This, too, was fated never to be built. However the general plan—a bowl attached to a long structure—was greatly expanded to become the library at Florida Southern College (see pp. 204-205). In this application, the round area served as a reading room and the long section as stacks for books and periodicals.

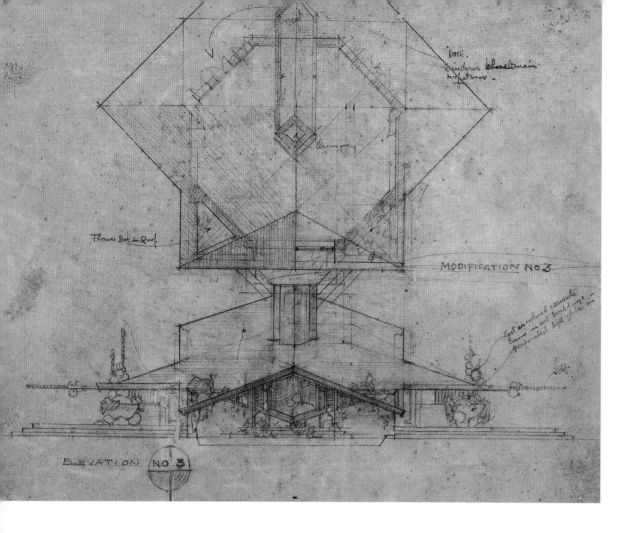

PLAYHOUSES, "KINDERSYMPHONIES"

For the Oak Park Playground Association
Oak Park, Illinois. 1926, Project

"Kindersymphonies" is the name that Frank Lloyd Wright gave to a group of five playhouses designed for the Oak Park Playground Association. How the commission came to him, and who the clients were, is not on record. Yet this was at the time, in 1926, when Wright, unable to pay a mortgage, was evicted from his home Taliesin. Without any support staff, these drawings therefore were made by him, from sketches to final renderings. He gave them names such as "Hob Goblin" and "Two for a Penny—Toyland." He also gave them the names of his grandchildren "The Betty Lloyd," who became the architect Elizabeth Wright Ingraham, and "The Ann Baxter" (left, bottom) who became the film actress Anne Baxter and starred in such outstanding films as *The Razor's Edge* and *All About Eve*. He then named one for his own daughter, "The Iovanna." The plan is the same for all five, but they differ in the elevations. As playhouses, they also served as education—through recreation, designed to delight children and spark their imaginations.

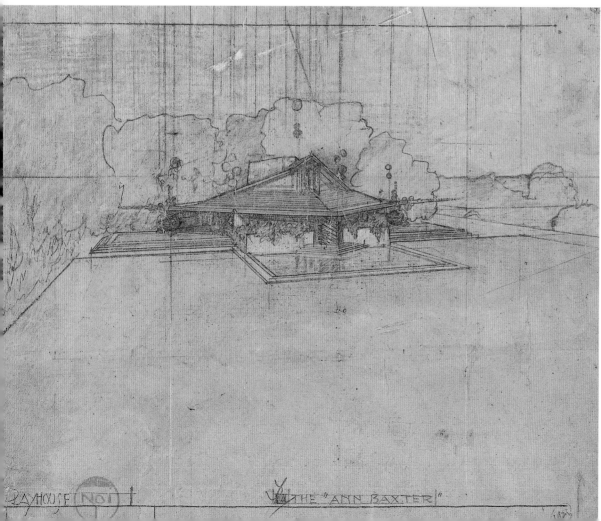

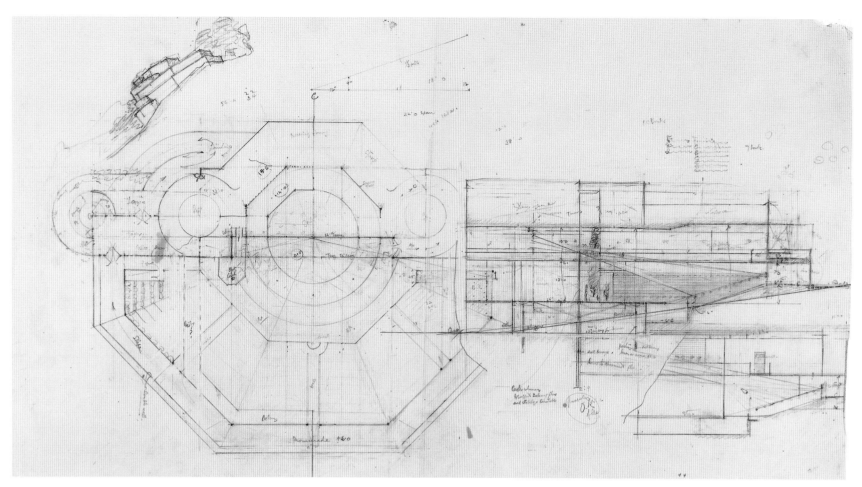

THE NEW THEATER

For J. P. McEvoy
Woodstock, New York. 1931, Project

Above: Plan. FLLW FDN # 3106.003.
Right, top: Perspective. FLLW FDN # 3106.027.
Right, bottom: Perspective for Dallas Theater Center.
FLLW FDN # 5514.002.

Following pages: Perspective for proposed theater
in Hartford, Connecticut. FLLW FDN # 4922.001

Wright was certainly disappointed that his theater design for Aline Barnsdall never came to fruition, thus it must have pleased him when, in the summer of 1931, J. P. McEvoy commissioned him to design a theater at Woodstock, New York. The site was a hill slope, and Wright positioned the theater so that it was nestled into the hill, the entrance via two exterior covered ramps that ascend from the lower level of the theater up to the ticketing offices and lobbies, one on each side. The plan is set within a large form that is basically hexagonal. He named the project "The New Theater," since it did away with the old concept of a proscenium which divided the theater into two "boxes," one for the audience and one for the performers. By using the hexagon for the seating, he figured that seeing the performance slightly in the reflex, that is, slightly at an angle, as opposed

to dead on, as in the square plan he employed in the Barnsdall theater, would be more pleasing. His plan for a revolving stage and a musicians' balcony above the stage is obviously the result of the years spent in Tokyo at work on the Imperial Theater. Unquestionably he admired the performances he witnessed in the Kabuki theater, wherein the circular, revolving stage was a prominent and dramatic feature, as well as the music coming from above the stage rather than in front of it. Also, by eliminating the proscenium, he has drawn the audience closer to the action on the stage. The entire structure was planned to be constructed using reinforced concrete.

Unfortunately, the project coincided with the Great Depression that swept over the United States following the stock market crash earlier. Funds for building projects were hard to come

by as a circumstance. Only those projects that were federally funded—the roads, highways, dams, and national parks, for example—that came as a result of President Roosevelt's "New Deal"—went forward, in an attempt to generate jobs for a labor force that suffered at that time from massive unemployment.

In 1949, Paton Price and Associates, along with the actor Don Murray, approached Wright for a theater to be built in Hartford, Connecticut (pp. 198-199). This design, likewise titled "The New Theater," was strongly based on the earlier one for Woodstock, New York. It was not built, but Wright's desire to design and see that design for a theater took shape later for the Dallas Theater Center, in Dallas, Texas (opposite page). Named The Kalita Humphreys Theater, it was finally constructed in 1955, based on the design for the 1949 "New Theater."

THE NEW THEATER
DALLAS THEATER CENTER
FRANK LLOYD WRIGHT   ARCHITECT

THEATER FOR THE NEW TH
FOR PATON PRICE AN
FRANK LLOYD WRIG

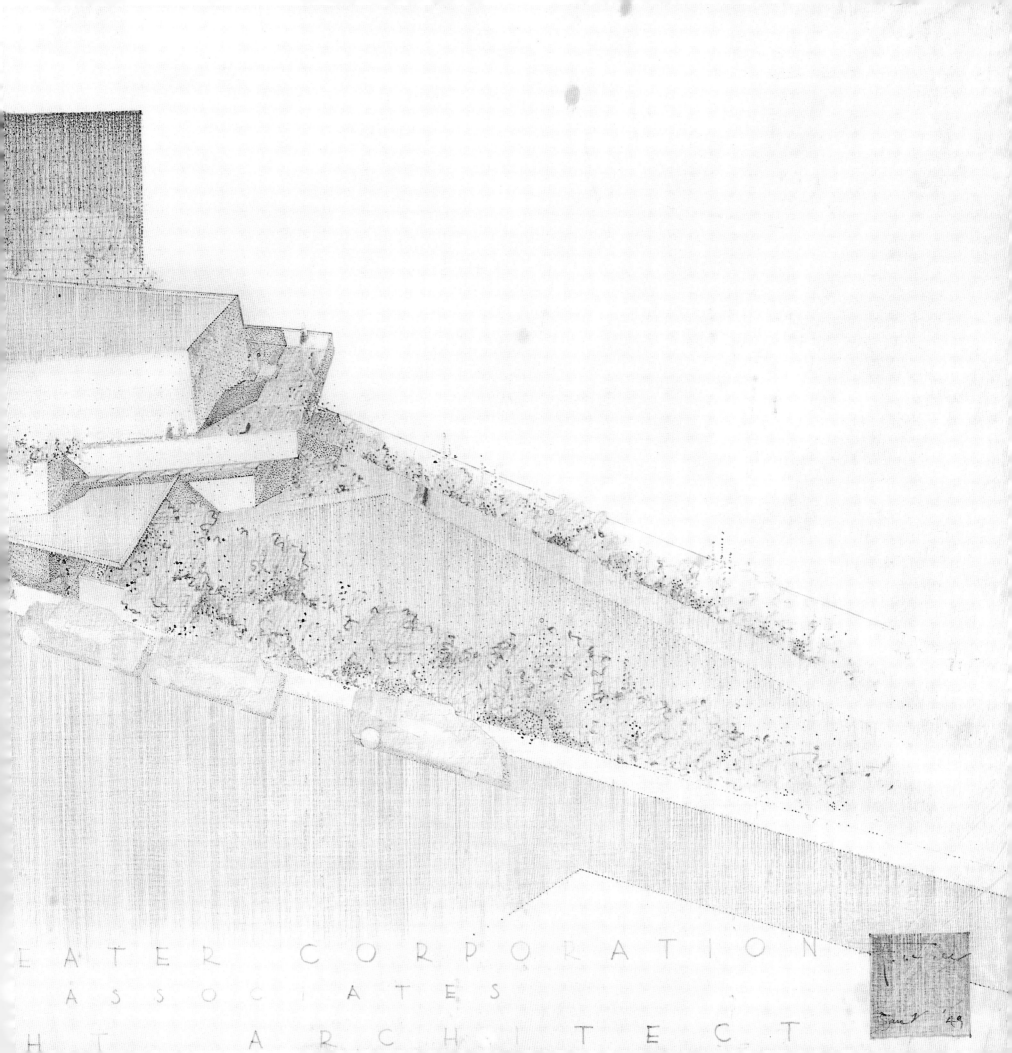

EATER CORPORATION

ASSOCIATES

HT ARCHITECT

FLORIDA SOUTHERN COLLEGE

For Dr. Ludd M. Spivey
Master Plan
Lakeland, Florida. 1938–1953, Executed in part

Mr. Ludd M. Spivey first met with Frank Lloyd Wright in 1938 to discuss the construction of a new college campus for Florida Southern College. He told Wright that he came to him as much for his philosophy as for his architecture. Wright assured him that the two were inseparable. Spivey explained that he wanted to give the United States at least one example of a college wherein modern life was to have the advantages of modern science and art in actual building construction.

Wright's first master plan for the new campus was mainly rectilinear in concept. Situated as it was, on a gentle slope of citrus trees bordering Lake Hollingsworth, he soon revised the plan to spread out along a different axes with all the buildings connected by an esplanade providing shelter against the hot sun and tropical rains. The height of the esplanade roof coincided with the trim lines of the citrus trees. In this manner, the shade from the trees spread into the esplanade to offer cool comfort in this Florida environment. The master plan (right) was devised in such a way that buildings could be constructed as funds were raised to build them.

Dr. Spivey's knack for raising such funds was purely genius. The original master plan called for a chapel, library, administration building, and seminar buildings. Added to these were plans for a theater, an industrial arts building, a smaller chapel, a music building, an arts and crafts center, and a science and cosmography building. Over the years, Dr. Spivey was able to build, along with the original four, the industrial arts building and the building for science and cosmography. Thus, out of twelve designs, nine were built. Adjacent to the administration building a large water dome was considered but too costly at the time. This dome is evident in the aerial perspective. In recent years, however, the Frank Lloyd Wright campus has been undergoing extensive conservation to remedy much

damage that time and neglect has wrought upon some of the structures. Among the new work to bring the campus back to its former glory is the recent construction of the original water dome.

Wright's master plan for Florida Southern College began in 1938. This was at a time when American colleges were Neoclassical, neo-Gothic, neo-Romanesque, neo-Spanish Colonial, neo-whatever, but certainly not American in any sense of the word.

"Ever since, owing to Dr. Spivey's unremitting efforts, this collection of college buildings has been in a continuous state of growth. Their outdoor-garden character is intended to be an expression of Florida at its floral best . . . you will see in these buildings now standing at Florida Southern College the sentiment of a true educational saga along the cultural lines of an indigenous Architecture for our own country." [6]

Right: Master plan.
FLLW FDN # 3805.013.

Following pages:
Perspective. FLLW FDN # 3805.001.
Pages 204-205: Perspective
view. FLLW FDN # 4118.002.

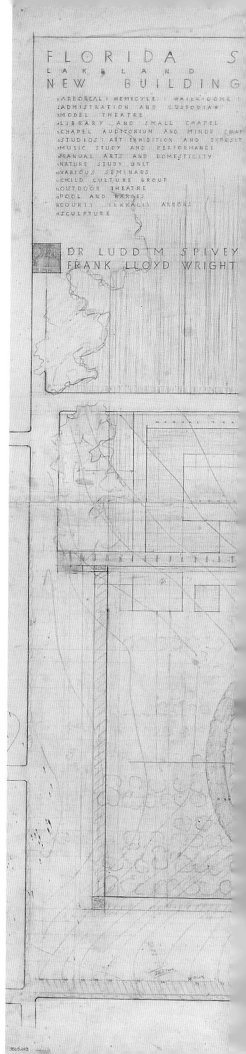

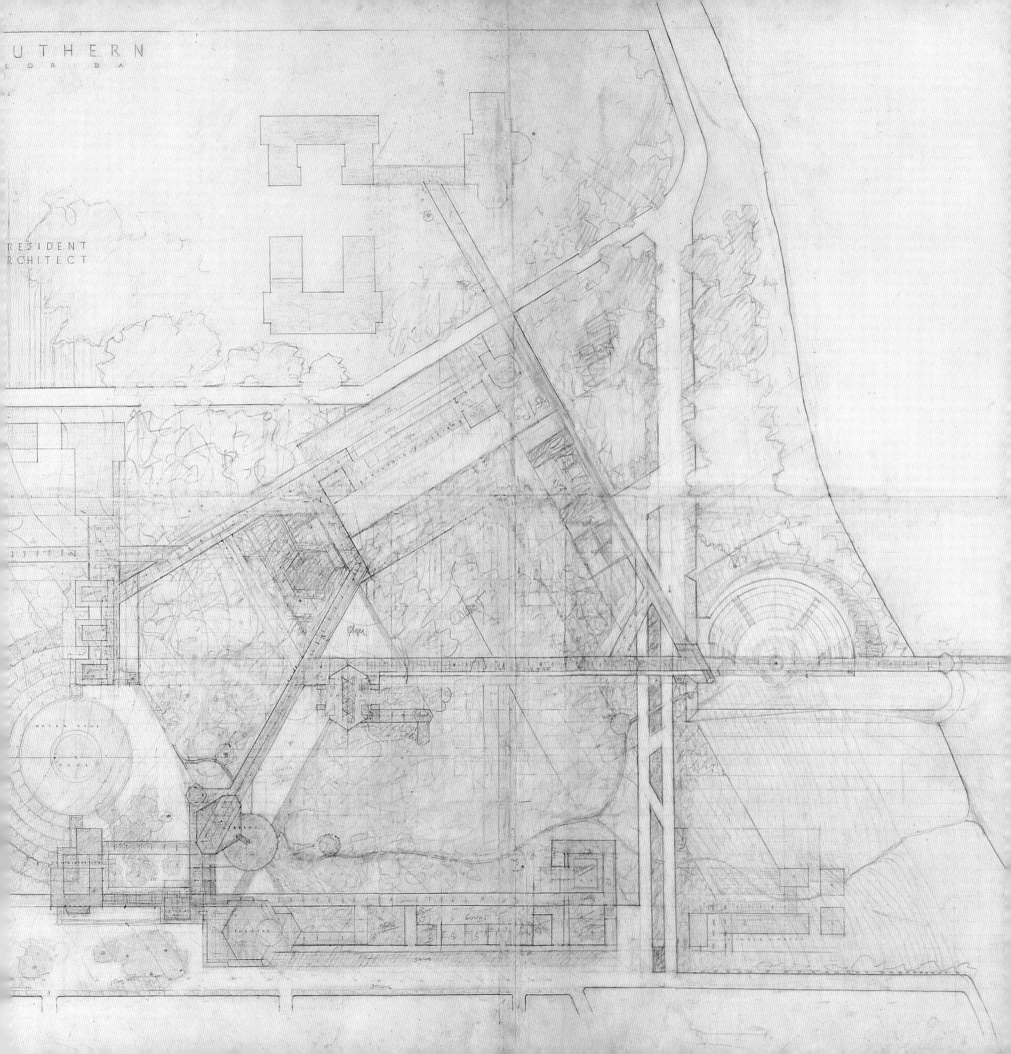

RESIDENT
RCHITECT

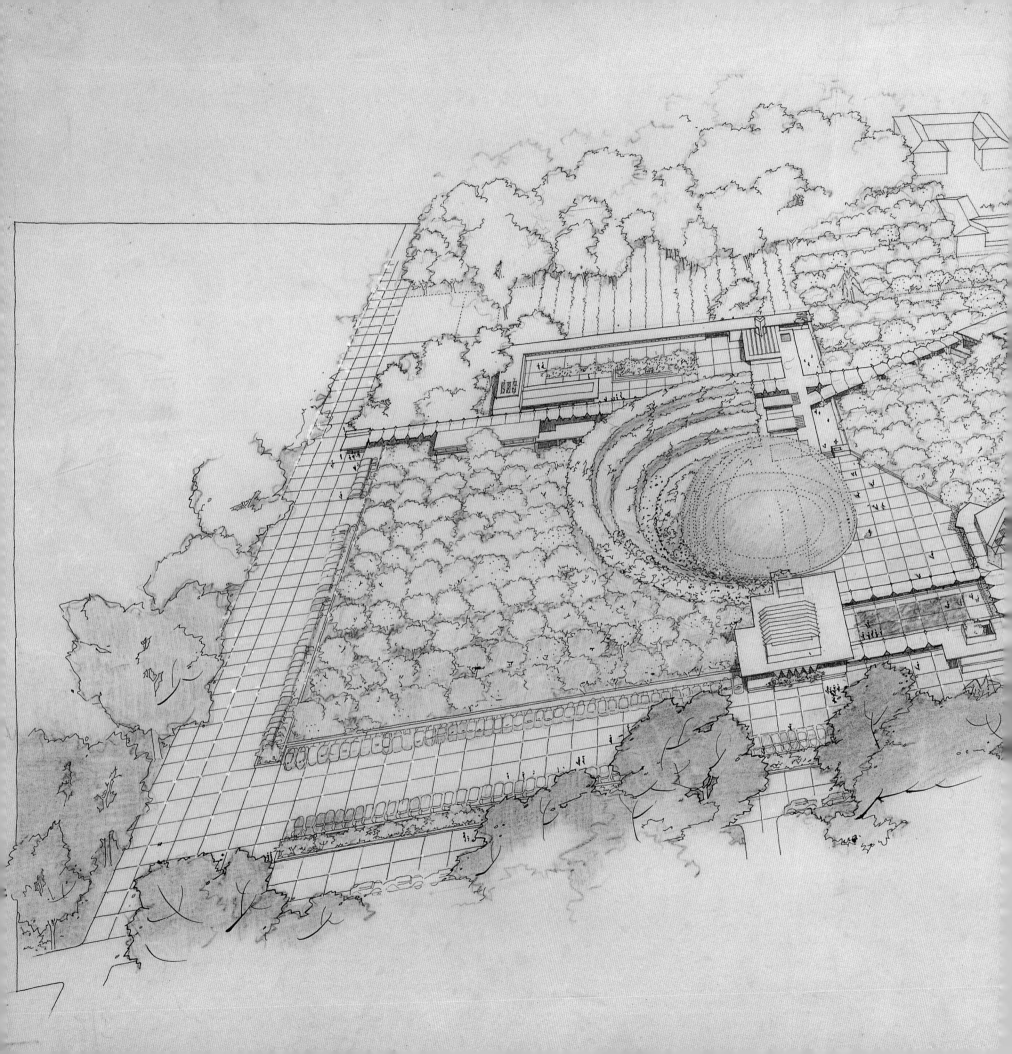

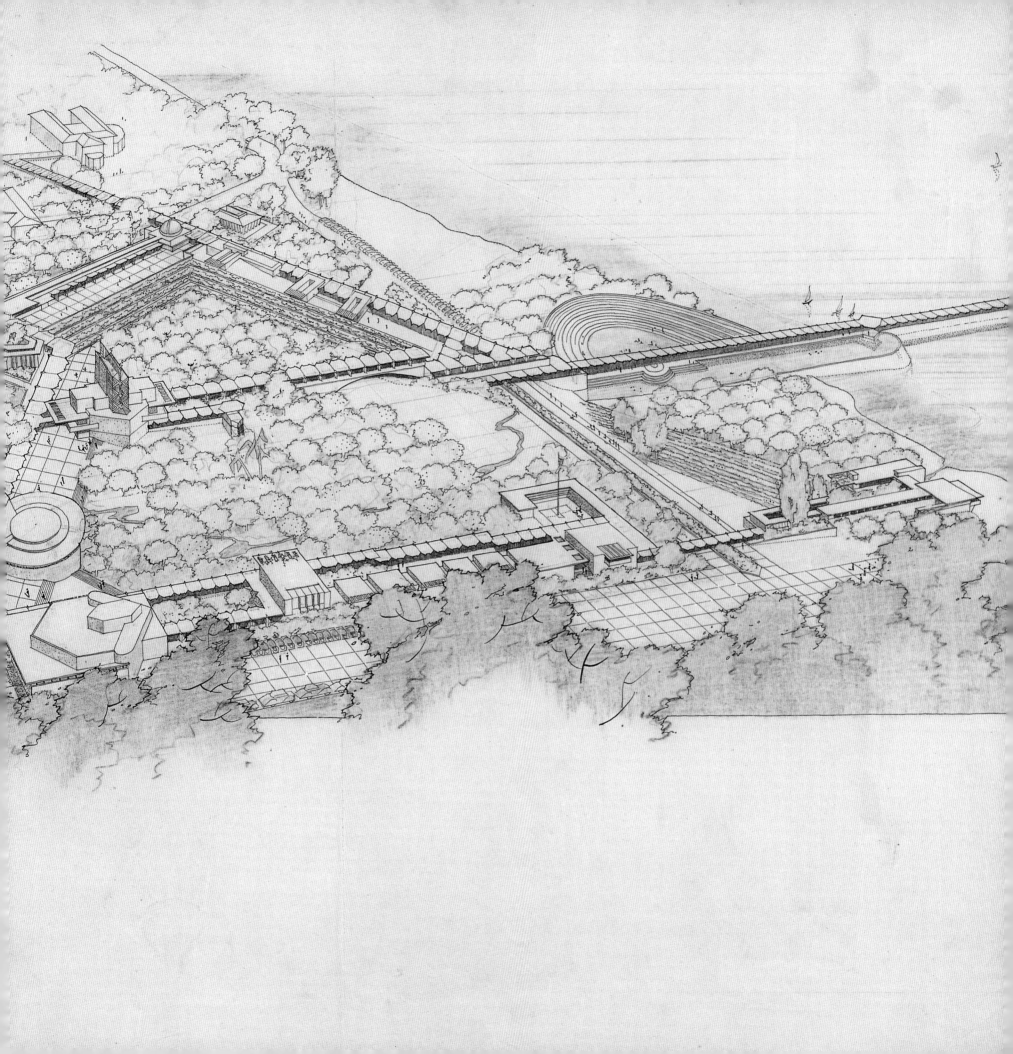

FLORIDA SOUTHER

LAKELAND FLORIDA

MONONA TERRACE CIVIC CENTER

Madison, Wisconsin. 1939–1959, Project

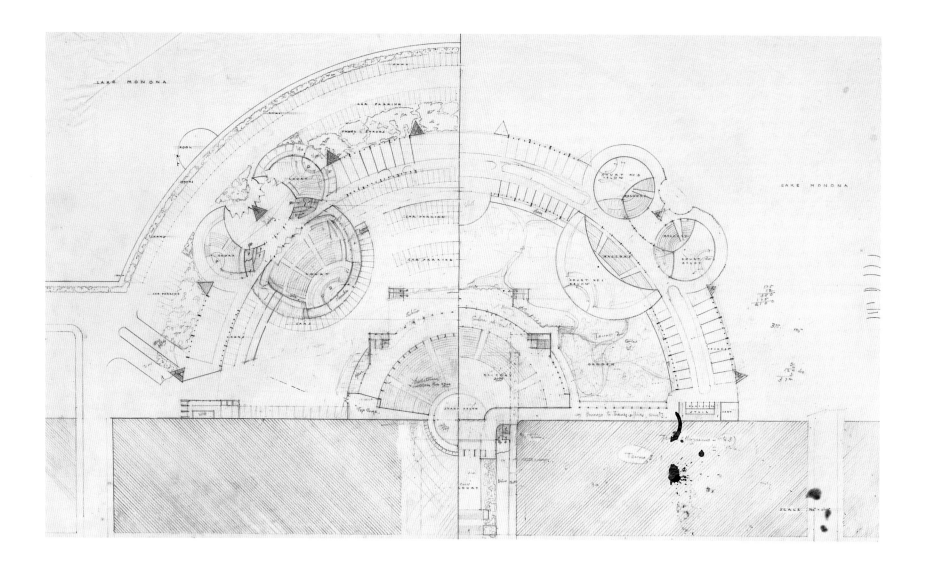

Although Madison is the capital of the state, in 1939 some concerned citizens lamented that it had no decent facilities for concert halls, exhibitions, dramatic presentations, or much-needed office space for county and city officials. In other words, Madison needed a civic center. The state capitol, a Neoclassical structure, is located on the part of Madison that stands as an isthmus between two of the city's four lakes, Lake Mendota and Lake Monona. A park leads down from the capitol building to an abutment, called Olin Terrace, which overlooks Lake Monona. When Wright was offered the possibility of designing a civic center, it seemed most logical for him to locate the structure proceeding out from this abutment, over the railroad tracks below and over the lake. A project which originally was called "Olin Terraces" soon became "Monona Terrace." His initial sketch shows how he conceived it in relation to the capitol on the hill above. Great circular terraces

EXTENSION AND TERMINAL OF MONONA AVENUE

EVEN ACRES OF MADE OVER EXISTING RAILROAD TRACKS. FOR PARKING.

AKE WATER THROWN UP INTO MONUMENTAL FOUNTAINS. MONONA AVE. "THE CITY GOES TO THE LAKE" SEVER MONTHS WATERDOMES, FIVE MONTHS

IVIC AUDITORIUM SEATING 10,000, FRONTING OLIN TERRACE.

OUNTY JAIL, AND OFFICES, CITY HALL, UNION RAILROAD DEPOT. COST $17,500,000, RAISED BY—? (SEE KAUFMANN A LA PITTSBURG)

Left: Initial plan. FLLW FDN # 3909.008.
Above: Early perspective.
FLLW FDN # 3909.002.

Following pages
Top: Section of second iteration.
FLLW FDN # 5632.011.
Bottom: Perspective of second
iteration. FLLW FDN # 5632.010.

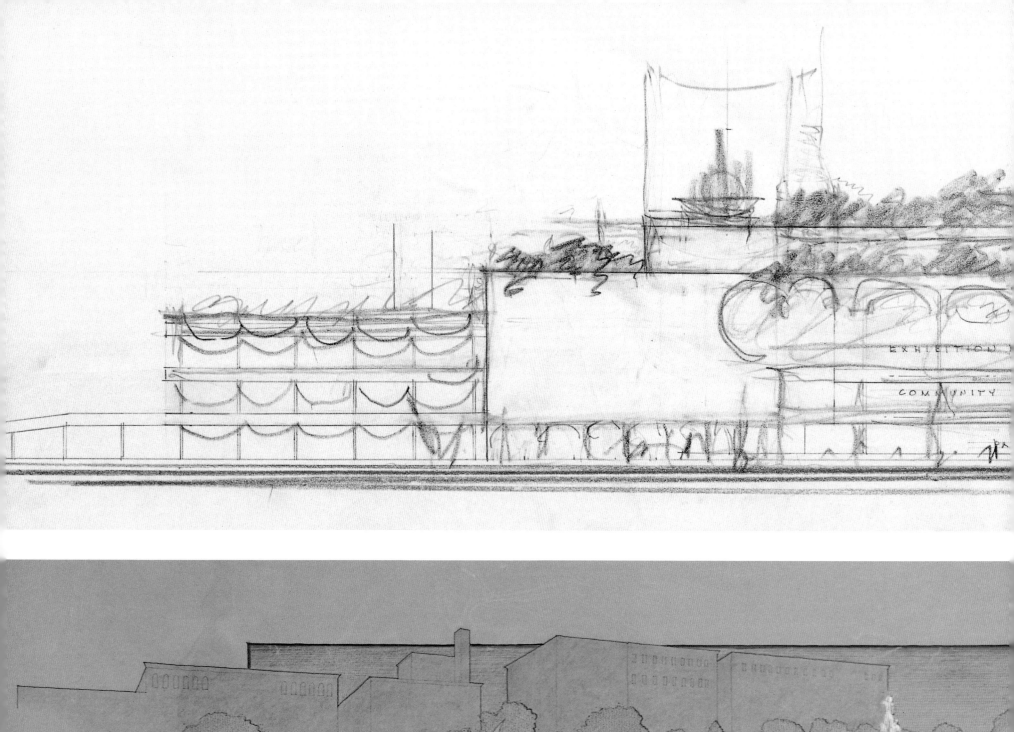

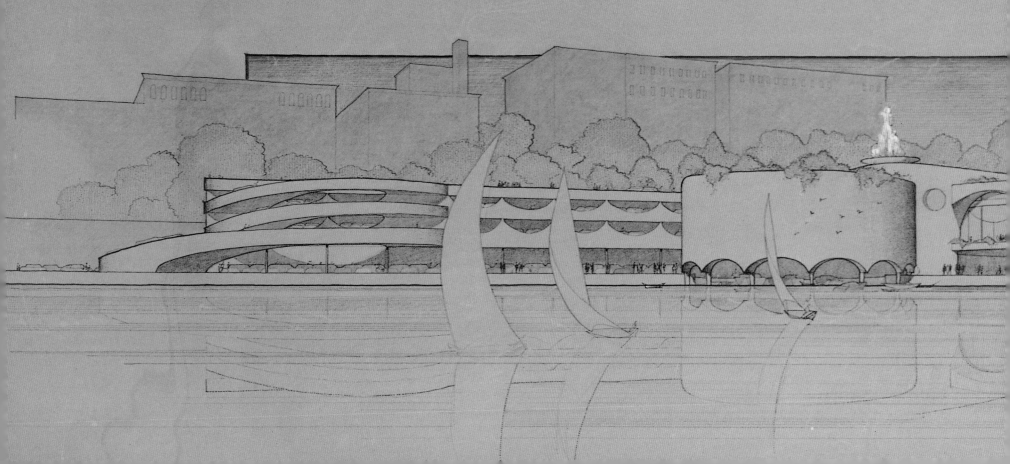

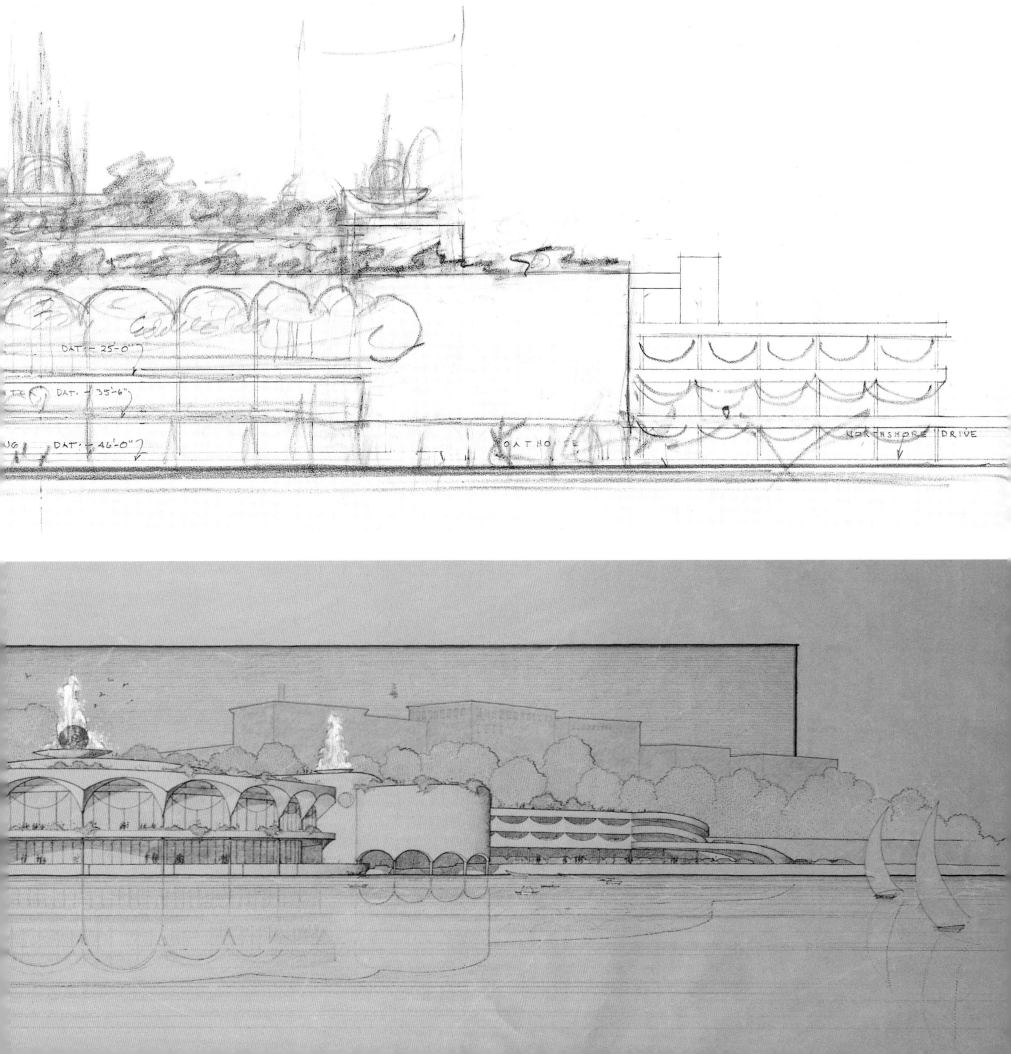

DAT. – 25'–0"

DAT. – 35'–6"

DAT. – 46'–0"

BOATHOUSE

NORTHSHORE DRIVE

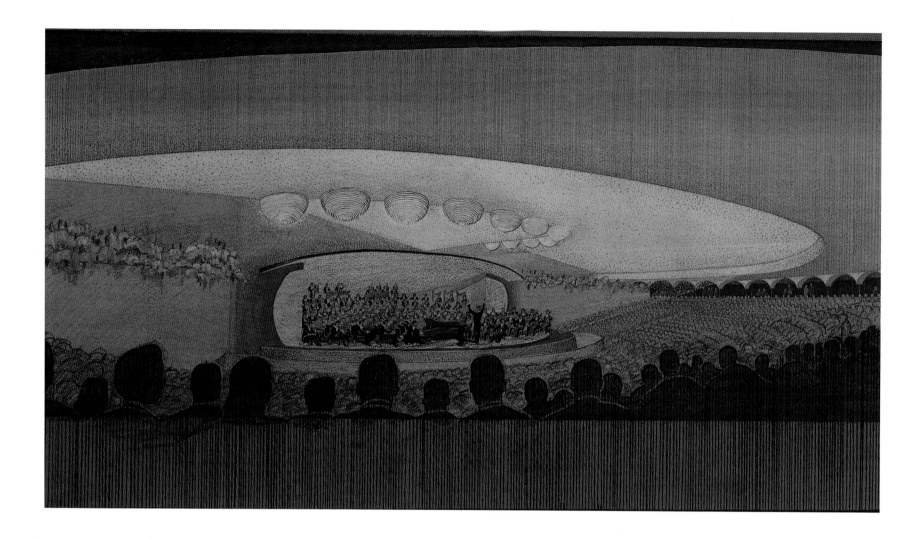

project over the lake, the topmost terrace a park, the ones below to provide a concert hall, exhibition spaces, and offices on one side for the city, on the other, for the county. At water level there are two goals, one for the city and one for the county. Ample parking is provided on the outer circles of the terraces, and openings in the uppermost terrace allow natural light to fall into offices and further parking spaces below.

The commission languished since it was not "official" but rather sponsored from the private sector of this group of citizens who wished for something better and more beautiful for their city. Politics, as is usual with anything involving city or county officials in a project of unconventional architecture, caused the scheme to fail.

Sixteen years later, again the citizenry brought the project up for consideration, with certain modifications and new requirements. But that too, became what is known as "political football." During the deliberations over Monona Terrace, the mayor remarked, "I don't think it is very attractive." To which Wright countered, "Well, I don't think his honor is very attractive as well!" Although it became a battle that went on for three years, Monona Terrace was defeated by the state legislature. The drawings and model were returned to Wright's office.

The night rendering (opposite page), drawn by Allen Lape Davison using tempera on black illustration board, is a spectacular drawing of the Monona Terrace Civic Center with its fountains lit from within and the peripheral spheres and tall light finials representing the twelve signs of the Zodiac at the outer edge of the terrace.

Above: Interior perspective of theater from second iteration.
FLLW FDN # 5632.052.
Right: Perspective.
FLLW FDN # 5632.001

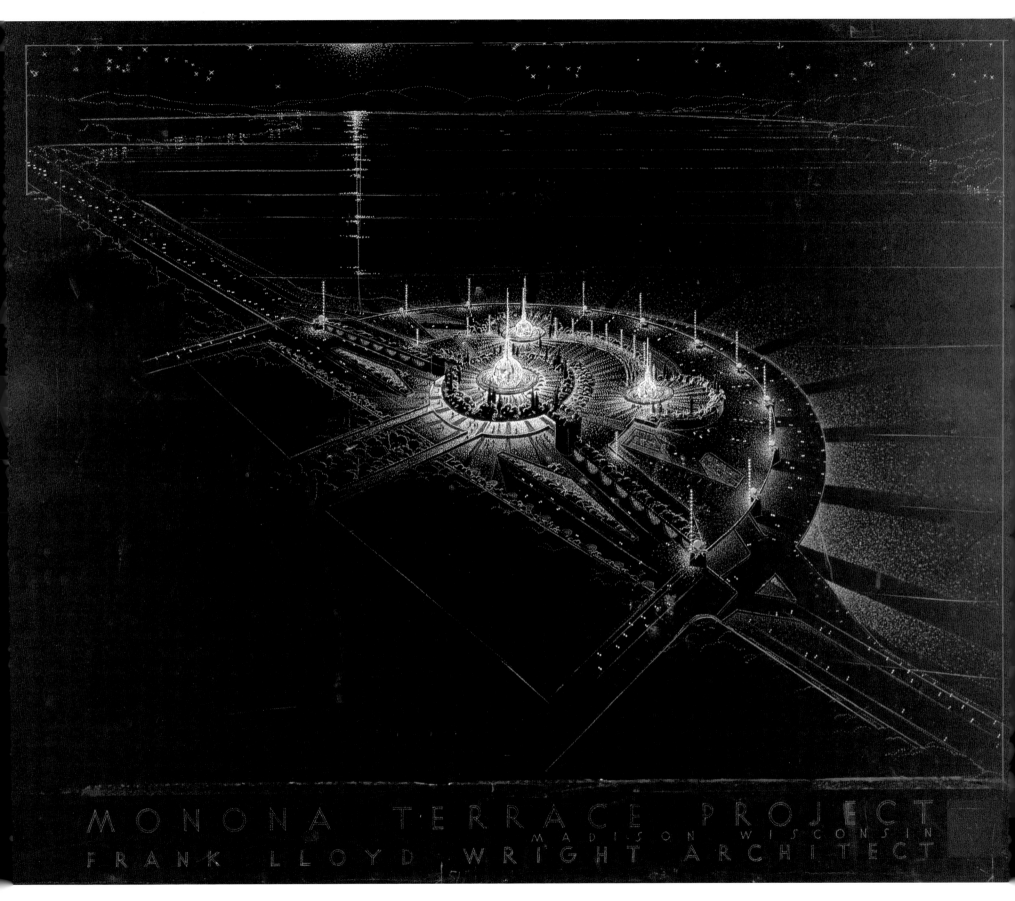

MONONA TERRACE PROJECT
MADISON WISCONSIN
FRANK LLOYD WRIGHT ARCHITECT

THE WALTER L. FISHER
MEMORIAL CHAPTER HOUSE

Chi of Sigma Chi, Hanover College
Hanover, Indiana. 1941, Project

Below: Elevation and plan.
FLLW FDN # 4108.001.
Right: Perspective.
FLLW FDN #4108.015.

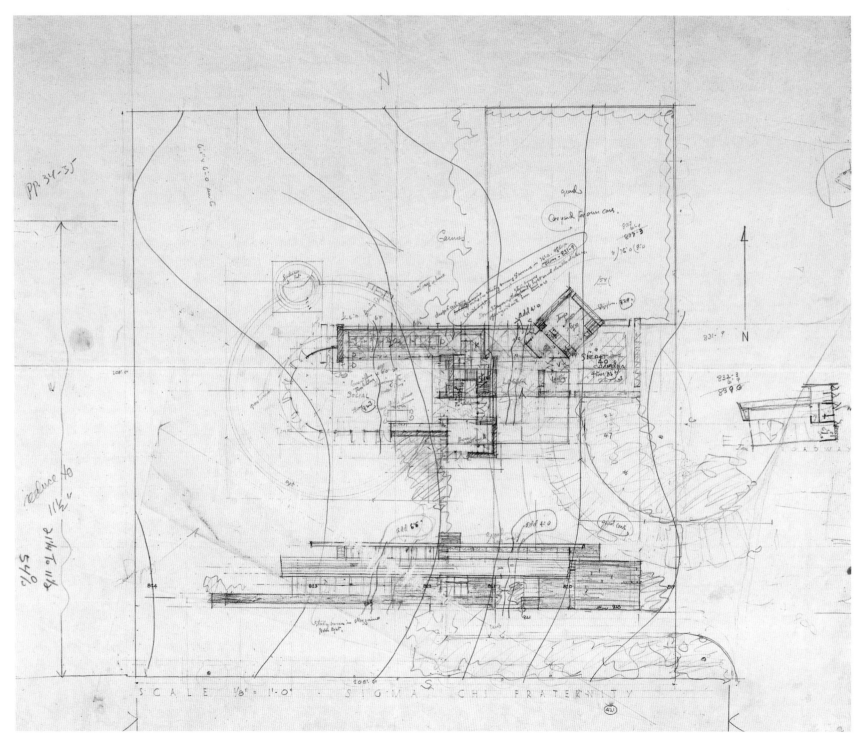

In November 1940, the chapter house Chi of Sigma Chi, at Hanover College, in Hanover, Indiana, suffered damage from a severe fire. Although it was made somewhat habitable afterward, the pledges and brothers discussed the possibility of building a new chapter house. In the discussion of whom to select as their architect, one member suggested something along the lines of Georgian Colonial. But another member, Russell Leavenworth, said to them, "Why not go to the top and ask Frank Lloyd Wright to be our architect." His first contact with Wright was on November 10, 1940, when he outlined the property and their requirements. Wright had previously designed a fraternity house for Phi Gamma Delta in Madison, Wisconsin, but its unconventional design was met with disapproval, and it was subsequently not built. With this new commission in the offing, Wright replied to Leavenworth:

"My dear Leavenworth: I am not unfamiliar with the fraternity house problem and when you are ready I'll be ready." [7]

On April 26, 1941, Wright wrote to Leavenworth that he had received the topographical survey and their list of requirements and he was starting to work on the preliminaries. But, later, Leavenworth wrote to Wright: "The battle is on! The Hanover College Board of Trustees took one look at our plans and blew up. They will probably refuse to allow us to

build on the site for which we originally planned." [8]

The situation became serious, the trustees were adamantly opposed to a Frank Lloyd Wright building on their campus. Leavenworth then asked Wright if he and three others could drive up to Spring Green to confer with him. Wright's apprentice Eugene Masselink, who also was his secretary and business manager, informed Leavenworth that he and the others would be welcome to come to Taliesin and stay for the weekend.

When they arrived at Taliesin on a pleasant sunny day in July, they were confused as to how to enter the building. Olgivanna spotted them outside, went out, greeted them, and took them into the loggia. Presently, Wright arrived. As Leavenworth recounted, "It took me an effort to stop my knees from buckling, so powerful was the impact of his presence." [9] Wright led them to a screened porch nearby, and there they met the other household guests, Mr. and Mrs. Erich Mendelsohn. Their visit with the Wrights included dinner in the Taliesin living room, a picnic to a nearby woodland site, a program in the theater with music and a film, and Sunday breakfast with the fellowship and the Wrights. It was a memorable weekend for them, and Leavenworth wrote of it:

"It took days to float down to earth again. I am still in awe of the Wrights' graciousness and

generosity. To have invited us to come on a weekend when we would be thrown together with the Mendelsohns was an extraordinary gift. And every hour was loaded with entertainment of the highest order, far beyond our capacity to appreciate fully. We were like four peasant louts plucked from our farmyard chores to spend a weekend at Versailles in the glow of the Sun King. How could we ever repay? Perhaps Wright was fully aware of his power, of the indelible impact he was making on four boys who would never again be the same." [10]

Ultimately, the students were unable to secure either the rights to the property (the trustees were determined not to have a Frank Lloyd Wright building on their campus) or the funds to go into construction. America's entrance into the Second World War also made it impossible to get building materials for any new project except those related to the war effort. Any hope of building it was abandoned.

However, the Sigma Chi project clearly illustrates, all along the way, the interest and consideration Wright had for Russell Leavenworth and his colleagues. He obviously maintained the utmost of patience in his hope that they could build this fraternity house. His and Olgivanna's kindness to them on their visit to Taliesin is a touching and heart-warming example of generous humanity.

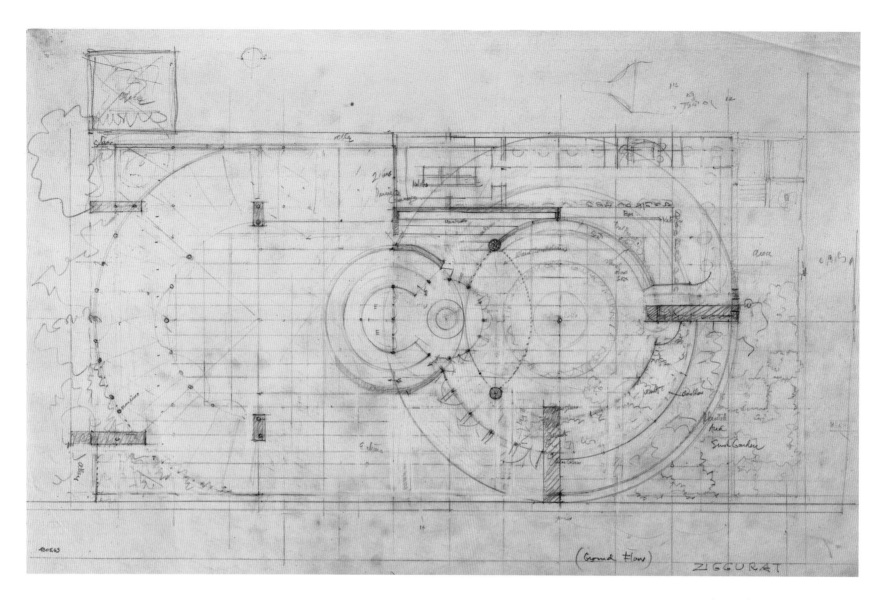

THE SOLOMON R. GUGGENHEIM MUSEUM

New York, New York. 1943–1959

Above: Plan. FLLW FDN # 4305.063.
Right: Section and elevation.
FLLW FDN # 4305.014.

Frank Lloyd Wright once made the remark, "Give me enlightened businessmen and I can change the face of the Nation." Of course that was a rather broad statement, but what he meant was that given the opportunity, clients with vision could build buildings not for themselves but for humanity. Throughout his career Wright had such clients. Darwin D. Martin built the Larkin Company Administration Building, Dr. Ludd Spivey built a college in Lakeland, Florida, Herbert F. Johnson built the Johnson Company Administration Building, and Harold

Price built the Price Tower, which served as offices for his own company as well as office spaces and apartments for others. Solomon R. Guggenheim built the museum that bears his name.

"You have noticed that all American millionaires, when it comes to their time to die get very respectable and sentimental where the past is concerned. They will build monuments à la the Greeks, make repositories and museum à la ancient styles. Not one of them has looked toward the future so far as I know except one

man: and that was Solomon Guggenheim, who died betting his accumulations on the future. He is the only American millionaire on record to have done any such thing! I think that the de Medicis were less praiseworthy than Mr. Guggenheim. They never bet on the future either. They took the best in the contemporary scene and subscribed to it. Mr. Guggenheim took the thing they were all laughing at in the present, believing it had a great future, and put his fortune behind it. That is what I call the right kind of act for a man to perpetrate when he has

ZIGGURAT

ZIKKURAT

TARVEGITZ

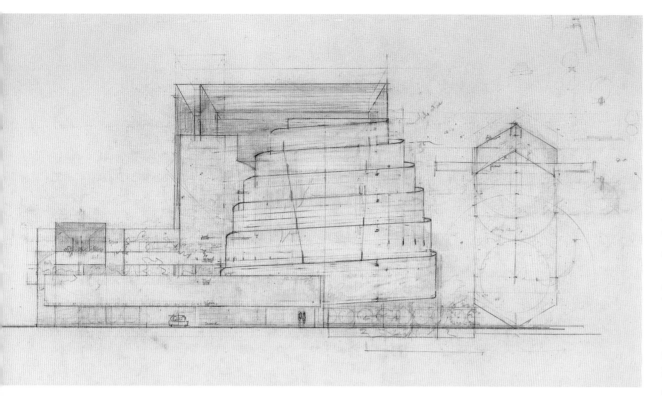

Left: Elevation. FLLW FDN # 4305.076.
Left, bottom: Perspective. FLLW FDN # 4305.747.
Right: Perspective. FLLW FDN # 4305.008.

a great fortune. Now if we had more American millionaires of that stripe, think what we would have in the future."[11]

Wright's first contact for the museum commission came from its curator, Hilla Rebay, who was acting on behalf of Solomon Guggenheim. Some sources claim that it was Guggenheim's wife Irene who prompted him to select Wright as his architect. The Guggenheims, along with Rebay, had made several trips abroad to purchase contemporary paintings, mostly the work of Wassily Kandinsky. It was a genre of work called "non-objective painting." Other artists were included in the Guggenheims' purchases, and eventually the collection was turned over to The Solomon R. Guggenheim Foundation and a gallery was set up for its display. As the collection increased, it became obvious that a more spacious building to house it was needed. When Wright was approached in June 1943, no particular site had been found. At one point a site up near The Cloisters on the upper tip of Manhattan was seriously considered. For such a site, Wright thought of a museum as a series of pavilions set amongst gardens and fountains.

On the other hand, Wright knew that Guggenheim loved Manhattan and would most likely find a site there. Six months had passed since Wright received notice of the commission and yet no site had been selected. He wrote to Rebay, "I am so full of ideas for our museum that I am likely to blow up or commit suicide unless I can let then out on paper."[12] Strongly believing in hunches, he felt he had to design something, knowing that Guggenheim was still searching for property. Assuming that such a property would be a city block in downtown Manhattan, he made several designs for a museum based on the spiral—some preliminaries represented the spiral decreasing as it rose, others, increasing. In both cases, the idea of a spiral ramp was constant. He wrote to Rebay:

"A museum should be one extended expansive well-proportioned floor space from bottom to top—a wheel chair going around and up and

down throughout. No stops anywhere and such screened divisions of the space gloriously lit within from above as would deal appropriately with every group of paintings or individual paintings as you might want them classified." [13]

"When I've satisfied myself with the preliminary exploration I'll bring it down to New York before going West and we can have anguish and fun over it. The whole thing will either throw you off your guard entirely or be just about what you have been dreaming about. Anything more modern, less stuffy and conventional, you have never seen. Nor anything so ideal for your purpose". [14]

An early plan (p. 214) reveals that from the outset, he envisioned the museum as one employing a spiral ramp. On this particular drawing he also wrote "Ziggurat" in further confirmation of the spiral nature of the design. Obviously, at this time he had already made some preliminary studies, and he began to develop them believing that the museum should go vertical rather than horizontal. His elevation and section drawings illustrates this, and off to the side he has again produced a small thumbnail sketch of the building (p. 215). Although this drawing represents his concept of a spiral ramp that increases as it rises, another sketch (p. 216, top) suggests a spiral that decreases as its rises. Several perspectives were rendered in water color by Wright's apprentice Peter Berndtson, and he took them to New York to show Guggenheim what sort of a museum design he had in mind. One of the perspectives represented the spiral growing smaller as it rose (p. 216, bottom). When Guggenheim saw the drawings, he said to Wright, "I knew you could do it, Mr. Wright, but I had no idea you could do it so well!"

The drawings assumed a full block would be found, and thus the museum/exhibition part, called the Rotunda, was placed on the right side of the block, with an apartment for Rebay on the left, and offices, work areas, and storage at the back of the block connecting the apartment and the rotunda. Rebay was a dedicated person who deeply believed in the spiritual aspect of non-objective painting—a belief that bordered on obsession. She wanted a theater in the basement of the museum in which the audience would be seated in chairs that reclined, so that they would

view, on the ceiling, projections of paintings while a string quartet played the music of Mozart and Beethoven. Such an ocular chamber, on a smaller scale, was provided for her own apartment.

Finally, in March 1944, a site was found and purchased between 88th and 89th streets. A narrow apartment building was located on the 88th Street side, which was not included in the purchase. To account for this, Wright revised his scheme and placed the rotunda on the left, the 89th Street side, and the apartment for Rebay adjacent to the existing building on 88th Street (p. 217).

In 1952, fortunately, the apartment building was purchased, and therefore the entire Fifth Avenue block—88th to 89th Street—was available. Wright then revised the scheme and moved the rotunda to the right, as it stands today (opposite page).

Many publications have been written about the details of this commission, which lasted from 1943 until ground was broken for construction in 1956. During this period of time, Guggenheim at first hesitated after the war, believing that costs of labor and materials would go down. Instead they rose, and he himself died in 1949, never to see his monument completed. Rebay continued as curator and took the role of client until she herself resigned in 1952 due to poor health.

Following her resignation, a new director took over and the general character of the museum changed. Originally it was "The Modern Gallery" and was established to house and display the collection that Guggenheim had acquired. Now, however, the museum would function in the nature of traditional museums, arranging exhibitions from its own expanding collections and taking in exhibitions from other sources. This meant a drastic change in its original program, and Wright changed and modified his design accordingly. There was also a matter of cost, and his changes had to take that into account as well.

The museum's director and several of its Trustees were fearful that the building would not be appropriate for the display of fine art. A letter sent to the trustees, and signed by twenty-seven contemporary artists, strongly urged that con-

struction be halted. To demonstrate to the trustees that the building would indeed function well for the display of fine art, he had several drawings prepared in 1958 to illustrate this point. One, called "The Masterpiece" (not shown), was rendered by apprentice Ling Po, who carefully "reconstructed" a large Kandinsky in the bay, with the spectators viewing the work, except for a little girl intrigued by the view down the open well. When Wright came into the drafting room to sign the drawing, he took a pencil and carefully drew a yo-yo in the hand of the girl. Turning to his apprentices, with the usual twinkle in his eye, he remarked, "In all of this endeavor, boys, we must never lose sight of a sense of humor!"

Even during construction the battle went on between Wright and the trustees. Guggenheim's nephew, Harry Guggenheim, took over the role of president of the foundation, and Wright constantly urged and implored him to save the building that his uncle had so cherished. Wright was accused of creating a building that would overpower anything exhibited within it. "No," he wrote, "it is not to subjugate the paintings to the building that I conceived this plan. On the contrary, it was to make the building and the painting as an uninterrupted, beautiful symphony such as never existed in the world of Art before." [15]

The night rendering (pp. 220-221), again a drawing by Wright's apprentice Allen Lape Davison, portrays the museum with a backdrop, a tall building that Wright proposed as an apartment tower with studios. The rental income from the studios would help support the museum's operation and educational programs. It was, indeed, a project that the museum was not able to fund at that time.

No commission in Wright's long career exacted such a toll on him as those thirteen years, with seven sets of working drawings prepared in order to respond to the changes demanded of him. It was a continuing struggle—with the director, with the trustees, with the codes of the City of New York. He established an office for himself in the Plaza Hotel to further oversee all that needed to be accomplished in relation to this Guggenheim work. And yet, during this same period of time, he was designing and

THE MODERN GALLERY
MUSEUM FOR THE SOLOMON R. GUGGENHEIM FOUNDATION
FRANK LLOYD WRIGHT ARCHITECT
HOLDEN AND McLAUGHLIN ASSOCIATES

Above: Perspective. FLLW FDN # 4305.017.

Following pages: Perspective. FLLW FDN # 4305.062.

building homes, factories, religious structures, educational buildings, and commercial buildings across the nation as well as writing and publishing six books.

The building opened to the public on October 21, 1959. An anxious throng lined the streets and swarmed in to see the building, some enthused about it, others incredulous, others shocked. Opinions about its feasibility as a museum ran the gamut from adulation to deprecation. Throughout it all, Wright never veered from his conviction that the building would work as a place for the exhibition of fine art. Time, fifty years later, has proven him right. The only tragic note to this saga about the Solomon R. Guggenheim Museum is that its creator did not live to see it completed. He died five months before its opening.

However, Frank Lloyd Wright lived long enough to see the building firmly fixed, if not completed, in the third dimension, one of the greatest creative acts ever achieved by man. It stands now as a profound exemplar of interior space—a fluid, moving, emotional, and intelligent entity. Solomon R. Guggenheim's great gift to humanity will forever inspire those who come within its walls.

A note about leeches and bad teeth:

Hilla Rebay was a firm believer in the ancient remedy of bloodletting. She often saw a doctor, a German by the name of Meyers, in New York, that applied long black leeches to her throat while she reclined on a black leather chaise longe. She insisted that not only Wright, but Olgivanna too, undergo the same procedure. She also believed that much of human sickness was

due to bad teeth. Only six months after meeting Wright, she had him remove several teeth, Olgivanna as well. Their young teenage daughter Iovanna was living in New York at that time studying at a private school. Hilla Rebay took Iovanna under her wing. One day, early in 1944, when Rebay was extolling the benefits of getting rid of bad teeth, she looked rather strongly in Iovanna's direction. At that juncture, Olgivanna told her husband, "I knew you were having trouble with some of your teeth, and it was about time to have them extracted. I, myself, let Hilla insist on having some of mine taken out. But not Iovanna. I shall put my foot down when it comes to that issue. Hilla is not going to get her teeth as well. Frank, this is a building for which you, for which we, have quite literally given out blood."

PITTSBURGH POINT PARK CIVIC CENTER, SCHEME 1

Pittsburgh, Pennsylvania. 1947, Project

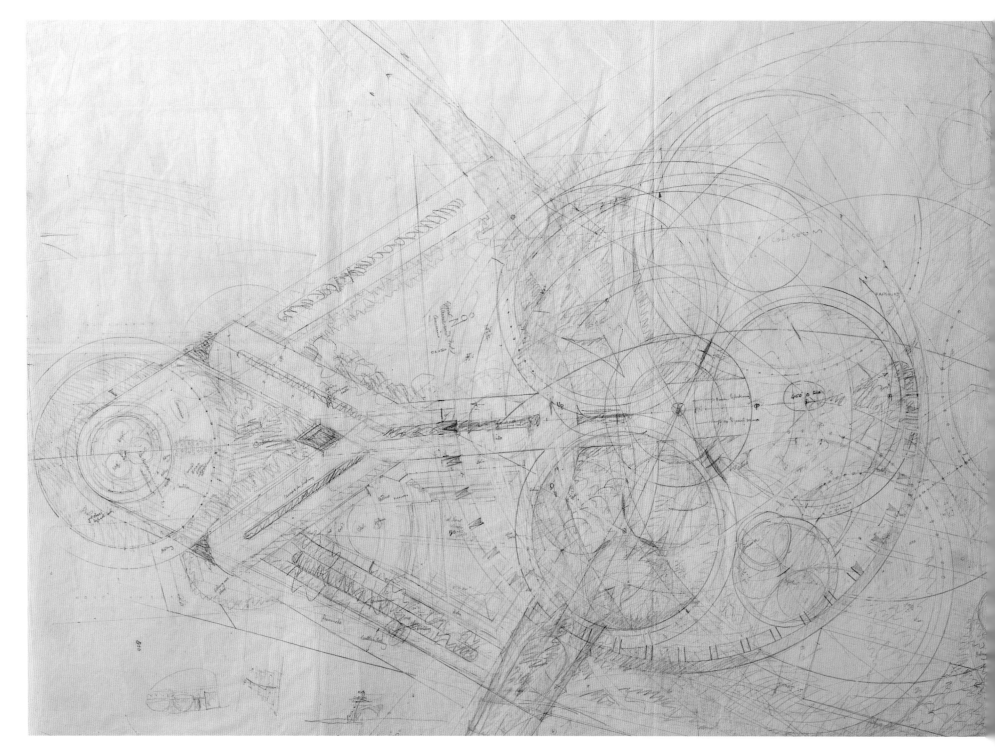

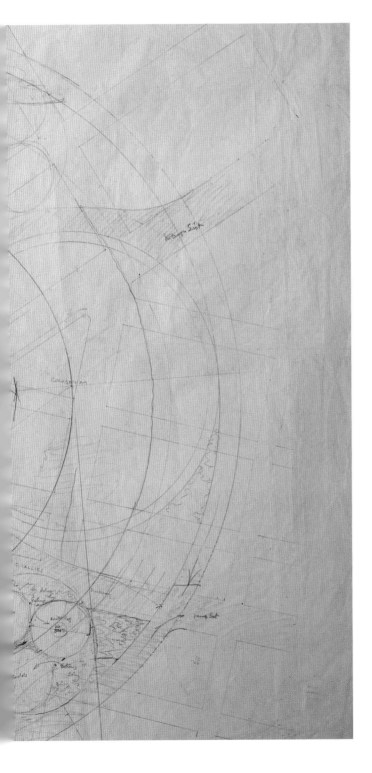

When Frank Lloyd Wright visited Pittsburgh in 1935 while he was consulting with Edgar J. Kaufmann on the design of his home, Fallingwater, he saw the city immersed in pollution and congestion due to the steel industry located practically in the very heart of the city itself. His reaction about the fate of the city was his suggestion that it was such a disastrous circumstance that the only hope would be to "abandon it." However, many concerned citizens realized the plight of the city and began to take measures to alleviate the situation and beautify the city. Among those was Edgar Kaufmann who was prominent in the cultural and civic affairs, and who frequently offered his advice and financial help. He was a charter member of the Allegheny Conference on Community Development. One of the goals of the Allegheny Conference was to develop the Pittsburgh Point State Park, a triangular tract of fifty-nine acres called the Golden Triangle where the Monongahela and the Allegheny rivers join to form the Ohio River.

In 1946, Kaufmann urged the Allegheny Conference to commission Wright to make a plan for the Point. The original plan was to develop the Point into a park, but Kaufmann had something more in mind than just a park, a more urban solution, a civic center in fact. He was aware of the civic center that Wright had proposed for Madison, Wisconsin, seven years earlier. The Madison project was designed in relation to Lake Monona, from which it took its name, Monona Terrace Civic Center. Here, in Pittsburgh, the element of water was the two rivers and their becoming one when joined. Seeing how Wright had made an inherent feature of the lake in the Madison project, Kaufmann was convinced that Wright would be the perfect architect for this project as well. Armed with a detailed site plan, and a general list of requirements, Wright set to work on the scheme and wrote to Kaufmann, "The magnum opus is

thrown up to scale on the draughting [sic] board . . . it is good to be working with you once more before the inevitable drift to the beyond."[16] His concept sketch (left) is one of the most remarkable drawings in the collection. Again he has transposed several levels on one sheet, and it took the genius of apprentice John Howe to decipher Wright's multilayered drawing to eventually produce the perspective views (one of which is seen on the following page, top).

And "magnum opus" it certainly was. This was the largest and most complex architectural project of his life. Gigantic in size, it was truly a megastructure. An immense spiral ramp four and a half miles long rose 175 feet above street level. On this ramp were located several hundred commercial concessions of all kinds, as Wright described it "The Grand Ramp within would resemble a county fair."[17]

Within the building itself there was a grand opera seating 10,000 to 20,000, three cinemas seating 1,500 each; with both the opera and the cinema having adequate parking. Further provisions accommodated a convention hall seating 12,500 and a sports area with 20,000 seats for both summer and winter events. On the top level of the building, there was a nine-acre "sky park," planted with trees, shrubs, and flowers. The park also provided landing space for helicopters and balloons. The central area of the park was a great fountain rising out of a glass bowl, the bowl providing daylight for the sports arena below. Outside the great circular structure on the street level was a concert garden on one side, and a zoo on the other. Extending out from this complex was a building containing a restaurant, aquarium, aviary, swimming pools, and access to floating docks on the Ohio River for the convenience of river traffic. Attached to the circular building was a triangular addition with a tower of twenty stories to provide offices for the city, county, and state officials. Two bridges, one crossing the Allegheny

River, the other the Monongahela River, gave direct access to the main ramp. Also attached to this ramp was a smaller one that provided quick access to any level desired on the larger one.

The main structure was, indeed, an expansion of the idea he had first proposed for the Gordon Strong Automobile Objective and Planetarium. In the Strong project, the support for the exterior parts of the building was intended to come from the large dome of the planetarium itself. Here, all the interior halls were likewise supported by the domes over the halls. The various halls and spaces within are constructed out of lens-shaped structures anchored to gigantic pylons. The materials were prestressed steel or col-drawn mesh, such as was used in the Johnson Wax Building dendriform columns, cast in high-pressure concrete with vertical and horizontal glass enclosures. Throughout the entire structure ninety-two acres were set aside for parking, twenty-four acres for rentable commercial purposes, and fourteen acres for terraces planted with greenery. "The entire scheme is arranged with adequate trees, shrubs, grass and flowers, all of which taken in connection with the broad expanse of flowing river surface render the whole architectural mass gentle and humane."[18] The section drawing (opposite page, bottom) but hints at the complexity of the project.

The scheme was far more expansive than the Allegheny Conference had expected. It surpassed any economic or technical feasibility as well. They expressed concern that it would be in conflict with the Pennsylvania legislatur, which intended to create a park on the site to commemorate the original Fort Duquesne of colonial times. When Park Martin, the executive director of the Allegheny Conference, sent Wright a full report on how the conference planned to memorialize the old fort, Wright replied:

"My dear Park Martin:

"While reading the fulsome report of the 'Triangle' which you have just sent me, I could not rid myself of the feeling that some practical joke was being played upon me.

"I kept seeing the famous black-robed widow of 'Campo Santo'—white handkerchief in hand, weeping, still standing in that famous cemetery beside her dead husband. When he died she had an effigy made of him dressed just as he stood at

Right: Perspective. FLLW FDN # 4821.003
Right, below: Section. FLLW FDN # 4821.005.

their wedding and placed in a large glass case—meantime leaving a bequest to have an effigy of herself in deep mourning (white lace handkerchief in hand) made and placed in another glass case beside him when she died. She wanted the public to see her affectionately mourning him beyond the grave.

"And of course this foolish attempt to preserve the old fort is in no better case. Such stupid things do occur but would only add to Pittsburgh's present lack of human grace—a note of pathos no self-respecting community should tolerate, no self-respecting architect would accept.

"But if among you there is sufficient interest not turned toward the grave (an empty sleeve of the G.A.R.) but racing toward the recreation of a happy life for her citizens now and in the future and I am so commanded, I will work.

"I should be happy to go into this with your conference if so desired. Otherwise I am hamstrung.

"Sincerely yours, Frank Lloyd Wright."

Kaufmann urged Martin not to stress the historical aspect too strongly and to encourage Wright to try again with a more moderate plan.[19]

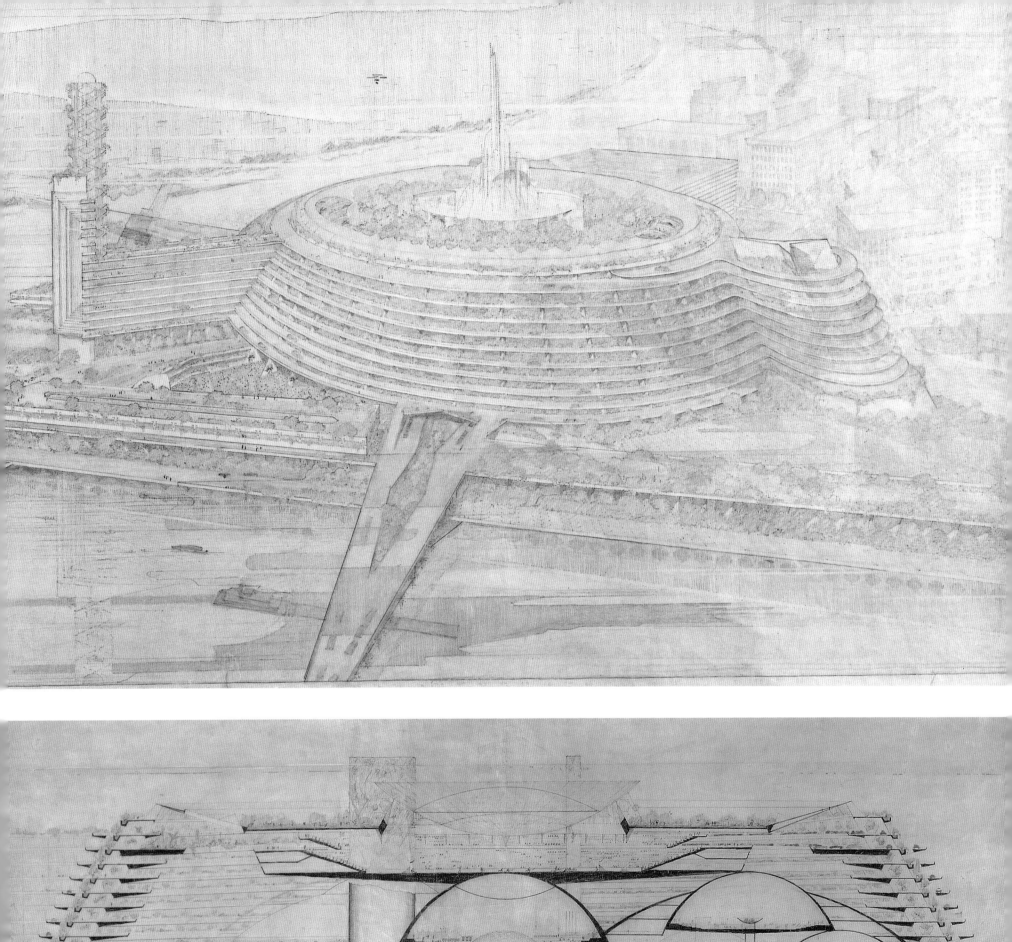

PITTSBURGH POINT PARK CIVIC CENTER AND TWIN SUSPENSION BRIDGES, SCHEME 2

Pittsburgh, Pennsylvania. 1947–8, Project

For the second proposal, Wright has concentrated on two bridges spanning the Allegheny and Monongahela rivers. He referred to these bridges as "cantilevered bridges," as they spring from a great concrete bastion seen as a mammoth concrete "sail." Stayed-cable construction is evident in the decorative but utilitarian cables that reach from the concrete bastion to the roadbeds of the bridges (pp. 228-229). This typed of bridge construction was used first in Europe, after the Second World War, as contrasted to the usual suspension-bridge type.

In 1940, a hurricane struck the Tacoma Narrows Bridge, virtually whipping the roadbed around, throwing vehicles and passengers off the bridge, into the water below. This became a lurid example of the necessity of finding a safer type of bridge construction. With the Seattle Narrows Bridge, the cables were in tension only at the points where the roadbed was under pressure from the passing vehicles. With stayed cables, each cable all along the bridge is in tension. Also, as the drawing indicates, Wright has designed the cross-section of the bridge to resemble a ship's keel, thus making it more stable against strong winds and hurricanes. The decorative network of cables and, most probably, metal panels in-between the cables attached to the bridges was a further means of ensuring the continuous tension of each cable. The bridges themselves are divided into three separate lanes, the lower one for trucking, the middle one for automobiles, and the top one for pedestrians, planted as a garden all along the way. An open well on the top level allows daylight to descend onto the level below for passenger cars, while the truck level below receives daylight from a continuous opening along the side (opposite page). There is a cantilevered observation deck protruding out from the reinforced concrete bastion near the top, with a finial rising above as a decorative shaft for light at night.

Certain elements that are seen in the perspectives and elevations do not appear in the plans. It might well be that the project was put together somewhat in haste, so as to quickly show the Allegheny Conference a revised scheme after they had rejected the first one. To further demonstrate the romance of the project, a night rendering by Allen Lape Davison shows how Wright envisioned the scheme with its sparkling lights reflected in the waters of the three rivers: shimmering, jewellike, and ethereal (see page 184).

As impressed as the Allegheny Conference must have been with the exuberance and imposing drama of Wright's drawings, they were not sold on the scheme and the project was abandoned. In retrospect, Wright's bridge design demonstrates his awareness of the new engineering techniques being used at the time and how he adapted those techniques into a safe yet beautiful solution of his own. As he admitted so many times, he never turned his back on a good idea.

The two designs for the Pittsburgh Point Park quite naturally raise the question about how feasible each would have been, if accepted and construction had proceeded. Wright himself was quite certain about the feasibility, yet it would have required some unconventional and totally innovative engineering to bring these projects into reality.

SECTION AT ... HARBOR TUBE

Section. FLLW FDN # 4836.053.

Following pages: Perspective.
FLLW FDN # 4836.003.

PASSENGER CARS

TRUCKS

Parkway

SECTION AT ℄ OF EITHER BOWL

SCALE ⅛" = 1'-0"

Y. W. C. A. BUILDING

For the Young Women's Christian Association
Racine, Wisconsin. 1949, Project

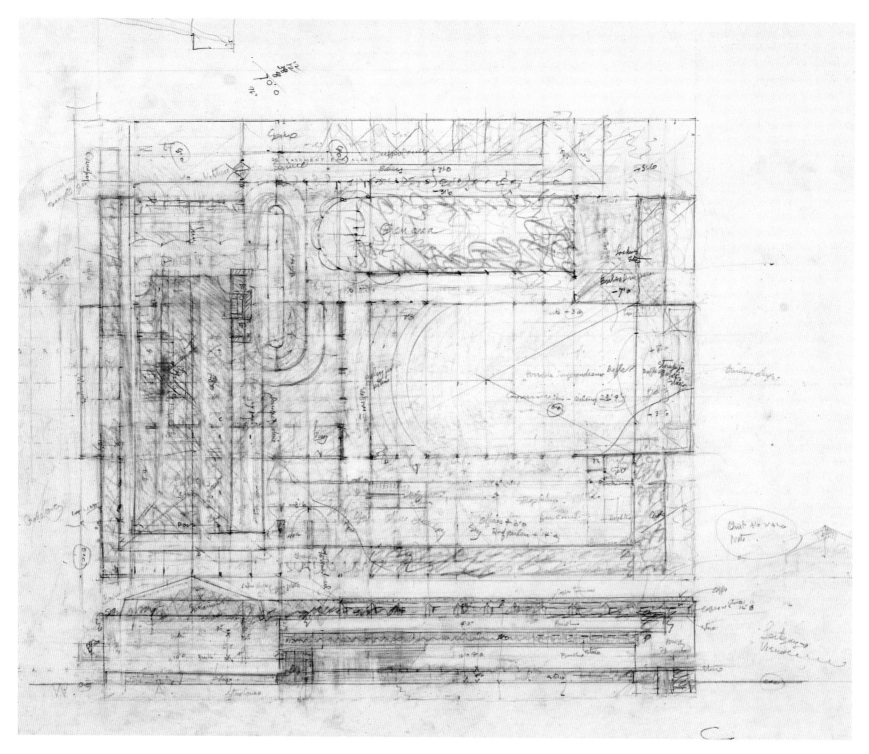

In 1949, the Y. W. C .A. in Racine, Wisconsin, was sorely in need of a new and better facility. How Herbert F. Johnson—of Johnson Wax—became involved in this commission is not clear. Perhaps his daughter Karen was a member of the "Y," but that is purely conjecture. In a telegram to Wright at the beginning of 1949, he wrote "The Y. W. C. A. intends to build soon. At a building committee meeting, I said you could best symbolize in a building the private initiative free enterprise and American way of life. Can you send more information if interested?"

Of course Wright was interested, and he subsequently prepared sketches to show the ladies of the Y what sort of building he proposed. To compare the finished perspective (following page, top) with Wright's first sketch plan and elevation (opposite page) is to see how closely the final rendering adhered to his original concept. It was an all-brick structure with reinforced-concrete-slab floors. The most distinguishing feature of the design was the innovative glass-enclosed swimming pool on the third or uppermost level. Panels of glass could be opened to bring in fresh air so as to combat the fumes of chlorine. In the winter, the glass would allow the pool to be heated by the sun, helping to reduce the expensive cost of heating by an oil-burning furnace.

The scheme provided for a bowling alley in the basement along with the usual heating and cooling provisions. On ground level, a two-story gymnasium along with a viewing balcony on the second level was long and large enough to provide for basketball games. Located on this ground level were lobby, locker rooms, offices for the staff, and a hall for lectures and cinema. The mezzanine provided a balcony for the gymnasium as well as another balcony for the cinema. Also on the mezzanine were placed the lobby, kitchen, and snack bar, along with party rooms, hostess rooms, and a residence for the caretaker.

Left: Plan and elevation.
FLLW FDN # 4920.014.
Above: Interior perspective.
FLLW FDN # 4920.001.

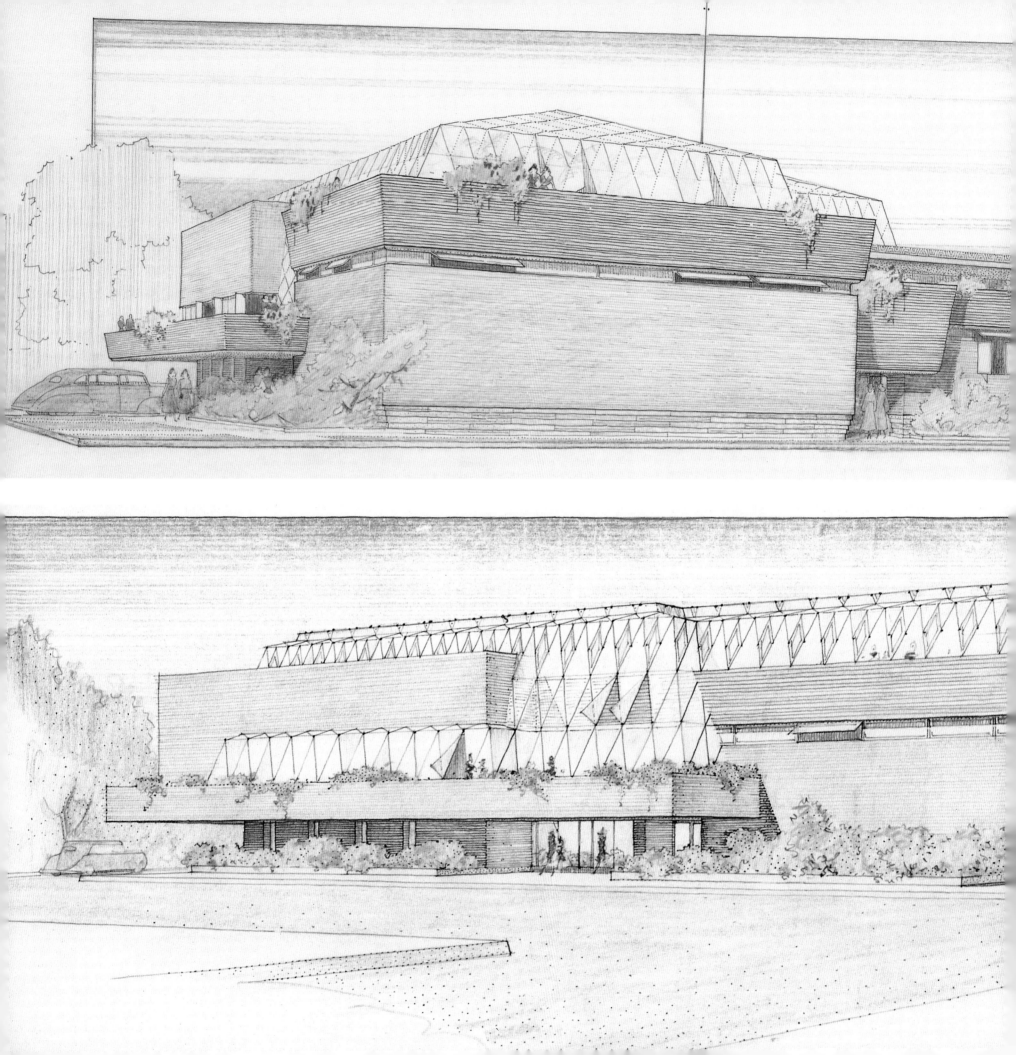

Left: Perspective.
FLLW FDN # 4920.002
Left, below: Perspective.
FLLW FDN # 5041.001

On the top level, adjacent to the swimming pool there was a lounge, changing rooms, and a sun deck. All levels were connected by ramps, and the central space of the building was open to all levels, as the interior perspective indicates (p. 231).

When this plan was submitted, the clients asked for some substantial changes, among them more office space on the entrance level. Wright complied with their demands, however the glass-enclosed pool remained on the third level with access to a roof garden for sunbathing (left, bottom). The plans for both versions were drawn showing split levels, somewhat confusing to read on the plans themselves, but quite clear on the sections.

A year after the commission was begun, however, Johnson notified Wright that the Y decided not to go further with the building. He included his check to cover the cost of Wright's work to date and the drawings were returned to Wright's office.

MASIERI MEMORIAL

Student Domicile and Library, Grand Canal
Venice, Italy. 1952, Project

In May 1951, Frank Lloyd Wright's exhibition *Sixty Years of Living Architecture* opened with resounding acclaim in the Palazzo Strozzi, Florence, Italy. It was the largest exhibition of Wright's work ever assembled and arguably the largest architectural exhibition ever assembled, anywhere, or by anyone, up to that time. On large eight-by-eight-foot panels were mounted photographs of Wright's buildings, over 600 original drawings were lent for the show, and models that had been previously made for a show held at the Museum of Modern Art in New York in 1940 were repaired, repainted, and made ready for a fresh venue. The model of Broadacre City, in particular, was repainted. In 1934 it represented a city in the throes of midsummer: stands of trees were painted deep forest green to represent the foliage of midsummer. When the model was spread out in the Hillside drafting room, Wright commented that as the model was originally made for midsummer, and the show in Florence was to open in the spring, he wanted the foliage of the model repainted to represent the fresh bloom of spring. The foliage was then painted light chartreuse first leaves of spring, other areas of planting were painted pale lavender, white, peach, soft rose to represent the blooming fruit trees, and long hedges of lilacs.

In Italy, Wright was honored at the Palazzo Vecchio in Florence. In Venice, at a ceremony of medieval splendor in the Doge's Palace, he was presented, by Count Sforza on behalf of the State of Italy, the coveted Star of Solidarity. While in Venice, Wright, Olgivanna, and their daughter Iovanna toured that watery, mysterious, and historical city accompanied by the architects Carlo Scarpa and Angelo Masieri. It was a most memorable tour, and Wright later told his apprentices about his trip and all that happened:

"Italy is the heart, really, if not the soul of all we call architecture, music, and painting. When you see Italy, you see the fields as you see in Umbria, you will see them all through Italy for that matter, but particularly in Umbria – you will see how cultivation, tillage, is architecture, how it makes a pattern, how carefully, how imaginatively they treat everything they do. Then you look at the buildings and they go along with the tillage, and the tillage and the buildings are, of course, part of the ground. It is all one beautiful harmony with a synthesis that exists nowhere in the world except in China and Japan. I think that our work—I noticed it in the exhibition—there is hardly a building there that wouldn't fit in Italy—in old Italy. . . . They gave us a wonderfully warm, heartfelt recognition, in spite of all the ceremonies and decorative pomp and glory—there was a heart in it all. It all came through in that fashion, which was immensely touching and convincing. The Italian heart is really the heart of the creative artist and the creative mind. So it was all very gratifying and peculiarly gratifying because it reaches you, too. I can't keep it to myself. You all shared in it, all of you at Taliesin who shared in this work. While it comes through me, it comes to you. So you have occasion to be grateful to Italy."[20]

The following year, Angelo Masieri and his wife Savina made a trip to the United States and motored to Wisconsin in order to pay homage to Wright. On their return trip, Angelo was killed in an automobile accident on the Pennsylvania turnpike. His widow, who survived the accident, wished to memorialize him in some manner. The Masieri family owned a tract of land bordering the Grand Canal in Venice. Knowing of her husband's deep admiration for Wright, she asked him to design a memorial library and domicile for architectural students on that site. The four story building he designed took into account that the property was triangular, and thus the plan (pp. 236-237) responded likewise, with balconies on the side facing the canal. When he sent the design (opposite page) to Savina Masieri, he later sent the following letter:

Perspective. FLLW FDN # 5306.002.

"Dear Madam Masieri:

"I intended to write a letter with the drawings explaining what I had in mind in the design of the little Library and Domicile but perhaps it was better to let you get your own impressions more directly. I would love to please Samona, Carlo and Bruno and hope they will like what I have done.[21] My best to them all.

"Loving Venice as I do I wanted, by way of modern techniques, to make the old Venice Tradition live anew. I am sure you will notice that the building affords views up and down the canal where no one in Venice ever looked out before— the corners of the rooms. This is modern; so are all the techniques.

"Alongside these corner features a glass lighting feature rises—lighting outside and inside by way of neon tubes (low candlepower) when appropriate . . . I hope you will all like the scheme in general. We will do anything we can do to meet any suggestions you make.

"Faithfully, Frank Lloyd Wright,
"February 19, 1953." [22]

In describing the structural system for the building, Wright wrote, "Venice does not float upon the water like a gondola but rests upon the silt at the bottom of the sea. In the little building I have designed slender marble shafts firmly fixed upon concrete piles (two to each) in the silt that rise from the water as do reeds or rice or any water plants. These marble piers rise to carry the floor construction securely—the cantilever slab floors thus made safe to project between them into balconies overhanging the water—Venetian as Venetian can be. Not imitation but interpretation of Venice."[23]

Savina Masieri was immensely pleased with what Wright had created, as were many of the others to whom she showed the drawings. The city fathers also believed that Wright had caught the spirit of Venice, albeit it in a modern idiom. However, the city's officials, who overlook the tourist aspect of Venice, became fearful that a modern building, situated in such a prominent location on the historic Grand Canal, would bring severe criticism and injure the tourist trade. The project was therefore abandoned.

When Ernest Hemingway, living in Africa at the time, heard about the possibility of Venice constructing a Frank Lloyd Wright building on such a prestigious location, he remarked, "If Venice builds that building, Venice should be burned!" When Wright was apprised of Hemingway's caustic remark, he was asked what he thought of it. He responded, "Not much, it is, after all, just a voice from the jungle."

FROM A HEIGHT OF 45'-11"-3/16 TO 55'-1"-7/16
2ND. SUPERIMPOSED STOREY

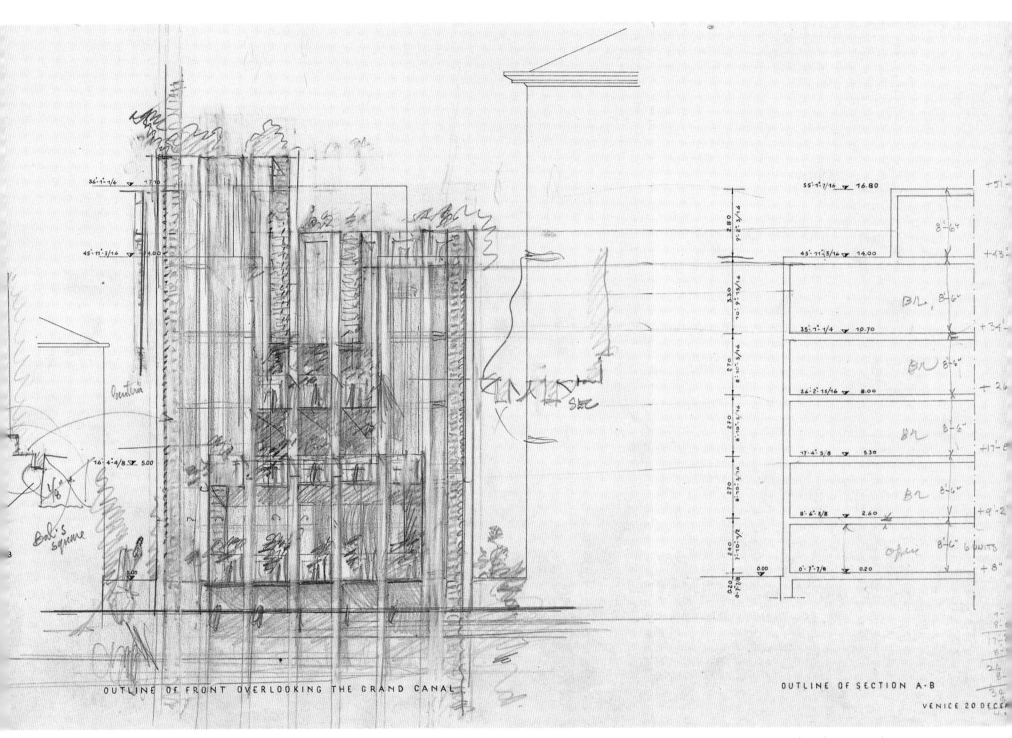

OUTLINE OF FRONT OVERLOOKING THE GRAND CANAL

OUTLINE OF SECTION A·B

VENICE 20 DECE

Plan, elevation, and section.
FLLW FDN # 5306.008.

PLAN FOR GREATER BAGHDAD

Crescent Opera, Museum, Gallery, Monument, and University
Baghdad, Iraq. 1957, Project

Below: Plan for Opera House.
FLLW FDN # 5733.009.
Right: Plan for Opera House.
FLLW FDN # 5733.028.

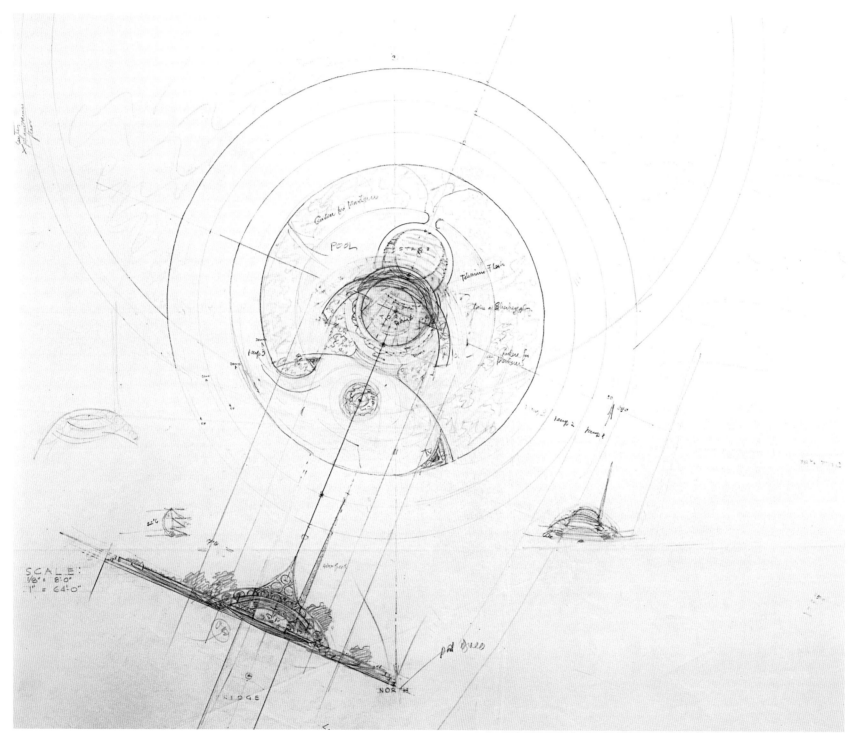

As a young boy, Wright was enthralled by the *One Thousand and One Nights*—he always referred to the book as the "Arabian Nights." In 1957, seventy-five years later, the commission to design an opera house for the city of Baghdad. Concerning this new work, he made the following comment: "I felt really that my boyhood had come forward and captured me again. The opera house is on a little promontory of the Tigris. It is the most beautiful spot in the world—Euphrates, Tigris, Garden of Eden, Baghdad."

The location for an opera house was originally intended to be within the city of Baghdad itself, but as Wright was flying into the area, he noticed a bare island, really a sandbar, in the Tigris River adjacent to the main portion of the city. He thought to himself that that would be the ideal place to put the building, because there would be ample room for parking. He often stated that when designing any building for large public occupancy, the first consideration must be the problem of parking. He brought the suggestion of using that island to the commission that retained him for the design of an opera house. They explained that the island was the personal property of the king. Wright then asked to be taken to him, and he would present the idea of the opera house on the island to the king himself, in person.

As Wright entered the audience hall in the king's palace, a dignitary of the court gravely announced, "His Royal Majesty, Faisal II, King of Iraq." Wright bowed graciously and then replied, "His Majesty, the American Citizen." The king invited Wright to sit down beside him and asked what he wanted. Wright explained that an opera house built in the heart of the city would be faced with the enormous problem of parking. However, that island in the Tigris River would be the ideal place, but the problem was the fact that the island was the king's personal

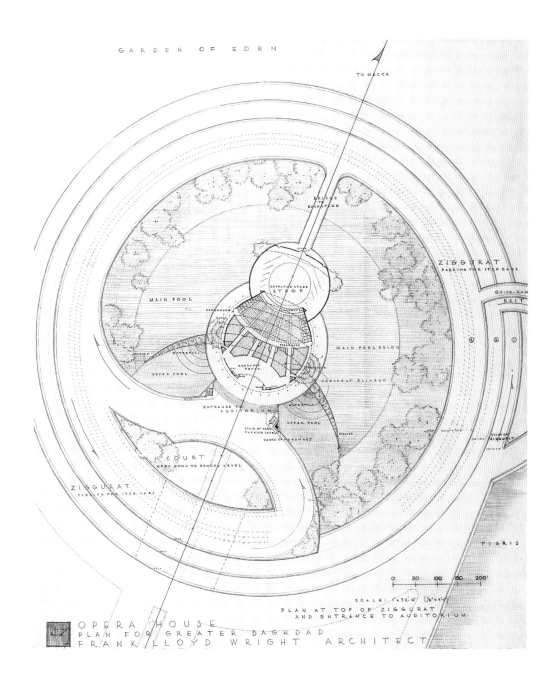

property. The king thought for a few seconds, and then turned to Wright and said, "Mr. Wright, the island is yours."

Realizing that this area was truly the cradle of civilization, on his preliminary drawings, the title block included "Dedicated to Sumeria, Isin, Larsa, and Babylon." During his trip to Baghdad he was taken to the museum that exhibits the arts of the ancient Sumerians. "I've been enlightened for the first time regarding the Sumerian priority in the arts connected with our own Western civilization. The Sumerians really did invent civilization and as I now see the Greeks didn't have so very far to go with it as I thought. I now think from what I've seen of Sumerian arts

and sciences and culture of that period, as inspiration and fresh. There is a vigor and a strength astoundingly refreshing. To see it is, I find, an education. We have gone very far from the deep roots of primitive culture and we have got to be pretty careful and farsighted not to make the mistake of going in the wrong direction by way of materialism and so betray those deeper simplicities of the ancient Spirit."[24]

The island on which Wright was to design his plan for the opera house and what he labeled the plan for greater Baghdad was originally called "Pig Island," but he renamed it "Isle of Edena." In the center of a garden, which he envisioned as a citrus grove, adjacent to the opera house, he

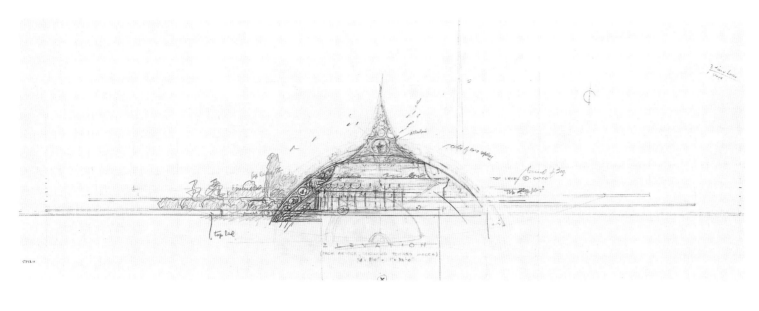

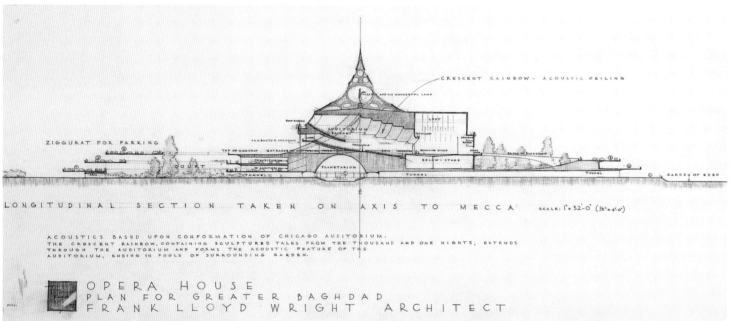

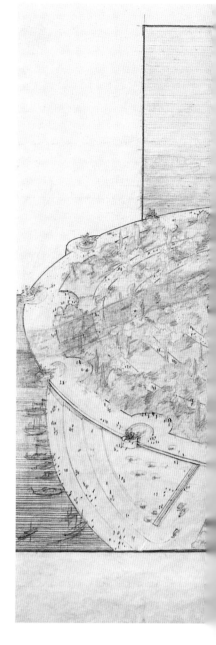

CRESCENT RAINBOW — ACOUSTIC CEILING

ZIGGURAT FOR PARKING

LONGITUDINAL SECTION TAKEN ON AXIS TO MECCA' SCALE: 1"=32'-0' (⅛"=4'-0")

ACOUSTICS BASED UPON CONFORMATION OF CHICAGO AUDITORIUM.
THE CRESCENT RAINBOW, CONTAINING SCULPTURED TALES FROM THE THOUSAND AND ONE NIGHTS, EXTENDS
THROUGH THE AUDITORIUM AND FORMS THE ACOUSTIC FEATURE OF THE
AUDITORIUM, ENDING IN POOLS OF SURROUNDING GARDEN.

OPERA HOUSE
PLAN FOR GREATER BAGHDAD
FRANK LLOYD WRIGHT ARCHITECT

Top: Perspective sketch for Opera House. FLLW FDN # 5733.011.
Above: Perspective section. FLLW FDN # 5733.031.

proposed two large sculptures, one for Adam and the other for Eve, with smaller sculptures around the periphery close to the edge near the river, to represent the various races of the world. (About the historic reference of Eve giving the apple to Adam, he claimed that here in the Middle East she did not give him an apple, but rather an orange.)

Wright had always maintained a strong admiration for the architecture and culture of Islam. His writing on the architecture of Persia—such as the buildings in Isfahan—are some of the most poetic and illuminating explanations of

historical work that he ever put down on paper. In this work for Baghdad, he was honoring the tradition of ancient Sumeria and Islam without copying from the past nor insulting the region with the then-current work going on around the world, as in the International Style's boxes of steel and glass. He claimed that the so-called International Style was neither international nor had any style.

When he presented the drawings to King Faisal and Crown Prince Abdul Ilan, he wrote: "If we are able to understand and interpret them, there is no necessity to copy our ancestors. These

designs are so intended. But also to revive the vision of natural beauty of form in the ancient crafts of the kiln and the use of the ground that produced the ancient architecture of the Middle East. It is worth noting here that the original city of Baghdad built by Haroun al Rashid was circular and so walled when the ziggurat of earth and masonry was a 'natural.'" [25]

Concerning his plan for the opera house which also included a civic auditorium, he explained:

"The Crescent Opera and Civic Auditorium are set in a natural water-garden surrounded by the motor ziggurat either one, two or three

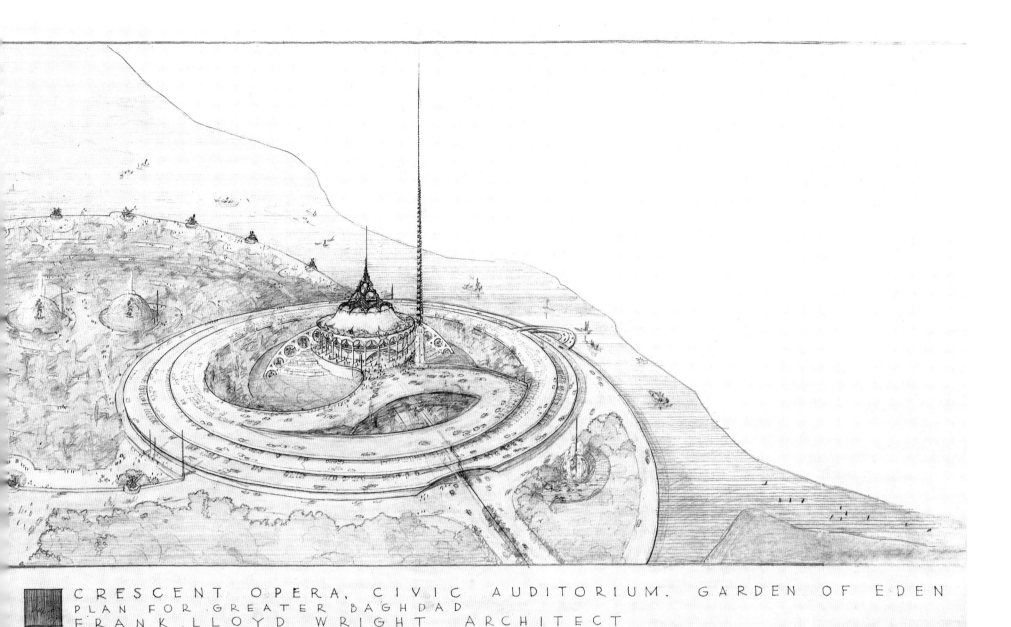

CRESCENT OPERA, CIVIC AUDITORIUM. GARDEN OF EDEN
PLAN FOR GREATER BAGHDAD
FRANK LLOYD WRIGHT ARCHITECT

Perspective of Opera, Civic Auditorium,
and Garden of Eden. FLLW FDN # 5733.007.

stories in height as traffic would allow. The opera: good acoustics are determined by the crescent ceiling of the great room as it curves upward and outward over the audience and sweeps outward on each side of the building as sculptural wings. The stage proscenium itself is the focal point of the crescent. In this case the crescent—like a great horn—extends outward. Each wing descends behind a series of fountain waterfalls on either side of the opera. These wings are seen from inside the promenades of the opera as well as outside. This feature of the crescent divides the opera from the civic auditorium and thus

cupped over the proscenium to carry sound as hands would be cupped above the mouth. Sensitivity to sound and intimate quality of occupation by opera and large civic meetings would be easy to make. The Chicago Auditorium by Adler and Sullivan successfully uses similar acoustics and this auditorium is recognized as the most successful room for opera and large audiences in existence.

"The house itself may be divided on this same crescent curve of the ceiling into two parts — 1600 seats next to the stage for specific opera and easily expanded, by pendent easily movable

screens hung on this same line of the ceiling sliding easily on the curve to additional space for 7,500 more seats, these for civic demonstrations, such as political meetings, conventions, or grand-concerts. A building of this sort is, as it should be, the apex of our Western Culture and would become increasingly useful to the East.

"Tales of the classic *One Thousand and One Nights* are employed to decorate the gardens with appropriate sculpture as seen set into the wings of the dividing crescent as they emerge from the building interior and descend on either side over the waterfalls of the garden. A golden figure of

241

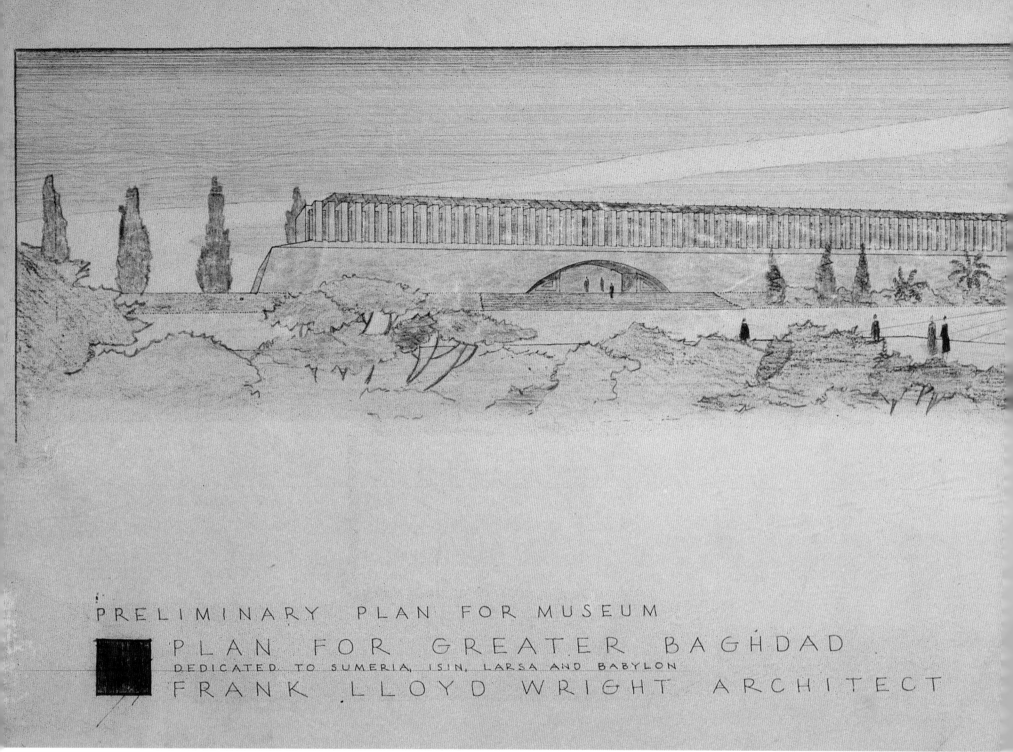

PRELIMINARY PLAN FOR MUSEUM
PLAN FOR GREATER BAGHDAD
DEDICATED TO SUMERIA, ISIN, LARSA AND BABYLON
FRANK LLOYD WRIGHT ARCHITECT

Perspective of museum for antiquities. FLLW FDN # 5748.007.

Aladdin holding his wonderful lamp (symbol of human imagination) stands overhead at the center of the crenellated canopy terminating the main edifice as seen against the sky."[26]

He made numerous sketch studies for the opera house, and they all proceeded along the same line as his earliest one, a constant development of one idea. His presentation plan drawn to show the top level of the ziggurat, places the

opera in the center, surrounded by the water garden, with a periphery of trees and planting. The ziggurat not only provides access to the opera, but also ample parking as well. The section (p. 240, bottom) explains the stacked levels of the ziggurat, with parking in under protection. Beneath the opera there is a planetarium. Throughout the drawings, Wright has always indicated "Taken on Axis to Mecca." This is in

respect to Muslim tradition. The section also explains the additional seating that can be lowered down for larger occasions. The Garden of Eden is shown adjacent to the opera, with its two statues of Adam and Eve in the center (p. 241).

As well as the opera house, he designed a large museum (above) for the archaic sculptures and arts of the ancient occupants of the region: the Sumerians, the Assyrians, and the Babylonians. This

museum for antiquities was a long, bold, most masculine-looking structure with three arched entrances, the center one flanked by two Assyrian winged bulls, each with the head of a man, the body of a bull, and the wings of an eagle.

Another museum was proposed for contemporary art. A group of kiosks made up the grand bazaar. This gallery for contemporary art was, in contrast, more curvilinear, more feminine in character (following pages, top). Another large drawing (following pages, bottom)represents the plan and elevation of the gallery, but on this sheet Wright has drawn a sketch section of the opera, a sketch section of the gallery, a sketch of the kiosks in the grand bazaar, and a sketch of the monument to Haroun al Rashid. On this drawing, an apprentice has drawn the elevation of the gallery, but Wright has interrupted it on the left side with a sketch elevation of the museum for antiquities. A design for a casino was indicated on another drawing but was never fully explained with any detail drawings. However, above the right side of the gallery on this drawing, Wright has drawn a section of a building labeled "Casino."

At the end of the isle he planned for a tall statue dedicated to Haroun al Rashid, who first

243

constructed Baghdad. The statue represents a caravan of riders encircling the tower up to the final statue of the caliph. One reason Wright planned for the monument was to place it at the tip of the isle facing the flow of the Tigris River. Since the isle is basically a sandbar, the concrete monument would act as a deterrent against erosion.

Spanning by means of a bridge over to the mainland, he designed a university, with the buildings tangent to a large three-tiered circular roadway, which he again called the ziggurat, that provided access to the various school buildings, as well as shaded parking, in the same manner that he proposed for a three-tiered ziggurat surrounding the opera house.

When he presented the drawings for the university to the king of Baghdad and the development board, he wrote:

"This age—the Motor-age—has yet given no practical recognition of changed character to the record in appropriate modern building. Baghdad is in danger of similar extinction.[27] But I have here hoped to see the Middle East put first things first. The vision and will to do so might be hers now in Baghdad. These drawings are voluntarily submitted for the purpose of this new freedom and are sent to the development board with this in mind—prompted by respect and affection for the ancient East of the Middle East.

"The use of the ziggurat has been already explained elsewhere in this thesis. Flexibility on the new time-scale has been sought everywhere. Extending one level to two or three levels or more as needed and according to demand becomes a most valuable attribute of this generic form for parking the entire university. The plans in general keep the campus free of cars and afford intimate parking with entrances to the entire campus from the ziggurat at every building alongside its inner circumference.

"Here the various university department buildings have been so directly associated on one side with the traffic and by open central courts connecting the entire building scheme with the interior lower level of the campus free of cars. The campus is thus not only free of cars but is directly available to the student life of the student-body of every department level. Beauty and economy of building is thus enhanced. Time-scale on the ramps is proportioned to the build-

ing scale on the campus. As a matter of course as many buildings as are needed could join the curriculum which the ziggurat thus becomes. A flexible basis for development is a natural consequence of this general form. The ziggurat winds in full view of the Tigris and travel to and fro upon it is safe and a pleasure."[28]

In developing the aerial perspectives of the university, Wright had his apprentices make three views, all from the same angle, but with variations as to certain elements outside of the actual university itself. On the lower left portion of one of the drawings (pp. 248-249), palm fronds are evident as well as a mosque-like dome at the rear. However, on this particular drawing Wright has used Wite-Out to block out the palm fronds and a domed building seen behind the tall spires in the center of the university. Those spires represent television towers, along with becoming a startling vertical contrast to the general overall horizontal nature of the scheme.

Above: Perspective of museum for contemporary art. FLLW FDN # 5749.005
Right: Plan and elevation. FLLW FDN # 5749.003

Following pages:
Perspectives of Haroun al Rashid Monument.
Left: FLLW FDN # 5751.001
Right: FLLW FDN # 5751.004

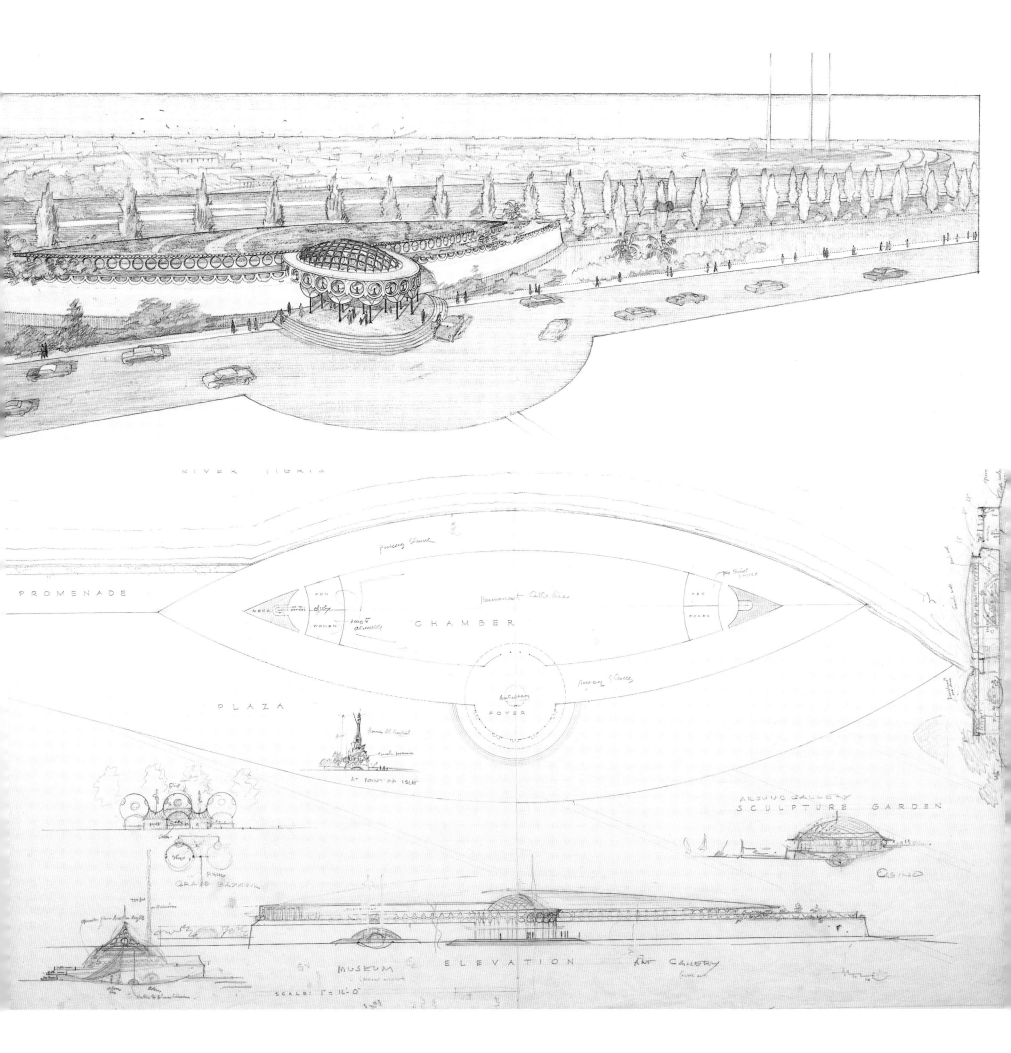

RIVER TIGRIS

PROMENADE

CHAMBER

PLAZA

FOYER

SCULPTURE GARDEN

MUSEUM ELEVATION ART GALLERY

SCALE: 1" = 16'-0"

HAROUN AL RASHID

HAROUN AL RASHID

FRANK LLOYD WRIGHT ARCHITECT

AERIAL VIEW OF THE UNIVERSITY   AT HEIGHT

PLAN FOR GREATER BAGHD

DEDICATED TO SUMERIA, ISIN, LARSA AND BABYLON

FRANK LLOYD WRIGHT   ARCHI

OO FEET

Wright's trip to Baghdad in May 1957 was obviously one that inspired him. The drawings for all the projects for Greater Baghdad were completed and signed by him on June 20, 1957 —an amazingly short period of time from the beginning of the commission until the moment when drawings were ready to be shown to the king and the development board. It was, as he often would admit, as if he just "shook the designs out of my sleeve and onto paper." He was originally commissioned to design only the opera house, yet when he had at his disposal the entire island, which the king had generously given him, it was as if he couldn't hold back—he went ahead and developed the entire island with its museums, grand bazaar, and statue to Haroun al Rashid. And further, he crossed over the river to another tract of land and proposed a large university. Tempted by the site, inspired by the region and its remarkable history (as the cradle of civilization), he often spoke of what happened to him as a result of these circumstances—he was like, as he would often admit, "a hungry orphan let loose in the bakery shop!"

Other architects were called upon to develop Baghdad, but it goes on record that what they proposed was just another application of the cold steel-and-glass idiom of the West. Wright, on the other hand, has reached into the past of the ancient Middle East, respected the culture of Islam, and created new forms and new concepts of engineering that are truly of the present with a deep reverence to that past.

An overall perspective view of the Plan for Greater Baghdad (right) shows the entire project: the opera, the museum, the art gallery with the avenue of kiosks running from the monument to the opera. Across the river is the university.

A year following his presentation of the designs for Greater Baghdad, the young king was brutally assassinated during a coup that overtook the royal government. Wright's project for the opera house was abruptly terminated. The designs he made for the Baghdad Post and Telegraph building, at the same time that he proposed his ambitious scheme for Greater Baghdad, lingered on for a while under the consideration of the new regime, but eventually that, too, was dropped. For all his work in Baghdad, so far as the record goes, he received no compensation.

Previous pages: Perspective of University. FLLW FDN # 5759.006.

Right: Perspective of Isle of Edena and University. FLLW FDN # 5733.008.

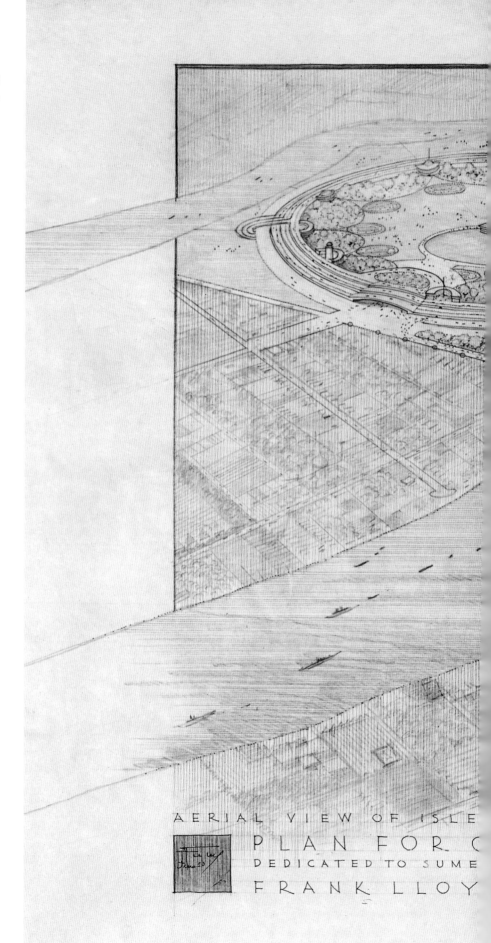

AERIAL VIEW OF ISLE
PLAN FOR C
DEDICATED TO SUME
FRANK LLOY

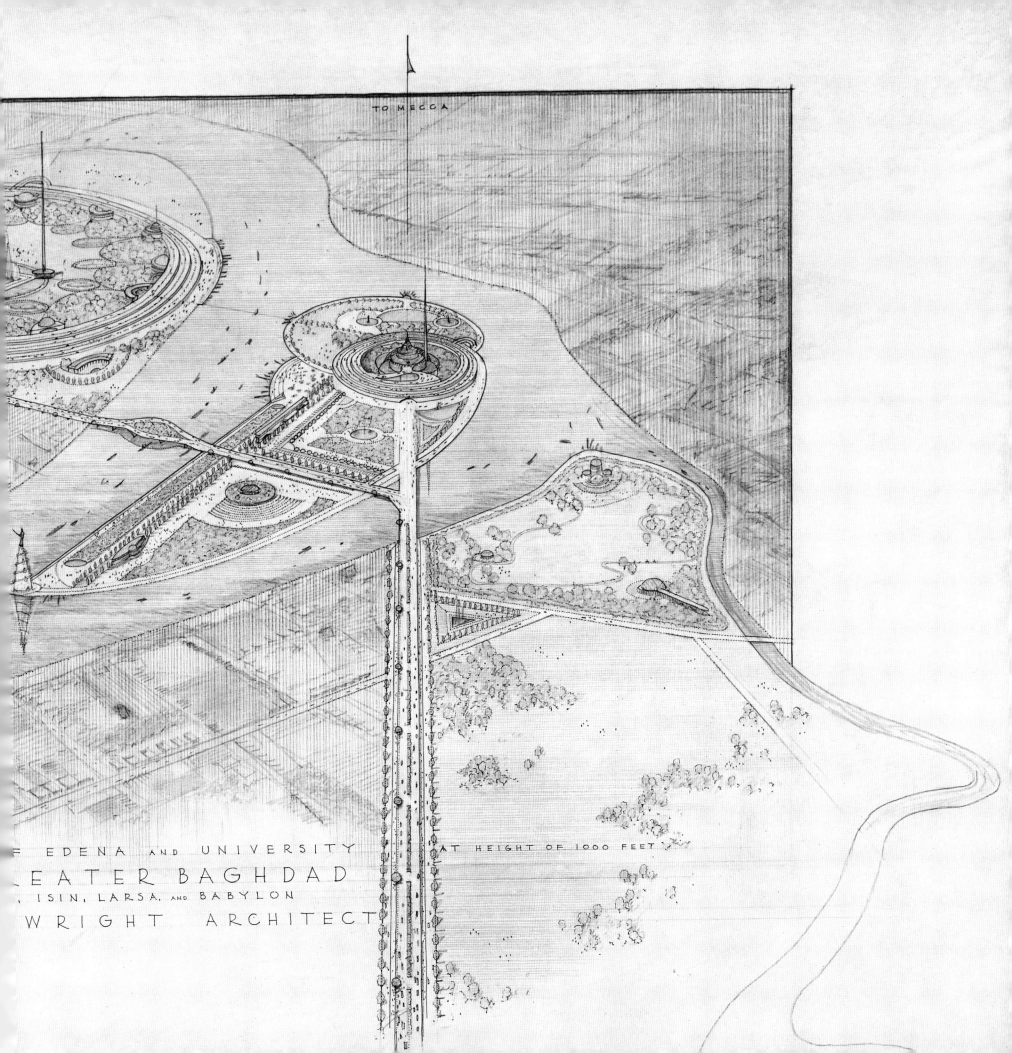

TO MECCA

EDENA AND UNIVERSITY ... AT HEIGHT OF 1000 FEET
EATER BAGHDAD
, ISIN, LARSA, AND BABYLON
WRIGHT ARCHITECT

PART FOUR

BUILDINGS FOR TRAVEL AND ENTERTAINMENT

The Wolf Lake Amusement Park was Wright's first design for a building dedicated to entertainment. In 1895, it showed his skill in designing a structure that housed a wide range of features for summer pleasures: swimming, boating, dining, dancing, and shopping in a mall with various enticing concessions among them. It was a grand scheme, and some of its design elements, such as the low spreading and projecting roofs, would figure as important features in his subsequent work. It was destined not to be built. In fact, of all Wright designs for buildings for travel and entertainment, only two were constructed, and eventually those two were demolished.

They were the hotel at Lake Geneva, Wisconsin, and the Midway Gardens in Chicago. The demise of Midway Gardens has long been considered a cultural tragedy. Here Wright was bringing to the pleasure- and leisure-seeking public a form of entertainment similar to what he had experienced earlier on his trip to Germany and Austria in 1909–1910: namely, the colorful and pleasant beer gardens. His design for Midway Gardens followed this precept, and expanded it in terms of modern design and construction. Added to the beer garden model, which functioned mainly in the summer, Midway Gardens also provided a Winter Garden, with the same amenities but closed in against cold or inclement weather.

The next three projects, Lake Tahoe Summer Colony, Gordon Strong Automobile Objective and Planetarium, and San Marcos-in-the-Desert were all places that were reachable by means of the automobile. It seemed only fitting that since the automobile played such a pivotal role in these works that a gas station by Frank Lloyd Wright is included along with these buildings for travel and entertainment.

When Chicago was planning a fair for the year 1933, to be called Century of Progress, it was assumed that Wright, so closely associated with this city in which he began his career, would be asked to participate with some design at least. This was not to be the case. Although neglected to take part in the fair, he nonetheless went ahead on his own and made three proposals. When he saw what the other architects were designing and whose designs were accepted, he remarked that the Columbian Fair of 1893 killed architecture while the fair of 1933 buried it.

Wright's brief, almost whirlwind connection with Elizabeth Arden gave rise to the design of a special spa for her clientele, but her uncertainty concerning what she really wanted from her architect, brought an abrupt end to the scheme.

The multi-millionaire Huntington Hartford had grand proposals for a resort hotel, a sports club, and a residence for himself in Runyon Canyon, near Los Angeles. However, Wright claimed that he was the sort of man who snuck up to an idea, pinched it in the fanny, and ran. His design for the Play Resort/Sports Club figures among his most ambitious and even out-of-this-world creations of his entire career.

His design for a tourist facility at Meteor Crater in Arizona provided him with the opportunity to design a structure that was truly a cliff-hanger, with provisions for tourists to view the crater from a high overlook rising out of the building itself, or take an elevator down along the same rock-faced structure to arrive at the base and stroll out on the vast crater.

Harry Guggenheim was the nephew of Solomon R. Guggenheim and a great horse-racing enthusiast. He commissioned Wright to design a new sports pavilion for Belmont Park. That design made innovative use of steel cables and translucent fabrics.

Finally, Mike Todd, of Todd-AO, collaborating with Henry J. Kaiser, of Kaiser Aluminum, and Buckminster Fuller, of the geodesic dome, all together commissioned Wright to design a series of prefabricated theaters that were intended to be constructed in shopping malls across the nation.

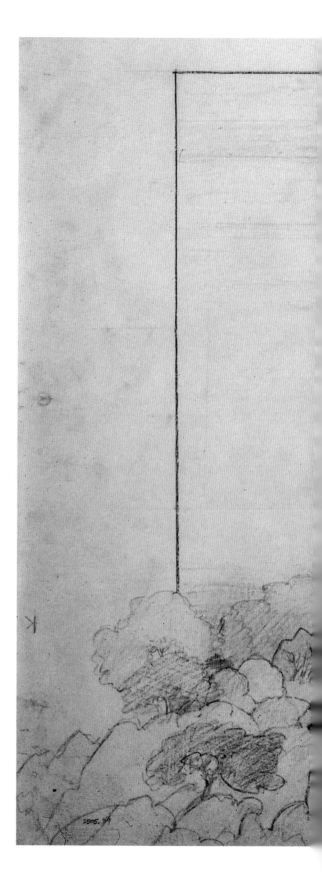

Perspective drawing of the Automobile Objective and
Planetarium for Gordon Strong (see p.270). FLLW FDN # 2505.039.

WOLF LAKE AMUSEMENT PARK

For Edward C. Waller
Wolf Lake, Chicago, Illinois. 1895, Project

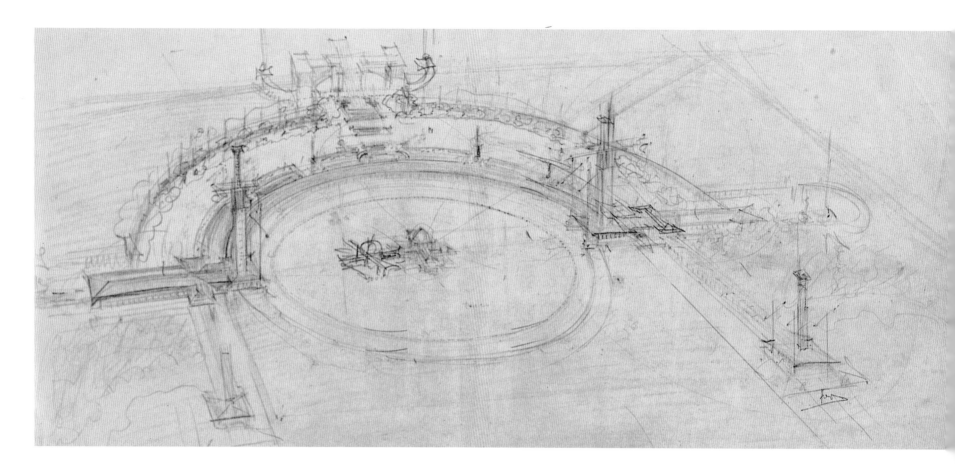

olf Lake, a tributary to Lake Michigan, lay on the Illinois-Indiana state line. Edward C. Waller, Wright's client for the Lexington Terrace Apartments, asked the architect to design a large amusement park for his property on the Illinois side of the lake. Wright's initial sketches placed the park as a large half circle nestled into the shoreline. Concessions, bandstand, viewing stands, casinos, and covered pavilions were planned within this half circle. A wide mall separated this half circle from another one that contained further concessions, separated by waterways. Bridges connected the two half circles so that small boats could navigate from the waterways onto the lake itself.

A large circle in the front contained a music pavilion. Stretching out on either side were long pavilions for boat landings, while two long arms projected out into the lake for bathing beaches, each one with a covered pavilion for the convenience of the bathers. At the back of the large half circle were water chutes spilling down into the waterways between the two half circles for concessions. Tall towers, carrying lights and balloons, rose all along the half circles to add a joyful and festive element to the entire scheme.

On an early sketch perspective (above), Wright has inscribed "Preliminary Study Wollf [sic] Lake Resort—1895 FLlW." The final rendering, done by his draftsmen in the Oak Park Workshop, is a stunning example of architectural drawing using watercolor and gouache on art paper (pp. 256-257).

Obviously the project proved to be far too costly, and Wright was asked to make a more moderate plan. In this second scheme he placed the entire park further back into the shoreline, taking advantage of two land projections, like the claws of a crab, to contain the necessary elements for the park. No further drawings exist as to how this second proposal was to be developed. The project was evidently dropped.

This was Wright's first large commission since he opened his office two years earlier. It was also two years after the immense Chicago World's Fair

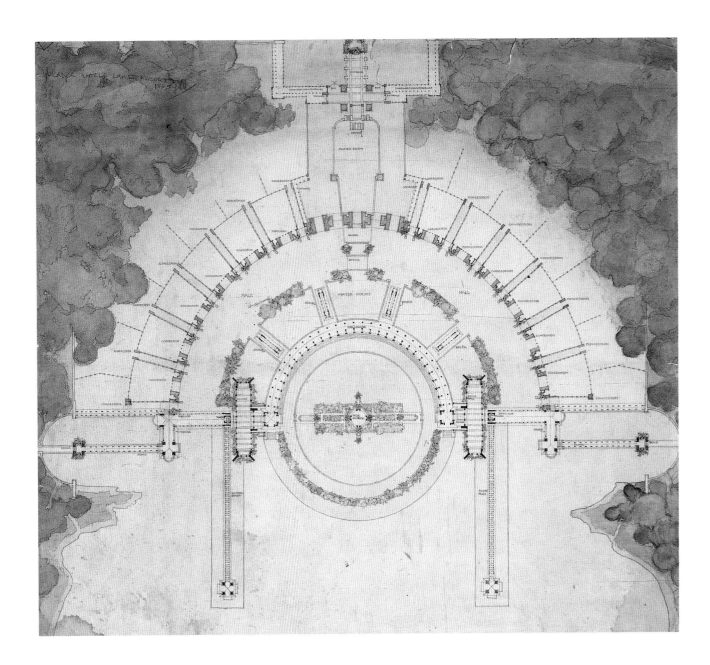

Left: Preliminary perspective.
FLLW FDN # 9510.002.
Right: Plan. FLLW FDN # 9510.016.

Following pages: Perspective.
FLLW FDN # 9510.001.

of 1893, called the Columbian Expostion, whose architecture trumpeted the Neoclassical forms throughout. Daniel H. Burnham was the architect of the fair and a friend of Wright's as well. Edward Waller, one of Wright's early clients, arranged a meeting between Wright, Burnham, and himself. Wright affectionately called Burnham "Uncle Dan." Seeing the enormous success of the fair, he said to Wright, "The Fair, Frank, is going to have a great influence in our country. The American people have seen the Classics on a grand scale for the first time. You've seen the success of the Fair and it should mean something to you too. We should take advantage of the Fair."[1] Burnham encouraged Wright to take a year off,

go to Paris, study at the École de Beaux Arts, and steep himself in Neoclassism. He generously offered to pay Wright's way for the year and also support his growing family at home. Wright replied, "I know. Yes—I know, Uncle Dan. You may be quite right but somehow it just strikes on my heart like—jail. Like something awful. I couldn't bear it, I believe. No, I just can't run away from what I see as mine, I mean what I see as ours in our country. I am grateful to you both, though, but I won't go."[2]

Of course both Waller and Burnham were deeply hurt by his refusal, but Wright believed that he was on a different course, one more true to an American culture no longer living in the

past. He had recently left the office of Adler and Sullivan, who were embarking on a new direction for architecture, leaving the old traditional forms behind them, and he chose to throw his hat in that ring.

In contrast to the Columbian Exposition with its flair for the classics, Wolf Lake Amusement Park, although a fair on a much smaller scale, was an indication of this new direction. This can be seen in the outstretched horizontal nature of the design, but with strong vertical accents, along with the low, pitched outspreading roofs which would become a prominent detail in his residential work, the whole emphasizing its association with the ground, and in this case, the water as well.

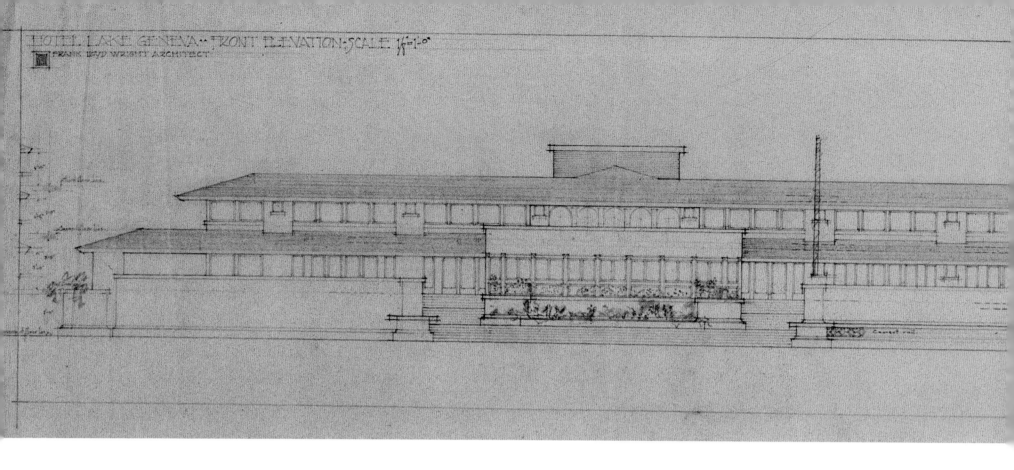

HOTEL LAKE GENEVA · FRONT ELEVATION · SCALE $\frac{1}{6}''=1'-0''$
FRANK LLOYD WRIGHT ARCHITECT

Above: Elevation. FLLW FDN # 1202.007.
Right: Perspective. FLLW FDN # 1202.001.

LAKE GENEVA SUMMER HOTEL

Lake Geneva, Wisconsin. 1911, Demolished

At the turn of the twentieth century, Lake Geneva, Wisconsin, was the summer "watering hole" for some of Chicago's more affluent families. When he was commissioned to design the Lake Geneva Hotel, his design considered the nature of the project: a summer resort inn on the shores of the lake. The perspective title block (right) reinforces this concept, as it reads "Summer Hotel Lake Geneva Frank Lloyd Wright Architect August 1911." The original design included a boathouse and pier at the water's edge, but this was never constructed. The first floor plan provided an entrance terrace which gained access to the lobby, which, in this case, was labeled "Lounge." This access was typical of Wright's way of entering a building: rather than a direct approach in the center, as one might expect, it was on the two sides. At the far end of the lounge there was an alcove with a fireplace and seats. Dining room, kitchen, offices for the management, and guest rooms are situated on this level. A broad terrace ran in front of the dining room and the guest rooms that faced the lake. The general atmosphere of the building is more residential in feeling than the usual hotel plan. This reinforced the character of a summer resort inn. The second floor provided for further guestrooms and a broad outdoor terrace over the lounge. As the perspective indicates, the original plan called for an extension at the end of the building, projecting out front as the front terrace and lounge do, but with a private entrance on the far end and a space inside labeled "Ladies' Parlor." In the final construction, this addition was not considered.

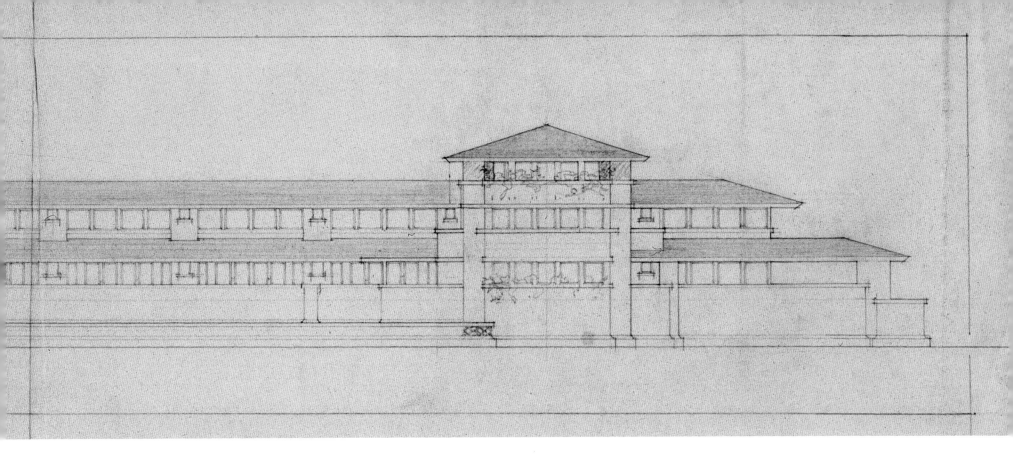

SUMMER HOTEL ON
LAKE GENEVA
FRANK LLOYD WRIGHT
ARCHITECT AUGUST 1911

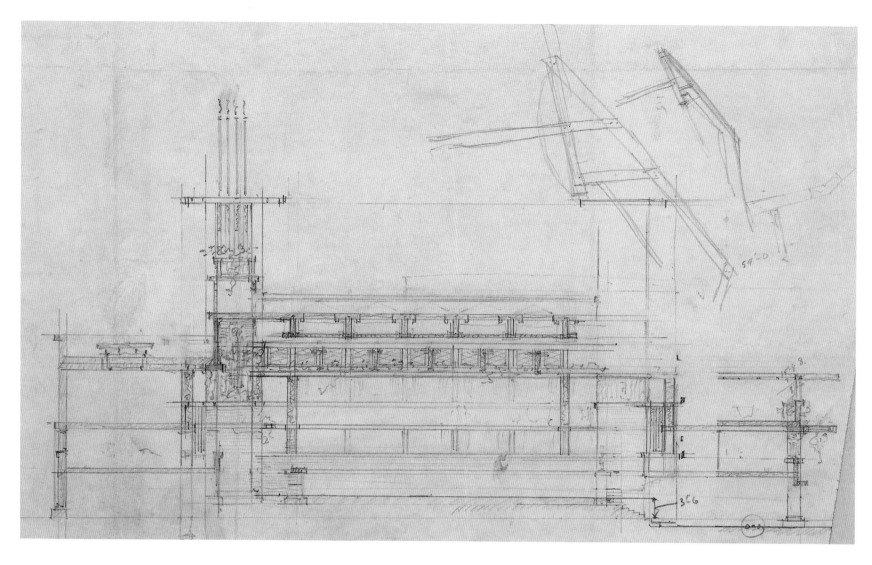

Above: Preliminary elevation. FLLW FDN # 1401.099.
Right: Decorative elements. FLLW FDN # 1401.081.

MIDWAY GARDENS

For Edward C. Waller Jr.
Chicago, Illinois. 1913, Demolished

Ed Waller, the son of one of Wright's Oak Park clients, came into his office one day in the fall of 1913 and said, "Frank, in all this black old town, there's no place to go but out, nor any place to come but back, that isn't bare and ugly unless it's cheap and nasty. I want to put a garden in this wilderness of smoky dens, car tracks, and saloons. I believe Chicago would appreciate a beautiful garden resort. Our people would go there, listen to good music, eat, and drink. You know, an outdoor garden something like those little parks round Munich where German families go. You have seen them. The dance craze is on now, too, and we could have a dancing floor inside somewhere for the young folks.

Yes, and a place within the big place outside near the orchestra where highbrows could come and sit to hear a fine concert even if they didn't want to dine at home. The trouble of course is the short season. But we could fix that by putting a winter garden on one side for diners, with a big dancing floor in the middle. And to make it all surefire as to money we would put in a bar [the "affliction" had not yet befallen] that would go the year round. We would run the whole thing as a high-class entertainment on a grand scale—Pavlova dancing—Max Bendix's full orchestra playing—light, color, music, movement— a gay place! Frank, you could make it unique." [3]

Wright knew exactly what Waller had in mind. Indeed, two years earlier he had experienced the pleasure and delight of the beer gardens in Munich and Vienna. They were not just saloons or bars, but delightful gardens with hanging lights at night, fine music, and fine food.

A few days later, Ed Waller came to Wright's office to see what the architect claimed "had simply shaken itself out of my sleeve. Young Waller gloated over it. 'I knew it,' he said, 'You could do it and this is it.'" [4]

Thus was born, in a remarkably short period of time, the scheme for Midway Gardens. A large three-story space provided a winter garden, the dance floor in the center, and balconies for

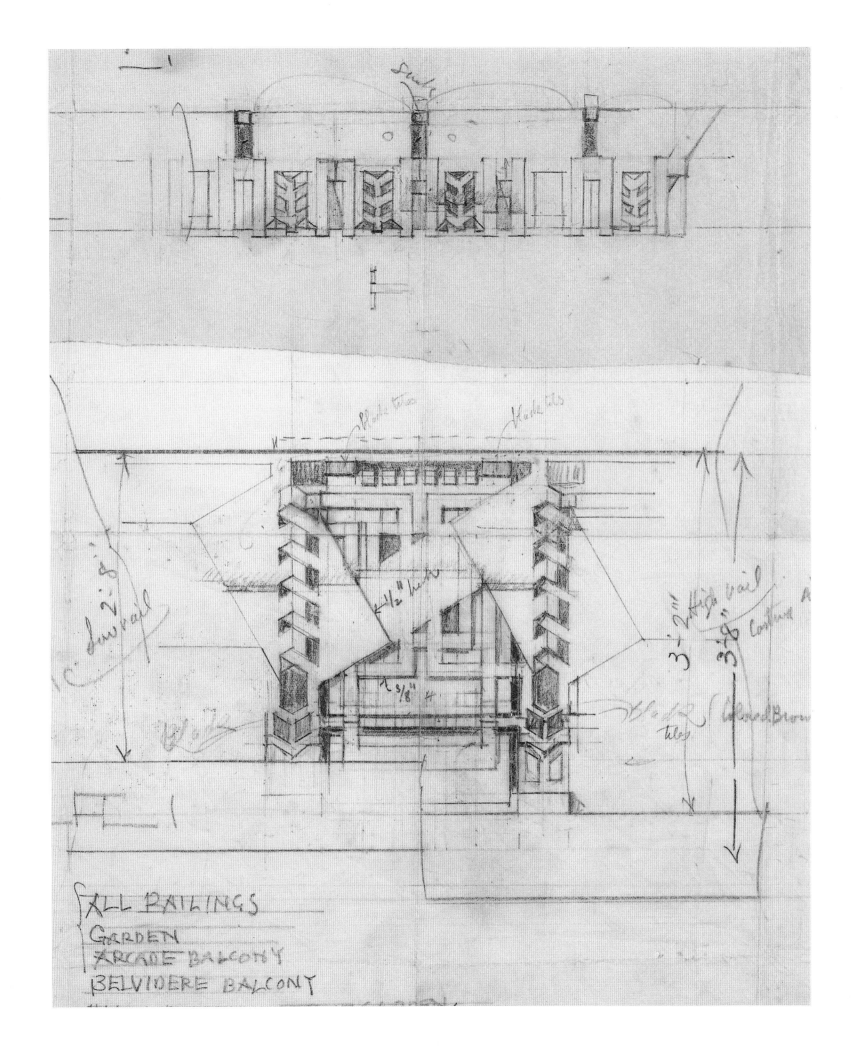

ALL RAILINGS

GARDEN

ARCADE BALCONY

BELVIDERE BALCONY

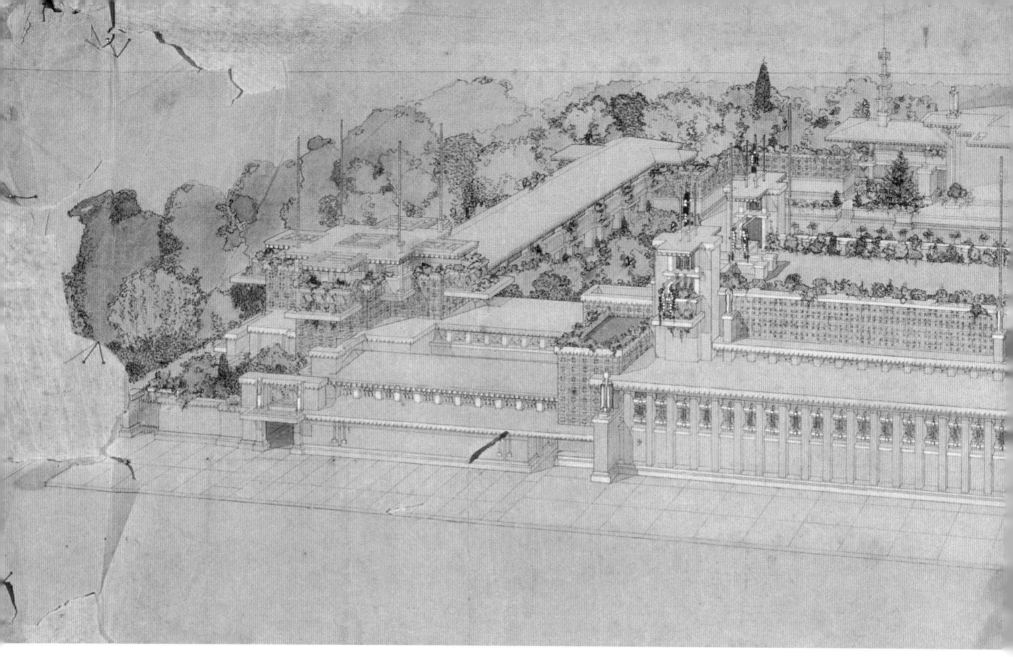

Perspective. FLLW FDN # 1401.004.

dining around and above. The famous Chicago restaurateur John Vogelsang was brought in to supervise the plan for the kitchen and serving facilities. He maintained that the success of any restaurant depended on quick service and hot food. The kitchen, therefore, was located in the basement with ramps and stairs leading to all levels of the winter garden. Outside, a large terrace formed the summer garden, and special ramps brought service from the kitchen below to the diners there. Running down either side of the summer garden were arcades roofed over, but open to the summer garden, and closed to the streets outside. At the end of the summer gar-

den, directly opposite the winter garden, was the orchestra shell:

"But the orchestra shell became a bone of contention. Out of a good deal of experience in such matters with Adler and Sullivan—they designed the Chicago Auditorium and twenty-six successful opera houses—I designed the shell, sure it would work out."[5]

Experts were brought in to see the scheme, and deemed it impossible. But Waller supported Wright, and told him if he was certain about the shell, then go ahead and build it. Wright based his conviction on the feasibility of the orchestra shell based on Adler's use of the sounding-board.

"Mr. Adler himself had invented the sounding-board as an architectural principle in earlier theaters he had built. That is to say, the sloping surface extending above the proscenium, opening into the audience room, was the sounding-board. Owing to this simple invention no public hall ever built by Adler and Sullivan was acoustically bad." [6]

The building was constructed of brick and reinforced concrete, with interior walls of brick and plaster. Decorative elements were cast in the concrete, integral with the building, such as the railings for the arcade balconies, main building, and roof gardens. Wright further designed the

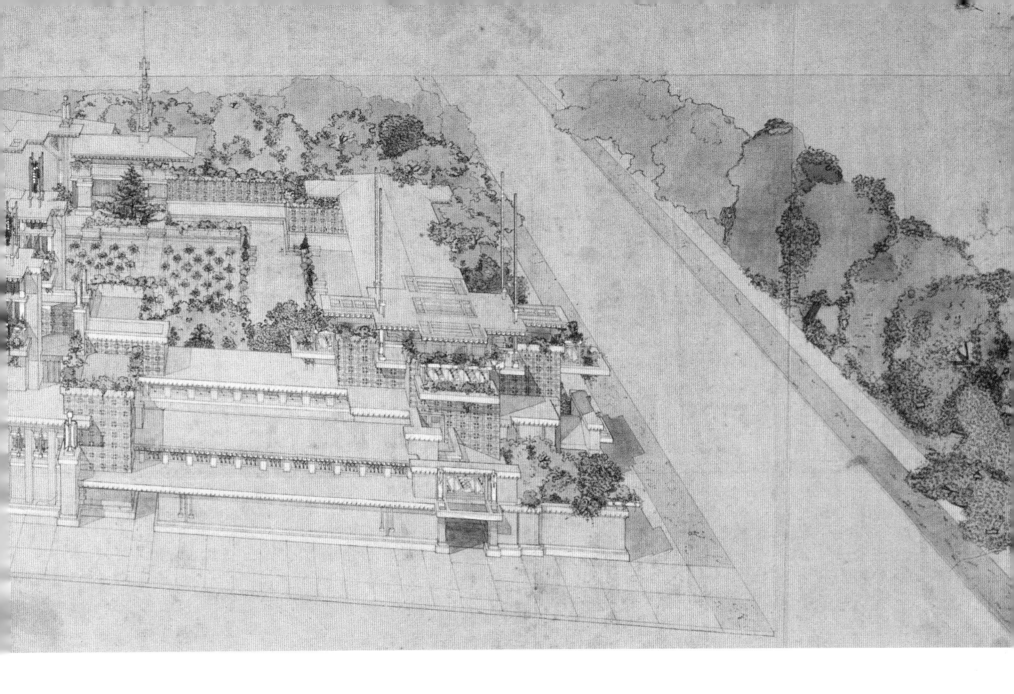

decorative elements of the building: sculpture, murals, and stained glass, as well as the furniture, tableware (dinnerware and table cloths), table lamps, and outdoor lighting. His designs for the stained glass he labeled "Dancing Glass," and unlike his other stained glass windows these patterns seemed to delightfully dance across the surface of the windows.

"Here in the Midway Gardens painting and sculpture were to be bidden back again to their original places and to their original offices in architecture, where they belonged. The architect, himself, was here again master of them all together."[7]

(It was during the last stages of construction, while Wright was at the site having a late lunch, that the news reached him about the tragedy at Taliesin. A servant had run amok, murdered seven people, and set the living quarters on fire. Wright returned home to see the bodies laid out on the court, and his home still smoldering as the sun went down.)

Meanwhile, the following year the Midway Gardens opened to a resounding success, indeed to Pavlova dancing to the music of Max Bendix's orchestra. However, debts accrued by the cost of construction and the unexpected theft of the office strongbox, forced the Gardens to sell. The

Edelweiss Brewing Company, taking advantage of a low price, bought them, painted over the murals and sculpture, and turned the place into a gaudy, cheap establishment. "A distinguished beautiful woman dragged to the level of the prostitute is now its true parallel."[8] Prohibitions then came in to deal the final blow, and the Gardens were turned into a skating rink. At last, they were mercifully destroyed to make room for an auto-laundry. Wright's only consolation was that they were so well constructed that the demolition contractor lost more on the contract than it was worth.

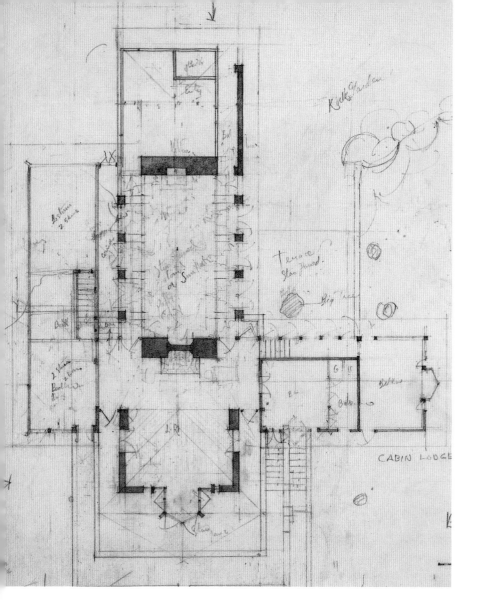

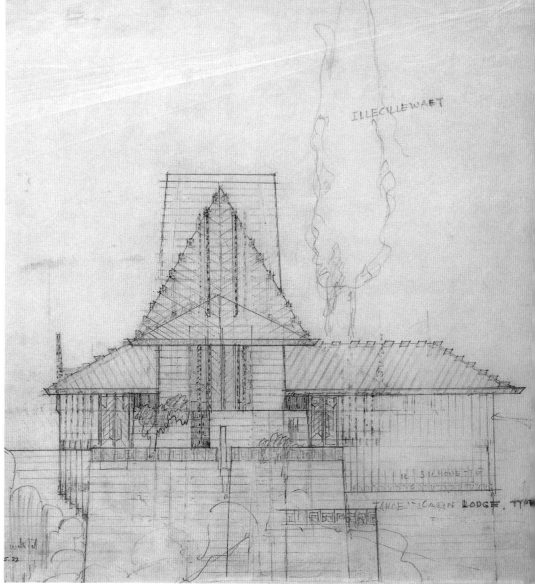

LAKE TAHOE SUMMER COLONY

For Jessie Armstrong
Lake Tahoe, California. 1924, Project

Frank Lloyd Wright's intense love for nature was deeply spiritual—one might even say religious. Often he claimed that while here on Earth, nature was the only body of God we would ever see. As one spells God with a capital "G," he spelled Nature with a capital "N." Of course this often brought down upon him strong criticism from the extremists of religious sects, but that never deterred him from his absolute belief in the sanctity and exuberance of the natural world around him.

One of the most romantic and intriguing architectural concepts in Wright's career is the

group of mountainside cabins and floating cabins that he designed for the Lake Tahoe Summer Colony. He came upon Lake Tahoe to meet with the client Jessie Armstrong who, along with her mother, owned two hundred acres of land along the shores and mountain slopes of Lake Tahoe's Emerald Bay. From his voyage across the lake on steamer from Tahoe City, where he first met Armstrong, to Emerald Bay Camp, she then took him in a small boat to her own camp. The heavily wooded slopes resplendent with majestic fir trees, the clean, white sands of the narrow beaches along the water's edge, and the cool,

deep blue spring-fed water of the lake obviously had a profound effect upon him.

When he returned to his office in Hollywood, he prepared his drawings for the project, which, along with cabins in the forest and on the lake included an inn that would have been located on a small island in the bay, connected to the mainland with a long pier. Few drawings survive for the inn, but several remain that detail the cabins for the forest, the shore, and on the lake. Clearly some of them reflect an inspiration derived from the fir trees that flourish in the region. His draftsmen at that time were Kameki Tsuchiura

Far left: Plan for "Cabin Lodge Type."
FLLW FDN # 2205.024
Left: Elevation for "Cabin Lodge Type."
cabin. FLLW FDN # 2204.022
Right: Perspective of the "Cabin Lodge"
type cabin. FLLW FDN # 2205.001.

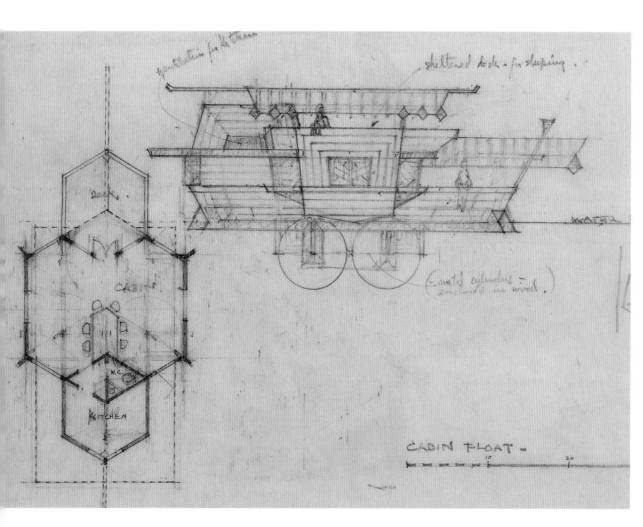

Above: Elevation and plan for
"Floating Cabin" type cabin.
FLLW FDN # 2205.008.
Right: Perspective for
"Floating Cabin" type cabin.
FLLW FDN # 2205.004.

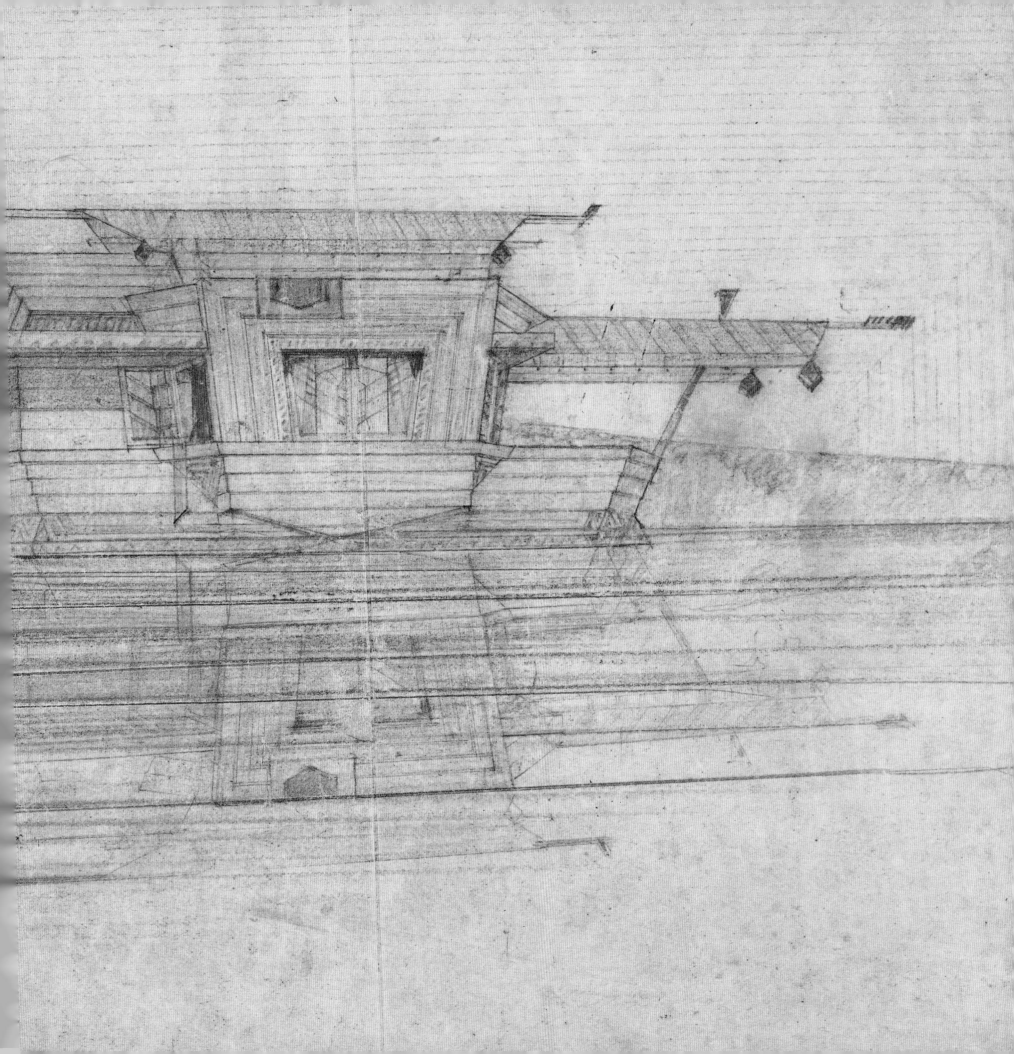

Conceptual sketch perspective for "Shore" type cabin. FLLW FDN # 2205.007
Right: Finished perspective for "Shore" type cabin. FLLW FDN # 2205.003

and his wife Nobu. Wright brought them back with him on his last return from Japan to America. They both were highly skilled artists, and it was Nobu who prepared some of the final perspectives for the Lake Tahoe project. She frequently included in the drawing, a figure holding a parasol as evidence of her work (opposite page). [9]

Beyond a great many conceptual sketches and several final renderings, nothing further exists for the project—no development drawings or construction details. Obviously the project was abandoned at an early stage. Ten years later, in a letter to his client Aline Barnsdall, he wrote:

"The Tahoe buildings were good form arising out of the nature of materials, circumstances, and site. I should say you had picked the place, up on a mountainside—that would be ideal for you. Why don't you buy the Emerald Bay property? There is nothing like it in the world for beauty I believe and it shouldn't cost much now? The Tahoe designs were tentlike and terraced—and belonged with the big trees—round about them. I loved the whole thing and was broken hearted when I discovered the realtors were merely exploiting my name to serve their own ends." [10]

Three cabin types are here illustrated: "Cabin Lodge Type" (pp. 264-5), "Floating Cabin" (pp. 266-7), and finally, "Shore Type" (above, and opposite page).

TAHOE CABIN - White Sand Black...
SHORE TYPE

Black technique
Taliesin

AUTOMOBILE OBJECTIVE AND PLANETARIUM

For Gordon Strong
Sugarloaf Mountain, Maryland. 1925, Project

Gordon Strong owned a tract of land leading up to and including the top of Sugarloaf Mountain in Maryland. He knew of Frank Lloyd Wright through his Chicago friend Albert Johnson, who had been a client of Wright's for an office building in Chicago. (See p. 370.) Strong was desirous of establishing a tourist facility at the top of Sugarloaf Mountain, and he approached Wright with the prospect of designing such a structure. The site was located in an area where motor travel is possible both from Washington, D. C., and Baltimore. Therefore, the automobile played an important role in this particular design. This greatly appealed to Wright, a fervent collector of fine cars, and the project was titled "Automobile Objective and Planetarium."

The automobile's role, so to speak, was more than just a means to get to the site, but rather to become an important part of the experience, and a feature of the building itself. From the outset, as his early studies (at right and on p. 272) clearly reveal, he envisioned a circular structure surrounded by spiral ramps: one for the vehicles to ascend, another for them to descend, and a third for pedestrians, situated as a balcony overlooking the vehicle ramps, thereby safe from the traffic.

As the scheme progressed, the interior was reserved for a large planetarium which rose through the entire structure (p. 273, top). On this particular drawing he has shown the planetarium on the right side, with supplementary supports for the ramps and other elements in the plan, yet on the left side, the dome of the planetarium becomes the main supporting element throughout. The intention for the use of the exterior ramps was threefold: cars would drive to the top, turn around, and descend taking in the view all the while. Or, passengers could vacate their cars at the top, an attendant would then drive the cars down to a parking lot at ground level, and tourists would descend on the pedestrian ramp, able thereby to take in the vast

2505.23

Small Scale Study
(Birds eye.)

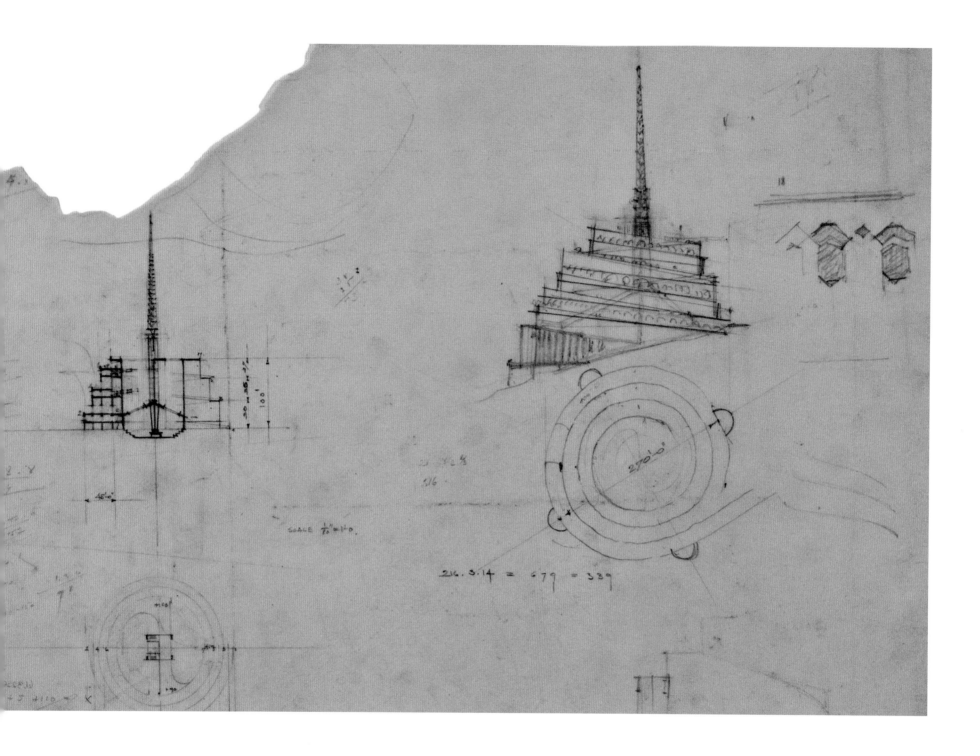

forests and streams from and around the mountaintop. Arriving inside, they would enter the planetarium or any of the two restaurants. An aquarium was also planned for the interior as well as other exhibits from the natural world. Here, then, was a structure offering an experience of seeing the earthly splendors from the mountain top, the starry skies, and the watery world within the building: an education as well as pleasure of the wonders of Earth and universe.

However, as Wright's drawings were developed into greater detail, Strong began to have doubts about the feasibility of the opus, even accusing Wright of creating a Tower of Babel. He finally decided to discharge his architect, and the project was never built.

Yet the idea must have appealed to Wright, even when it was defeated. Twenty-two years later, the concept of a great building—a mega-structure—enclosed by a spiral ramp for automobile access was vastly amplified from this Gordon Strong project to the largest single structure of Wright's career, the Pittsburgh Point Park Civic Center.

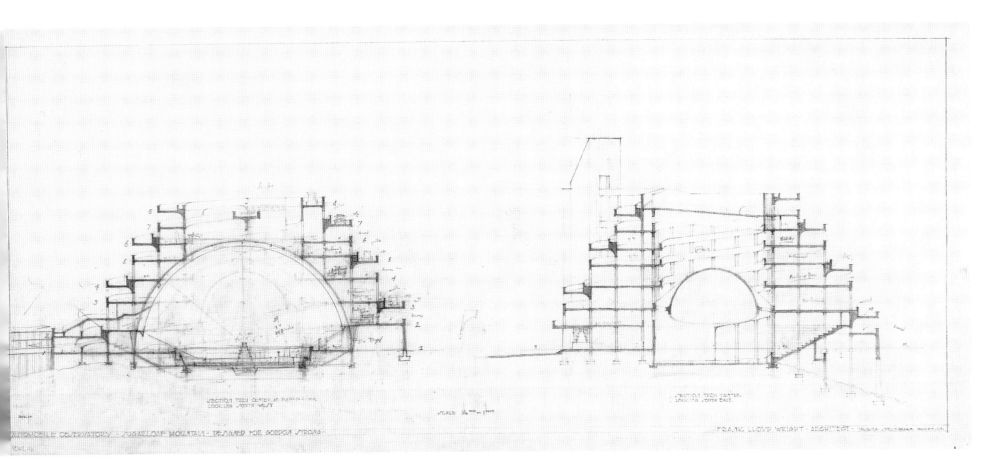

AUTOMOBILE OBSERVATORY · SUGARLOAF MOUNTAIN · DESIGNED FOR GORDON STRONG ·

SECTION THRU CENTER OF PLANETARIUM
LOOKING SOUTH WEST

SCALE ⅛" = 1 FOOT

SECTION THRU CENTER
LOOKING SOUTH EAST

FRANK LLOYD WRIGHT · ARCHITECT ·

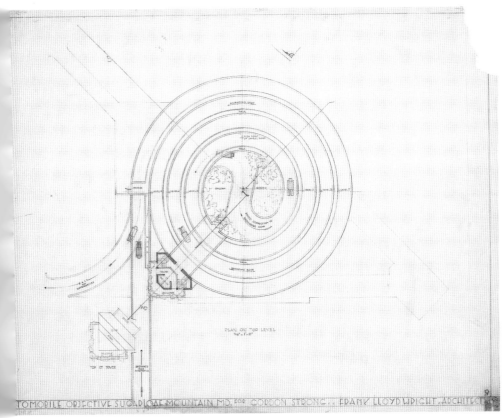

PLAN ON TOP LEVEL
¼" = 1'-0"

AUTOMOBILE OBJECTIVE SUGARLOAF MOUNTAIN MD. FOR GORDON STRONG ·· FRANK LLOYD WRIGHT ARCHITECT

Far left: Conceptual sketch elevation
and plan. FLLW FDN # 2505.018.
Above: Section showing planetarium.
FLLW FDN # 2505.034.
Left: Plan. FLLW FDN # 2505.04SR.

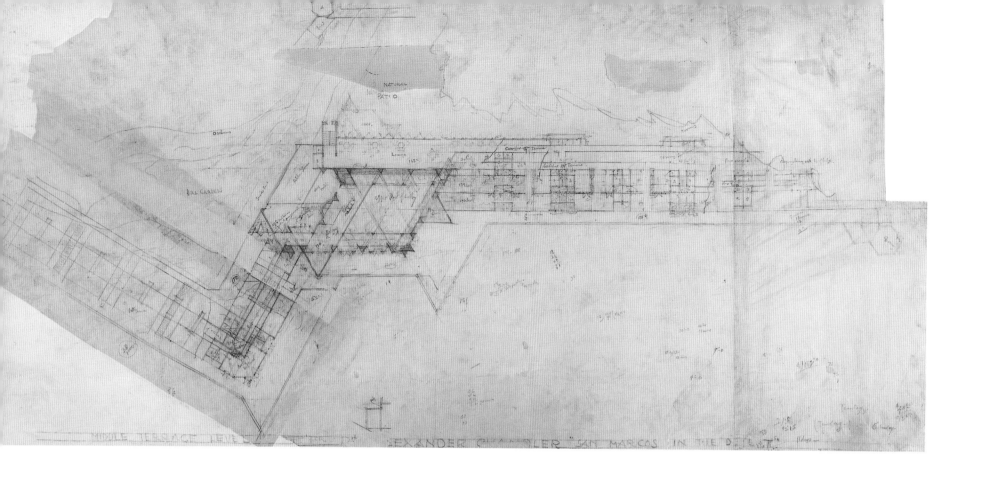

SAN MARCOS-IN-THE-DESERT RESORT HOTEL

For Dr. Alexander Chandler
Chandler, Arizona. 1928, Project

Frank Lloyd Wright's design for the resort hotel San Marcos-in-the-Desert was the apotheosis of concrete block construction. A system which he had pioneered five years earlier in southern California was now brought to perfection in this project. Every single element with which to build the hotel was arduously worked out in minute detail. Twenty-two sheets of working drawings were made using a hard graphite pencil on tracing paper, so hard, in fact, that the paper was practically incised by the pencil, and without any erasures whatsoever. His cadre of draftsmen included Europeans as well as Americans, and this set of drawings is perhaps the finest example of remarkable draftsmanship in Wright's entire collection of drawings. Along with the main working drawing set, seventy sheets of drawings were devoted to the hundreds of concrete blocks for every conceivable detail imagined.

The client for this prodigious work was Dr. Alexander Chandler, a veterinarian from the east who moved to Arizona, founded the town that bears his name, and established citrus groves and cotton fields. He also built the luxurious San Marcos Hotel.

"A dream of Dr. Chandler's it seems as an undefiled-by-irrigation desert resort for wintering certain jaded eastern millionaires who preferred the dry desert to green, wet fields. He wanted to build this characteristic resort on a tract of several thousand acres in great stretches of pure mountain desert. The site was over there in the Salt Range ten miles from his San Marcos, a successful hotel in his little town. So, learning I was in the neighborhood, he came over to invite my little family to come with him and stay awhile to talk it all over at the pleasant, aristocratic, Hotel San Marcos.

"Dr. Chandler had certain definite ideas concerning this new desert resort. He said he had waited ten years before planning the building because he knew of no one who could give him what he wanted, unless I could. And he said this with his beautiful smile.

"Well, there could be nothing more inspiring to an architect on this earth than that spot of pure desert in Arizona he took me to see, so I believe. At last here was the time, the place, and here was, in Dr. Chandler, the man. And he looked like the man of strength and independent judgment always necessary to characterize a thoroughbred undertaking or in anything else. I went to work for him and with him, making the first sketches for the building while living by the seaside at La Jolla. Held off so long from active creation, I could scarcely wait to begin. I could not get the project off my mind. The sketches were

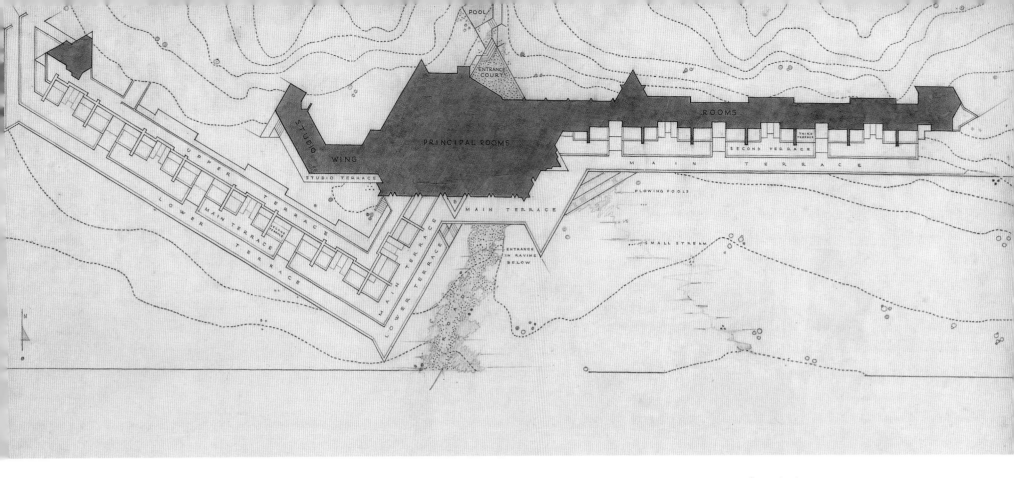

Left: Early plan. FLLW FDN # 2704.003.
Right: Early plan. FLLW FDN # 2704.052.

Following pages: Elevation.
FLLW FDN # 2704.007.

successful. And important too. I had pretty well mastered the block technique by this time— a good desert technique. With a man like Dr. Chandler to work for and this mastery I felt certain of results."[11]

Wright had been in Arizona at that time working for Albert Chase McArthur as a consultant on the Arizona Biltmore Hotel. While living in central Phoenix with his wife and family, he took motor trips out into the surrounding desert with its vast mesas and majestic mountains. He noticed that the vegetation in the desert, especially the cacti, all appeared constructed along dotted lines, never a hard straight line, and he reasoned that any building in that desert should also refute the hard, straight line to the more graceful dotted one. For one thing, in the hard, arid environment under a sometimes merciless sunlight, shadow was a welcomed relief, and the

dotted line made shadow more pleasant. He often called these dotted shadows that fell upon the desert floor "eye music," and he designed his desert building to have the same effect created by architectural forms and minute details.

He also studied the saguaro cactus, that great sculptural form rising like an ominous sentinel above all other cacti, with its ribbed sides and thorns. "The building was to grow up and out of the desert by way of desert materials. The block system naturally as the Sahuaro [sic] grew up. The Sahuaro should be the motif that inspired its style and the details."[12]

The site was up against the Salt Range Mountains, on a location where a deep ravine came down to a deep wash running along the desert floor. Since the ravine separated the mountain slopes in two directions, his first sketches (above) responded to this condition: the hotel was planned

to account for that change, a wing to the east in one direction, to the west for the other. The central portion (as seen on following page) rose over the ravine, a tall mass (again the Saguaro) would provide for a tower, in which there was to be an organ loft, with music drifting across the desert silence from time to time. The guest rooms ran along three terraces, each one further back along the slope so as to provide sun terraces with pools and gardens for each room. No overhangs or the protecting roofs so characteristic of his work, for here, in the winter, the warming sun was a welcomed relief. Since the desert nights are chilled, each room was provided with a small fireplace in which to take the chill off the night air. The central portion was for the lobby, called "Living Room," and there was a reception area, dining room, and other facilities for a resort hotel. The dining room on the top level had a "cathedral"

BLOCK DESIGN ⅛"= 1 FOOT

AN MARCOS IN THE DESERT · FOR · ALEXANDER CHANDLER · FRANK LLOYD WRIGHT · ARCHI

...CT • PERSPECTIVE FROM GATE LODGE

Left: Perspective. FLLW FDN # 2704.047.
Bottom: Perspective. FLLW FDN # 2704.048.

ceiling of copper and glass skylights in a richly geometric pattern.

A perspective (left, top) taken from the gate lodge reveals the opus stretched along the mountain slopes. The gate lodge was set far to the south of the hotel, where the guests arrived and parked their cars, to be shuttled to the hotel. The arroyo, or deep wash, became the road that entered under the central portion of the building.

"So, of course, it was all too good to happen. Sometimes I think it was just a dream. But here are the completed plans, there you may see the carefully studied details. Responsible estimates were complete; the contract was signed by Paul Mueller[13] the good builder, awaiting the Doctor's signature.

"Then at that moment as Dr. Chandler took the train to complete the arrangements for coming to build came the crash of 1929. Where was Dr. Chandler? Now instead of a $40,000 fee I found myself with a deficit of $19,000 to add to the mounting mountain of debt at Taliesin. $2,500 was all there was to set against the whole."[14]

The debt at Taliesin referred to its rebuilding after the dramatic fire of four years earlier. Now Wright had to abandon any hope of seeing San Marcos-in-the-Desert ever built, although for the next three years Dr. Chandler tried, in vain, to secure funding. In the meantime, Wright left Arizona, discharged his draftsmen, and with his family returned to the newly rebuilt Taliesin in Wisconsin. He would have no significant architectural work for five years.

Later, when writing about San Marcos-in-the-Desert, he concluded:

"I have found that when a scheme develops beyond a natural pitch of excellence the hand of fate strikes it down. The Japanese made a superstition of the circumstance. Purposefully they leave some imperfection somewhere to appease the jealousy of the gods. I neglected the precaution. San Marcos was not built. In the vault at Taliesin is this completely developed set of plans, every block scheduled as to quantity and place. These plans are one of our prize possessions."[15]

RALPH AND WELLINGTON CUDNEY HOUSE

San Marcos-in-the-Desert
Chandler, Arizona. 1928, Project

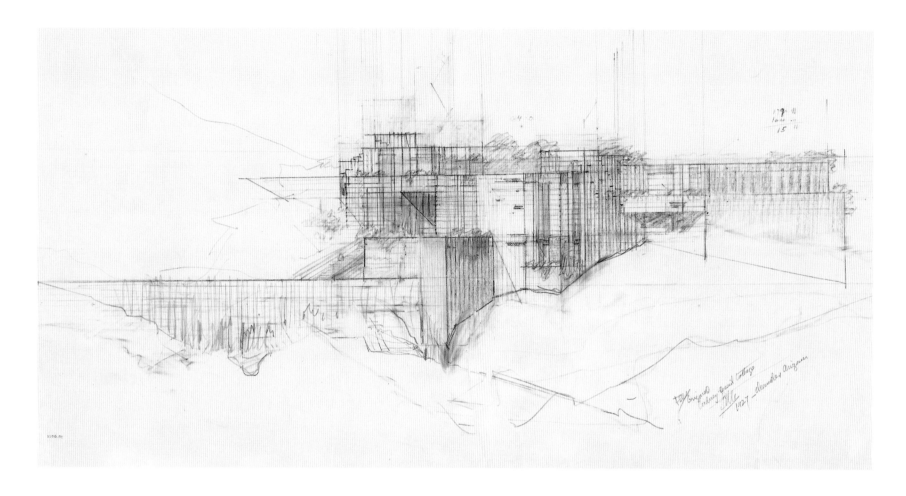

Owen D. Young and Ralph Cudney, both from the East Coast, both philanthropists, were two men whom Dr. Chandler had commandeered to help raise funds to construct San Marcos-in-the-Desert. Each family also desired a winter home in conjunction with the hotel, one at each end.

The client for the Young House, according to the title sheet on the drawing, was Mrs. Young, while the Cudney House was for Ralph and Wellington Cudney. Both schemes employed concrete blocks, but in the design for the Young House, Wright devised a system of block construction in which the blocks were turned at a 45-degree angle. This resulted in an extraordinarily novel appearance, and one might justly wonder how it could ever be constructed, but no further designs explain how this would happen.

The Cudney House made use of the same blocks as the hotel and was planned, like the hotel, on a 60-30-degree triangle grid. On one of the San Marcos-in-the-Desert perspectives (p. 278, top), the Cudney House can be seen at the far eastern edge of the drawing.

With the demise of the hotel following the stock market crash, these residences also fell victim to the same fate.

Above: Elevation.
FLLW FDN # 2706.001.
Right: Perspective.
FLLW FDN # 2706.007.

SAN MARCOS IN THE DESERT "SAHUARO"

FOR WELLINGTON AND RALPH CUDNEY   FRANK LLOYD WRIGHT ARCHITECT

THE STANDARDIZED SERVICE STATION

1932, Project

Below: Elevations.
FLLW FDN # 3206.021.
Right: Plans and early elevation.
FLLW FDN # 3206.002.

Wright's cousin Richard Lloyd Jones, for whom he eventually designed a large home in Tulsa, Oklahoma, was the editor and publisher of the *Tulsa Tribune*. Through business connections, he knew the officials of the Skelly Oil Company, and based on that connection, he encouraged Wright to make some preliminary designs for a service station. The usual service station, or gas station, of that time was a rather ugly makeshift nondescript cabin. Given Wright's strong conviction that the automobile could free the American family from the confines of the city, it was only natural for him to welcome the chance to design a more attractive station. "Public service stations now no longer eyesores but expanded as good architecture to include all kinds of merchandise, appear as roadside service along the roads for the traveler."[16]

The most unusual features of this gas station are the overhead supply hoses carried along cantilevered beams, the nozzles of the hoses fitting into a drain receptacle at ground level when not in use. The plan of the station itself is composed of two squares offset from each other, the lower square at ground level houses the service section, with counter, cash register, and cases for merchandise. Steps down a half-level access a storage room. On this lower level behind the storage room is a space for the attendant, with a cot and small lavatory. Steps on either side mount to the rest area, again a half-level up above the lower storage room. Here there is a small room with seats and a display table, with a deck for further display and restrooms for women and men. Planting boxes soften the structure of concrete and steel. The cantilevered beams are counterbalanced by a concrete mass, or anchor, over the restrooms.

To add a decorative element to the scheme, the steel cantilevered beam has steel or copper inserts in a geometric pattern. The copper roof over these beams is also richly ornamented.

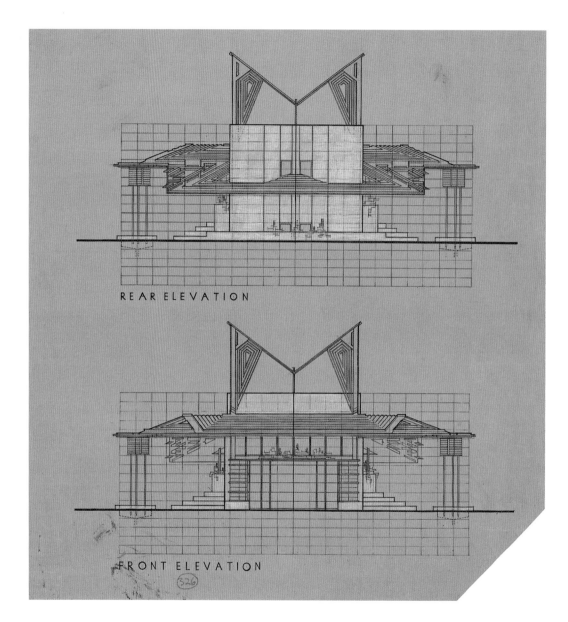

REAR ELEVATION

FRONT ELEVATION

Sheet steel was then coming into use, and Wright has made innovative use of it in this project. The station was designed to make use of prefabrication, Wright's solution of what he termed as the factory coming to the site with the materials ready to be assembled. No particular location was denoted for the project, indeed Wright envisioned these stations as planted all across the nation in multiple applications, with provisions to expand as needed for each particular circumstance. The prefabricated nature of their construction prompted him to refer to them as "standardized."

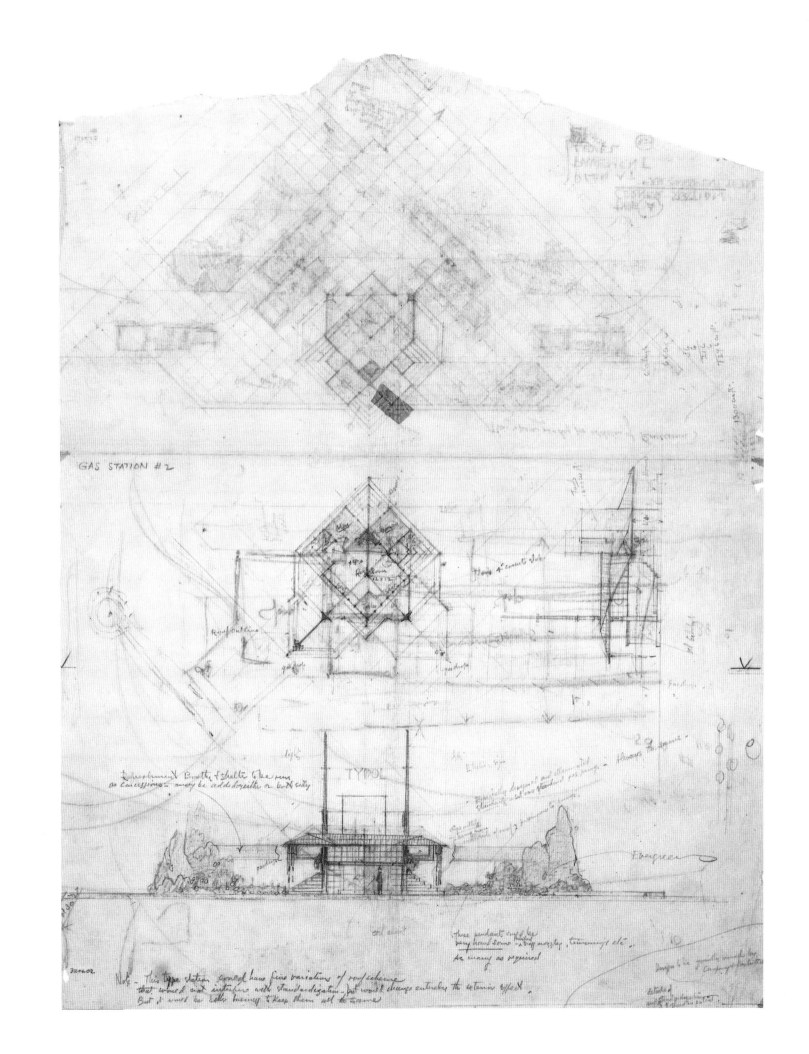

GAS STATION #2

TYDOL

CENTURY OF PROGRESS

Chicago World's Fair, 1933
Chicago, Illinois. 1931, Project

Below: Elevation for scheme 2. FLLW FDN # 3103.001.
Right: Elevation and plan for skyscraper (or scheme 1). FLLW FDN # 3103.003.

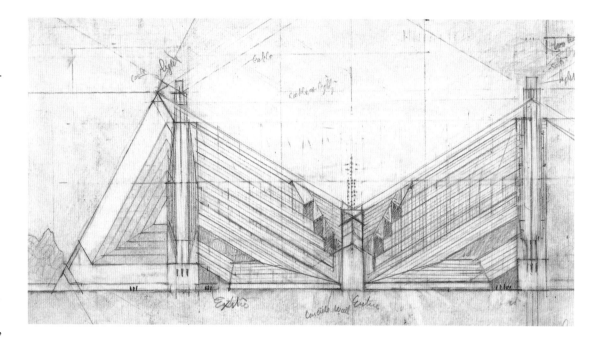

In 1931, a group of architects began formulating and assembling material for the 1933 world's fair to be held in Chicago under the name "Century of Progress." Paul Cret, the architect who was selecting the other architects, proposed that Wright be selected as one to design a structure for the fair. The other architect on the selection committee was Raymond Hood, who was also a personal friend of Wright's. Hood responded to Cret by saying that Wright was temperamentally unsuited to work on this commission. As he wrote to Wright, "I felt that you were a strong individualist, and that if an attempt were made to harness you in with other architects, the result would be more apt to be a fight than a fair."[17]

Nevertheless, although he was not selected, in an address to the American Union of Decorative Artists and Craftsmen (AUDAC) on February 26, 1931, Wright outlined what his proposal would be for the fair.[18] Since most fairs were constructed of materials that could be easily taken down once the fair was ended, he presented three possibilities, each of which would be a permanent structure available for other uses after the fair was over. His designs included a skyscraper, a series of connected steel and translucent fabric pavilions, and a series of floating pontoons out on Lake Michigan moored behind a breakwater.

For the skyscraper design (opposite page), he counted the stories to add up to 175. At various setbacks as the building rises, he has indicated six garden restaurants. He has also indicated certain spaces as 20 feet high with "galleries" running all around. For parking, he planned four terraces extending out on all sides around the building. He located the building adjacent to the waterfront of Lake Michigan and indicated a harbor for watercraft with docks and wharves to access the tower. Off to the side, he has sketched in the Empire State Building rising just a little over halfway up his own tower. "Every floor

would be a practical resource for future affairs of every sort. The business of the city itself might move into it with all its multifold minor branches. Still there would be room enough left for a mighty, continuous, never-ending industrial fair that would embrace the products of the entire civilized world in Chicago. Something accomplished worthy of a century of progress?"[19]

Scheme two (above) in the fair contained pylons, each one 500 feet square, and composed of steel cables carrying a translucent fabric canopy, as a glass substitute, rising 500 feet. The canopies are arranged in such a way that rainwater would cleanse them and cascade down into fountain basins at ground level. The geometry of this particular scheme is much in the same character as that of the Steel Cathedral (p. 168). On the drawing, to illustrate the sense of scale, at the base of the pylons, on ground level, he has indicated people with small dots. Further describing the scheme, he wrote, "All trees, foliage, and waterways could be combined for the beholder

by moving walkways to reach the individual plots allotted to the individual exhibitors. Little footwork. Each individual exhibitor would thus be free to set up his own show and ballyhoo it how he pleased."[20]

The third scheme he proposed was one in which the fair is set on pontoons in a protected harbor on Lake Michigan. The drawing for this (not shown) lacks the detail and explanations that he produced for the other proposals, but his description in his autobiography fully explains his idea for the project.[21]

There are no dates on the drawings for these proposals, but since Wright explained his plans, verbally at that meeting of February 26, 1931, it is most likely that upon returning home to Taliesin he then put the ideas down on paper. This would place the design in the early part of 1931, most likely sometime in March or April as this is when Wright finally returned to Taliesin after two long months of traveling.

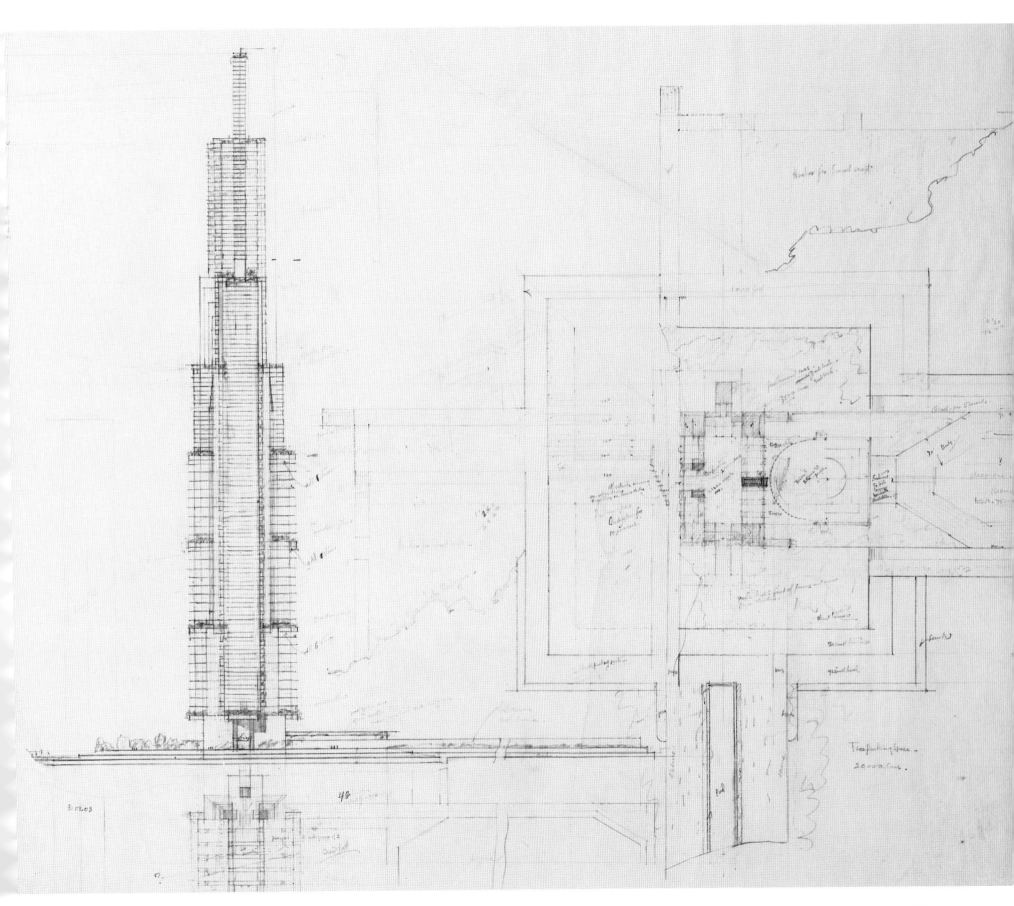

DESERT SPA

For Elizabeth Arden
Phoenix, Arizona. 1945, Project

Elizabeth Arden, the cosmetic queen, ran an establishment called Maine Chance in Mt. Vernon, Maine, where women of substantial means came to lose weight, recover from cosmetic surgery, or become rejuvenated. She also ran a series of salons called Red Door. These were located in cities all across the nation. She revolutionized the use of cosmetics, which before were relegated to makeup for the entertainment industry. Instead, she provided makeup for women not involved with the stage or screen. She eventually opened and ran another Maine Chance similar to the one in New England, located in the outskirts of Phoenix, Arizona, up against the spectacular Camelback Mountain. In 1945, desiring to enlarge the spa with a new building, she commissioned Wright to prepare some sketches for her.

Apprentice Eugene (Gene) Masselink, who was also Wright's secretary and business manager, wrote of Arden's arrival at Taliesin West: "Yesterday Mr. Wright and I went in to the valley to collect items of beauty for decorating the house. Elizabeth Arden and some Count and others of note were expected to dinner." [22] (The "count" was her second husband, a Russian prince.) Gene's letter went on to recount, "Elizabeth Arden is a tremendous disappointment—I had expected an elaborate horse—with many trimmings—she is just a frustrated looking mousy business woman—slight of build with no style whatsoever. She certainly is the product of her own fabulous advertising. The others were nondescript too. The Count is a mess." [23] A second letter went on, "Mr. and Mrs. Wright were invited to her place for lunch. She bought 37 acres there and two houses and is commissioning Mr. Wright to build a hundred thousand place. We came back to pick them up and they were just having dessert so we were asked in—very fancy barbeque arrangement but the people were swell —two nieces of Arden and both very pleas-ant—one is a singer-actress understudy for Dorothy McGuire in 'Claudia' and Jean Arthur—also reducing—but awfully sweet and nice." [24]

On April 9, 1945, Gene also wrote to Jack: "Mr. Wright is at work on the Arden project. It is of sandblasted concrete covered with roof gardens of flowers and looks like almost anything from an elaborate private residence to a 'spa.'" [25] His first sketch elevation (opposite page) reveals the garden-like nature of roofs and planting all around. The perspective further emphasizes this. The drawing of the mountains was by Wright, and the circle cut into the paper represents the sun (or the moon, as the case may be) (pp. 288-9).

However, after their meetings, Wright sensed the equivocal nature of Elizabeth Arden, and also perceived that what she wanted was not really what he was proposing—she wanted a house just for the purpose of selling. It was the type of speculation that was odious to him and two weeks later the project seemed to have come to an abrupt end.

Gene wrote, "Elizabeth Arden and her retinue came and went on Sunday afternoon—evidently that is that—she doesn't know WHAT she wants—doesn't like Arizona—and the plans Mr. Wright had prepared aren't what she expected—wants a house she can sell—it is just as well. I also I think she is a plenty tough customer—more of a plumber than a beautician." [26]

Thus what would have been a most exciting structure in an extremely beautiful setting was lost. However Wright included the Arden Spa in the January 1948 *The Architectural Forum* and wrote thus of the project:

"Elizabeth Arden made an excursion to Taliesin West with the high purpose of doing something for her clientele in the Arizona desert as inspiring in point of appropriate relationship to environment as is her practice with female recon-stitution. Soon, all mixed up where that affair was concerned, we lost sight of her. The arrangement is sufficiently obvious, the roof in the instance becoming earth-on-terrace and developing as an overall garden. It would seem that the fundamental error in this essay lay in the emphasis placed on sunlight when twilight or moonlight was preferable. Project abandoned."

Yet, for some inexplicable reason, after the issue was closed, he sent the original perspective to Arden with this note attached: "My dear Elizabeth Arden: So many fine things are born into 'the Here' and vanish . . . pass on into an unrealized Future—probably the best things of all do so? . . . This being 'just one of those things' at which you glanced in passing—I thought you might like to see it again—just because. Frank Lloyd Wright, Taliesin West, April 27, 1945."

SUN LIGHT
FOR ELIZABETH ARDEN

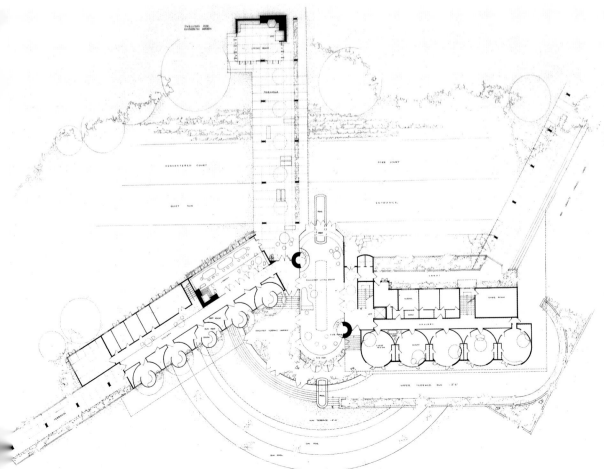

Above:: Elevation. FLLW FDN # 4506.001.
Left: Plan. FLLW FDN # 4506.009.

Following pages: Perspective. FLLW FDN
4506.002.

4506.02

MOONLIGHT
SUNLIGHT   FOR ELIZABET
             PRELIMINARY
             FRANK LLOYD

ARDEN
TUDY
RIGHT

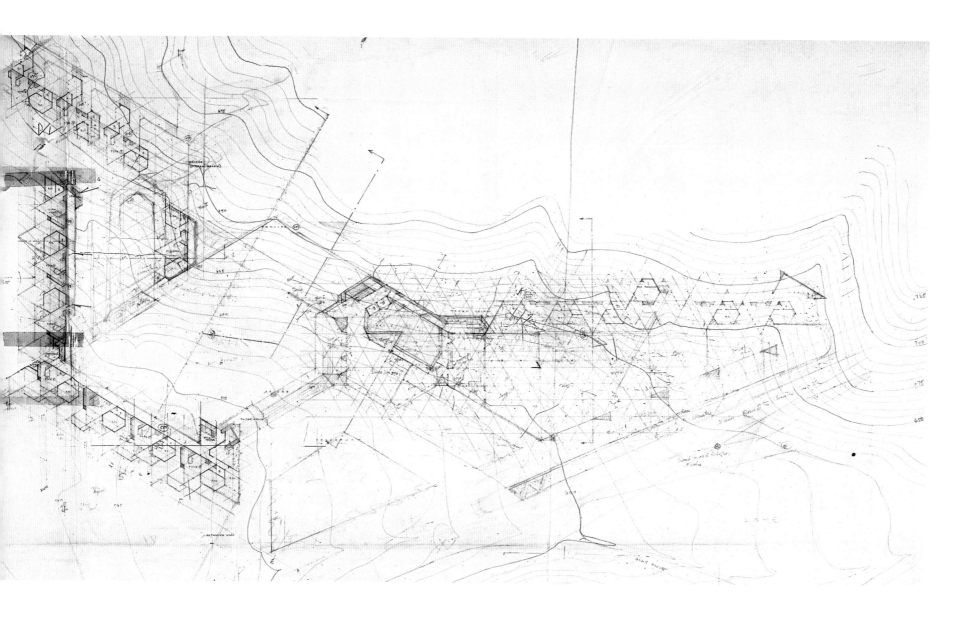

COTTAGE GROUP HOTEL, SCHEMES 1 AND 2

For Huntington Hartford
Los Angeles, California. 1947–48, Project

George Huntington Hartford II was heir to the vast Great Atlantic and Pacific Tea Company, which was known as A&P Grocery Stores. With over 16,000 stores in the United States, it rivaled General Motors as the largest retail chain in the world. Huntington Hartford soon dropped the name George; his personal fortune was estimated at $700 million. A man of diverse interests, along cultural lines, he built a theater in Los Angeles and a museum in New York City. Along the lines of development, he acquired Hog Island in the Bahamas and renamed it Paradise Island. Projects connected with this venture fell through, and he lost an estimated $25 million. This seemed to be a pattern in his life wherein several of his schemes were doomed to fizzle out and continually deplete his fortune.

The project he commissioned Wright to design was to be located in Runyon Canyon (later named Runyon Park). Situated in the Hollywood area of Los Angeles, it was close to the metropolitan part of the city. Hartford asked Wright to design a hotel (there were two versions of this), a sports club, and a residence for himself in this area. A brochure that Hartford put together about the hotel stated: "Completely secluded because of its fortunate and unusual topography, this sequestered canyon is nevertheless but four blocks from La Brea and Hollywood

COTTAGE GROUP CENTER FOR HUNTINGTON HARTFORD
FRANK LLOYD WRIGHT ARCHITECT
LLOYD WRIGHT ASSOCIATE

Left: Preliminary sketch plan of scheme 1.
FLLW FDN # 4721.006.
Above: Perspective for scheme 1.
FLLW FDN # 4721.035.

boulevards. Thus is made possible a fine metropolitan hotel retaining for itself and the community the beauty, health, and pleasure of a large acreage covered with century-old sycamores and pines. No city in the nation enjoys so near its center a hotel as refreshing and country-like."

The plan for the hotel was labeled "Cottage Group Center" rather than the conventional "Hotel." To be sure, there was a main section that provided reception, offices for the staff,

lobby, dining room, cocktail lounge, outdoor terraces, and a swimming pool. Grouped on the various levels of the steep hillside were cottages containing units of two or three bedrooms and sitting rooms connected by walkways to the main body of the hotel. The cottages also provided facilities for preparing meals. The entire group provided accommodations for approximately 130 guests, a rather small, perhaps elite, number considering the expansive, and complex,

nature of the design. Wright's first sketch plan (opposite page) explains the way in which he has positioned the hotel and cottages in careful relation to the topography of the site while the overall perspective (above) emphasizes the building's relationship to the lay of the land as well as the natural features. Although thirteen preliminary drawings were made and then signed by Wright on October 27, 1947, and presented to Hartford, Wright felt that a new scheme would be

291

infinitely more appropriate to the situation. It was a matter of light.

With the first scheme, on the west side, sunlight would pour into the rooms of the guests as it rose in the east. With the second scheme, placed on the east slope, the sun would rise behind them and cast light on the west canyon wall with all its sycamore and fir trees. Hartford was opposed to this change of location, preferring the original west side. Wright admonished him in a letter, saying:

"The assumption is that you are happier in a room looking out of sun into a dark landscape than you are in a room in shadow looking out into bright landscape."[27]

The letter was written scarcely one month after the first proposal had been made, and evidently the second solution was already in Wright's mind.

In both schemes, the main entrance and parking was on the ground level at the entrance to the canyon. With the Cottage Group Center moved to the east slope, the connection to the various cottages was closer and in better relation to the main body of the hotel. The basic accommodations were the same as in the original proposal. From the point of view of light, in Wright's way of thinking, along with the beauty of the rising sun illuminating the western slope in abundant light, sunsets would likewise be more enjoyable to the guests as the sky and clouds put on a splendid array of color and drama. Again, for the second proposal, he had made his plan on the topographical survey (not shown). A developed section (opposite page) explains the position of the hotel in relation to the mountain slope. One perspective is taken at the entrance (pp. 294-5) with a view of the sports club high on the upper left side of the drawing. A full front perspective (below) follows.

Below: Perspective for scheme 2.
FLLW FDN # 4837.047.
Right: Sketch elevation for scheme 2.
FLLW FDN # 4837.014

Following pages: Perspective.
FLLW FDN # 4837.046.

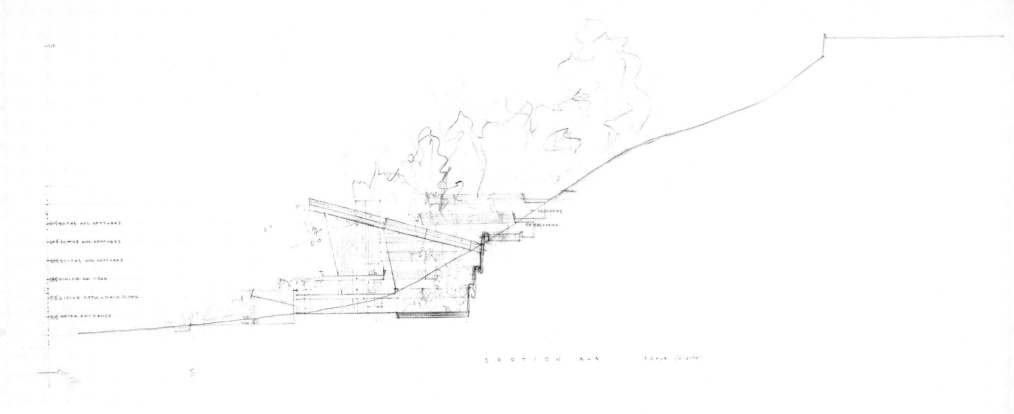

SECTION A-A   SCALE 1/8"=1'0"

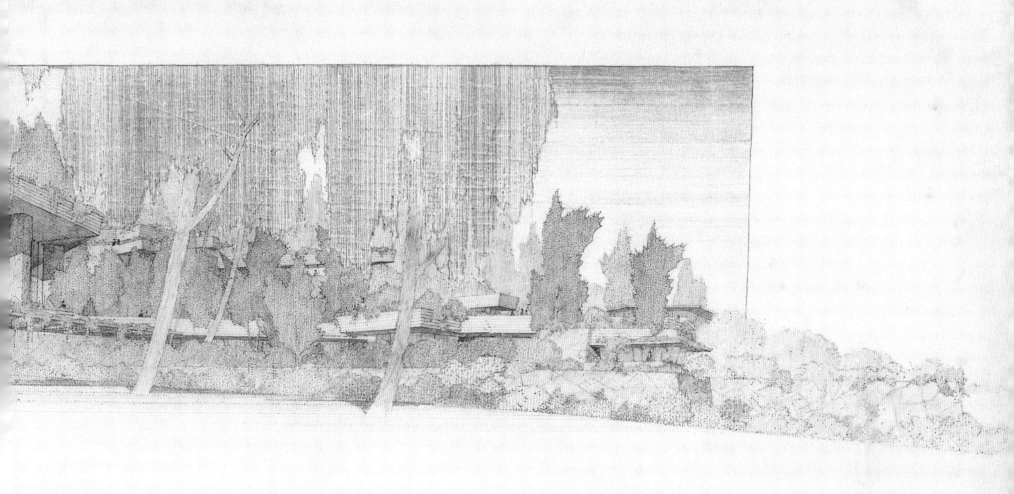

V I E W   F R O M   E N T R A N C

C O T T A G E   G R

F O R   H U N T I N G T O

F R A N K   L L O Y D   W

L L O Y D   W

4837.046

E D R I V E

U P   C E N T E R

N H A R T F O R D

R I G H T   A R C H I T E C T

R I G H T   A S S O C I A T E

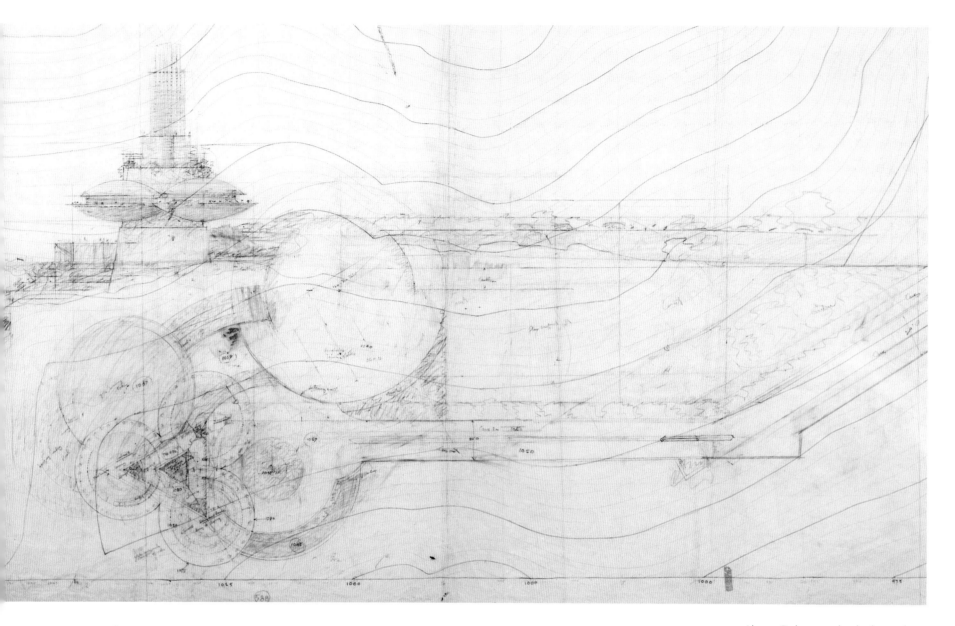

PLAY RESORT AND SPORTS CLUB

For Huntington Hartford
Runyon Canyon
Los Angeles, California. 1947, Project

At the very apex of the canyon, looming out over the trees, Wright proposed one of the most radical, innovative, and extravagant designs of his entire career. The client, ambitious and flighty, along with his hotel at the entrance to Runyon Canyon, asked Wright to design a sports club —play resort—for the use of tournament tennis and in general a good-time place for guests in the hotel. Wright's design featured three great disks springing out of a solid masonry core: one disk for dining and dancing, another for a lounge, and the third for cinema. Each disk was roofed with shallow domes of concentric circles set with glass tubes, similar to the ones he employed in the Johnson Administration Building and Tower. Each disk also had an outside balcony for viewing the expansive canyon below. At the top, a smaller disk was reserved for sunbathing.

His first sketch (above) contains both the plan and elevation of the project. A tall tower is seen rising out of the building, but his next elevation (p. 299) does away with the tower and clearly shows the main disks and the sunbathing disk at the top.

PLAY RESORT IN HOLLYWOOD HILLS FOR HUNTINGTON HART
FRANK LLOYD WRIGHT   LLOYD WRIGHT ASSOCIATE

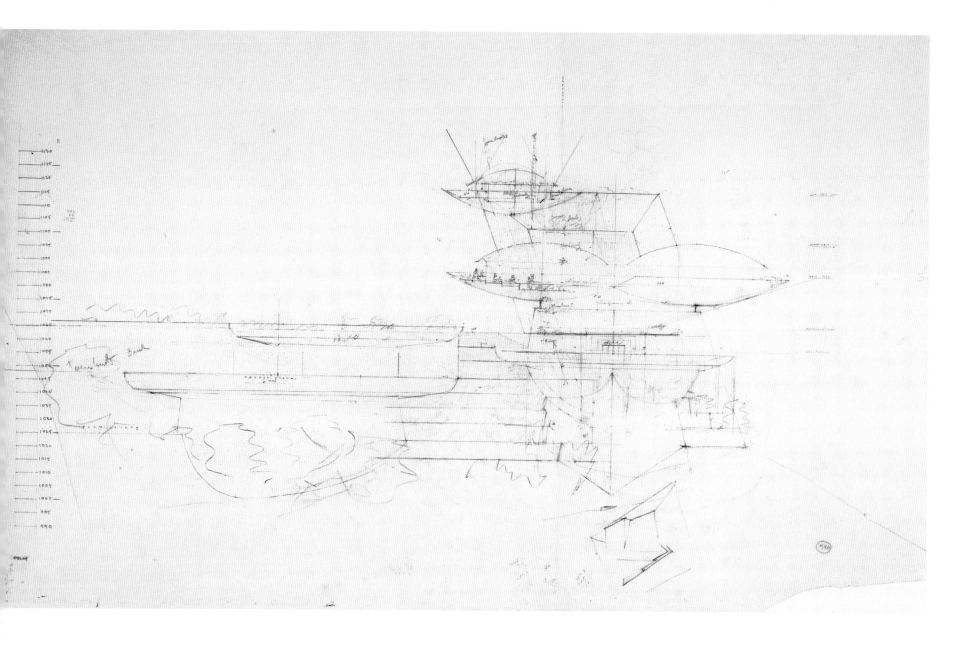

In the masonry core were provisions for entrance lobby, office, card room, pool room, kitchen, changing rooms for the outdoor swimming pool, and a two-level apartment for Hartford himself. Extending out along the hill slope adjacent to the play resort was a special court for tournament tennis with viewing stands on each side, and further, other play courts, for tennis, badminton, and croquet.

What prompted this design? It came as a result of a terrible tragedy that struck Wright and his family when their older daughter Svetlana and her two-year-old son Daniel were killed in an automobile accent on the highway near Taliesin in 1946. On the sunset terrace at Taliesin West, Wright erected, as a monument to her, a redwood triangle, about three feet tall, that carried three shallow disks made from plowshares. Painted his typical Cherokee red, they held oranges and grapefruit brought from the orchard of his son David Wright in Phoenix. When citrus was not in season, glass bowls, such as those fishermen used to float their nets, were placed there instead. On the redwood base was inscribed in gold leaf "Svetlana."

One day, when Wright was out on the terrace, he looked at the memorial and thought to himself, "This would make a great building."

Obviously Hartford did not think so, and all the work on Wright's part was for naught, but on record is a fine collection of most dramatic and impressive drawings.

Above: Elevation.
FLLW FDN # 4731.004.
Right: Elevation.
FLLW FDN # 4731.002.

Following pages: Perspective.
FLLW FDN # 4731.020.

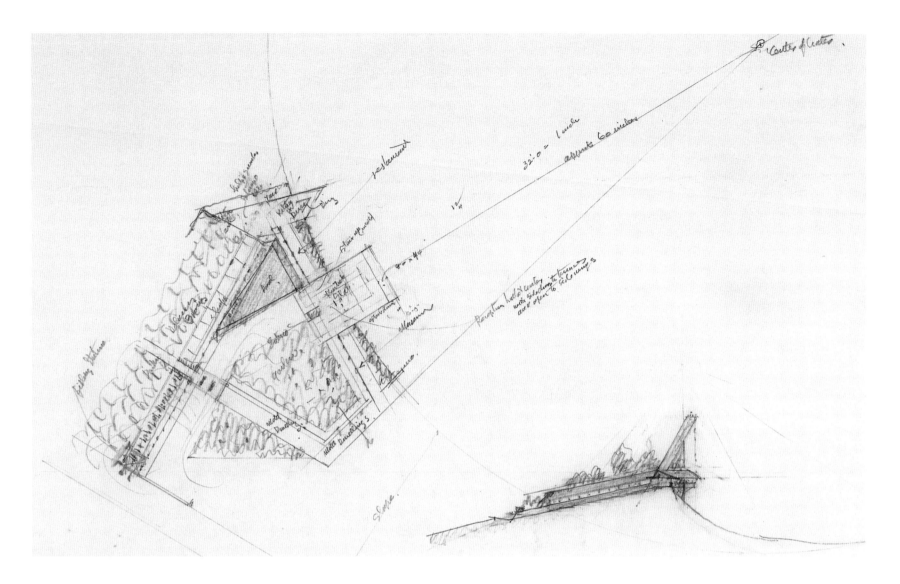

RESORT INN AND TOURIST FACILITY

For Burton Tremaine
Meteor Crater, Arizona. 1948, Project

Above: Preliminary sketch plan and
elevation. FLLW FDN # 4822.003.
Right: Plan. FLLW FDN # 4822.008.

Approximately 50,000 years ago, during the Pleistocene epoch, a gigantic meteor struck the desert in northern Arizona. The meteor vaporized on contact, but left a crater 4,000 feet in diameter and 170 feet deep—the depth of a seventeen-story building. It was first discovered by European settlers in the nineteenth century and considered to be the result of some volcanic action, not meteoric, and controversy prevailed over the years. The realization that it was indeed a meteor that made the crater was finally proven in 1960 when research revealed that the formation of rare silica in the crater could only have been accomplished by an impact of great magnitude and at a speed of 28,600 mph (or artificially by a nuclear explosion).

The property around the crater remained in private control, until it was designated a National Natural Landmark in 1967. In 1948, however, it was owned by Burton Tremaine. He and his wife Emily were philanthropists and avid art collectors, amassing a great collection of paintings by living artists such as Jasper Johns, and other works by Braque, Picasso, and Paul Klee. In the Spring of 1948, they wrote to Frank Lloyd Wright that they wished to build a visitor center on the rim of Meteor Crater. On May 17, he signed the perspectives that his apprentice

John Howe had prepared and took them to New York to show the Tremaines.

The impact of the meteor had caused the rim of the crater to rise up slightly from the desert floor to the edge. This condition prompted Wright to design a building that would follow the slant of the site, rather than bulldozing it away to make it flat or placing a building on stilts so that it, too, could be totally horizontal. In other words, it is a clear example of how Wright appraised a given circumstance and made the best of it. At the very edge of the rim, he designed a tall stone structure that provided a high vantage point looking over the crater and

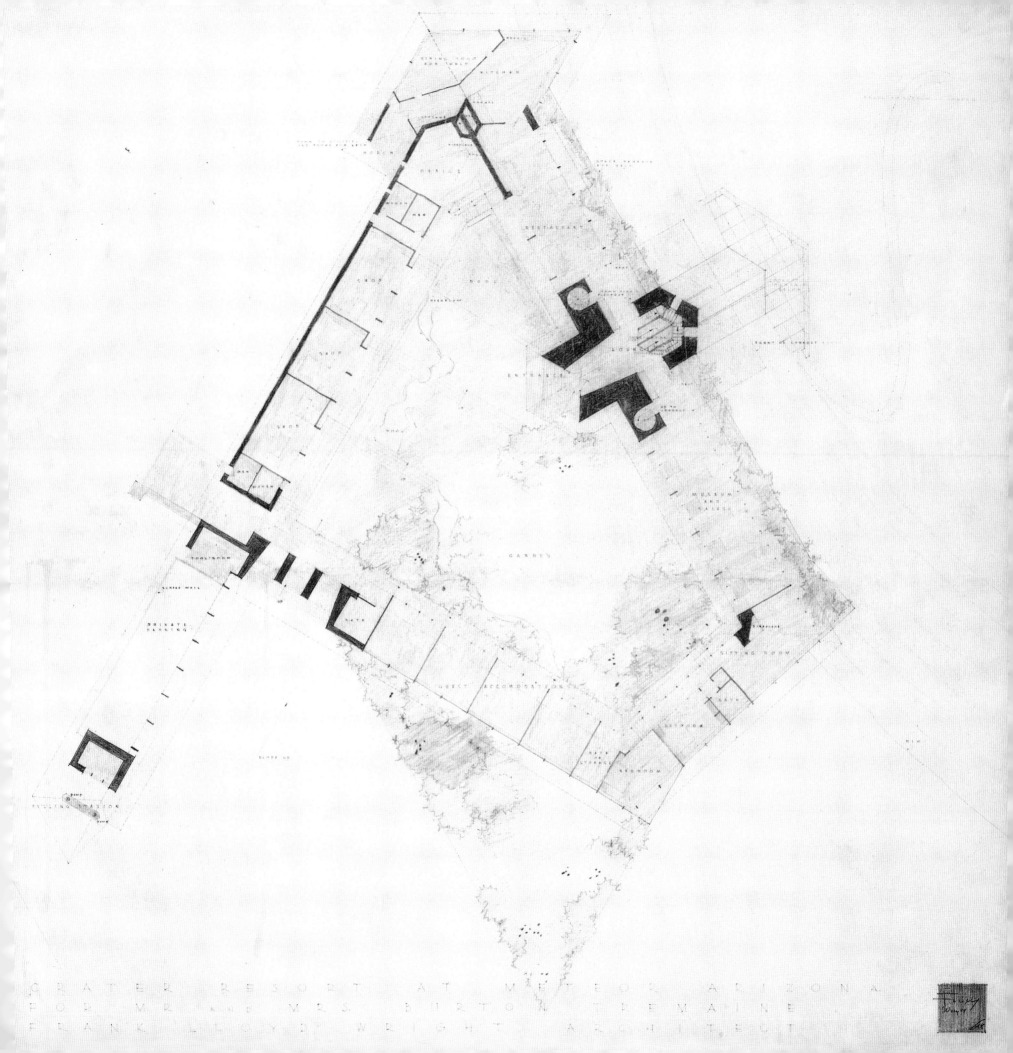

CRATER RESORT AT METEOR ARIZONA
FOR MR AND MRS BURTON TREMAINE
FRANK LLOYD WRIGHT ARCHITECT

at the same time clung to the edge of the rim and rode it down to the base of the crater. With this provision, tourists could either climb up stairs to the top of the stone mass or descend down and step out onto the crater itself (right and p. 1). Other provisions were designed for the usual tourist center, to include a restaurant, shops, a museum, and guest accommodations.

The commission was fraught with difficulties and misunderstandings. Although the Tremaines were pleased with Wright's preliminary plans and even asked to publish them in a book about their other art collections, to which Wright acquiesced, they were alarmed at his fee of 3 percent of the estimated cost, or $1,500 for the structure of $50,000. They declined to pay, having consulted other contractors in New York who came up with a figure of $200,000. This infuriated Wright, since most of his life he was aware of the cost of building his buildings, whereas many contractors tended to be immensely skeptical. When he located a contractor who better understood the work, he usually took that contractor on for other jobs as well, a practice he had begun in his early years in Oak Park. With the Tremaines he was adamant about his fee, and a great deal of work had gone into the project, including detail sections and elevations right from the very beginning. He then suggested they build in sections. They reneged, but eventually paid him $750 for the work and returned the drawings to his office, telling him that they considered any obligation or contractual arrangement between the Tremaines and Frank Lloyd Wright as terminated. Knowing of their connection to the Brazilian architect Oscar Niemeyer, Wright's final letter to them suggested, "Now why don't the Tremaines try Brazilian Rococo."[28]

The commission lasted exactly one year from the first communication to this final one. In Wright's work, however, this is a significant building in that it is a "cliff-hanger" designed a few years after the V. C. Morris House, his first cliff-hanger. Both represent remarkable solutions to dramatic sites in which the buildings do not impede upon the natural conditions, but respect and glorify them.

AT METEOR ARIZONA
BURTON TREMAINE
RIGHT ARCHITECT

NEW SPORTS PAVILION

For Harry Guggenheim
Belmont Park, New York. 1956, Project

Below: Preliminary sketch elevation.
FLLW FDN # 5616.001.
Right: Section. FLLW FDN # 5616.012.

Following pages: Perspective.
FLLW FDN # 5616.020

Frank Lloyd Wright regarded the miracle of steel as "the spider spinning." In other words, steel was not treated as timber, the way it had been traditionally employed ever since its discovery as a building material, formed as a post-and-beam construction—old wooden post-and-beam of ancient times.

"I love the natural materials for their beauty and their character and I use them continually, but the structural materials in my category now are fully the steel strand. Steel strands on which you can pull, buried in concrete which is the flesh. Just the way you're made and the way God made you is the way I want to make a building."[29] One example of how he admired the steel strand was its use in a suspension bridge. He said of John Roebling's Brooklyn Bridge that Roebling was the first prophet of steel in tension.

Harry S. Guggenheim, the nephew of Solomon F. Guggenheim, took a profound interest in racehorses and racing. Along with that interest, he wanted to see a newer and finer stand for spectators, and he asked Wright to design a new building for Belmont Park. Wright's design made full use of the steel cables that supported the gigantic canopy over the spectators. This was a project very dear to him for two reasons: one, Guggenheim played a key role in the final stages of the design for his uncle's museum, standing by Wright's desire to see the building built, and two, Wright again made a feature architecturally as well as structurally for the steel strand in a most innovative and imaginative way. Concerning the project he wrote:

"The New Sports Pavilion (for racetrack and other sports), Belmont and Aqueduct. New York. A Massive slab, with four levels reached by twelve or sixteen escalators (depending on size of stand), covered by a translucent plastic roof, suspended on a lacework of slender tensile steel cables. There will be no pillars of any kind,

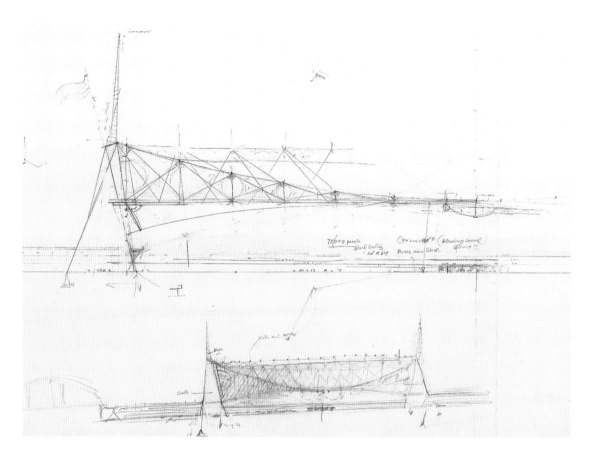

affording total visibility for 65,000 or 80,000 people. Parking space for from 3,500 to 5,000 cars, again depending on the size of the structure. Two tall towers situated at end of stand are to be banked with floodlights capable of lighting the entire structure, the illumination pouring through the translucent roof. Water pipes embedded in the floors at the various levels will carry hot water to warm the structure in cold weather. All wagering facilities, restaurants, snack bars, and restrooms will be directly under each bank of seats or boxes on four levels with easy access from the seats, arranged to eliminate long queues. A structure that is organic in character, and this principle can be applied, and

ultimately must be, to every human endeavor architecturally."[30]

His first preliminary study (above) shows the elevation of the project, with a closer elevation drawn above it detailing the network of steel cables. At the bottom of the drawing he has lettered "The Manhattan Sports Pavilion" but in a later one he called it "The New Sports Pavilion." A section drawing (opposite page) illustrates the approach to the Pavilions via a series of escalators passing through and accessing the other facilities of the building. On the final perspective (pp. 308-9), Wright has again gone back to his earlier title and labeled the drawing "The Manhattan Sports Pavilion."

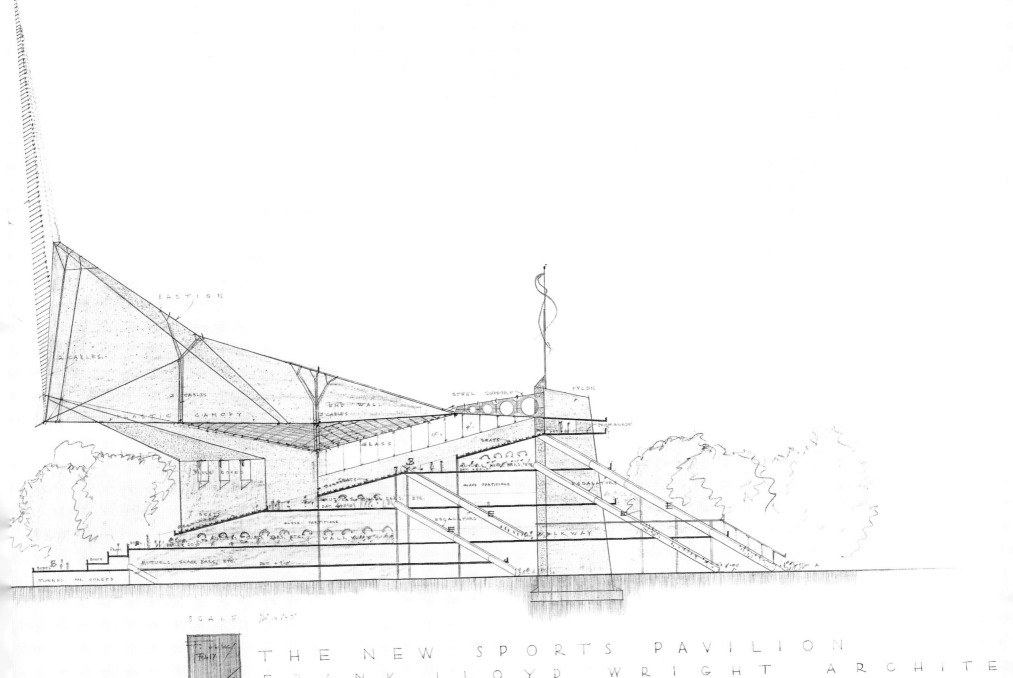

THE NEW SPORTS PAVILION
FRANK LLOYD WRIGHT ARCHITE

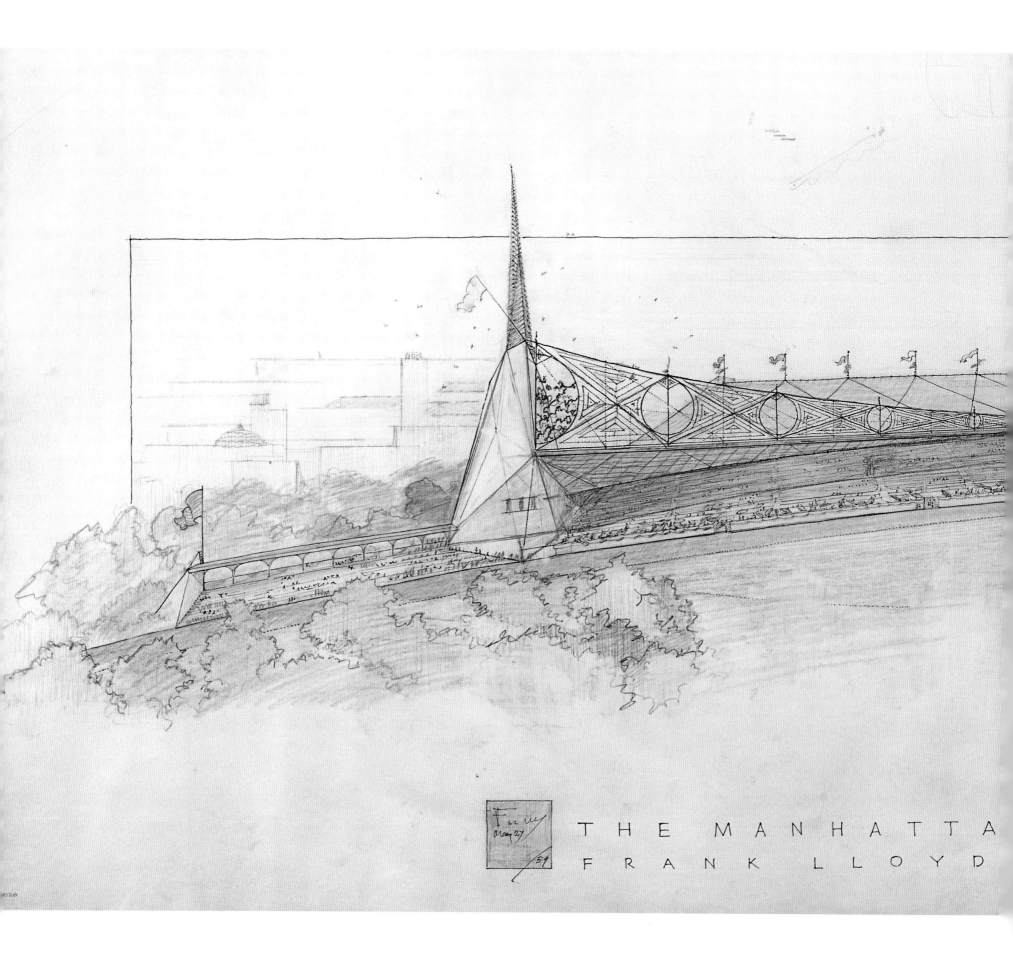

THE MANHATTA

FRANK LLOYD

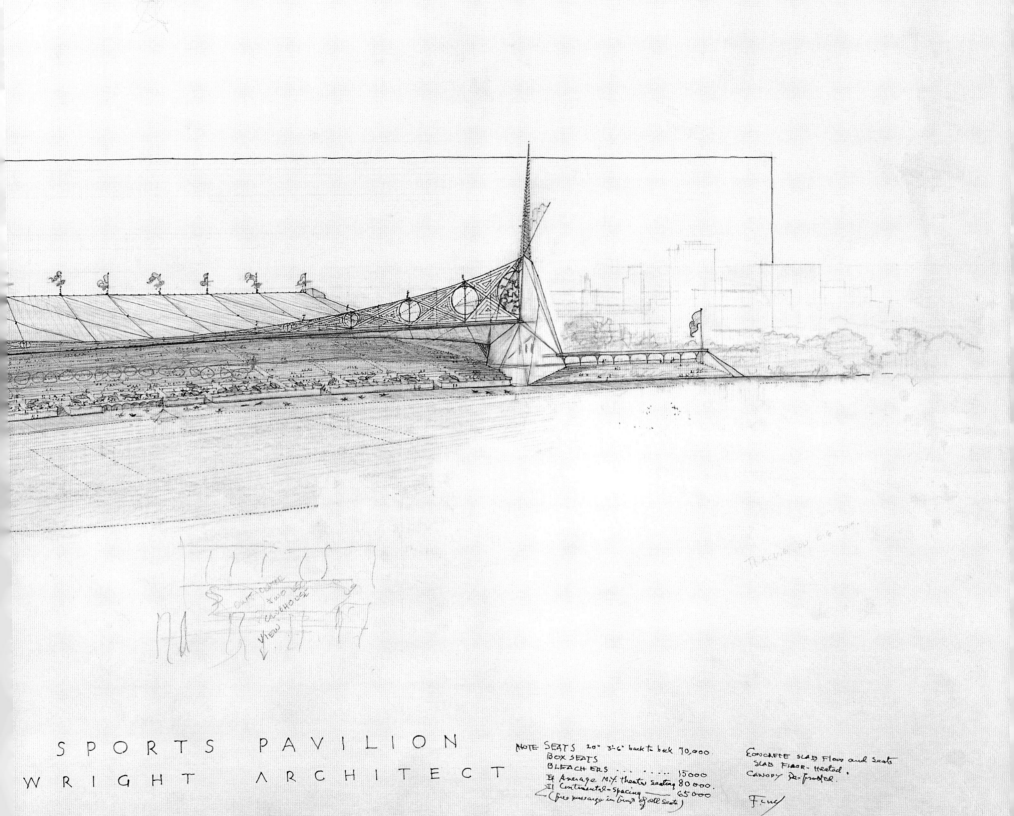

S P O R T S   P A V I L I O N

W R I G H T   A R C H I T E C T

NOTE SEATS 20" 3'-6" back to back 70,000.
BOX SEATS
BLEACHERS 15000
I Average N.Y. theater seating 80 000.
II Continental-spacing —— 65 000
(free passage in front of all Seats)

Concrete slab floor and seats
Slab floor- heated
Canopy See-proofed.

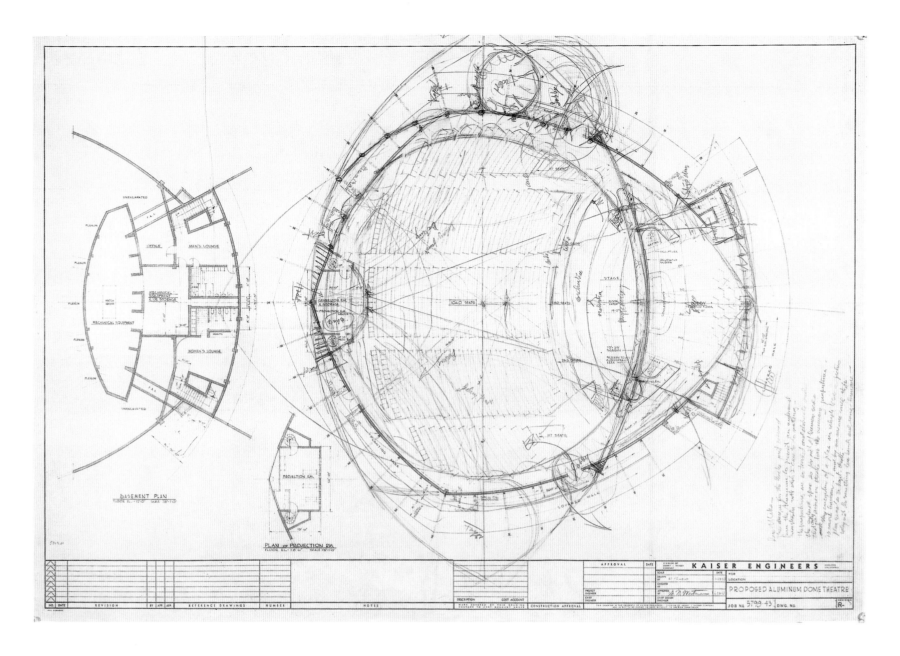

TODD-AO THEATERS

For Mike Todd
1958, Project

Michael Todd, best known as Mike Todd, was an American theater and film producer. In 1950 he formed the Cinerama Company along with Lowell Thomas and Fred Waller. Waller had invented the process of three cameras, using three films, to project one image from the three on a wide curved screen. There were certain flaws in the system, namely that it required expert skill in projecting so that the three would merge seamlessly.

Soon Todd left that company and developed a new widescreen process called AO, designed by the American Optical Company. This employed one projector with a special lens projecting a wide film on a large screen, without the seams that plagued Cinerama. Mike Todd then wished to develop a series of theaters, using prefabrication, and place them in shopping malls where the parking for theatergoers would be available at night, during the time when the stores were closed.

To accomplish this, he went into collaboration with Henry J. Kaiser, of Kaiser Aluminum, and Buckminster Fuller, the genius of the geodesic dome manufactured by Kaiser. The three of them then approached Frank Lloyd Wright to work with the existing plans and come up with a new design for the Todd-AO Theaters. The idea of designing a building that would make use of prefabrication—the aluminum dome and precast concrete panels for the walls, greatly appealed to Wright.

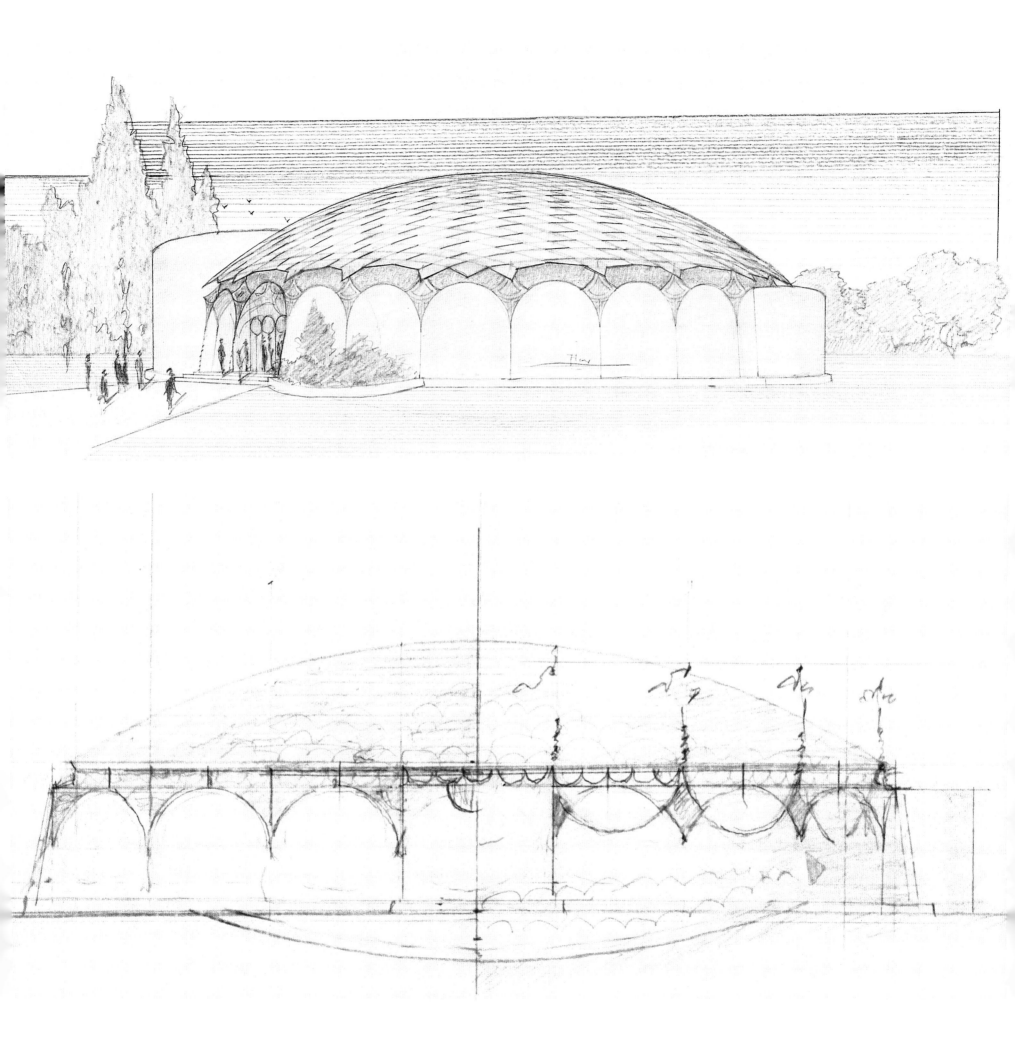

THEATER FOR MIKE TODD
FRANK LLOYD WRIGHT ARCHITECT

This was, however, an instance where a theater design had already been made and Wright's role was to modify and enhance it. The first thing he did, working on the prints that Kaiser Aluminum had sent him, was to modify Fuller's dome to bring it down to a more graceful proportion. This is evident as he set to work directly on the prints (p. 310) of the existing design that were sent to him.

In the final stages of the project, two theaters were proposed. One, in a complete circle, provided seating for 650. This was a version for cinema only (p. 311). A second proposal (above and opposite page) was considerably larger, basically circular in form but with extensions to provide facilities for dramatic productions, if desired. This larger version had seating for 1650.

Tragically Mike Todd, along with a screen writer, the pilot, and copilot, were killed when their private airplane crashed on March 22, 1958, near Grants, New Mexico. Certain Wright drawings also went down with the plane, but several others survived. Understandably, the sudden and unexpected death of Todd brought the theater project to an abrupt end.

Above: Perspective for second version. FLLW FDN # 5816.016.
Right, top: Perspective for second version. FLLW FDN # 5819.011.
Right, bottom: Perspective for second version. FLLW FDN # 5819.012.

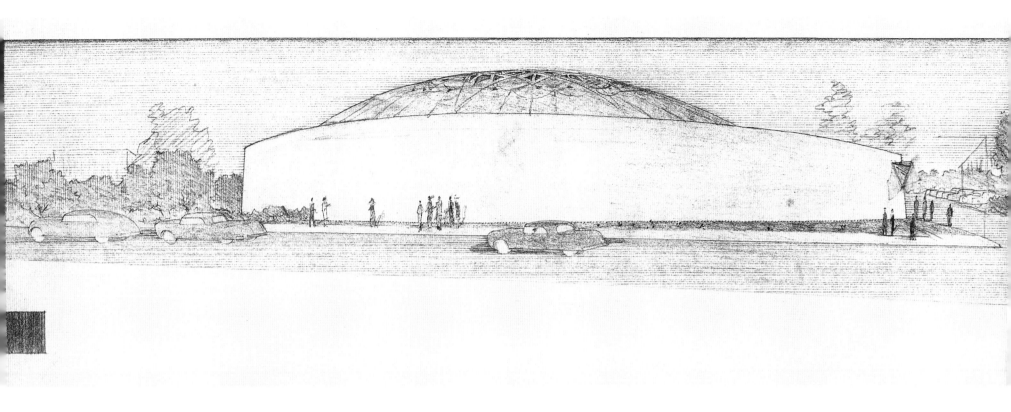

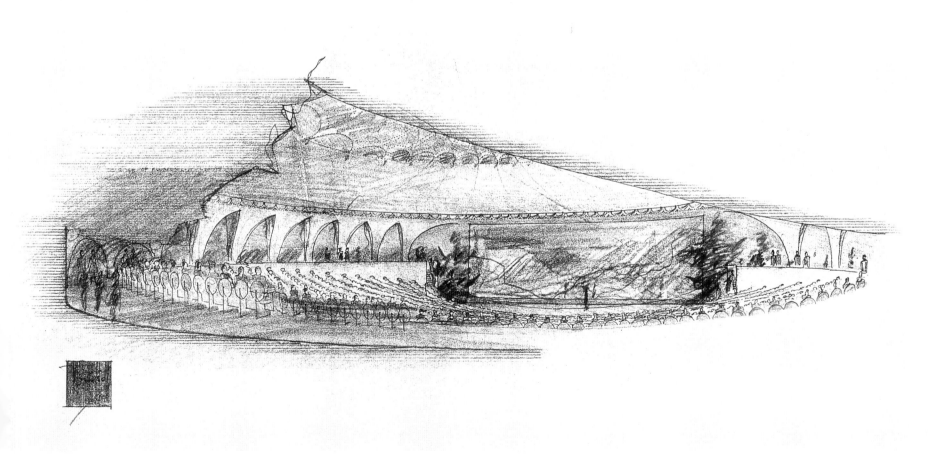

PART FIVE

BUILDINGS FOR COMMERCE AND WORK

Whether it was a building for commerce or a building for work, Frank Lloyd Wright strove to make it not only functional, but beautiful as well. Of his famous administration building for the S. C. Johnson & Son Company, he wrote, "Organic Architecture designed this great building to be as inspiring a place to work in as any cathedral ever was in which to worship."[1]

His first design for an industrial building was the office building for the Larkin Company, Buffalo, in 1903. The same principle at work, albeit thirty years later in the Johnson opus, was here applied for the first time.

He believed that a bank should evoke a sense of security in its overall design, "the village strong box" as he called it. For a bank in Mason City, Iowa, 1909, his commission required not only a bank, but a hotel adjacent and connected to it.

When the Johnson Wax building was complete, the company then requested a design for a research tower. This gave Wright the first opportunity to put into actual practice his theory of the taproot foundation.

A small dress shop for Leo Bramson, in Oak Park, Illinois, revealed his approach to a building located on a city street, crowded in on other sides by existing structures. This same condition prevailed when he made his design of the V. C. Morris Gift Shop in San Francisco, and the Anderton Court Shops in Beverly Hills.

The Valley National Bank, with branches in Tucson as well as in Phoenix, commissioned Wright for designs in both places. Here illustrated is the one he created for Tucson, which he named "The Daylight Bank" because of the great hexagonal skylight that provided light for the interior as opposed to customary windows—again emphasizing the feeling of the strongbox.

In 1955, Wright's design for the Lenkurt Electric Company, albeit an industrial factory, was nonetheless more in the nature of an office

building, and the same principle he applied to the Johnson administration building worked well in this particular application.

His design for the Arizona state capital provided him with the opportunity to create a beautiful government building for the state which he dearly loved and in which he spent his winters during the last twenty years of his life.

Of the eleven projects illustrated here, Wright was fortunate enough to see six of them go into construction, but he also lived to see the great Larkin Building demolished in 1950—truly a cultural tragedy if there ever was one.

Arizona State Capital
(see p.354). Perspective.
FLLW FDN # 5732.001.

314

LARKIN ADMINISTRATION BUILDING

Buffalo, New York. 1903, Demolished

Below: Perspective. FLLW FDN # 0403.010.
Right: Drawings for reception desk.
FLLW FDN # 0403.025.

Following pages: Perspective.
FLLW FDN # 0403.001.

The Larkin Company of Buffalo, New York, was a manufacturer and distributor of soap and other household products. In 1903 they were in need of a new administration building to house the officers and employees of the company and space for its business of responding to and mailing its products: an early example of the mail-order business. Darwin D. Martin was secretary of the company and was already a client of Wright's for a home he was building in Buffalo. His brother William had already built a Frank Lloyd Wright house in Oak Park, Illinois. Another officer in the Larkin Company, William Heath, was also about to build a Wright-designed home in Buffalo. Although Darwin Martin was assigned as the client for the new administration building, the final choice for architect would rest with John Larkin, the president of the company. Larkin was a deep admirer of Louis Sullivan, and realizing this, Wright's initial sketch for the building showed the annex, or entrance, enhanced by a large Sullivanesque arch (right).

Once the commission was gained, however, the arch was forgotten (pp. 318-9). What both Larkin and Martin wanted in a new building was a space that was clean, functional, and above all a healthy and inspiring place in which to work. Larkin, who remembered the great fire of 1951 that consumed Chicago, was also adamant that the building be fireproof. Thus, a steel-frame structure with brick interior and brick exterior seemed the perfect solution.

There is a revealing story behind one of the Larkin drawings (unshown), as told in a letter by the draftsman who made the drawing, Henry Klumb. In writing to the historian Donald Hoffmann, he explained: "Having come from Germany I was aware that in Europe, the younger architects, especially the critics (after the 1926 publication of *Frank Lloyd Wright* by H. Ds Fires) had a strong negative feeling about F. LL. W.'s spiritual and poetic exuberance inherent in his work, considering it an expression of the superficiality of American Culture. Anything that did not fit the contrived formula of intellectual rationalization was considered a crime against this rigidly adhered to formula of the ir two-dimensional architecture, the so called 'International Style.' Assembled and sitting with F. Ll. W. around a fire in the studio one winter day in 1929, discussing this and other matters of Organic Architecture, I suggested that we might try to reduce his delicate renderings of his best known buildings to a two-dimensional black-on-white graphic presentation *Modern Architect* were addicted to. His answer: "DO IT." Okami[2] and I went to work and produced several including in addition to the Robie House (drawn by myself), the Winslow House, Yahara Boat Club, Bock Atelier, Unity Temple, and the Larking [sic] Building. The result was that even the stark graphic black-and-white surface presentations did not produce a two-dimensional effect, but rather emphasized the depth of his poetry and the power of the third dimension. Nothing 'International Architecture' had to show could equal it."[3]

These drawings were included in the large exhibition of his work that traveled across the United States in 1930, and were shown in the same exhibition as it traveled to Holland, Germany, and Belgium in 1931.

This was Wright's first great industrial commission, and in it he pioneered along several new lines: one of them a system of air-conditioning.

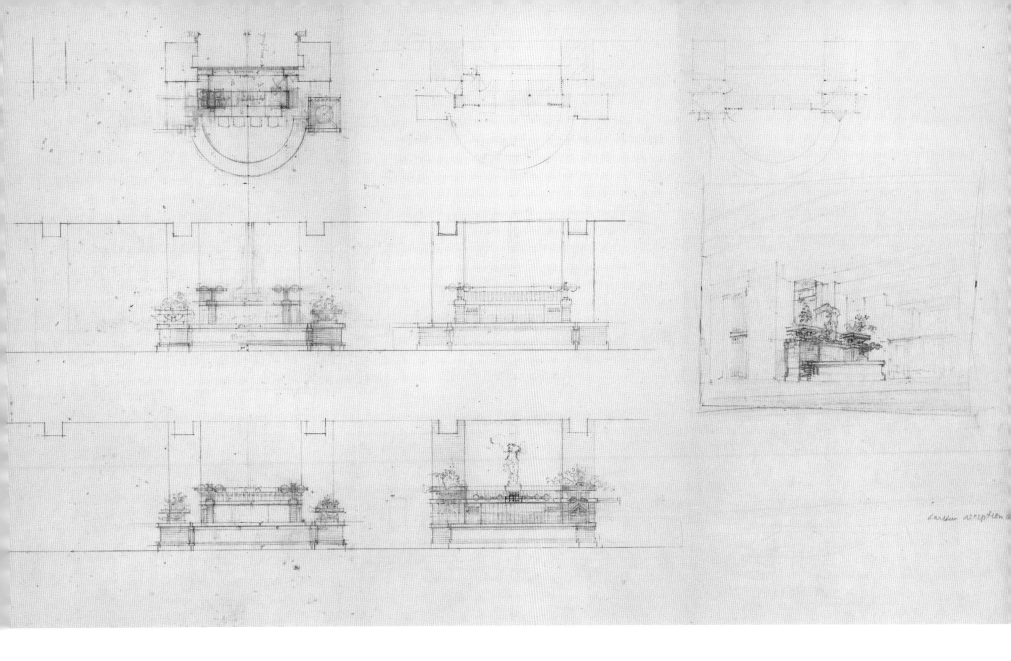

The building was located in the midst of railroad tracks and industrial factories. As such, he designed the building to be sealed from this environment, and air brought in was forced through a washing and filtering system, and then cooled or heated depending upon the season. He also devised the wall-hung water closet, along with wall-hung partitions in the toilets so that cleaning would be simpler and more efficient. The desks and chairs were made of metal, the first of their kind in the nation, and specially manufactured in Cleveland, Ohio. The chairs in many instances were hinged to the desk, this also to provide for easier sweeping and washing of the concrete floors.

On the drawing for the reception desk (above) Wright has made seven studies to represent seven solutions, and then he has drawn a thumbnail view of the desk he finally approves.

The exterior brick was red, but the interior was a soft tan color, to be more pleasing to the eye. Central to the building was a large five-story atrium, topped by a skylight. On the ground floor of this central court were the desks of the officials of the company, along with their support staff. The surrounding balconies provided desks for the employees who received and processed the mail orders. High windows, above the walls with built-in filing cabinets, provided daylight. On the top floor there was a restaurant with a pipe organ that played music during lunch, and a conservatory with plants. In the annex, as well as being the main entrance and reception, rooms provided for rest and relaxation, toilets and dressing rooms, a branch of the Buffalo Free Public Library, and classrooms. Employees were encouraged to attend classes whenever they could. This was indeed a revelation in the American work place, and Wright was central to this endeavor.

When the Larkin Building was published in the Frank Lloyd Wright monograph by Wasmuth, Berlin, in 1910, and again in a Wasmuth photographic publication of his work 1911, it exerted a strong influence on a new generation of architects and may be considered seminal to the burst of modern architecture as we know it today. Despite its influence overseas and its enthusiastic acclaim worldwide for several decades, in 1950 the building was demolished to make way for a parking lot.

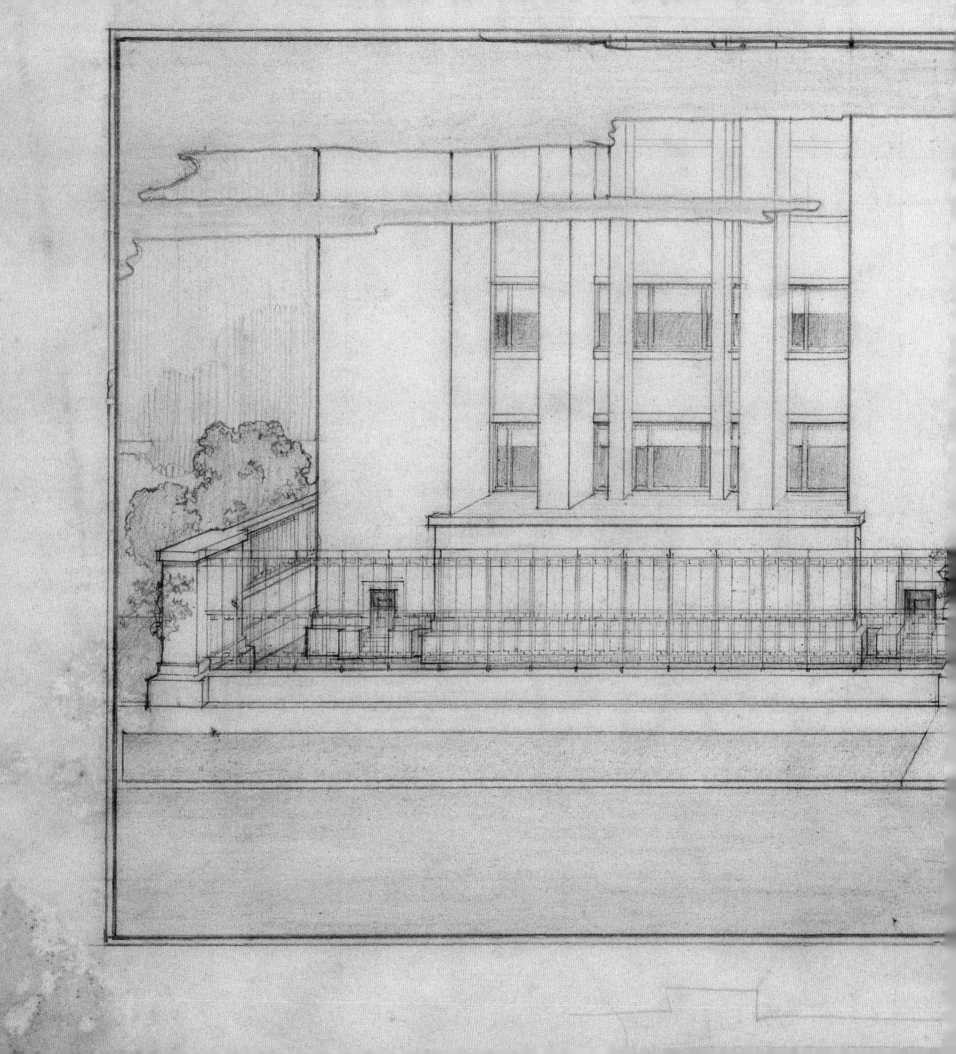

Larkin
1904-05
H.R.H.

CITY NATIONAL BANK AND HOTEL

Mason City, Iowa. 1909

Concerning the design of a bank building, Wright wrote: "While there is probably little romance about a bank—less poetry in the bray of Sancho Panza's substantial, positive gray donkey than in the sound of Rosinante's spirited neighing—yet the community likes to feel that that same bank is there to stay. It is, in fact, the town strong-box, and it is a temple to the God of Money, as modern temples go. This design has taken shape with some conception of the dignified character of the mercantile machine, and some concession to the time-honored love of ornament."[4]

This text referred to a design he first made in 1894 and called "One Story Concrete Monolith Bank," as one constructed in concrete but revised as one in brick in 1901. The somewhat monumental character for the design illustrated Wright's sense of a bank as a strongbox. It was never built (above).

However in 1909 a bank design of his was built, based on the some premise as the one of 1894–1901.

The commission for the City National Bank and Hotel was actually a three-part work: a bank, a hotel, and law offices for the clients of the entire scheme. The bank, situated on a corner lot, is three stories tall, with the third story relegated to offices while the bank is a two-story space lit by high windows. The strongbox atmosphere that Wright wrote about is achieved by the high brick walls with windows at the top set between brick piers. The ornamental aspect is achieved by the tile inlay in the piers, and the stained glass windows. At ground level, a monumental bronze gate at the entry emphasizes this sense of security.

The hotel design, with its projecting roofs overhead, a detail Wright consistently used in his residential work, and extensive plate glass windows at ground level, lends a more human scale and welcoming aspect to the project. The law offices are set between the bank and the hotel, and serve not only the purpose for which they were intended but also act as a separation between the mercantile and hospitality elements. The materials, however, and the way in which they are treated, connect the three elements into one cohesive structure.

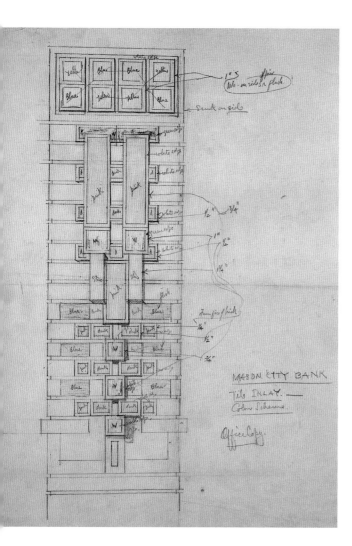

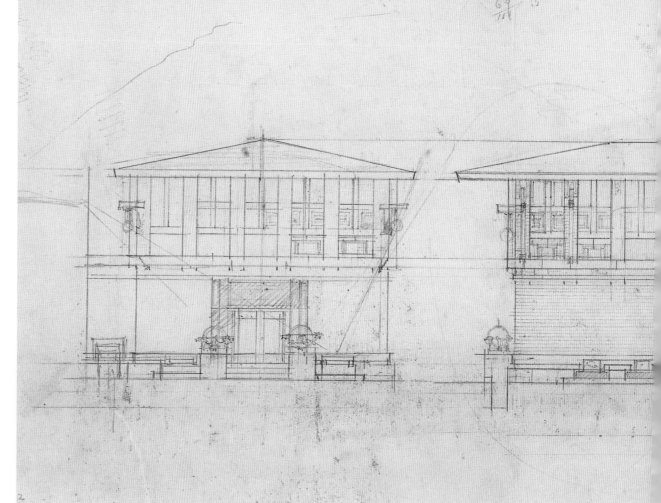

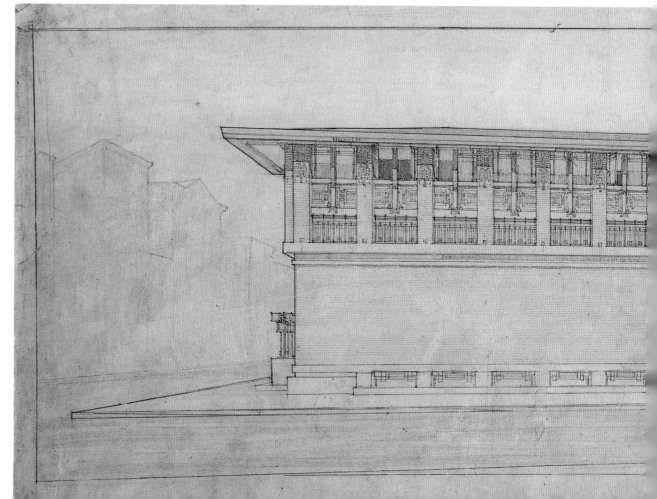

Above: Detail drawing of tile inlay
for bank piers. FLLW FDN # 0902.010.
Right, top: Elevation.
FLLW FDN # 0902.012.
Right, bottom: Perspective.
FLLW FDN # 0902.001.

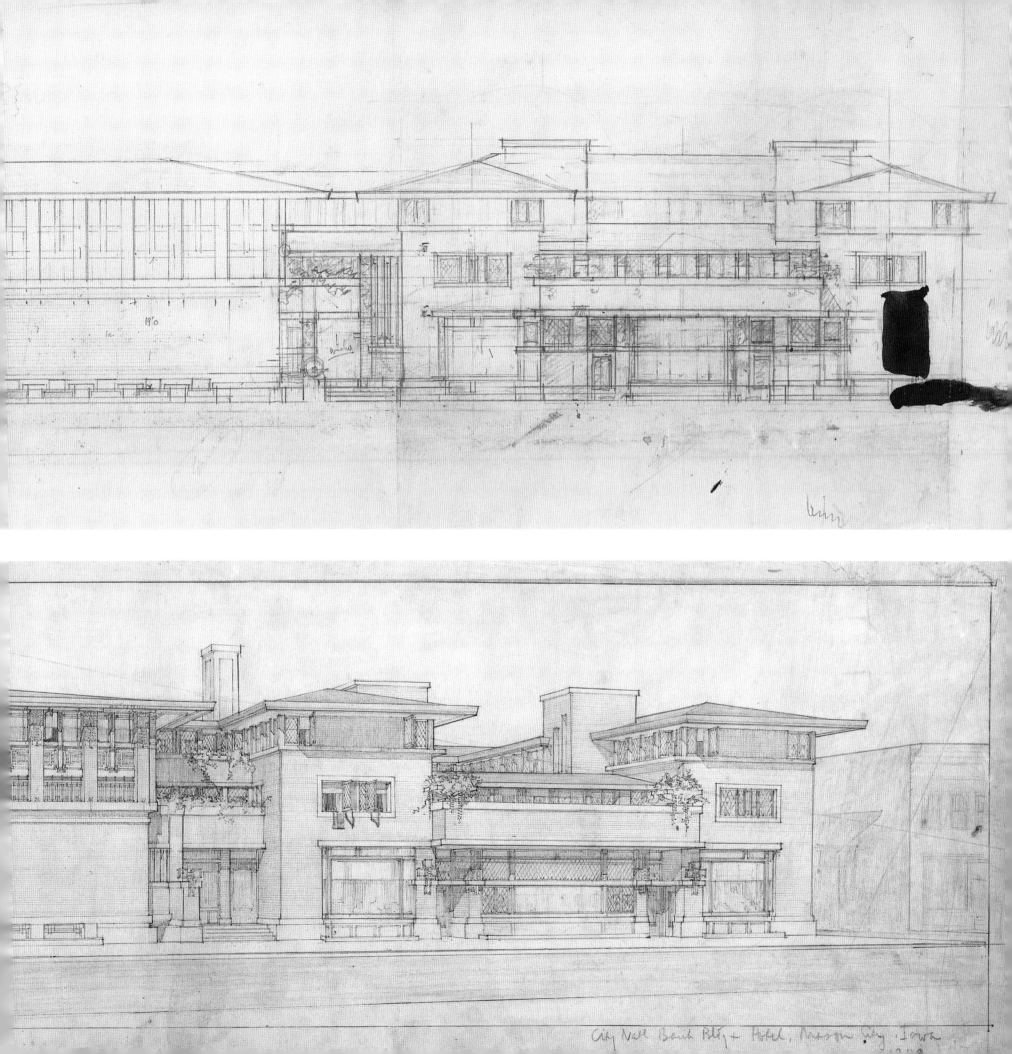

City Nat'l Bank Bldg + Hotel, Mason City, Iowa

ADMINISTRATION BUILDING

For the S. C. Johnson & Son Company
Racine, Wisconsin. 1936–1939

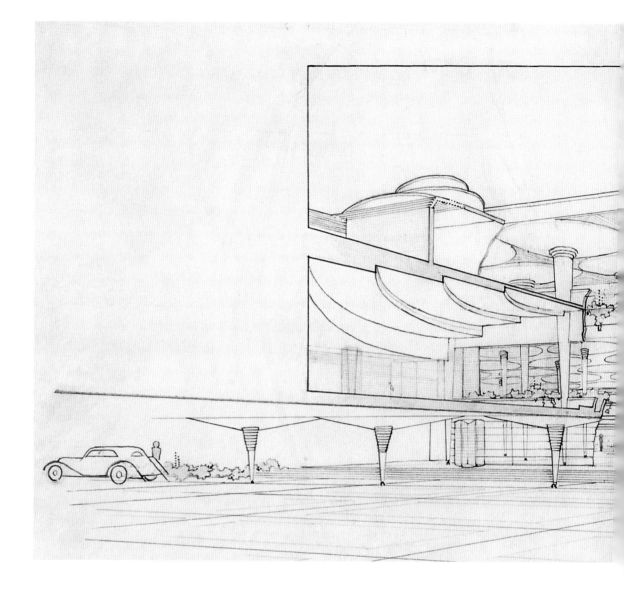

On July 20, 1936, Herbert F. Johnson, president of the S. C. Johnson & Son Co., along with Jack Ramsay, the company's general manager, drove from Racine, Wisconsin, the company's headquarters, to Taliesin in order to confer with Frank Lloyd Wright about the design of a new administration building. Ramsay and William Connolley, another executive in the company, were both aware of Wright's work. Another architect had already been retained to design the building, but Johnson and the others were not satisfied with the plans. Ramsay and Connolley urged Johnson to approach Wright. It was important to Johnson that the building respect his father's ideal, as he expressed it: "Call it enlightened selfishness if you like, for when people get proper wages and proper working conditions, they don't feel the need to organize to fight for what they want."[5]

The first thing that Johnson noticed, upon arriving in the motor court at Taliesin, was that the architect's car, a Lincoln Zephyr, was just like his own. This seemed a good omen. However when they were discussing the type of building that was needed, Olgivanna recalls that Johnson said to Wright, "Please don't make the building too unconventional!" Laughing, Wright replied, "Then you came to the wrong man. You'd better find yourself another architect. The Johnson administration building is not going to be what you expect. But I can assure you one thing— you'll like it when it is put up." Johnson then said, "It's okay with me then, if you think so. We'll have your kind of building, not the kind of building I had in mind."[6]

What Wright had in mind was a newspaper plant that he had designed six years earlier for the *Capital Journal*, in Salem, Oregon. He used a type of column, dendriform-like, that rose to the second level and then spread out like lily pads. In the Salem building, the columns supported a second floor. With the Johnson building, an even more graceful application of the columns rose to support and become the roof, with the interstices between the tops of the spreading pads containing skylights. In this manner, the light for the clerical workers in the main large workroom would fall down between the columns, like daylight drifting down through a forest of slender birch trees.

Following this first meeting, three days later Wright received a letter from Johnson asking him to proceed with the plans, and enclosed a check for $1,000 as a retainer. Wright showed the letter and the check to his apprentices and exclaimed, "It's all right boys, we got the job." His use of "we" was indicative of how he always referred to architectural work. Not "I" but "we." As with his draftsmen in the early years, Wright was always keenly aware of the support team that worked alongside him. "No man flies high on his own wings" was a statement by William Blake, the English poet whom Wright deeply admired. And Wright certainly lived up to that dictum.

Wright's original sketch plan of the building (not shown) has been lost, but a photograph of the drawing indicates his general idea for the administration building. One side contains what is called the Great Workroom, another side is a covered carport, with a covered entrance between the two. Above the entrance and carport is a theater for films and lectures, and on the third level

are the executive offices. From their offices on this level, the executives can see the great workroom by means of the three-story lobby to the main building, which gives them clear view of their employees. Another example of the connection between employer and employee is here made an important feature, as it was in the Larkin Building thirty years earlier.

The similarity between the Larkin and the Johnson buildings is evident in that both clients, Darwin D. Martin and Herbert F. Johnson shared the deep belief that the workplace should be modern, clean, comfortable, and—most important— inspiring. As Wright himself wrote, "Organic architecture designed this great build-

ing to be as inspiring a place to work in as any cathedral ever was in which to worship. It was meant to be [the] socio-architectural interpretation of modern business at its top and best."[7]

Some, in comparing the Larkin Building with the Johnson, find the Larkin rather strong and masculine in character while the Johnson is curvilinear, fluid, and perhaps more feminine. Certainly that is what the critics thought when a feature article in *Life* magazine on May 8, 1939, reporting after the public opening of the building wrote: "It is like a woman swimming naked in a stream. Cool, gliding, musical in movement and manner. The inside of an office building like a woman swimming naked in a stream? Yes, that's right."

Above: Perspective.
FLLW FDN # 3601.006.

Following pages:
Left: Column detail. FLLW FDN
3601.487.
Right: Plan. FLLW FDN # 3601.485.

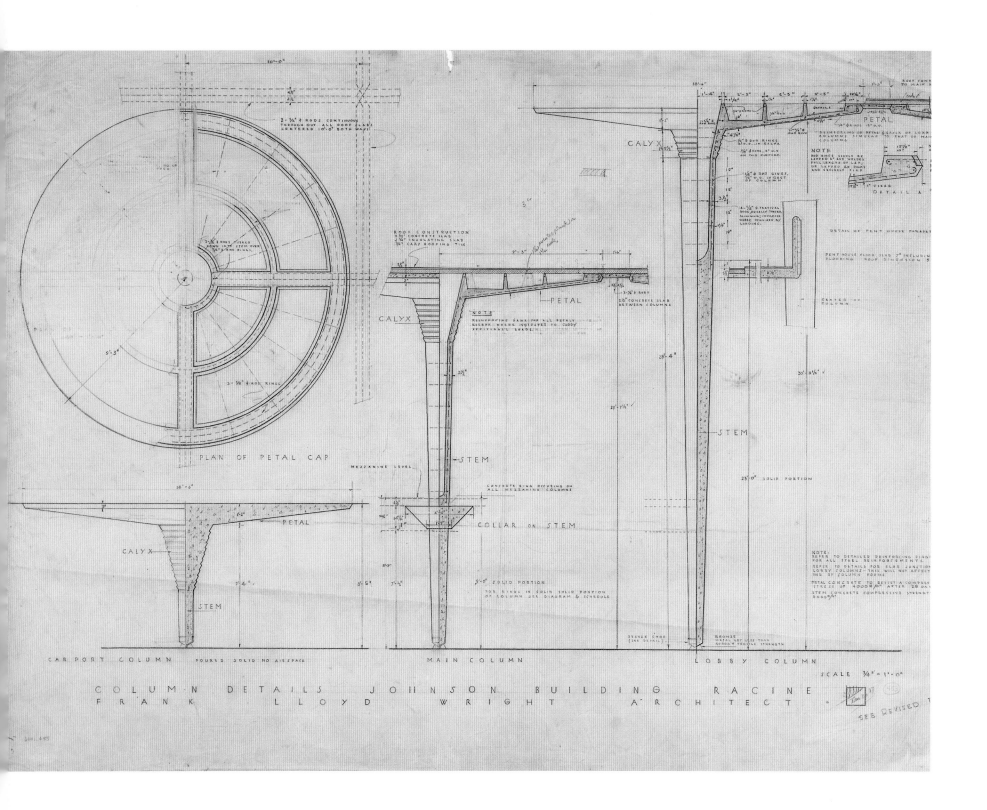

PLAN OF PETAL CAP

CALYX

STEM

PETAL

CAR PORT COLUMN — POURED SOLID NO AIRSPACE

COLLAR ON STEM

MAIN COLUMN

STEM

LOBBY COLUMN

SCALE ¾" = 1'-0"

COLUMN DETAILS   JOHNSON BUILDING   RACINE
FRANK   LLOYD   WRIGHT   ARCHITECT

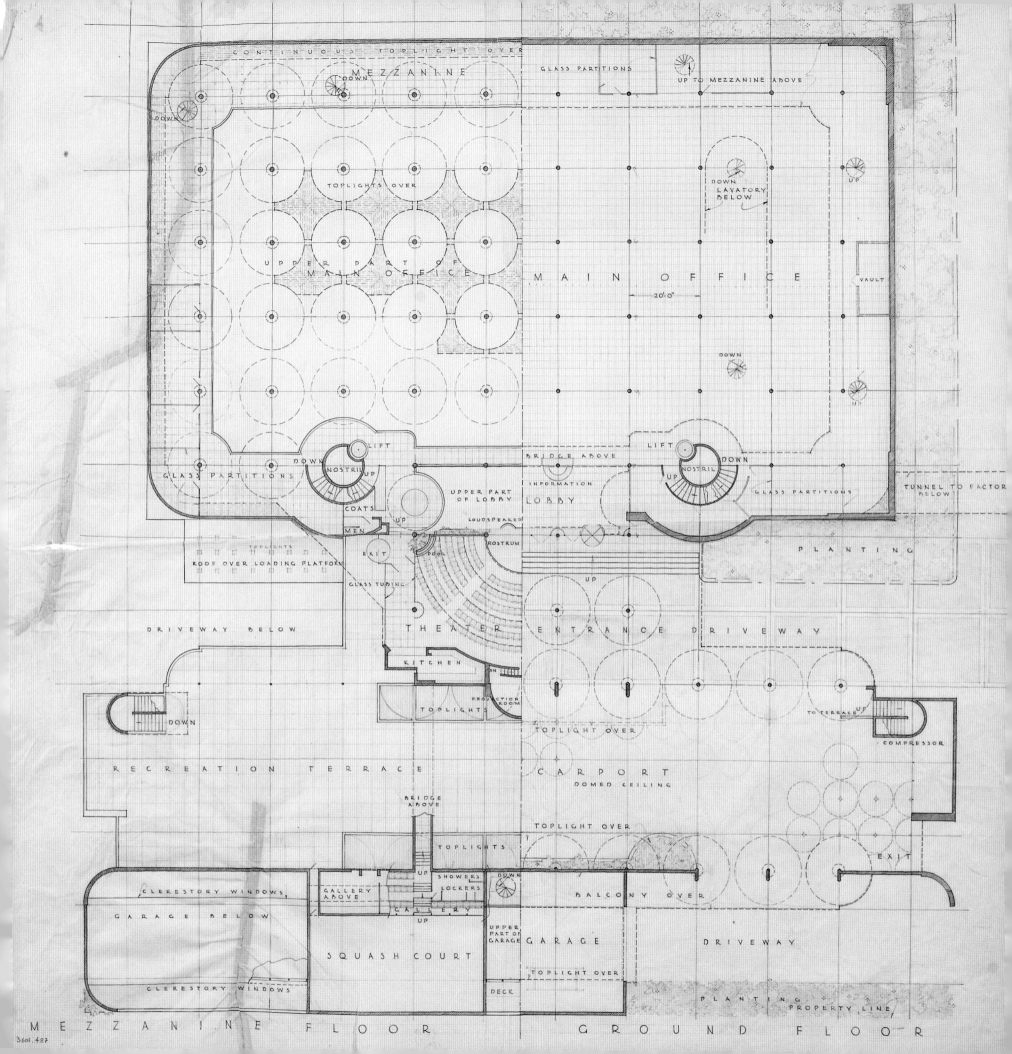

MEZZANINE   F L O O R   G R O U N D   F L O O R

RESEARCH TOWER

For the S. C. Johnson & Son Company
Racine, Wisconsin. 1943–1951

When the Johnson Company decided to expand their products from wax to household items, including furniture polish even insect repellent, they found it necessary to construct a special building in order to carry on the research and development of those products. Herbert Johnson explained to Wright the type of building he wanted: "It is a plain factory kind of job that should be built by an engineer or contractor like our other factory buildings. Yet because of its proximity to your masterpiece, it should have a relationship thereto and we feel it would be unfair to you and mistake on our part if we didn't ask how you think you would want to fit into such a picture."[8] Wright responded with the proposition that the laboratory should be in a tall structure, not placed along the street with views into the factory neighborhood of Racine. In fact Johnson himself had remarked, "Why not go up in the air, Frank?"

In one of the most remarkable letters of his entire career, he wrote to Johnson about the type of building he envisioned. Wright was enamored with the *One Thousand and One Nights*, and his letter is an intriguing improvisation in that style:

"O Caliph. Why build a heavy building sodden upon the ground—facing awkwardly upon unsightly streets when by creating a charming interior court space for parking—the lighting come from above or from the court. A gallery would follow above and around that court space, O master. And bridge tunnels would be seen connecting this space and the administration building itself to the research laboratory which is as a tall-shaft would rise from the center of the court, etc. . . . What a miracle of beautiful planning will be there to instruct thy foes, delight thy friends and convince thy subjects of the illustrious character of thy reign, O my Caliph."[9]

Johnson was won over by this romantic appeal but cautioned Wright that the cost of the structure must be held down to an original estimate. He reminded his architect of the cost nightmare associated with the construction of the administration building and warned him that the company would not go through that ordeal again.

Along with the tower for research, other offices were required, and these would be placed over the existing carport adjacent to the administration building. Wright called his design "Helio-Laboratory," remarking that all the floors in the tower would have the benefit of ample daylight. By December of the same year he wrote Johnson, "I have a good scheme ready for you to see . . . . I think you'll get a thrill out of the drawings."[10]

The original proposition for the tower showed a structure in which each floor projected slightly out from the one beneath it, in the same manner as he had proposed for the St. Mark's tower in New York fourteen years earlier. This proposal was abandoned, however, since it would entail making new formwork for each level, thus incurring a substantial increase in the construction costs. The tower, in its final version, is fourteen stories tall, twelve of the stories alternating between a square plan and a circular mezzanine. All floors are cantilevered out from a central core. This core rises the full height of the tower, and on each level there is a toilet and stairway as well as an elevator. Within this core are the vents and utility shafts required for heating and cooling and the removal of fumes from the use of chemicals. The core rises out of what Wright called a "taproot" foundation: a central shaft forty-four feet deep (right). A reinforced concrete flange, like the handle of a sword, attached to the tap root and sunk underground, assures stability. The outer shell of the tower is sheathed in glass tubes with a low brick wall on each of the square levels. The glass tubes, as with the main administration building, provide diffused daylight all around and on all levels.

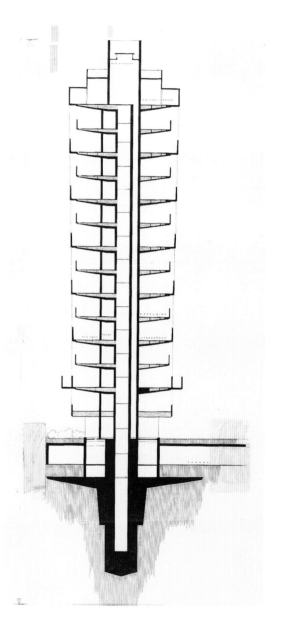

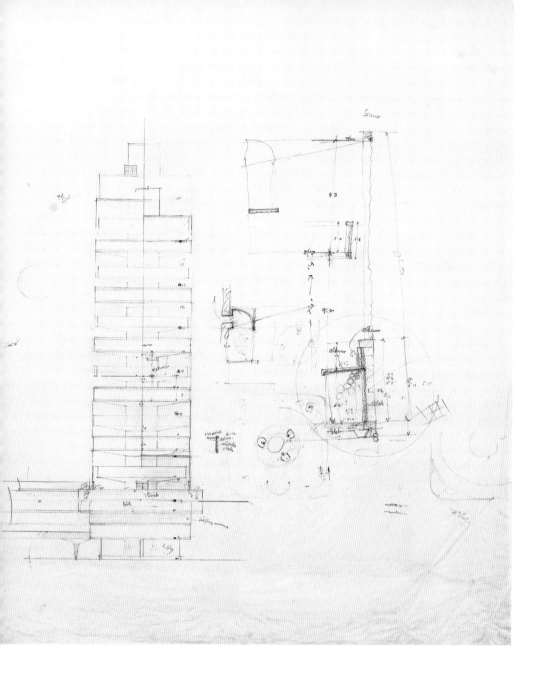

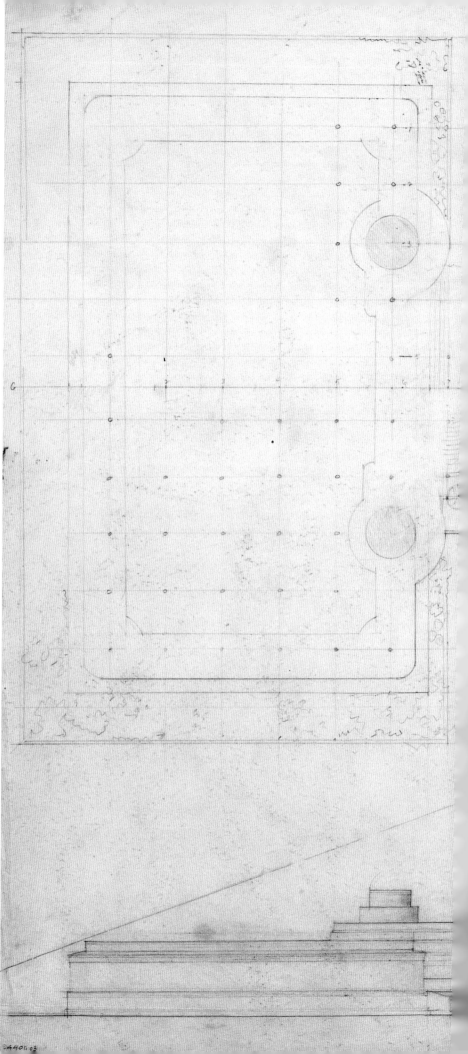

A basement level extends out from the tower in three directions in order to provide testing laboratories, storage rooms for chemicals, special climate-controlled rooms, and locker rooms for the employees and chemists. This sprawling subterranean area is a vast and complex arrangement. The largest room is the pilot laboratory, a two-story space beneath the west wing of the courtyard. Equipped with a ceiling hoist and a network of pipes, the ceiling reaches twenty feet above the floor with a mezzanine. Machinery throughout provides air filtering and exhaust systems to remove any poisonous or toxic gases that might arise in the process of experimentation as well as safety features in case of fire or explosion.

Above: Plan.
FLLW FDN # 4801.041.
Right: Plan and elevation.
FLLW FDN # 4401.003A.

Following pages: Perspective.
FLLW FDN # 4401.002.

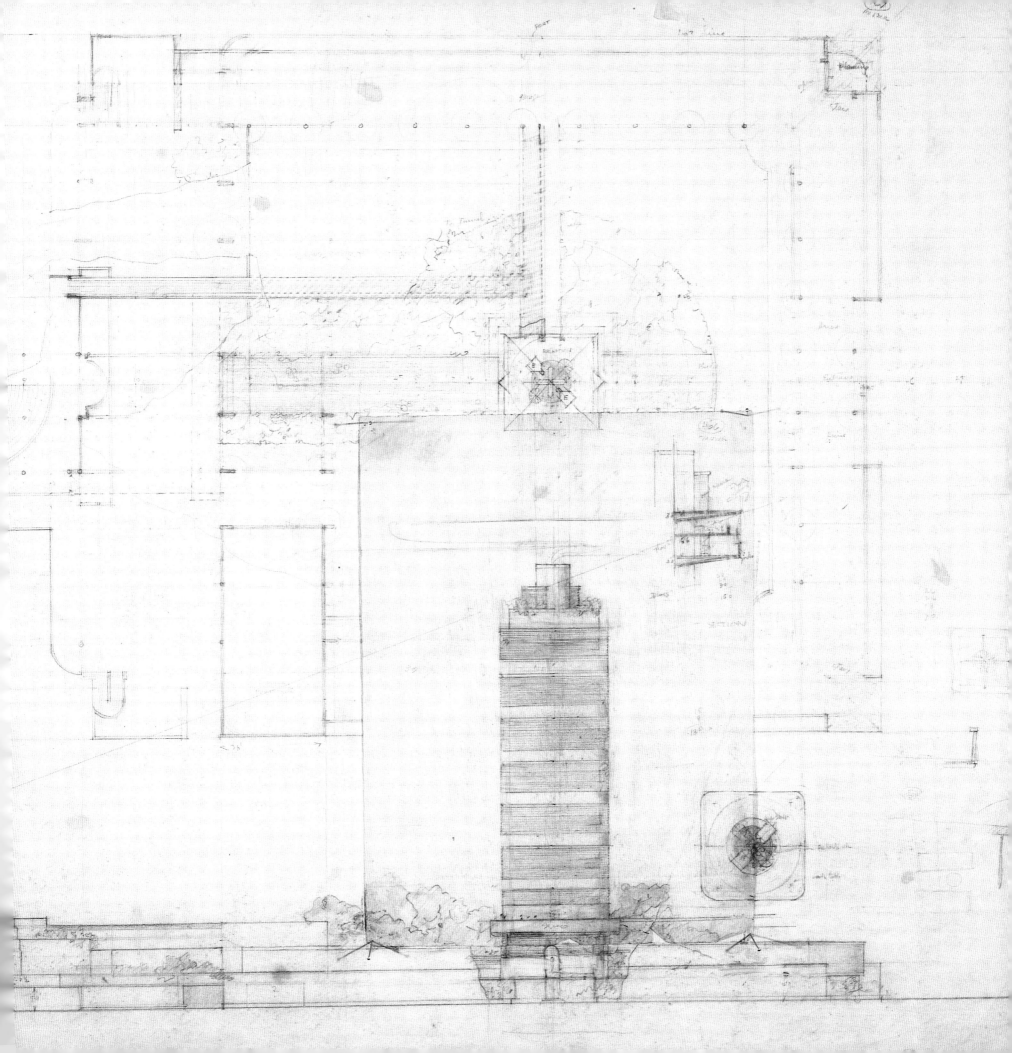

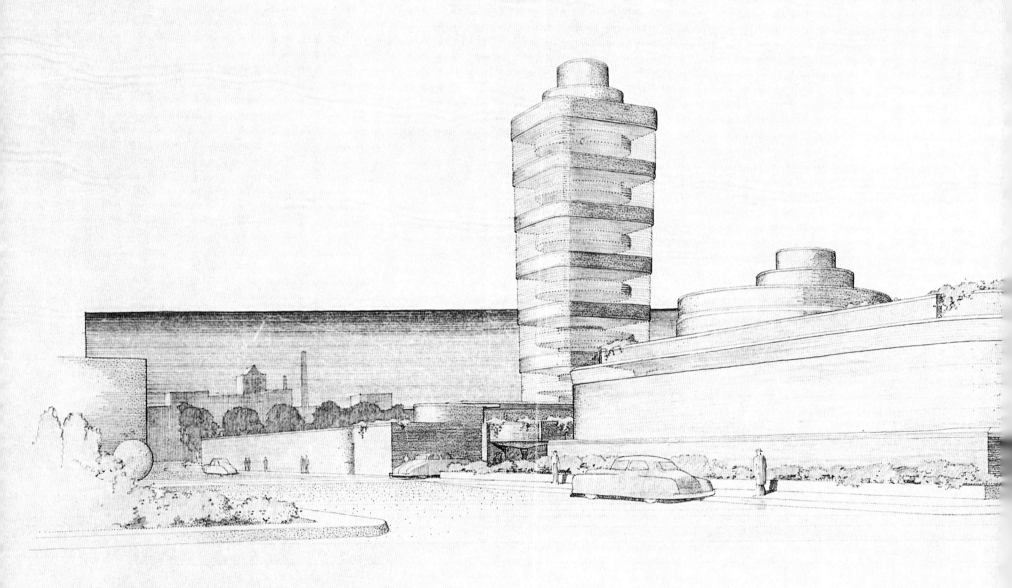

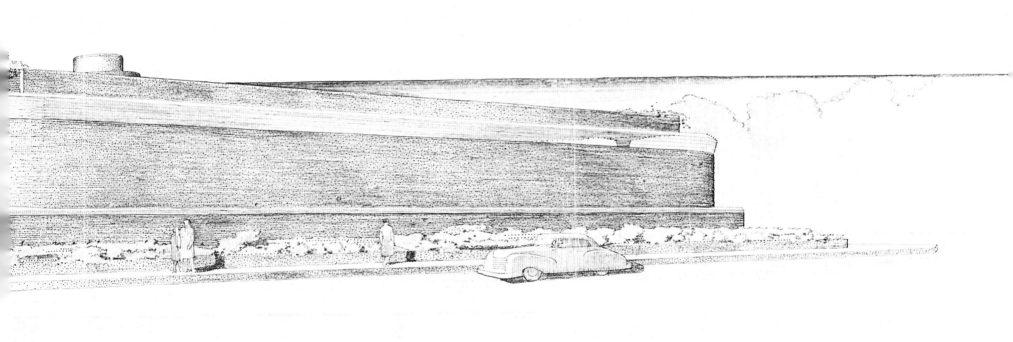

DRESS SHOP

For Leo Bramson
Oak Park, Illinois. 1937, Project

Below: Elevation. FLLW FDN # 3706.003.
Right: Perspective. FLLW FDN # 3706.001.

Following pages: Perspective of
Merchandising Building (project),
Los Angeles, CA., 1922. FLLW FDN
2203.006.

Bramson was a couturier living in Oak Pak, Illinois. He asked Wright to design an establishment for him that would include both a shop and a residence. The location was a long narrow city lot, and this prompted Wright's design to go "vertical." As for the storefront, which would need the customary shopwindow, Wright followed the same pattern that he did sixteen years earlier for a large merchandising building in Los Angeles (pp. 336-7). The typical storefront window display was in under an over-hang, to provide protection during inclement weather. In the daytime, this condition often cre-ates, because of the window being in the shade, a mirror effect. To account for this and throw more light on the merchandise, strong artificial light is required. In the merchandising building, Wright designed a three-story wall of glass running above the projecting overhang, but set back to allow daylight to fall from the edge of the over-hang onto a skylight over the display window itself. This allowance of natural light on the objects is understandably far more desirable than artificial light.

In the Bramson design a smaller version, but with the same effect, takes place. A cantilevered balcony projects over the display window, and daylight is brought in from above by way of a top-light glazed over in the floor above. A set-back in the second story allows this to be directly over the display window.

The ground and second floors provide spaces and accommodations for the shop, and the third floor becomes a penthouse residence. The rather confining situation of the narrow lot is relieved by the projecting balconies which lend a strong sense of the third dimension.

The final rendering is a one-of-a-kind draw-ing: a circle set into a square, and yet the circle is interrupted to let lines project out to the edge of the square in order to make a place for Wright's traditional red square and signature (opposite page; signature not visible). As an additional feature, a planting box is superimposed on the circle where this interruption takes place. This type of detail is consistent with Wright's perpet-ual sense of asymmetry not only in the design of a building, but in the manner in which that design is represented in preliminary form to show the client.

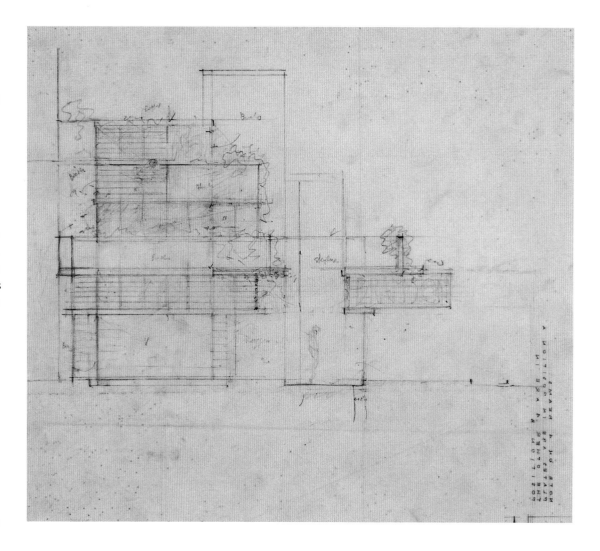

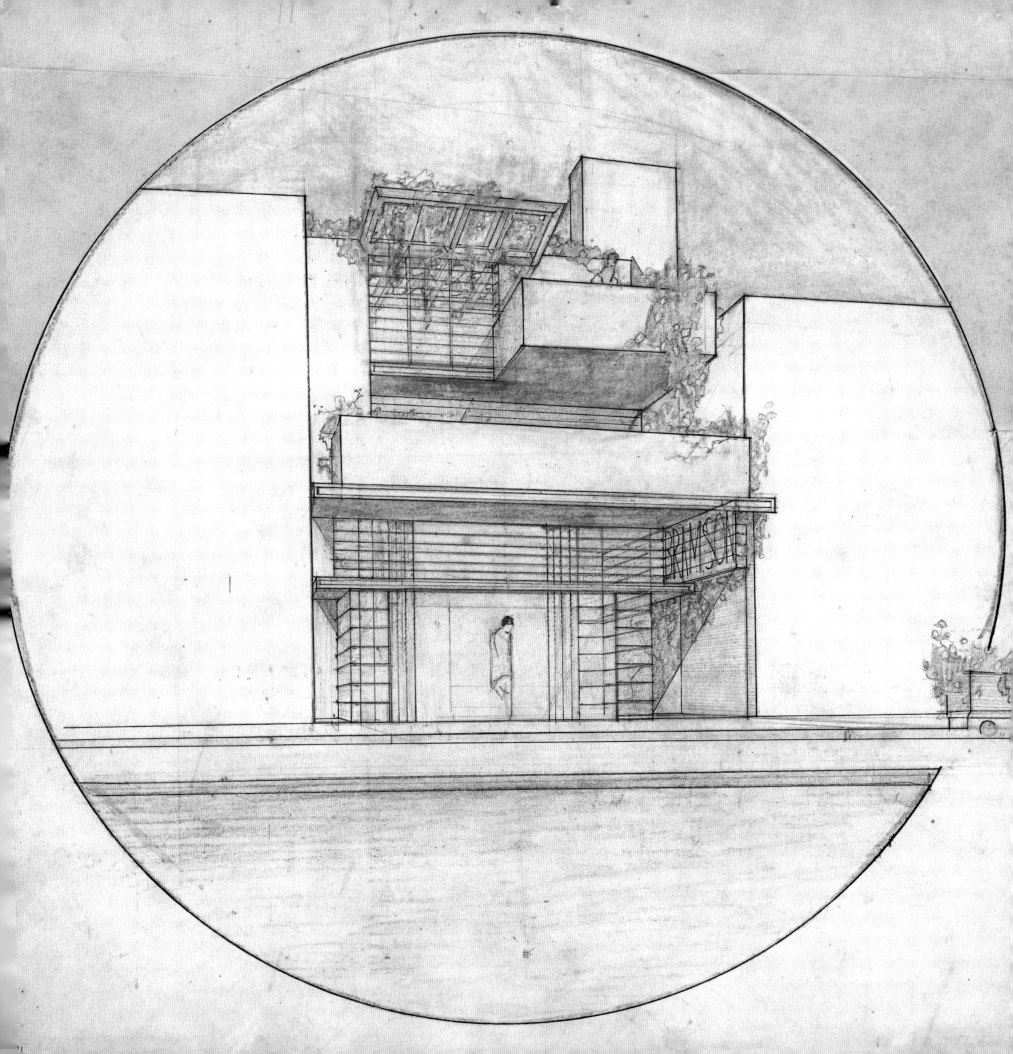

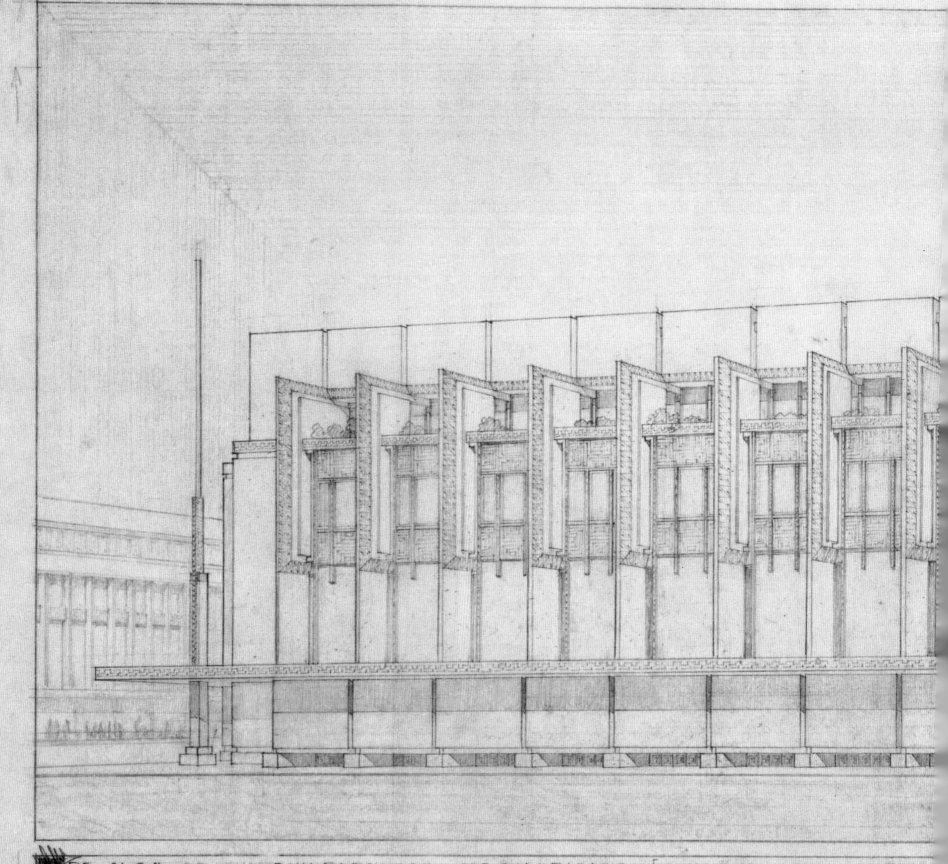

DESIGN BUILDING FOR MERCHANDIZING [CONCRETE SLAB CONSTRUC

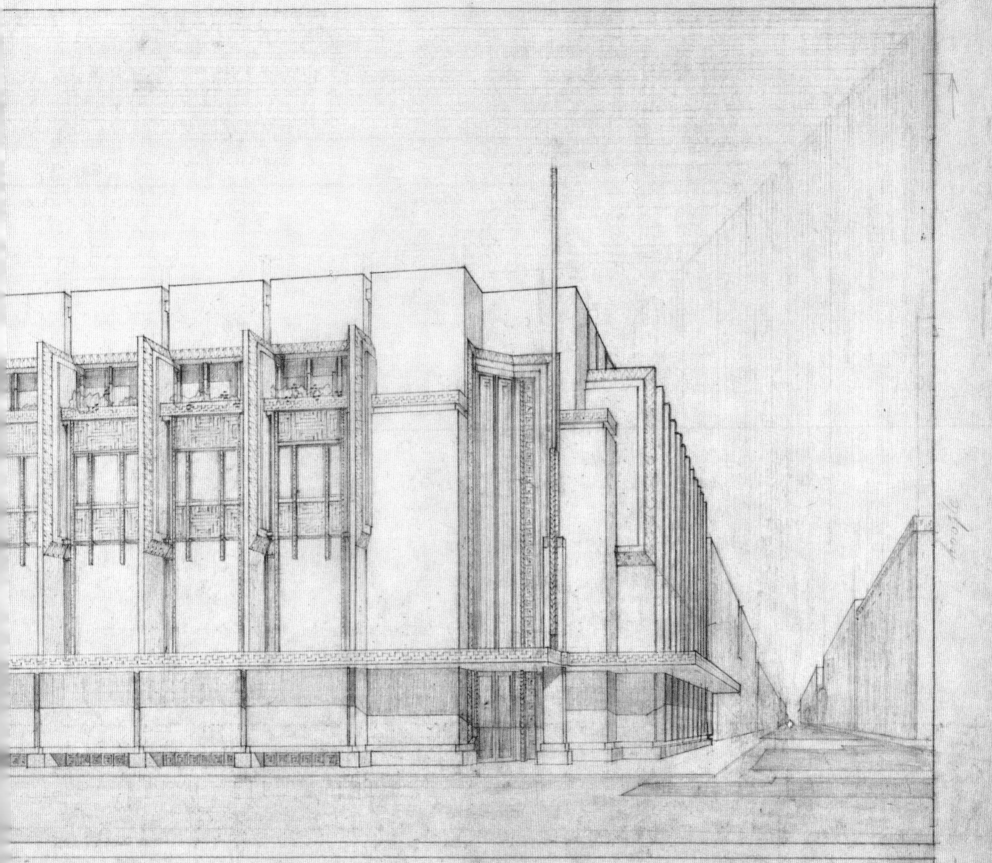

FRANK LLOYD WRIGHT .. ARCHITECT :: HOLLYWOOD .. CAL... ▥

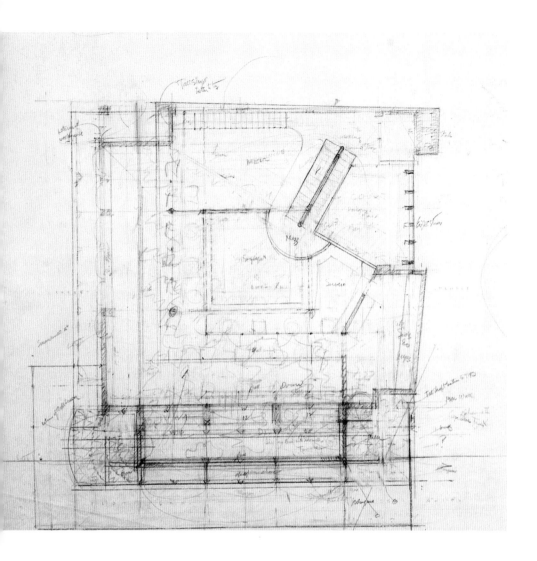

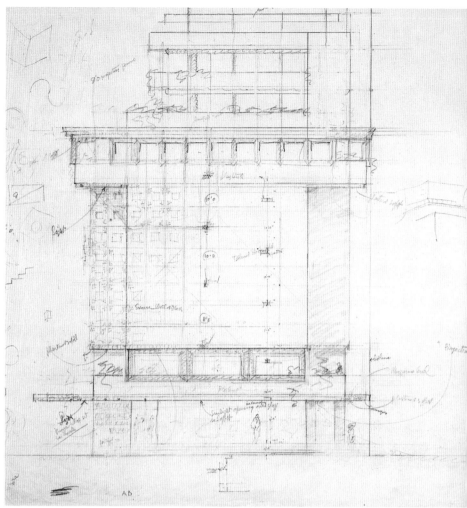

CALICO MILLS DEPARTMENT STORE

For Gautam Sarabhai
Ahmedabad, India. 1946, Project

Above left: Plan. FLLW FDN # 4508.002.
Above right: Elevation. FLLW FDN # 4508.003.
Right: Perspective. FLLW FDN # 4508.001.

The Gautam Sarabai family owned a factory called "Calico Mills," in Ahmedabad, India, that produced the fine textiles for which India is famous. In 1946 their daughter Gira joined the Taliesin Fellowship as an apprentice to Frank Lloyd Wright. At the same time, the family desired to build a department store that would serve the community as a general store and also feature their calico product.

The building that Wright proposed for them was an eight-story structure with an open well running down six of the levels on the center, while another open well was placed tangent to an exterior wall. The seventh level was reserved for a restaurant with an outdoor terrace, while above that was a level for rest and private dining.

The ground level was two stories tall, with a mezzanine. The feature of the store was its shop-window, two stories tall in this case. Wright here has employed the same method for bringing natural light into the window that he used in the Merchandising Building in 1922. The glass extends up beyond the projecting overhang at street level and permits daylight to come down from above. The fabrics are shown as long, luxurious bolts of cloth hanging down from their racks as a rich and tempting display.

The climate being hot and sultry, Wright wrote how he would address this situation: "Concession to the character of the climate is found in the carrying of all floors independent of direct contact on the outer wall shell, the shell itself being a perforated screen allowing inlet and exit of air on all floors."[11]

Wright's preliminary plan and elevation (above) clearly explain the project, followed by the presentation perspective (opposite page).

It seemed that the engineering required to construct a reinforced concrete building with perforated concrete-block walls was insufficient in that particular region of India, and after much work on the project, it had to be abandoned.

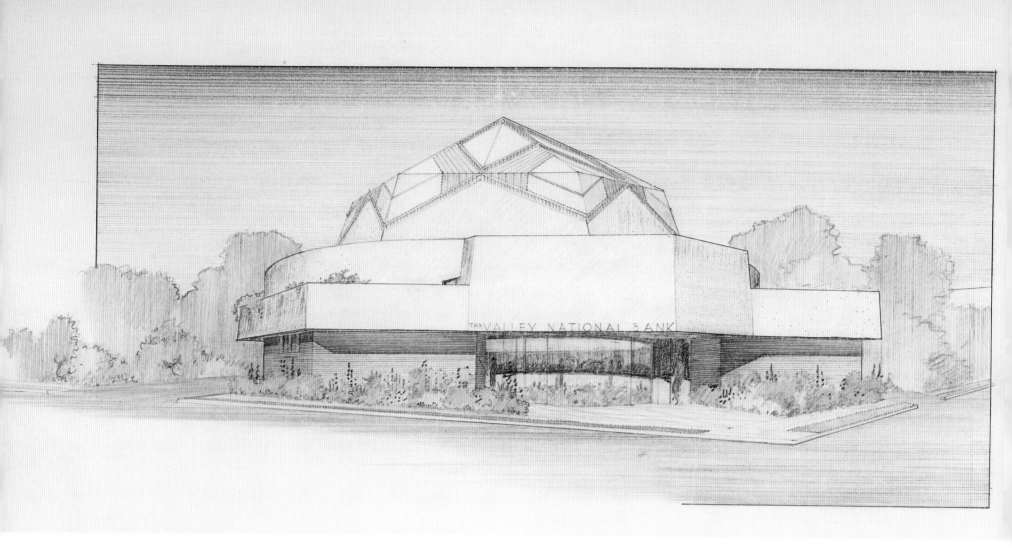

THE DAYLIGHT BANK

For the Valley National Bank
Tucson, Arizona. 1947, Project

Early in his career, Frank Lloyd Wright wrote that a bank is the "town's strongbox," and should evoke a feeling of security, a feeling that one's money is safe and protected. Here the bank is placed in a hexagon, with a hexagonal skylight above the mezzanine level filling the entire interior two levels with natural light, hence the name "Daylight Bank" that Wright gave to the project. The only windows on the ground level are at the entrance into the building. The main floor provides the general banking area, with ramps up to a mezzanine for offices, a lounge, and restrooms. Ramps from the main level descend to the basement level for safety-deposit boxes and the main

vault. The lower level also contained restrooms for the employees.

A feature of the interior is the open well in the center of the ground floor, giving a view down onto the impressive vault door. A smaller adjacent circle, with a writing desk for customers running along the parapet, is also open to this view of the vault door below. The tellers' windows and further office space run around the periphery of the room. On the outer edge of the bank, at ground level, are four tellers' windows for drive-in convenience. The upper floor projected just enough over the drive to provide protection from inclement weather to the drivers in

their cars. To some of the officials of the bank, this was an unnecessary detail, as one of them stated, "Drive to a teller's window? No, people will always want to park their cars and walk into the main building itself."

Since the Valley National Bank was, at that time, the premier bank in Arizona, Wright proposed fine materials for the work: an exterior with the ground level walled in Roman brick, the upper level reinforced concrete, the floor surfaces within of marble, and the tellers' screens bronze. Such luxurious materials seemed to raise the cost of the building more than the client desired, and the project was abandoned.

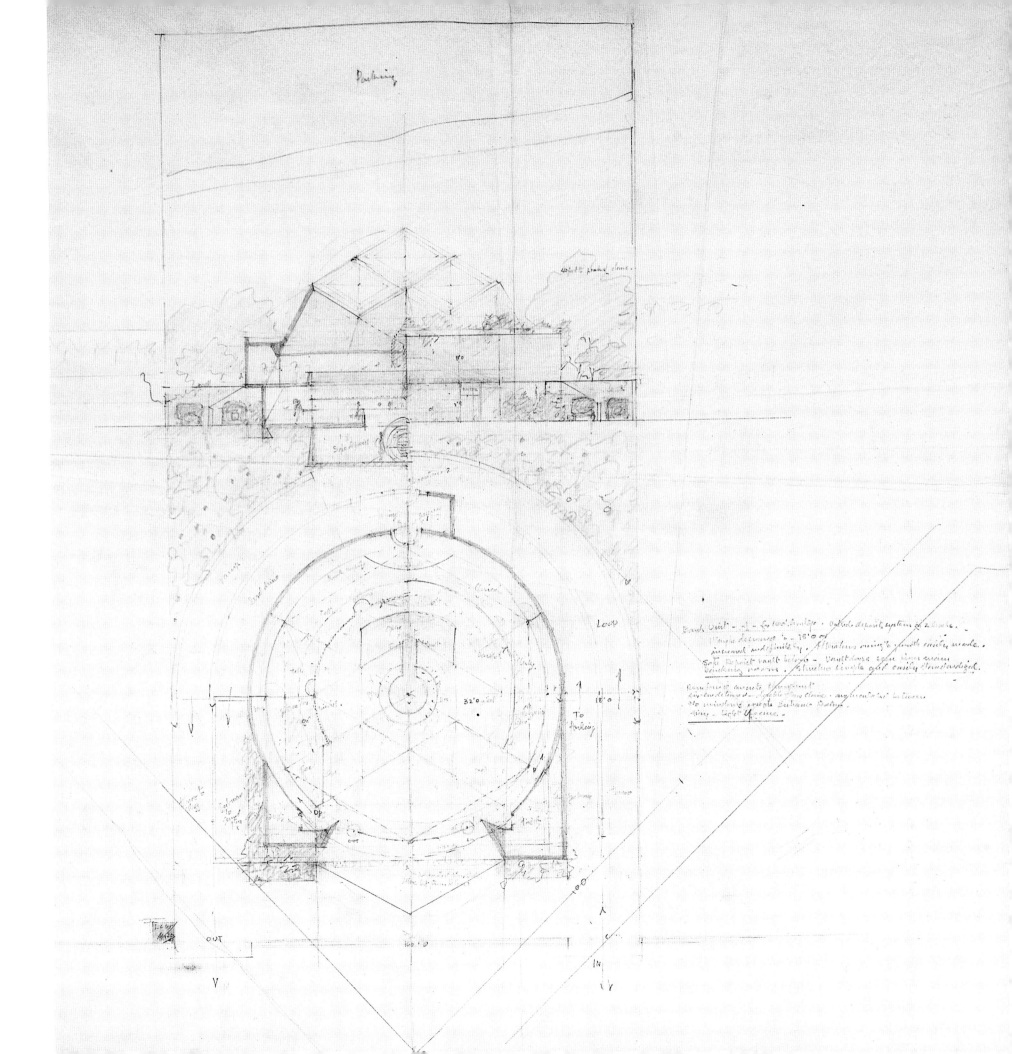

GIFT SHOP

For V. C. Morris
San Francisco, California. 1948

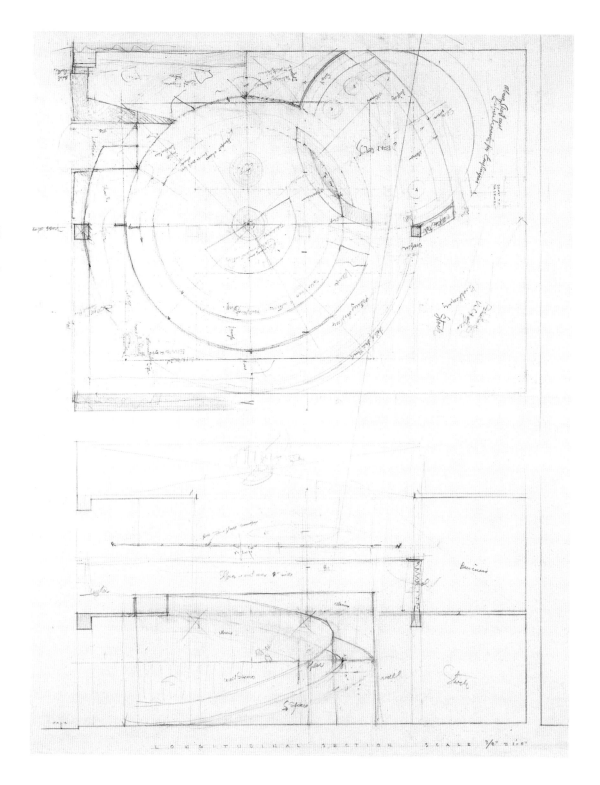

The V. C. Morris Gift Shop is a remodeling installed in a current building on San Francisco's prestigious and fashionable Maiden Lane, near Union Square. The shop was dedicated to the sale of fine china, exquisite tabletop ware, and crystal, along with table linens and luxurious accessories. Wright's first sketches, plan and section on one sheet, represent the concept of a ramp connecting the main floor with the mezzanine (right). The former space of the tenant had a large skylight, which Wright kept, adding a dropped ceiling light composed of frosted glass halfglobes alternating large and small to provide a rhythmic pattern overhead. The facade (opposite page) is a simple brick wall with a line of horizontal square lights running along the front of the wall, about three feet above the ground, and another line of lights next to the arched doorway running vertically up the wall to the top of the building. The brick wall is without the customary shop-windows. Only a striking arch gains entry to the store.

When Wright showed this concept to Mr. and Mrs. Morris, they expressed alarm at the thought of no shopwindow. Wright reassured them that "you are not going to dump the merchandise on the street," but rather designed a better solution: the entry arch was provided with a glass-enclosed wide stone ledge for the display of objects. The arch entered a short tunnel, with the ceiling overhead half enclosed by brick, the other half by glass. People passing by could look into this brick-and-glass "tunnel," and glimpse a few assorted items on the stone ledge. Their curiosity piqued, they then could venture in and arrive at the shop's glass door. This unique entrance prompted Wright to call it "a mousetrap" since a person venturing further in was suddenly in the shop and a salesperson would greet the person with "Welcome, may I help you?"

The interior is a two-story space, with a circular ramp rising from the ground floor to the mezzanine. The wall along the ramp on one side is pierced in several places with circular and semicircular opening, some of them displaying items. The other side of the parapet overlooks the main floor. Hanging from the ceiling is a large circular planter with vines and flowers. The Morrises kept Siamese cats. When the cats were in the store they would roam up and down the edge of the ramp, passing by objects but never disturbing them. In the shop, everywhere one looks the eye is met with elegance, while the cats cast an unexpected aura of calm.

FOR DETAILS OF ENTRANCE AND FACADE SEE SHEET 7

Left: Plan and section. FLLW FDN # 4824.005.
Above: Elevation of front facade. FLLW FDN # 4824.008.

Following pages: Section. FLLW FDN # 4824.009.

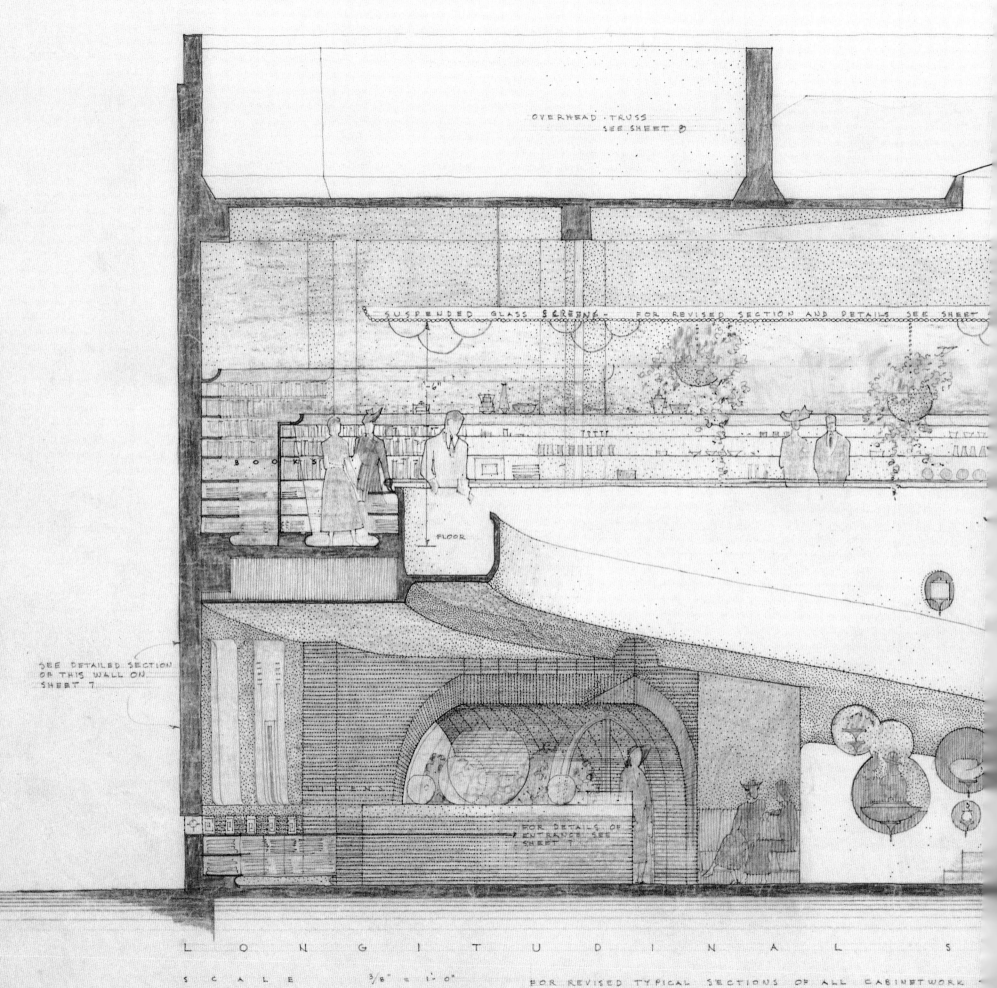

OVERHEAD · TRUSS
SEE SHEET 8

SUSPENDED · GLASS · SCREENS · FOR · REVISED · SECTION · AND · DETAILS · SEE SHEET

B O O K S

FLOOR

SEE DETAILED SECTION
OF THIS WALL ON
SHEET 7

FOR · DETAILS · OF
ENTRANCE · SEE
SHEET 7

L O N G I T U D I N A L   S

S C A L E   3/8" = 1'-0"   FOR · REVISED · TYPICAL · SECTIONS · OF · ALL · CABINETWORK

FOR · DETAILED · STRUCTURAL · SECTIONS · SEE SHEET 9

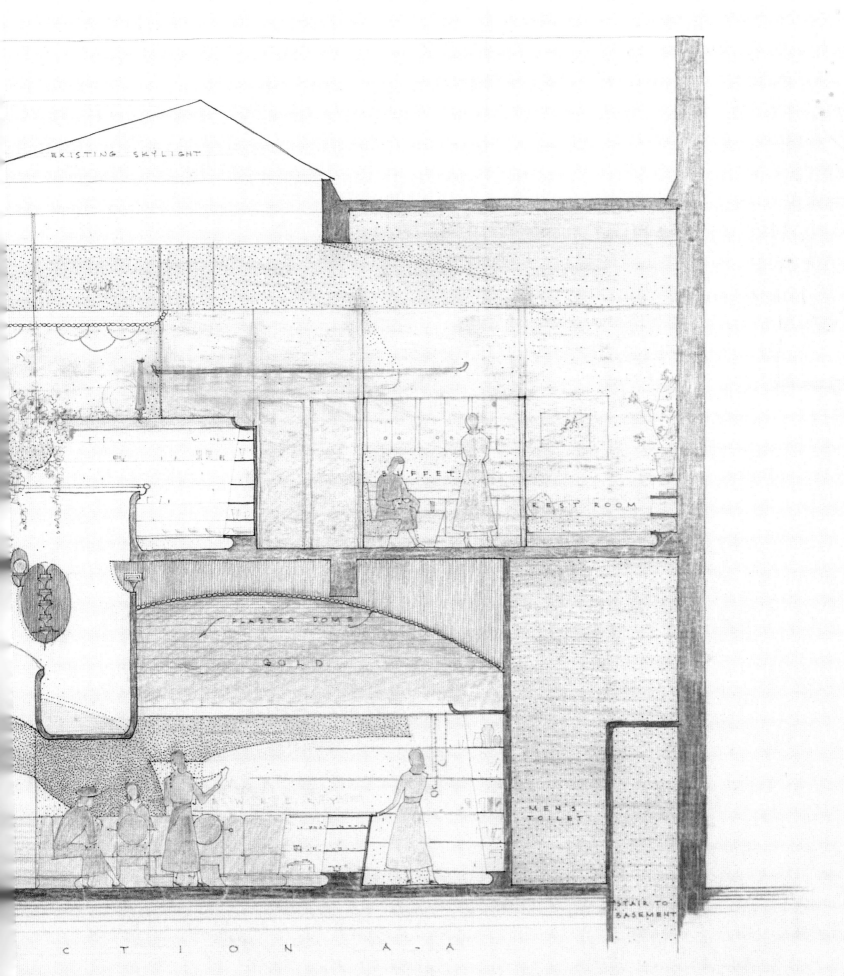

EXISTING SKYLIGHT

BUFFET

REST ROOM

PLASTER DOME
GOLD

JEWELRY

MEN'S
TOILET

STAIR TO
BASEMENT

CTION   A-A

N HERE SEE SHEET 10

ANDERTON COURT SHOPS

For Nina Anderton
Beverly Hills, California. 1952

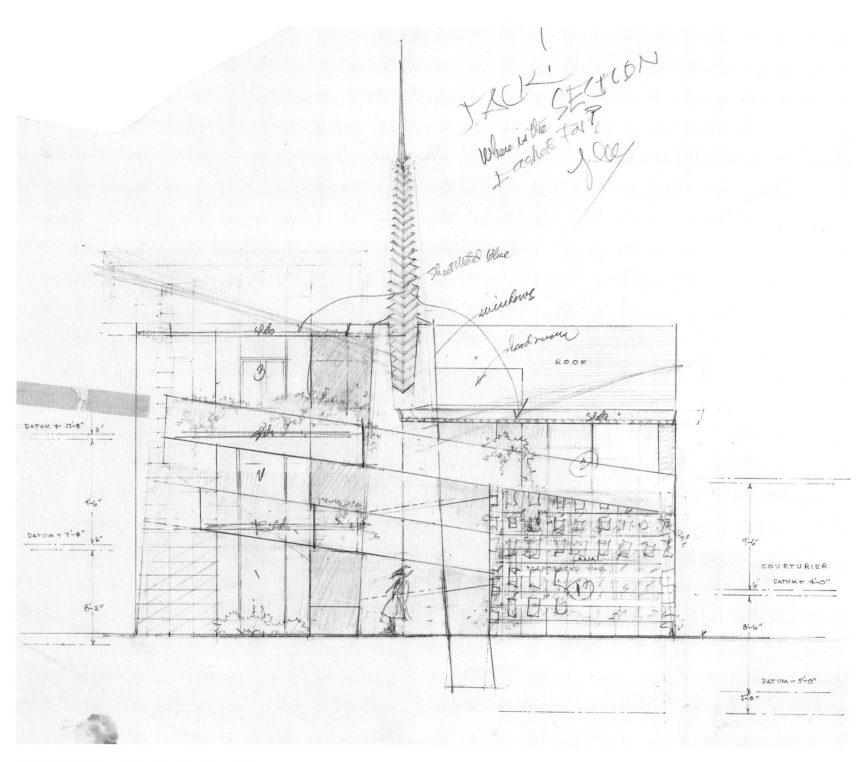

The couturier Nina Anderton was the client for this building of five shops and a penthouse located on the prestigious Rodeo Drive in Beverly Hills, California. One of the shops, on ground level, was to be hers, while the others were scheduled for rental units, with the penthouse reserved for Anderton herself. Wright's plan was conceived as a building of three levels, with an exterior ramp in the front connecting all the shops. The plan was laid out with the unit system of parallelograms and split levels. Although the ramp is basically out-of-doors, it is protected by the parapets, while a totally enclosed stairway accesses all levels at the rear of the building. On his concept elevation (opposite page), along with the drawing of the building he has inscribed certain notes about the details of materials. His large note at the top is a reminder to Jack (his apprentice John Howe) that he is waiting for a particular drawing.

Anderton Court Shops is a relatively small building tucked in amongst its larger neighbors. In comparison with them, it makes those neighbors appear stiff and unfriendly. Wright's typical application of human scale results in the quiet character of a structure composed of a charming array of geometric angles, shapes, and forms. In the hands of a lesser architect, such an array would spell confusion, but Wright was always a master of whatever forms he chose to employ for his ideas in architecture.

LENKURT ELECTRIC FACTORY

San Carlos, California. 1955–56, Project

Below: Section. FLLW FDN # 5520.029.

Right: Perspective. FLLW FDN # 5520.004.

Over and over again Wright declared that in designing a large public or commercial building, the first thing to consider was the problem of parking. What was reprehensible to him was a building surrounded by a sea of automobiles. In his design for Lenkurt Electric, a factory that manufactured microwave and telephone systems, he has solved the parking problem by placing it on ground level beneath the building, but with access to the work area above at certain stations in the building. In so doing, he had not only solved the parking problem but provided for covered parking in California's constantly changing weather conditions. An early study (right) illustrates this concept. Here he has shown a section with the column rising to support the upper level, the pagoda-like skylight above, and with the ground level reserved for parking.

The name of the factory is derived from its two founders, Lennart Erickson and Kurt Appert. At the beginning of the commission, they explained to Wright that the type of work going on in their factory required a building that could expand. Considering this, his conceptual plan is based on the unit system, capable of expansion as needed. Due to the rather delicate nature of the work, rather than the heavy machine work of the usual factory, Wright's plan was more similar to what one would design for an office building. With this in mind, he fashioned the scheme with the Johnson administration building in mind (see p. 324). As with the Johnson building, he again employed the dendriform columns as support for the overhead, but with this important change: at the interstices at the top, where the lily pad–like flanges of the columns meet, rather than a flat skylight, he provided a type of pagoda composed of copper louvers and glass. These pagodas, which he called "sunshades," are equipped with motors so that the louvers may open or close, depending upon

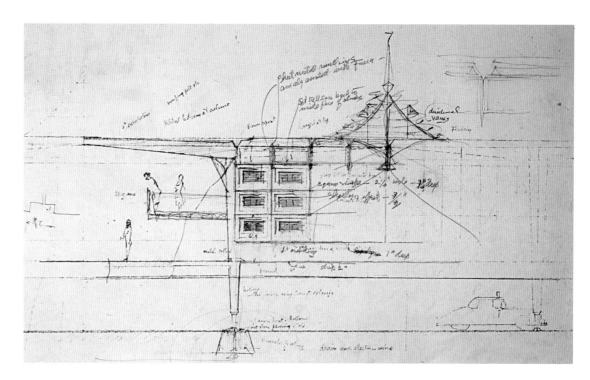

the amount of light desired at any one time. The exterior walls are perforated concrete blocks set with glass for further fenestration.

Originally he planned for separate towers rising out of the general plan to provide offices for the company's officials. Later he eliminated that plan and created a large pavilion-like structure at the corner of the factory, adjacent to an existing lagoon. Part of this pavilion engages the water. All the executive offices, a library, auditorium, committee rooms, and an employees' lounge are located in this three-story structure. In the center, on the ground floor, under a great sunshade—an expanded version of the sunshades in the factory area—the plan provides for a café, with kitchen facilities adjacent. The ground floor is open to surrounding trees and shrubs and the waters of the lagoon.

The rendering of the factory at night (pp. 352-3), with light pouring out from the

sunshades, from the perforated concrete-block walls, and from the large sunshade over the café, presents a shimmering spectacle of such beauty as to make one wonder, "Is this really a factory or some mysterious object from another planet set down on the California landscape?"

It was an enormous project, detailed in every way, and a complete set of working drawings and specifications were produced. Geared and ready to go into construction, suddenly the work was halted. The company decided to sell out to Sylvania Electric, and the plans to build this factory were shelved.

Like the Larkin Building and the Johnson Administration Building, the Lenkurt Electric was another instance where Wright has provided for a workplace of beauty as well as utility in every way possible for all working in it.

VELLION

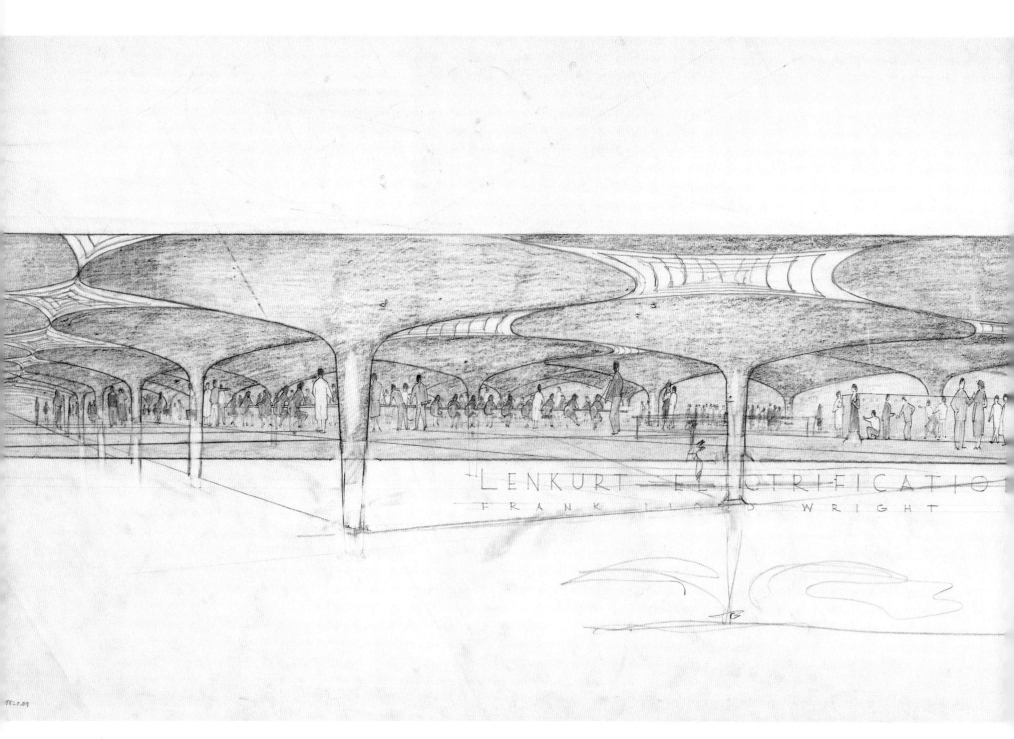

Above: Perspective. FLLW FDN # 5520.009.
Right, top: Presentation plan. FLLW FDN # 5520.007.
Right, bottom: Conceptual plan. FLLW FDN # 5520.041.

Following pages: Perspective. FLLW FDN # 5520.015.

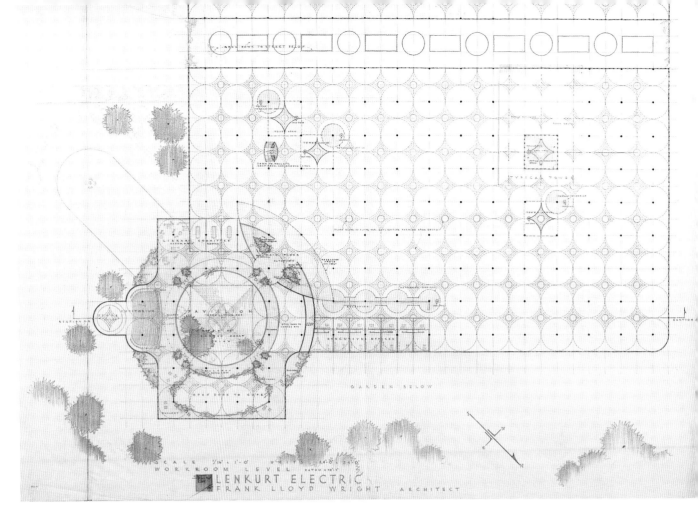

SCALE 7/16" : 1'-0" UNIT □ 34'-0" 34'-0"
WORKROOM LEVEL DATUM 0'-0"
LENKURT ELECTRIC
FRANK LLOYD WRIGHT ARCHITECT

TYPICAL
WORKROOM
INTERIOR

RCHITECT

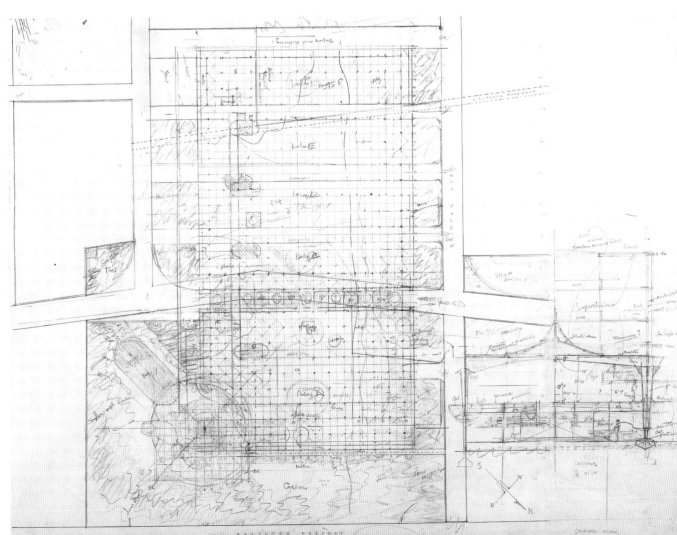

THE
LENKURT ELECT
FRANK LLOYD W

ARIZONA STATE CAPITOL

Phoenix, Arizona. 1957, Project

In 1957 the Arizona State Legislature proposed constructing a new building in downtown Phoenix for the state capitol. The nondescript and totally mundane design that was selected was a typical tall building. When Wright learned of this, he expressed serious concern, as an Arizona citizen, that the proposed building would be a mistake located in the already heavily congested downtown area. As for design, it expressed nothing of the beauty of Arizona nor did it seem appropriate for its citizens.

When news of his reactions to the design spread to the public, Lloyd Clark, a reporter on the *Phoenix Gazette* asked Wright for an interview. Wright usually did not give impromptu interviews, but he told Clark that the "Lloyd" in his name gained him entry. Clark drove out to Taliesin West, and the two of them sat down in Wright's office. Naturally Clark asked Wright what sort of design he

envisioned for a state capitol. Wright replied that it should move out of the downtown area and locate over to the nearby Papago Park, amid the spectacular red rock formations. He then took a sheet of eight-by-ten-inch piece of paper and made two sketches, one a rough elevation showing a large central perforated dome hovering protectively over a spacious public area below and partially over two hexagonal structures that represented the two houses of the legislature (above). A second sheet of paper showed a sketch plan (not shown). He went on, while drawing, to tell Clark what sort of building he was drawing. When the interview was concluded, he bid Clark goodbye and gave him the two pieces of paper upon which he had put down his concept for an Arizona state capital.

A little later, when talking to his apprentices about the meeting with Lloyd Clark, he explained:

"I spent at least 20 minutes this morning — have you seen the glad tidings, the news that the

legislature of Arizona had approved the plans of a new state capitol? You may have seen it in the newspapers. It is a curious hybrid. It's a terrible, terrible thing."

Although he had given those first two sketches to Clark, he went on to explain:

"But I have a design—it's easy—and I put it on paper this morning and I think I'll draw it out when I get to the drawing board."[12]

Continuing his discussion with the apprentices, (it was as though while he was talking about it, at the same time the design was germinating in his mind), he went on to explain how the dome was usually placed in state capitols as a symbol of authority, harking back to the dome of Michelangelo. Considering the fierce heat of the Arizona sun, especially in summer, he proposed a dome here, as he had shown it to Lloyd Clark, that would be constructed in reinforced concrete

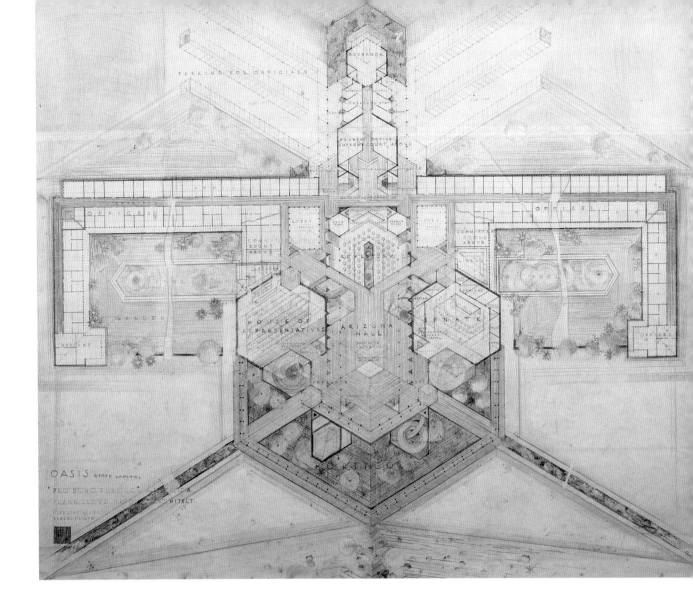

Left: Elevation. FLLW FDN # 5732.017.
Right: Plan. FLLW FDN # 5732.008.

Following pages: Perspective.
FLLW FDN # 5732.004.

and perforated, so as to create shade and shadow patterns below. Water, being a special luxury to the Arizona desert, would come into play as fountains and pools (see p. 314). The main area between the two legislative structures—one for the senate, the other for the representatives—would be a shaded public space, "Pro Bono Publico," as he inscribed on the drawing. Here there would be gardens, sculpture exhibits—all becoming a veritable cool, shaded, park. Between the senate and the house, a long gallery would be reserved for further exhibitions dealing with Arizona's natural wonders and history. Further back would be the offices for the governor as well as courts and offices for the judiciary (see p. 4). Spreading out on either side would be offices on ground level for the senators, representatives, and their staffs, opening onto gardens and pools. Adjacent would be ample parking.

Seven days following this talk with his apprentices, the design, as he would often claim, "was just shaken out of my sleeve," and the final drawings were signed. A special press conference was set up to show them.

A few days later, addressing the students of the Phoenix Union High School along with a presentation of the drawings, he told them:

"I have had my faith pinned on you youngsters, you teenagers, for a long time. I think this capitol for our state is going to be built for you and your generation more than for the present generation. And that is why I am standing here. I believe that our sense of the beautiful—let us say artistic, let us say creation—resides more with you now than it does with your parents, your grandparents, your uncles, your aunts. You are the coming power that is going to be called Democratic, in America.

"If I do nothing more than awaken your young minds to the possibility of architecture as a great creative element in your life, then I will have done all I expected to do. I never expected to build your capitol—do not expect it now. But what I do expect to do is to bring home to the fresh young minds of Arizona the possibility of a great architecture, a humanistic architecture that makes life itself more beautiful".[13]

Many years later, in 1990, when the Frank Lloyd Wright Foundation was preparing an exhibition of Wright drawings at the Phoenix Art Museum, Clark brought the two drawings and gave them to the Frank Lloyd Wright Foundation. He further explained that one time a burglar broke into his house and stole the TV set and some other items, but these two drawings were framed and on the wall above the TV, yet they were not taken.

PRO BONO PUBLICO ARIZONA

PART SIX

BUILDINGS FOR THE CITY

Many of the buildings that Frank Lloyd Wright designed for the city are already represented here in previous categories; residential, religious, commercial, educational, and cultural. In this section, however, a selection is made of other structures, some built, some projects that were never constructed, but all of which reflect his way of dealing with architecture in an urban setting.

The Press Building, a project for San Francisco, was truly his first skyscraper, while the National Life Building was a far more complex and innovative skyscraper design. The concept of floors being cantilevered out from a central support, the exterior walls as screens of metal and glass hung from the slab edges, was first introduced in this design and became a principle of structure that he would apply afterward in all tall building designs, culminating in his 1957 design for the Mile High Skyscraper.

In the category of hotels, the Imperial Hotel was a building constructed to honor Japanese culture, while giving the Japanese a building that could withstand the violence of their eternal nemesis—the earthquake—which it gallantly did in 1923 when most of Tokyo and Yokohama were destroyed in the worst earthquake in Japan's recorded history.

Another hotel for Dallas, the Rogers Lacy, was the first hotel in modern times to employ an interior atrium, a feature that was widely imitated by other architects.

His project of 1926, the Skyscraper Regulation, took the average gridiron plan, prevalent in most American cities, and gave it a new solution to better humanize the city. In 1934 he approached the urban problem by decentralization: Broadacre City. His writings in 1932, *The Disappearing City*, heralded this work, which he further expanded in another book, *When Democracy Builds*, in 1945. At the end of his life, he again approached this vision of a decentralized "city" in a further revision of the first two books, this time calling it *The Living City*, 1958. Obviously throughout his life, starting as early as 1913, he was deeply concerned with urban problems and solutions to urban conditions.

In the nation's capital he planned a group of buildings called "Crystal City" that included a hotel, apartment towers, shops, and a theater. Zoning as well as opposition to anything in Washington that was neither "Greek" nor "Colonial" defeated the project.

Individual buildings that he designed for American cities include a group of funeral chapels for San Francisco, a laundry and dry-cleaning plant for Milwaukee, and a self-service Garage for Pittsburgh. Also for San Francisco, he proposed an enormous reinforced-concrete bridge with the highest single span ever designed in order to connect the city with its outlying communities.

Each of these works is individual to the needs and requirements of the particular case. They represent a broad spectrum of architectural designs, and they further attest to Wright's constant application of Organic Architecture in which a building is appropriate to time, appropriate to place, and appropriate to man.

Perspective of interior of
Rogers Lacy Hotel (see p. 384).
FLLW FDN # 4606.003.

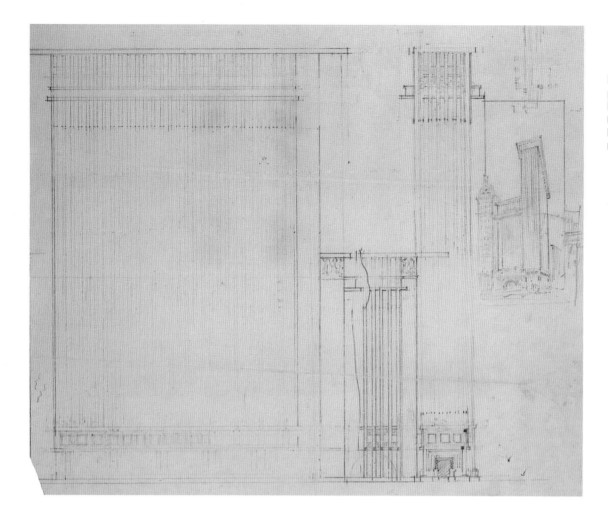

OFFICE BUILDING, "PRESS BUILDING"

For the San Francisco Call Bulletin
San Francisco, California. 1913, Project

The Press Building, as it is known, for the San Francisco newspaper *Call Bulletin*, was Wright's first tall building. He explained its construction when he included the model and drawings in his exhibition that toured the United States and Europe in 1930 and 1931: "To be run in concrete same as a grain elevator is constructed. Projecting slab at top is lighting fixture to illuminate the walls. Building set back so overhang covers only own ground space." Referring to the grain elevator, he means the use of a slip-form that rises, level by level, as each section is poured. When he exhibited the model of the building in his exhibition *Sixty Years of Living Architecture*, which was on tour from 1951–1954, he wrote in the catalog, "This project profoundly influenced the development of the American

skyscraper." Wright's former employer, Louis Sullivan, can justly be credited as the innovator of the skyscraper, not in construction—that was the work of Sullivan's partner Dankmar Adler—but in design, the sense of the building being tall. Up to the time of Sullivan's work, tall buildings were simply blocks of masonry piled one upon the other and ending with an elaborate cornice of some sort. Sullivan indented the window wall, giving accents to the vertical mullions that ran all the way to the top.

In this project, Wright has intensified the character of a tall building but replaced the usual decorative cornice with the projecting reinforced concrete slab. On the final perspective (oppoiste page, right), he has shown a companion building, less tall, but joined to its taller partner.

An early preliminary study with two elevations (above), also shows his thumbnail sketch. The floor plans are labeled "Design for Reinforced Concrete Skyscraper Slab Construction." Another drawing bears his inscription "Call Bldg S. F. Globe Bldg with Albright of L.A." Harrison Albright was the architect for the Spreckels family, the client for the Press.[1] A rudimentary perspective (oppoiste page, left) indicates that the Wright building was to be adjacent to a more conservative neighbor.

The two plans that survive are for the ground floor and the top floor. With so few plans and details, the commission is shrouded in mystery, and although Wright has signed some of the drawings "1912," research has placed the commission in the spring of 1913.[2]

THE IMPERIAL HOTEL

Tokyo, Japan. 1913–1922, Demolished

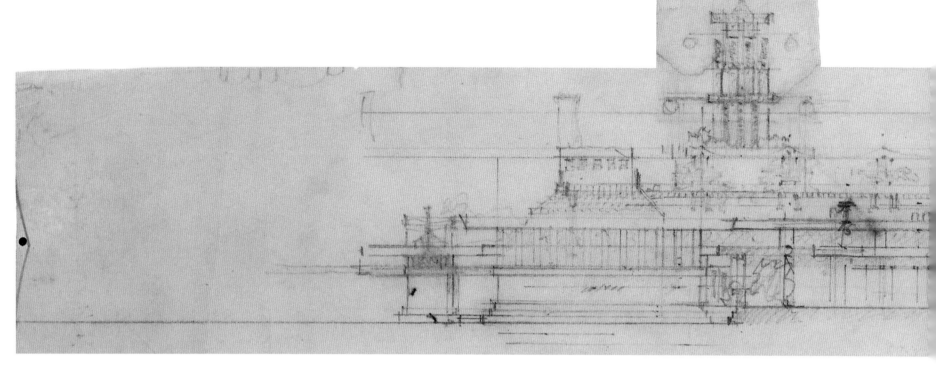

Wright's first journey to Japan took place in 1905, and he was accompanied by his wife Catherine and his clients Mr. and Mrs. Ward Willits. He claimed the reason for this trip was to get away from the exhausting work required to complete the Larkin Building in Buffalo. But why Japan, when the majority of Americans, when they ventured out of the nation, went east to Europe? Chicago happened to have a group of American collectors of Japanese woodblock prints. Wright was certainly cognizant of them and their collections, and thus he was drawn to the nation of their origin. Upon arriving in Japan, he remarked that it "looked just like the prints." Thus began a love affair between Wright and the masters of the Ukiyo-e wood block prints, and he began to acquire a collection of the prints for himself.

In 1911, the old Imperial Hotel in Tokyo proved insufficient for the flock of foreign tourists coming into Japan. The general manager, Aisaku Hayashi, set about to find an

architect for a new hotel. His selection of Wright was spurred on by Frederick Gookin, a noted authority on Japanese prints and a friend of Wright's. Gookin wrote to Wright:

"My dear Wright:

"Do you remember that when I saw you last I asked you how you would like to design a new building for the Imperial Hotel in Tokyo? Well, I wrote a long letter to Mr. Hayashi urging him that you were the right man for him to select as his architect. Today I have a letter from him in reply and this is what he says: 'Many thanks for your opinion of Mr. Wright. I shall write him shortly after completing a rough plan according to my idea. If he would not be too radical and would work under reasonable terms he would be the first one.' I presume that you will also hear from him before a great while, and I sincerely hope this may lead to your getting the commission. Somehow it seems to me that this would be a great opportunity for you to do a stunning thing."[3]

Two years later, in 1913, Wright again journeyed to Japan, this time accompanied by Mamah Borthwick Cheney, the wife of his client Edwin Cheney. Wright and Mamah had fallen in love, and both deserted their families to take up life together. The purpose of this trip, however, was to secure the commission for the new Imperial Hotel. On returning to the United States, he wrote to his friend and client Darwin D. Martin, of the Larkin Building, "I have just got into the office (an hour ago). The planning of the Imperial Hotel is up to me."[4] It was also in this trip that he bought a great number of Japanese prints not only for himself but for other American collectors as well.

By 1916, a formal contract had been signed by Wright and the Japanese for the design of the Imperial Hotel. Hayashi and his wife came to Taliesin and Chicago. They saw his work and were completely convinced that the correct architect had been retained. One noon, while Wright and Hayashi were having lunch in a Chicago

Below: Elevation. FLLW FDN # 1409.001.
Bottom: Elevation. FLLW FDN # 1409.018.

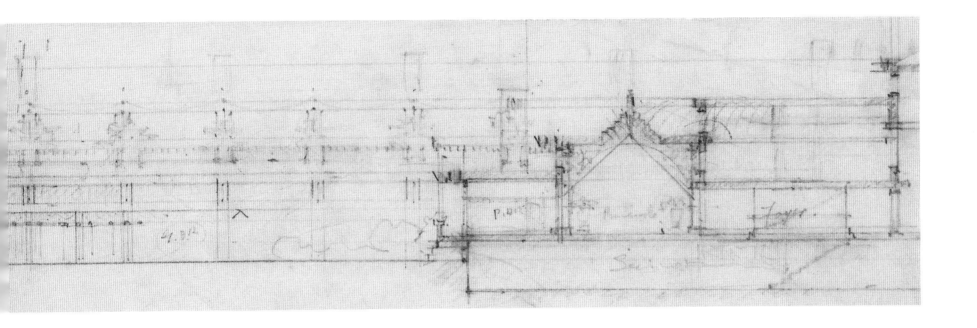

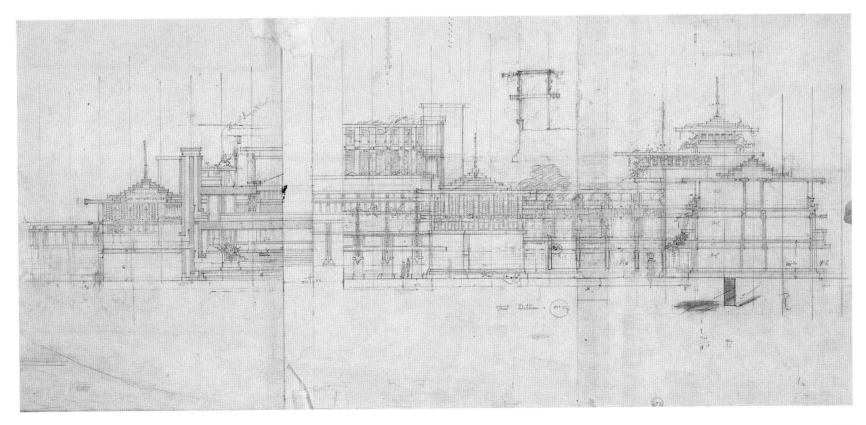

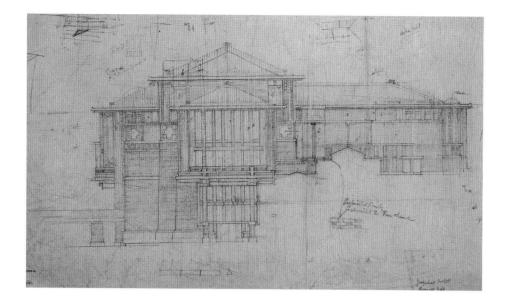

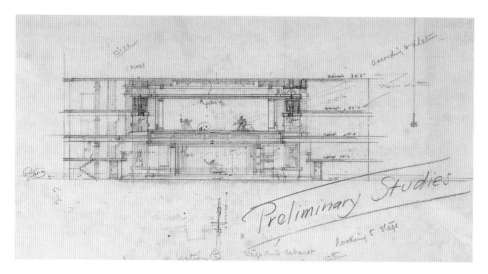

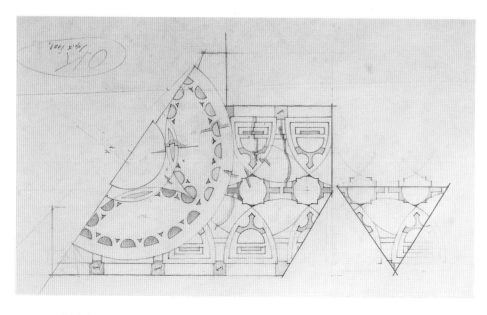

restaurant, the question came up about the constant threat of earthquakes, prevalent in Japan. How to build a building that could survive them, Hayashi asked. Wright pointed to a waiter carrying a tray, supported by his hand under the center of the tray, the tray balanced overhead on it. "Like that," Wright replied, "balanced loads." He was referring to the principle of cantilevered support, rather than support at the exterior walls, like a house of cards in which if the walls are moved, the whole comes tumbling down. Another factor in the design of the hotel was the use of reinforced concrete and brick masonry. The traditional buildings in Japan were of wood and paper, with heavy tile roofs. Fires customarily followed the earthquakes, and the wood and paper buildings were swept away while the heavy tiles thrown down on the streets fell upon the people running to and fro during the disaster. Wright proposed a roof of lightweight copper tiles instead.

When Wright was studying the site upon which the new hotel was to be built, he was informed that many years ago it had been filled in on a part of Tokyo Bay. Further investigation revealed that a strata of nine feet of topsoil rested upon a substrata of twenty feet of mud. He reasoned that if he could connect the foundations of the hotel to that substrata of mud, the building could quite naturally float, in a sense, and move with the movement of the quake rather than stand rigid and try to fight it. In other words, flexibility, not rigidity. This was a novel idea and met with a great deal of consternation and disapproval. Nonetheless, he instructed the workmen to bore holes two feet on centers and nine feet deep across the entire site. Into these holes concrete was poured, creating a network of dowels upon which pig iron was placed, and carefully weighed in order to record how much weight each dowel would support until it sank deeper. In this way, data was accumulated and Wright was able to design and engineer a structure that would rest on these dowels as a foundation. Here was the principle of flexibility combined with the principle of cantilever construction that Wright was convinced would allow the hotel to move with the quake and then return to normal.

Even before a final contract was in place, as early as 1913 Wright began to prepare sketches

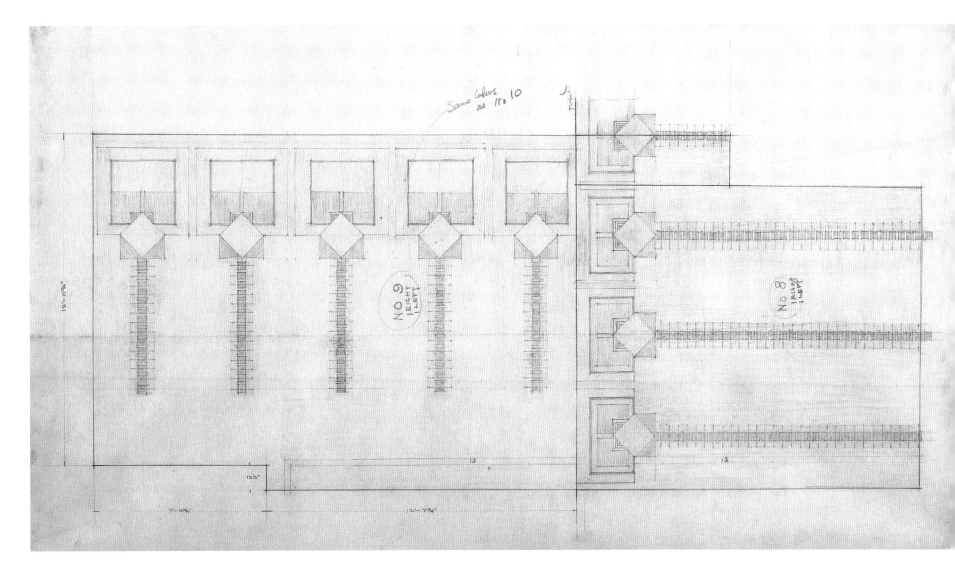

Same colors as No. 10

No. 9 (RIGHT) (LEFT)

No. 8 (RIGHT) (LEFT)

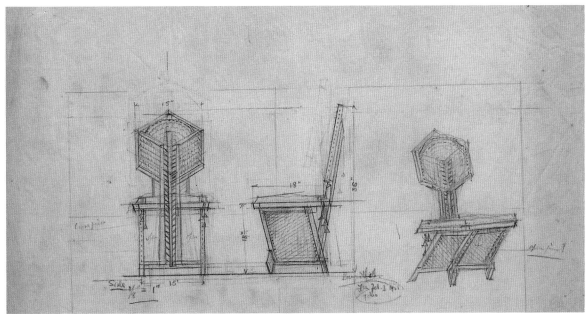

Left, top: Elevation. FLLW FDN # 1509.018.
Left, middle: Section. FLLW FDN # 1509.187.
Left, middle: Plan. FLLW FDN # 1509.196.
Above: Sketch for decorative elements.
FLLW FDN # 1509.036.
Near left: Sketch for chair.
FLLW FDN # 1509.057.

Perspective. FLLW FDN # 1509.003.

and preliminary studies. An imposing, large presentation rendering was made by his draftsman Emil Brodelle (pp. 366-7). As the work progressed, Wright designed sculptural elements in stone that were woven into the general fabric of the building, along with murals, furniture, tableware, rugs, and textiles. Like the Midway Gardens, this was to be a structure where again the

architect was master of all the arts.

During the construction, Wright was faced with the ongoing task of how to instruct the Japanese workmen to build a building of reinforced concrete and brick when they were accustomed to building with wood and paper. "On an average we employed about 600 men continually for four years. As a large proportion of them

came from the surrounding country they lived round about in the building as we built it. With their numerous families, there they were—cooking, washing, sleeping. And we tried faithfully—sometimes frantically and often profanely—to teach them how to build it, halfway between our way and their way . . . How skillful they were! What craftsmen! How patient and clever. So

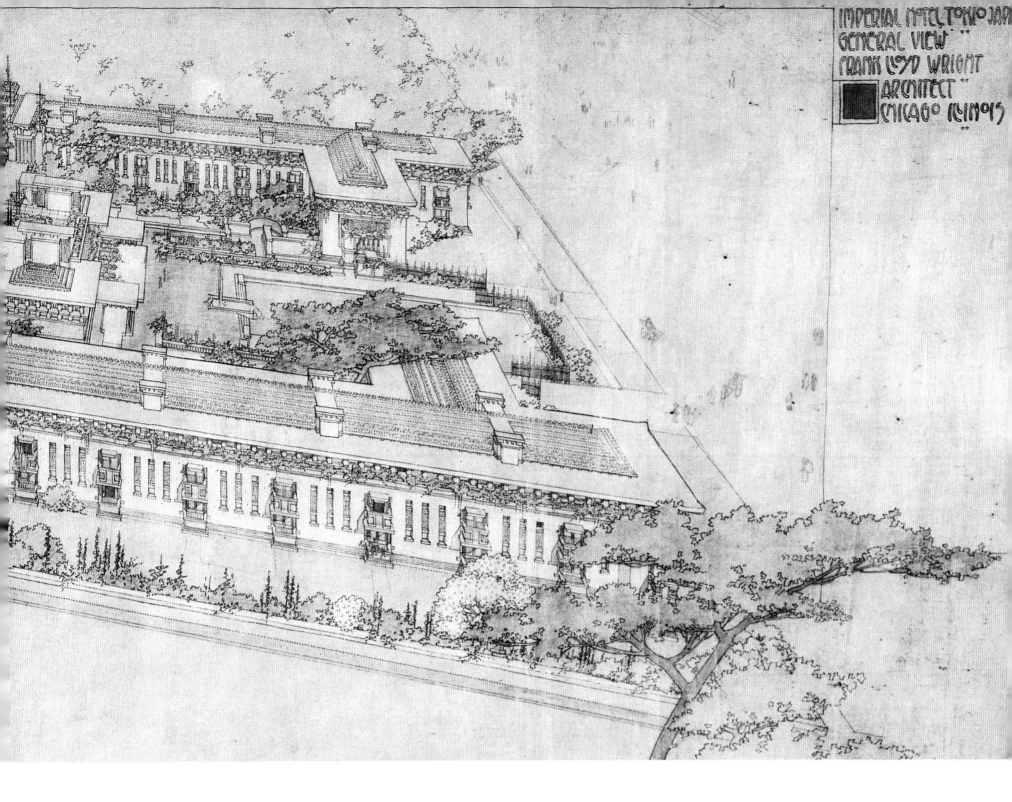

instead of wasting them by vainly trying to make them come our way—we went with them their way . . . The countenance of the building began to emerge from the seemingly hopeless confusion of the enormous area now covered by the building materials of its terraces and courts and hundreds of families. And the workmen grew more and more interested in it. It was no uncommon thing to see groups of them admiring and criticizing too as some finished portion would emerge—criticizing intelligently. There was a warmth of appreciation and loyalty unknown in the building circles of our country. A fine thing to have experienced."[5]

However, despite his conviction about the soundness of the innovative foundations, he was constantly met with doubts and disbeliefs. That is, until one day in 1922. Wright and the Japanese draftsmen had moved their workplace to the top of the left wing above the promenade entrance.

"Suddenly with no warning a gigantic jolt lifted the whole building, threw the boys down sprawling with their drafting boards.

A moment's panic and hell broke loose as the wave motions began. The structure was literally in convulsions. I was knocked down by the rush of the workmen and my own boys to save their own lives . . . . As I lay there I could clearly see the groundswell pass through the construction above as it heaved and groaned to hideous crushing and grinding noises. Several thunderous crashes sickened me, but later these proved to be the falling of five tall chimneys of the old Imperial, left standing alone by the recent burning of that building. At the time it seemed as though the banquet hall section, invisible just behind the workroom, had crashed down. Only one faithful assistant stayed through this terrible ordeal. Endo-San, loyal right-bower—white to the teeth—perspiring. Otherwise the building was deserted. We got up shaking to the knees and went together out onto the roofs. There across the street were crowds of frightened workmen. There they all stood strangely silent, pasty-faced, shaking. A strange silence too was everywhere over the city. Soon fires broke out in a dozen places. Bells rang and pandemonium broke. Women dragging frightened children ran weeping and wailing along the streets below. We had just passed through the worst quake in fifty-two years. The building was undamaged. A transit put on the foundation levels showed no deviation whatsoever. The work had been proved." [6]

But there would be an even worse test, the next year. Wright had already returned to the United States and left the finishing construction of a wing identical to the one he had supervised to his assistant Endo. On September 1, 1923, the hotel was preparing luncheon for its grand opening. At exactly noon, the worst quake ever recorded in Japanese history struck. Much of Tokyo and Yokohama lay in ruins, fires breaking out all over. All water mains and gas lines were torn up. Poles carrying electric and telephone wires were broken and tossed to the ground. Over a hundred thousand people perished. Direct communication was cut off, and the newspapers reported, erroneously, that the Imperial Hotel had been destroyed. For ten days Wright suffered through anguish and uncertainty. Finally, from Baron Okura, chairman of the board of directors of the Imperial Hotel, the following telegram was sent to Wright, who was in Los Angeles at the time: "Hotel stands undamaged as monument of your genius. Hundreds of homeless provided for by perfectly maintained service. Congratulations." [7]

"For once good news was news and the Baron's telegram flashed around the world to herald the triumph of good sense. Both the great Tokio [sic] homes of the Baron were gone. The splendid museum he gave to Tokio and all its contents were destroyed. The building by the American architect, whose hand he took and whose cause he sponsored, was all he had left in Tokio—nor could love or money buy it now or buy a share of stock in it. When the letters began to come in and nearly all the friends were found to be safe the news most gratifying to the architect was the fact that after the first great quake was over, the dead rotting there in unburied heaps, the Japanese in subsequent shocks came in droves dragging their children into the courts and onto the terraces of the building, praying for protection by the God that has protected that building." [8]

As with all grand hotels worldwide, the Imperial Hotel provided the necessary amenities to the public as well as the hotel guests. The more public areas were located in the central section of the building. The guest rooms were located in wings on each side, thus the whole forming a great "H." In the center a lobby, with two upper levels for balconies, led directly into the main dining room, a two-story space lit by high windows on both sides. On a lower level beneath the lobby were located a beauty parlor, barber shop, shops, and concessions. Also in the central section were located a cabaret, a theater, and on the top floor a banquet hall, called the Peacock Room, that could serve one thousand persons. Adjacent to this were two spacious "parlors" each with a fireplace above which were hand painted murals of Wright's design (right). A long alley stretched across the entire width of the building and provided for small gatherings along the way. Private dining rooms also served the need for the Japanese to entertain guests and clients, since, by tradition, such meetings were not held in private homes.

However, the Imperial Hotel provided another important role, perhaps the most important of all:

"When I built the Imperial Hotel in Tokyo, Japan, I tried to make a coherent link between

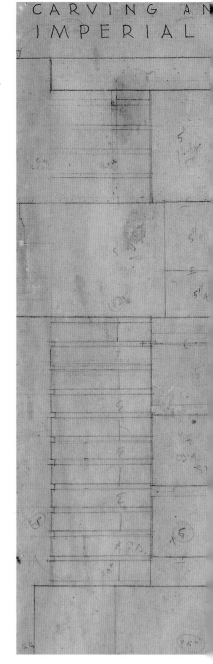

Design for mural.
FLLW FDN # 1509.005.

what the Japanese then were on their knees and what they now wanted to be on their feet. Every civilization that had gone to Japan had looted their culture. Because it was the only such culture, coming from their own ground as it did, I was determined as an American to take off my hat to that extraordinary culture. At the same time I was now faced with the problem of how to build a modern building earthquake-proof. This was mainly the Mikado's building. So I had also to consider the Mikado's needs for a social clear-

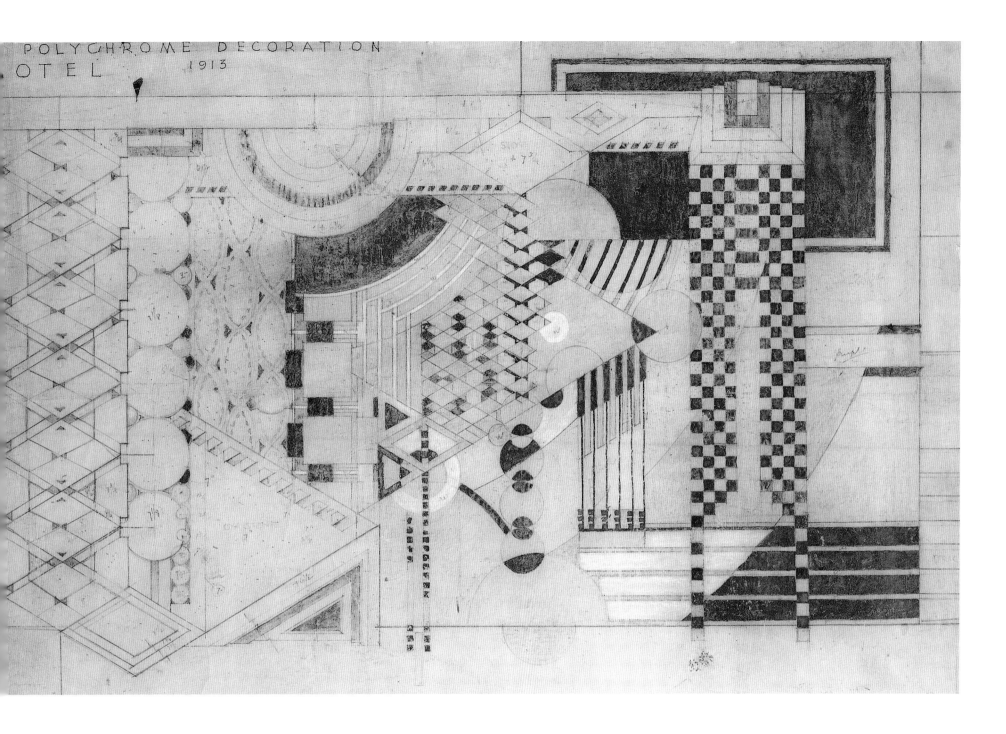

POLYCHROME DECORATION
OTEL 1913

inghouse for the official life that would inevitably now come to Japan. So the Impeho would have to be comfortable enough for foreigners, although it would need to serve the needs of the Japanese."[9]

Postscript: The Tragedy of Progress

By 1967, the word around Tokyo was that the most valuable real estate in the city was the air above the Imperial Hotel. In other words, the management of the hotel realized that it had become desirable to demolish the rather low

lying Wright building and in its place erect a typical multistory steel and glass hotel tower. Learning of this decision, former Japanese apprentices to Frank Lloyd Wright urged his widow, Olgivanna, to come to Japan and muster public support in order to save the building. She arrived in Japan in October 1967, accompanied by several members of the Taliesin Fellowship. It proved to be a fruitless quest: the hotel was a private property, and the owners had made up their minds to tear it down.

However, when Olgivanna arrived at the hotel, it was late in the afternoon, and the receding autumnal sun painted a golden glow across the yellow brickwork of the building. When she stepped out of the car in the porte-cochere, the long wings of the guest rooms stretched out on either side, a reporter asked her, "How does it feel, Mrs. Wright, to actually be in the hotel Mr. Wright built?" She replied, simply, "It is once again like being in the arms of my husband."

OFFICE BUILDING

For the National Life Insurance Company
Chicago, Illinois. 1925, Project

Below: Plan, section, and perspective. FLLW FDN # 2402.012.

Right: Preliminary section and plan. FLLW FDN # 2404.011.

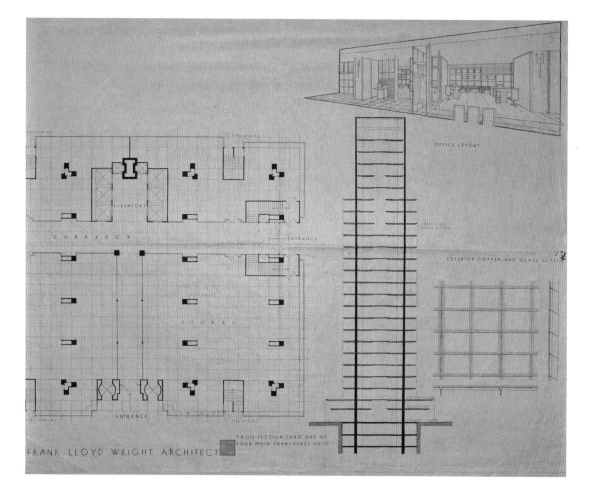

FRANK LLOYD WRIGHT ARCHITECT

Albert Johnson, president of the National Life Insurance Company, was immensely impressed with the performance of the Imperial Hotel in the Kanto Earthquake, and he agreed to pay Wright $20,000 for a design for an office building for his company. He wanted to see how the structural principle that saved the Imperial Hotel could be applied to a tall office building. Wright described A. M. Johnson as "a strange mixture of the fanatic and the mystic, Shylock and the humanist. Withal he was extraordinarily intelligent. Ideas attracted this insurance man. He kept saying 'Now Wright, remember!'—with his characteristic chuckle—'I want a virgin. I want a virgin.'"[10]

This was a much-needed commission for Wright at the time, and he set to work on a large skyscraper. His initial study (opposite page) reveals a tall building with an atrium court running down the center and rising up to a skylight above. Between the section and the plan he has drawn two minuscule thumbnail views of the building. Discarding this study, he then set to work on a completely different design, and described it in a letter written on October 30, 1925 to his friend and colleague H.Th. Wijdeveld in Holland:

"I am working on a great commercial building, a copy of a photograph of the perspective drawing enclosed—but not for publication yet. A new system of cantilevered floor construction— resting on interior pylons extending from 60 feet below ground to above the building as you see, where the setback occurs. The exterior is a screen all of copper and glass carried from floor to floor on the cantilever projections of the floors —a projection from the pylons of twelve feet all around. This shell or screen is a mechanized fabric some four or five inches thick and deducts nothing from rentable ground area as the glass is on the lot-line, and continuous. The fire escapes are integral stairways between floors (see center of each unit). There is nothing in the way of the commercial uses of the various floors—and nothing manufactured as features for effect. All is enclosed commercial space with clear outside glass."[11]

At the time that Wright was working on the National Life building, the American skyscraper or tall building was a structure of heavy masonry, blocks of stone adhered to a steel skeleton framework, a system of construction that was both labor-intensive and costly. His concept for the tall building, on the contrary, was something lighter in weight and made use of factory production for the individual units. The pylons, or central supports, as well as the floor slabs, were of reinforced concrete. The outer shell, the exterior wall of the building, was composed of two-by-two-foot units of glass and copper suspended from the edges of the floor slabs. These units could be made in a factory and shipped to the construction site.

"Thus, literally, we have a shop-made building in all but the interior supporting posts and floors, which may be reinforced concrete or con-

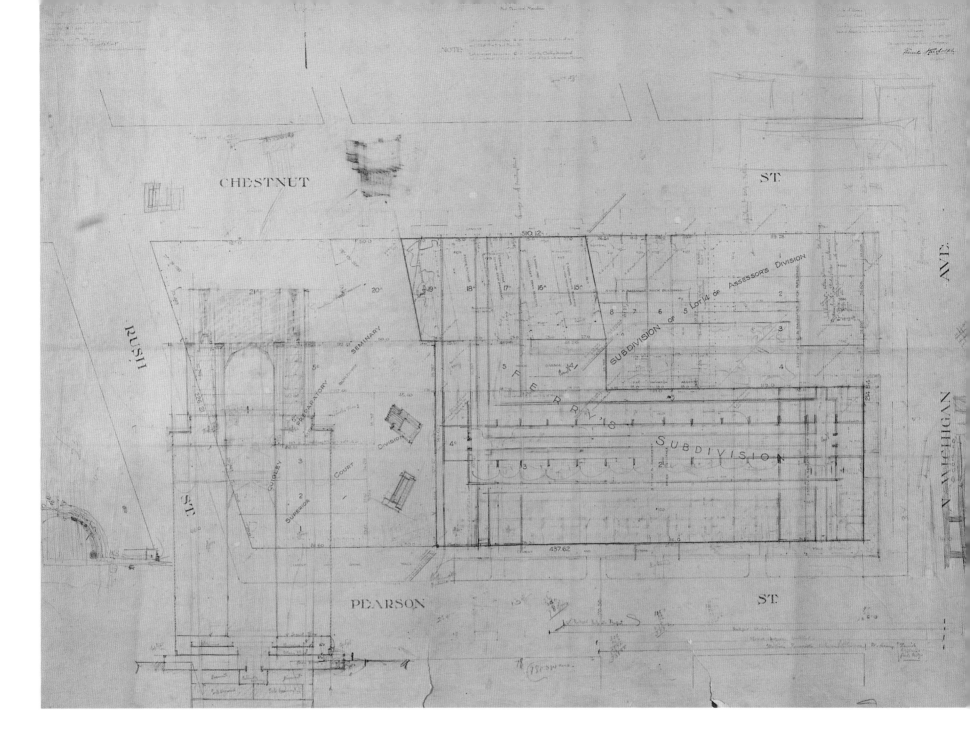

crete-masked steel cast in place in the field. In this design, architecture was frankly, profitably and artistically—why not?—taken from the field to the factory. A building is here standardized as any mechanical thing whatsoever might be from a pennywhistle to a piano, and it is dignified, imaginative, practical. The economic advantages are enormous and obvious."[12]

"I had the good fortune to explain the scheme in detail and show the developed preliminary drawings to Liebermeister Louis H. Sullivan shortly before he died. Gratefully I remember—

and proudly too—he said 'I had faith that it would come. It is a work of great art. I knew what I was talking about all these years—you see? I could never have done this building myself, but I believe that, but for me, you could never have done it.'

"I know I should never have reached it, but for what he was and what he himself did. This design is dedicated to him."[13]

While Johnson was admittedly enthusiastic about the scheme, he was not enthusiastic enough to build.

"Intensely interested in ideas, I believe, though not himself the kind of man inclined to build much, he seemed rather of the type called conservative who, tempted, will sneak up behind an idea, pinch it in the behind and turn and run. There is this type of man bred by our capitalistic system, not the captain, nor the broker or the banker, but a better sort not quite contented with the commonplace, not quite courageous enough to take risks. I have met many such men."[14]

DING FOR NATIONAL LIFE INSURANCE: CHICAGO FRANK LLOYD RIGHT ARCHITECT W TALIESIN

Left: Perspective. FLLW FDN # 2404.001
Right: Perspective. FLLW FDN # 2404.041 .

OFFICE BUILDING FOR NATIONAL LIFE INSURANCE CO OF USA CHICAGO — A M JOHNSON PRESIDENT   FRANK LLOYD WRIGHT ARCHITECT 1925

SKYSCRAPER REGULATION

Location unspecified. 1926, Project

Below: Elevation. FLLW FDN # 2603.002.
Right, top: Elevation. FLLW FDN # 2603.001.
Right, bottom: Plan. FLLW FDN # 2603.004.

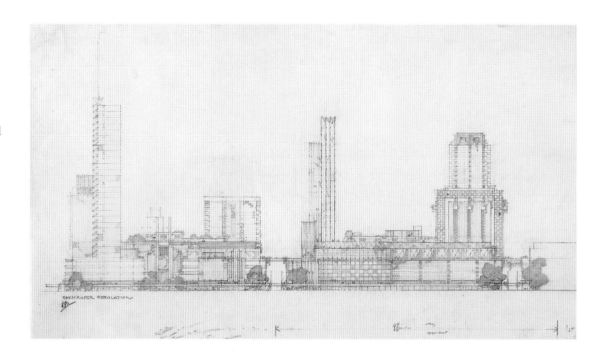

For Frank Lloyd Wright, city planning was a vexing problem which he first attacked in 1913 when the City Club of Chicago arranged a competition for the development of a quarter section of land on the outskirts of the city. Although Wright submitted a plan, it was not part of the competition, and it was published as "Non-Competitive Plan" in 1916 along with other projects in the book *City Residential Land Development: Studies in Planning* (University of Chicago Press).

His plan provided for commercial buildings, cultural buildings, recreation centers, religious centers, theaters, schools, a library, art museum, motion-picture theater, shops, fire department, post office, bank branch, apartments, and dwellings. The entire block was planned around spacious open parks and water lagoons, and placed the commercial buildings adjacent to the railway for the suburban trains, while at the opposite, quieter side were the residential units, both for expensive homes and less costly ones.

Further to his efforts concerning city planning, ten years after this plan was published, he proposed a scheme that would take into account the solution in regards to current cities. He called this new plan "Skyscraper Regulation."

In this project Wright has taken an average city block group of four or eight blocks on the usual grid plan of American cities and realigned the tall buildings and boulevards. The average city plan placed tall buildings—skyscrapers—in such a way as to create dark canyons for the citizens on the streets below. In this plan he had regulated the placement and height of the buildings in such a way as to avoid the "canyon" effect. If a tall building faces east, then the building across the street would face north, for example.

The rooftops of the buildings are flat, and in some cases simple architectural features, part of the main structure, conceal water towers and elevator machinery. The transportation and circulation plan locates heavy trucking on an underground level accessing storage areas, warehouses and loading docks. The ground level is reserved for light service vehicles and automobiles. The second level is for pedestrian traffic, crossing over the avenues and streets on bridges, protected from the street traffic. The sixth level is another pedestrian level, also crossing over the avenues on pedestrian bridges. On several buildings throughout the grid, this sixth level becomes a rooftop garden with outdoor restaurants and parks. The broad main avenues are planted with spacious medians to bring trees and planting into the scheme. The design of the buildings and skyscrapers themselves would closely follow that of the National Life Insurance Company office building: reinforced concrete cantilevered floor slabs are supported by a central core which also provides service, utilities, and elevators. The outer surfaces, no longer acting as supports, are screens of glass and copper hung from the slab edges. Illustrating this method are two drawings (above and opposite page, top) of staggering the tall buildings, expanding the avenues with trees and shrubs, and the top levels of some of buildings planted as garden parks.

On another drawing (opposite page, bottom) he has made copious notes concerning the concerning setbacks, height restrictions, parking, landscaping, access to subways, and underground power lines, further detailing this city plan, in which he has humanized the urban condition as much as possible by providing a crystalline cluster of geometric forms interspersed with light, air, and landscaping. At the bottom of these notes, he has written:

"Sky-Scraper Regulation
Augmenting the gridiron
Remodeling of the City—FLLW 1926
Beyond these provisions the city should spread out."

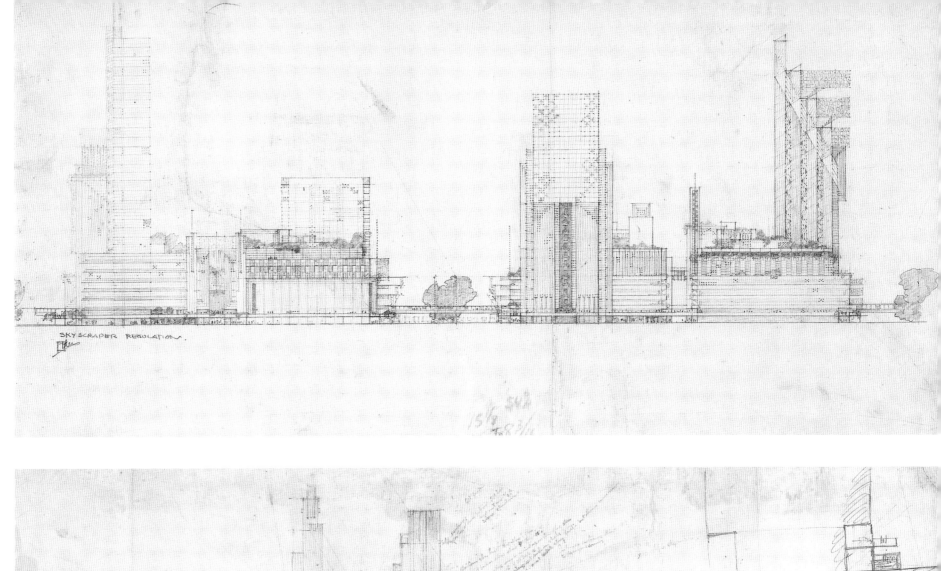

SKYSCRAPER REGULATION.

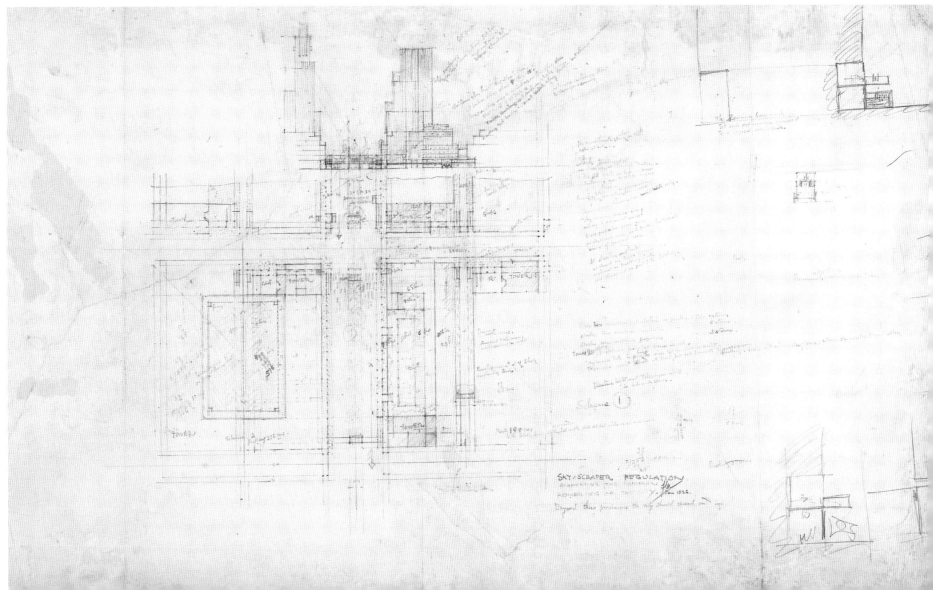

SKY-SCRAPER REGULATION

"CRYSTAL HEIGHTS" ("CRYSTAL CITY") HOTEL, APARTMENT TOWERS, SHOPS, AND THEATER

For Roy S. Thurman
Washington, D.C. 1940, Project

Below: Plan. FLLW FDN # 4016.005.

Right, top: Elevation.
FLLW FDN # 4016.002.
Right, bottom: Perspective.
FLLW FDN # 4016.004.

The property Roy Thurman planned to acquire for this project was called "Temple Heights." As Wright's design went forward, he suggested the name "Crystal Heights," but eventually it came to be known as "Crystal City." The site was vaguely triangular in shape, and sloped down from an oak tree garden at one end to the point of the triangle at the other. On the upper level of the site, eleven towers, based on the plan for St. Mark's-in-the-Bouwerie, were linked together, with three others freestanding. Each section was composed of two towers joined together. Five of the double towers and one triple tower constituted the hotel portion of the project, and formed an "L" in plan. The towers for apartments extended out from the L plan to the edge of the property on the other side.

Running along the Connecticut Avenue side down to the lowest part of the property where Connecticut Avenue meets Florida Avenue a theater with seating for 1,100 was planned. Between the hotel part at the top and the theater at the lower side were five terraces for shops, with parking located behind the shops underground. Access to the shops and parking was provided at the point where each terrace is tangent to the avenue. Wright has thus faced the problem of parking with ample space on top of the terraces adjacent to the hotel, as well as behind each of them. All concrete surfaces throughout the building were to be sheathed in blue-veined white marble, the metal components, such as the window sash, in bronze. With such extensive use of glass, Wright included an explanatory letter with the preliminary drawings:

"Crystal is the word when you see the buildings. I have assumed that you wanted the last word which is also the first word in all this and we have it—the apotheosis of GLASS. The floor surfaces which are extensive inside and outside will receive great attention—be of white marble with bronze shallow bas-relief inlays—at appro-

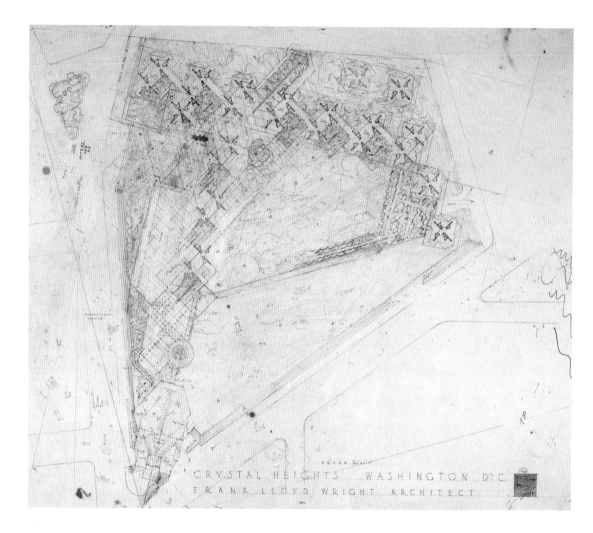

CRYSTAL HEIGHTS   WASHINGTON D.C.
FRANK LLOYD WRIGHT ARCHITECT

priate places emphasizing the great spaciousness in bright light of the whole structure. The gardens and terraces all contribute to this effect too. I've managed to save the better part of the oaks. The dining room, banquet hall and all private supper rooms are all sunlit overlooking garden terraces—gleaming crystal palaces, Versailles is no more."[15]

The project underwent trial after trial with the zoning authorities, since the neighborhood was primarily residential there was opposition to

a scheme that served so many commercial aspects. Underlying this problem of zoning, there was strong resistance on the part of some of the authorities to see such a modern structure take place in Washington. "Neither Greek nor Colonial therefore unfit for the nation's capital" was their opinion, but in order to make it seem "legal" rather than a mere artistic opinion, they relied on the excuse that it violated the conditions of "zoning" and it was thus defeated.

CONNECTICUT AVENUE ELEVATION   SCALE 1" = 32'-0"

CRYSTAL HEIGHTS WASHINGTON DC FRANK LLOYD WRIGHT ARCHITECT
FOR ROY S THURMAN

DAPHNE CHAPELS

Funeral Chapels for Nicholas Daphne
San Francisco, California. Project, 1945

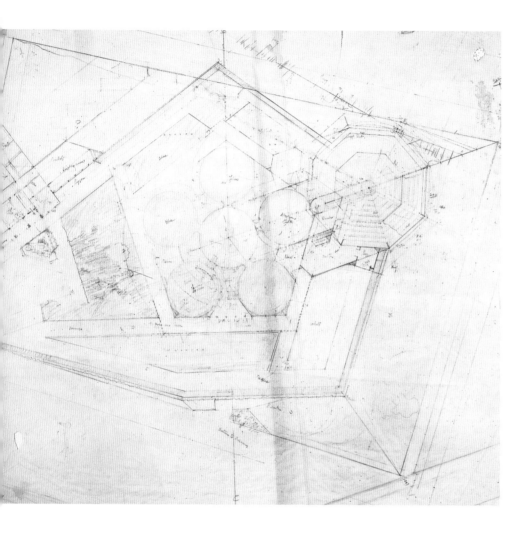

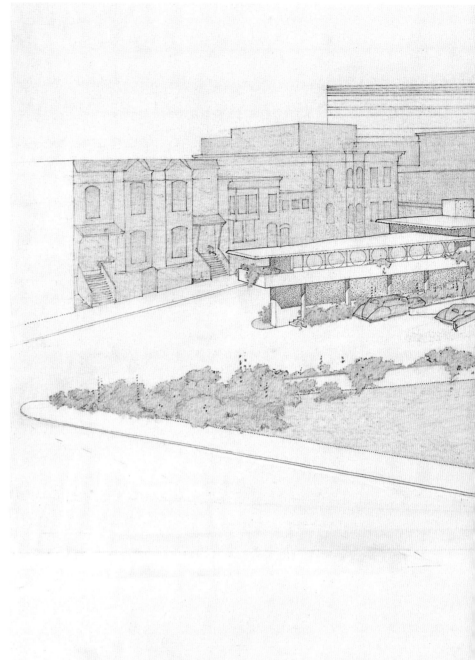

The commission to design San Francisco funeral chapels for mortician Nicholas Daphne was a most difficult one for Wright, not from the aspect of design, but rather because of the client's specifications and requirements. Wright was generally opposed to the customary ritual of embalming, cosmetic work, and final burial. He strongly believed in cremation. (When he himself died, however, his widow Olgivanna was prevailed upon by his surviving children to adhere to formal tradition and go through the entire burial procedure. Upon her death twenty-eight years later, her will specified that both she and Wright be cremated and their ashes interred in a stone wall at Taliesin West, Scottsdale, Arizona.)

For this particular project, the details and conditions of the program began to have an adverse effect on him. "Of course I had to 'research' a good deal and that nearly got me down. I would come back home, now and then, wondering if I felt as well as I should. But Nick had a way of referring to the deceased, always, as 'the merchandise' and that would cheer me up. I pulled through and you behold the result."[16]

His first sketch plan (above, left) represented a grouping of five chapels with a sixth one, very much larger, attached to the general plan. His elevation shows this as well (not shown). But the plan to add the larger chapel was abandoned early in the development stages of the project.

The final configuration represented five circular chapels arranged as a cluster within a penta-

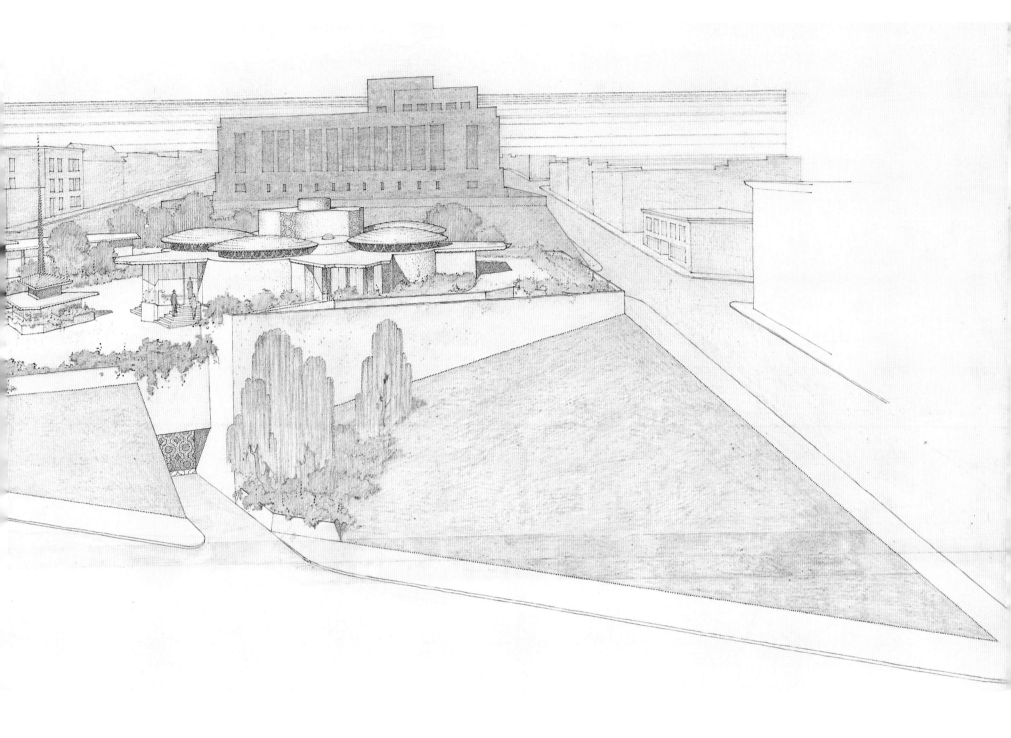

gon. Each chapel, which can seat 70 to 100 persons, had a "mourner's alcove" where the family of the deceased could look into the chapel yet not be seen. The chapels are lit by a narrow ring of high clerestory windows where the walls meet the edges of the domed ceiling, providing a pleasant but diffused light within. Each chapel has its own entry and is bordered outside by a garden. All workrooms are located in an underground level, beneath the chapels and independent of them. Parking is also located underground

with elevators to the chapel floor for access to the mourners and the chapels. A long building on the side of the property provides offices and basket displays, with a residence on the second floor. A triangular kiosk, separate from the chapels or office area, contains floral displays. Gardens are provided throughout the area, as Wright explained, "Every possible convenience designed to make the place helpful to the bereaved is here incorporated. The emphasis is here laid not on Death but on Life."[17]

Left: Plan. FLLW FDN # 4823.017.

Above: Perspective. FLLW FDN # 4823.006.

LAUNDRY AND DRY-CLEANING PLANT

For Benjamin Adelman
Milwaukee, Wisconsin. 1945, Project

At the beginning of 1945, Wright was at work for Nicholas Daphne designing funeral chapels. Work on the commission went on for some time. As Wright admitted, he became somewhat depressed due to careful study of all the methods and procedures used in the preparation and cosmetic work involved in a mortuary, and how to provide for them in his design. Therefore, it must have been somewhat of a relief when his next large commercial commission for the city was the laundry and dry-cleaning plant for Benjamin Adelman.

The site was an irregular property with a slight slope. Planned on two levels with a basement, the public area and workrooms are placed on the lower part of the site, on mostly level ground. Wright's first sketch (opposite page) shows how he has placed the building on a diagonal line on that part of the property that was flat. His drawing also included an elevation and a section within the general workroom of the plant. On the main floor plan, an entrance drive passes under the mezzanine level, with provisions for parking and exiting at the other side of the lot. Public access and the laundry workroom are located to the right of the entrance under this covered entrance drive. A sales counter extends the full width of the interior; there is, as well, a general office and two circular private offices.

The main laundry workroom is just beyond the circular offices. Here the space is two stories tall, and a large plenum is held overhead by reinforced concrete struts that engage the plenum and provide clerestory windows all along the plenum throughout the laundry room and the mezzanine. Another plenum is located in the basement below the laundry room. The plenum above provides warm air in winter and cool air in summer, while the plenum below draws the air down and out through special vent shafts. By this device, the usual dank air in a laundry

establishment is drawn out and fresh air brought in by the constant interaction of these two plenums.

A mezzanine above the general public area and office spaces overlooks the laundry room below and provides several additional functions: a cafeteria, with access to an outdoor roof deck, a kitchen, a private dining room, a lounge, and two rest rooms (equipped with beds). The large circular form supported by the pedestal is given over to dry cleaning and a gas room. Directly over the drive-through are eight open wells that bring natural light down to that level.

An angular shape, determined by the property, is adjacent to the main building and contains a covered court for trucks. Since the building was to be built on a sloped site, this truck court is level with the mezzanine, and a space next to the main laundry room is provided with a long opening to the bundle room below: the truckers thus drop their bundles down where they are sorted and brought into the laundry below.

The design takes into account the well-being of the workers in a clean and well-lit environment along with the provision for a cafeteria a nd outdoor dining during pleasant weather conditions.

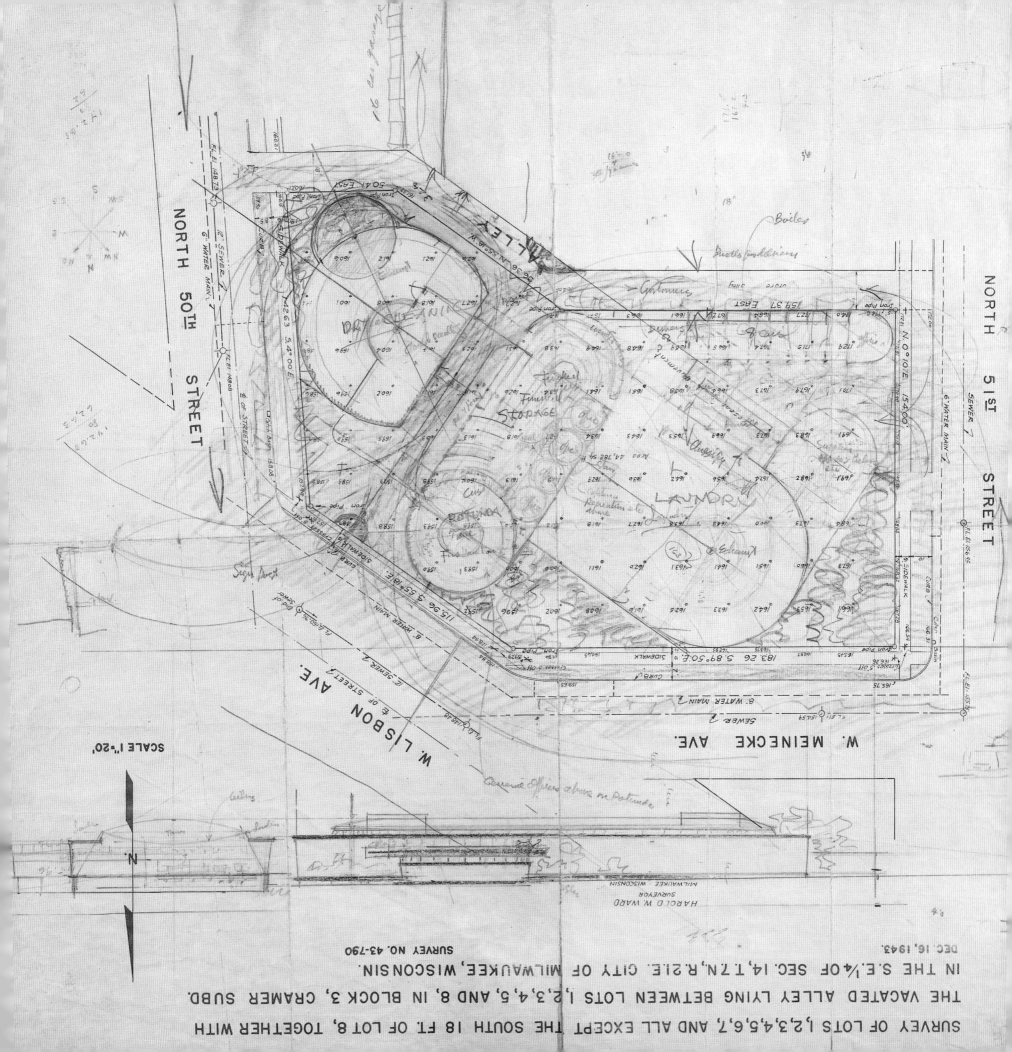

SURVEY OF LOTS 1,2,3,4,5,6,7, AND 8, TOGETHER WITH
THE VACATED ALLEY LYING BETWEEN LOTS 1,2,3,4,5, AND 8, IN BLOCK 3, CRAMER SUBD.
IN THE S.E.¼ OF SEC.14,T.7N,R.21E, CITY OF MILWAUKEE, WISCONSIN.

SURVEY NO. 43-790

DEC. 16, 1943.

HAROLD W. WARD
SURVEYOR
MILWAUKEE - WISCONSIN

SCALE 1"=20'

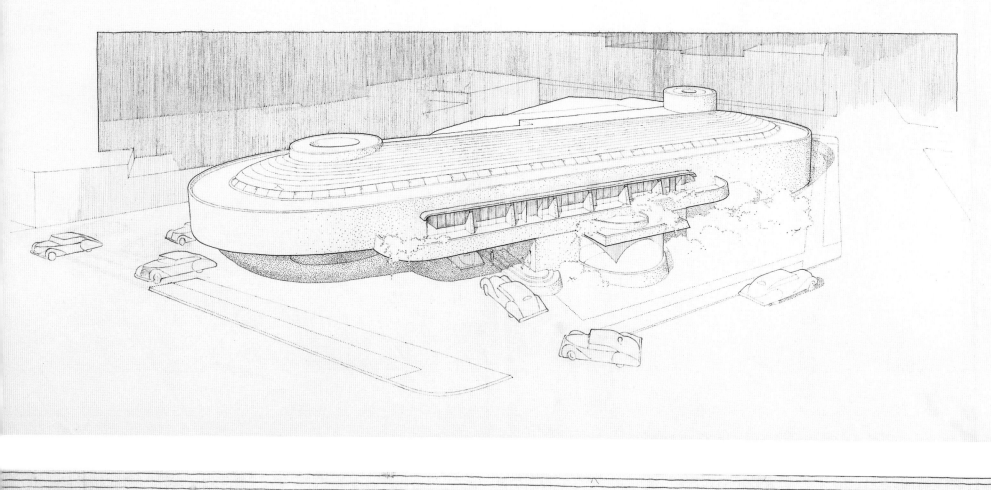

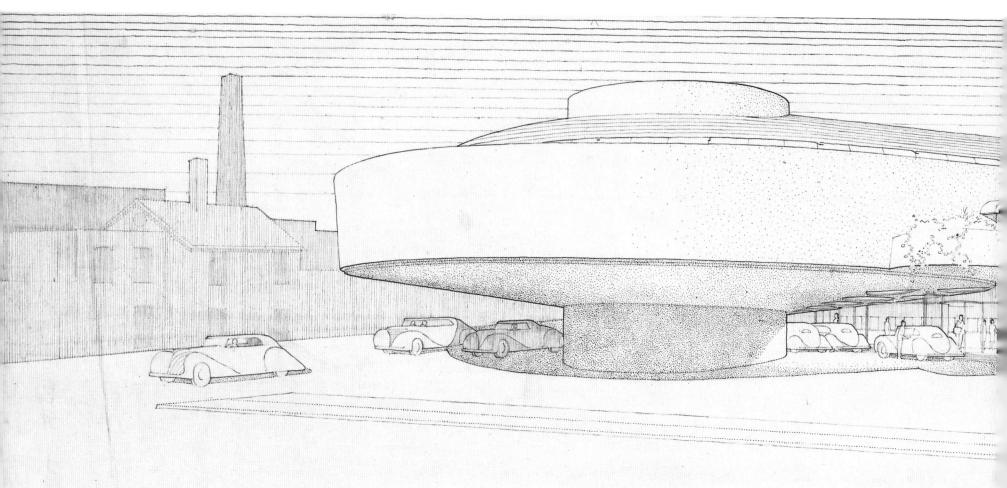

L A U N D R Y   F O R   M R.   B E N J A M I N   A D E L M A N
F R A N K   L L O Y D   W R I G H T   A R C H I T E C T

ROGERS LACY HOTEL

Dallas, Texas. 1946

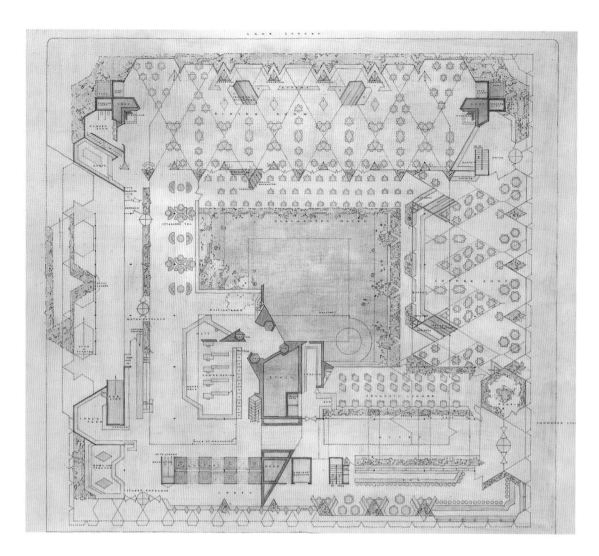

The Rogers Lacy Hotel was an extraordinary commission, and one for which Wright and his apprentices undertook an enormous amount of planning and work. Scheduled to be built on a downtown block in the city of Dallas, the structure was designed so as to place the major elements of the hotel in a fifteen-story block of rooms and guest facilities opening onto a central atrium. His conceptual drawing (oppoiste page) is another instance where he has drawn a plan with a section superimposed over it and off to the side, a thumbnail sketch perspective of the building. The presentation plan (at right) of the ground floor shows the openness of the space, arranged around a pool labeled "Ornamental Water." Above this pool rises the central atrium. Rising out of this block was a fifty-story tower, growing wider as it rose and providing further guest rooms. The exterior of both the main block and the tower was sheathed with double glass panes insulation in between the panes, but made of a type of glass wool that allowed light to filter through. These glass panes provided a soft, translucent light into the rooms. Certain panes could swing open to afford a view. But Wright reasoned that the view of downtown Dallas was not particularly attractive, and the focus should be on the atrium court. The construction of the tower was planned along the lines that Wright consistently employed for his tall buildings: from a central reinforced-concrete core the floors were cantilevered as branches of a tree, while the non-supporting glass exterior walls were hung from the edges of the slabs. To further stabilize the tower, a great concrete "sail" rose alongside it, which also provided space for heating and cooling ducts as well as ducts for all utilities and services.

To translate Wright's preliminary sketches and prepare the final rendering, the apprentices amassed a file of nearly seventy-nine drawings, of which thirty were the set prepared to show the client, Rogers Lacy. These were drawn on fine Japanese paper that Wright acquired from his former assistant Arato Endo in Japan directly following the Japanese surrender in 1945. Apprentice Curtis Besinger was assigned, along with John Howe, to work on the project. Besinger recollected:

"The final presentation drawings, done in the drafting room at Hillside, were traced on a Japanese paper which contained silk fibers. It came in a roll about twenty-four inches wide. Because of the height of the tower the drawings were organized vertically on the sheets. Drawing on this paper was a delicate operation. We could not erase since this destroyed the surface of the paper. We traced the drawings in brown ink. We could just touch the surface of the paper with a pen. Any pressure on the pen might catch the point in the silk fibers and cause a blot. To tint the drawings we used colored pencils applied to either side of the paper. Seeing the color on the reverse side of the transparent paper overlaid with another on the front side gave a kind of depth and airiness to the drawings." [18]

In writing about this work, Wright emphasized: "If our cities are to continue habitable, something like this turning inward, over ample parking facilities, all avoiding competition with surrounding mercantile establishments, introducing an element of repose and real harmony into building is absolutely necessary." [19]

It was a most imposing work, detailed in every aspect and beautifully rendered. Sadly, however, the client died during the preliminary stages and with him died any hope of building the Rogers Lacy Hotel.

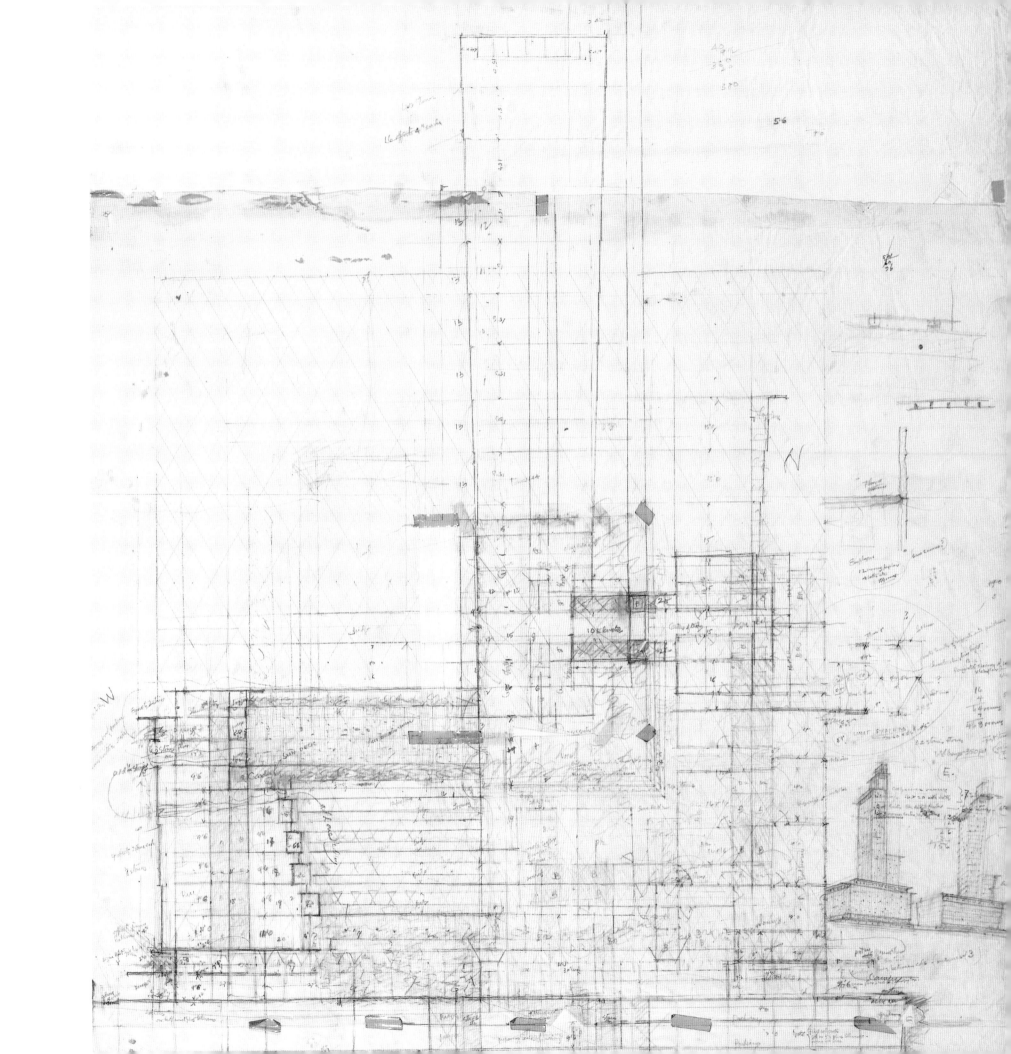

Previous pages:
Left: Plan. FLLW FDN # 4606.004.
Right: Plan, section, and thumbnail
perspective. FLLW FDN # 4606.031.

Far left: Section. FLLW FDN # 4606.002.
Left: Perspective. FLLW FDN # 4606.001.
Right: Perspective showing central
atrium. FLLW FDN # 4606.011.

Following pages: Interior view of hotel
room. FLLW FDN # 4606.010.

BUTTERFLY-WING BRIDGE

Southern Bay, Second Crossing
San Francisco, California. 1949, Project

Below: Perspective for Butterfly Wing Bridge, project.
Spring Green, WI. 1947. FLLW FDN # 4723.002.
Right, top: Perspective. FLLW FDN # 4921.001.
Right, bottom: Perspective. FLLW FDN # 4921.017.

Following pages:
Top: Perspective. FLLW FDN # 4921.027.
Bottom: Perspective. FLLW FDN # 4921.002.

Working in collaboration with the California engineer J.J. Polivka, Wright made a most unusual design for a bridge to be constructed over the San Francisco bay so as to further provide a second connection for the city with its neighboring cities and suburbs. A special requirement was a bridge high enough to allow the passage of tall ships below. For this design he expanded on his design for the Butterfly-Wing Bridge (right) that he had proposed two years earlier for the Wisconsin River, near his home Taliesin.

For San Francisco, the bridge is supported upon hollow piers penetrating the ground below the bay, and called by Wright "taproots," a system of foundations that he used successfully in the Johnson research tower in Racine, Wisconsin. Hollow reinforced-concrete curved slabs spread out, winglike, 80 feet on each side of a pier to carry six lanes of traffic and two pedestrian lanes.

Over the main shipping channel of the bay, twin arches spread apart and span 1,000 feet rising 175 feet above the water. Each arch carries the traffic in one direction, and the two are joined at the highest point by means of a suspended garden park. Vehicles and pedestrians can leave the main lanes and take advantage of the park and the view if so desired. Wright reasoned that this type of bridge, all reinforced concrete, was more practical than the traditional high-towered steel bridges.

When presenting the project, he composed a text for explanation which opened with:

"When the coefficient of expansion between concrete and steel was discovered to be the same, the perfect welding of fibrous steel in tension and concrete in compression was possible and a more organic modern world became inevitable. Modern construction has now made the rampant exposed construction of the upturned steel-truss bridges extravagant and obsolete, like corporation 'service' poles and

REGIONAL DEVELOPMENT WITH HIGHWAYS AND PARK SYSTEM PROPOSED BY THE FRANK LLOYD WRIGHT FOUNDATION

wires, they remain a devastating blemish on our landscape.

"It would be a shame to see the site of a great city so dependent upon good bridge construction for the comforts of decentralization as is San Francisco, made as unsightly by bridges such as Pittsburgh and even New York. Such destructive constructions as characterizes both cities (all except the Brooklyn Bridge) are becoming obsolete. They are no longer necessary, but all are now relatively extravagant in first cost and a strain in subsequent upkeep.

"Accordingly we herewith submit for your distinguished consideration a more simple,

coherent form of concrete bridge than most of those offered in the United States. These plans are for a great bridge that, befitting the landscape, would distinguish and beautify the San Francisco Bay region."[20]

TALIESIN WEST   4-21-49

SECOND BAY CROSSING   SAN FRANCISCO
FRANK LLOYD WRIGHT ARCHITECT
J. J. POLIVKA ENGINEER

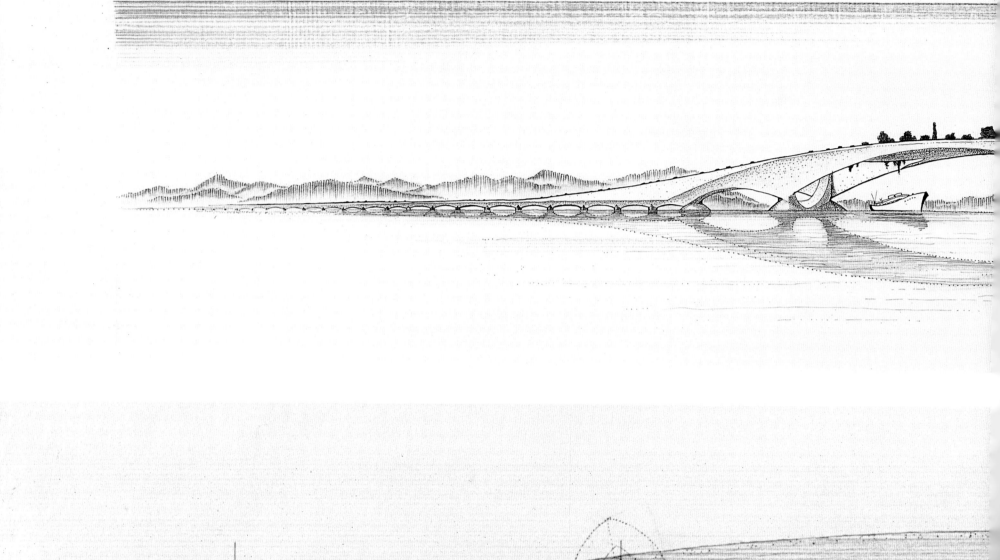

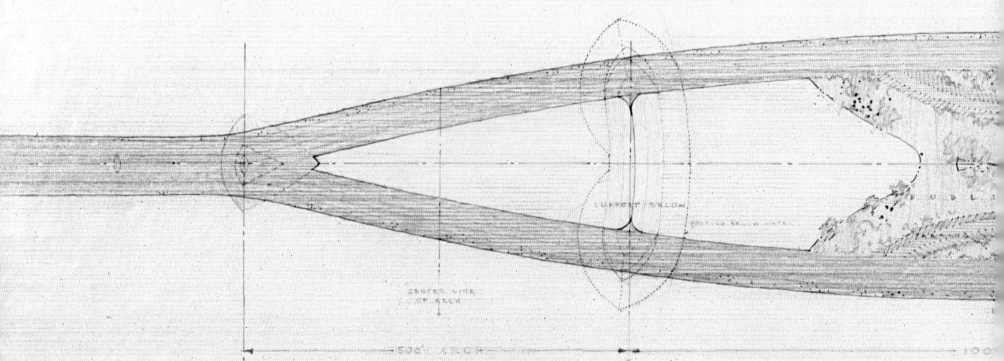

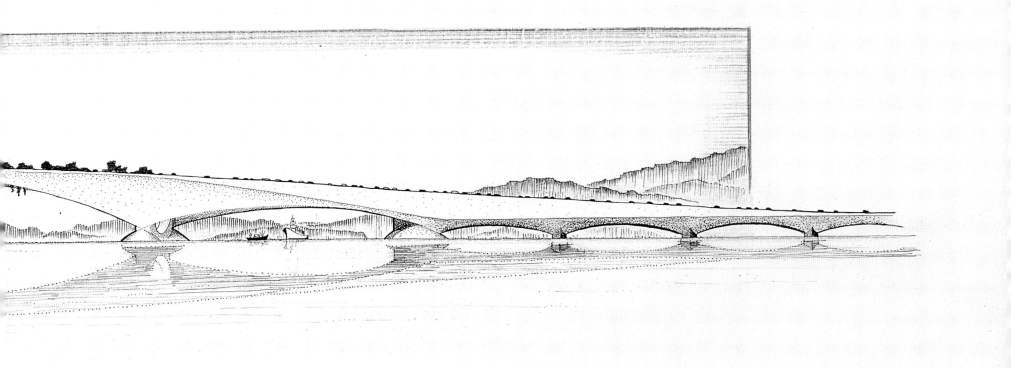

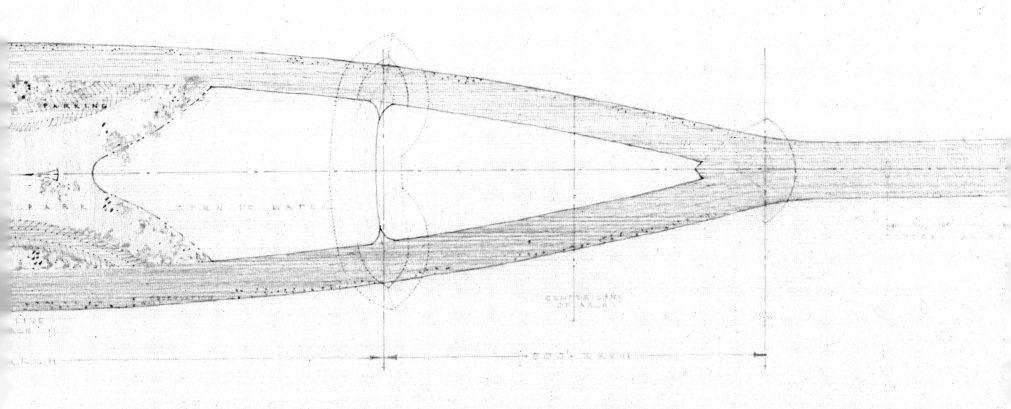

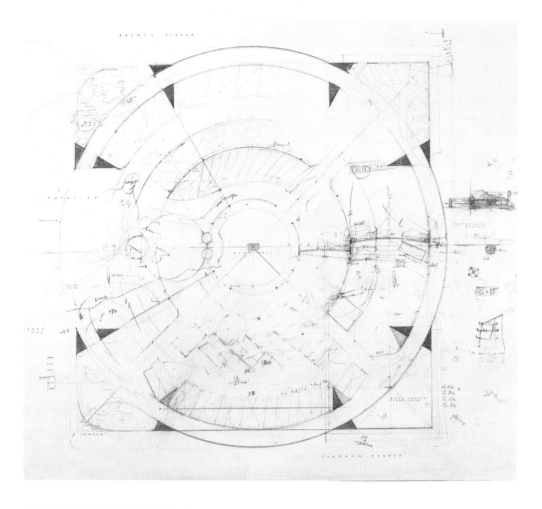

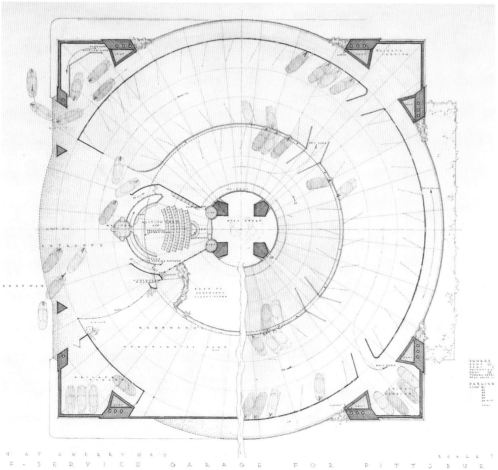

SELF-SERVICE GARAGE

For Edgar J. Kaufmann
Pittsburgh, Pennsylvania. 1949, Project

In 1949, Edgar J. Kaufmann asked Wright to design a self-service parking garage to replace a parking facility that existed on a lot adjacent to his department store. Rather than a structure of stacked levels, ramps connecting each one, Wright created a building with continuous spiral ramps from bottom to top. There are four ramps, two large ascending ones for parking and a narrow descending ramp at the outer edge for exiting. A fourth, smaller ramp, is located in the center as a pedestrian walkway. A wall separates the two inner parking ramps from the descending one, which is open to the elements at the side. At the four corners of the structure triangular reinforced-concrete masses, or bastions, support the outer descending ramp and the inner larger parking ramp. Located within these bastions are areas designated as "Private Parking." Four reinforced-concrete pylons in the center, spaced around an open court, help support the innermost parking ramp as well as the pedestrian walkway. These pylons rise above the building and join together at the top to hold suspension cables that further support the ramps in the nature of a suspension bridge.

At one point Wright had a perspective made that showed the ramps without the corner pylons. Why this was suggested is not on record, and no drawings accompany this particular version. However, there is a stunning drama to the drawing that somewhat staggers the imagination.

Calculations on one of the drawings indicate that the building would provide parking for 1,106 vehicles. Kaufmann was delighted with the project, but negative reaction on the part of local consultants who were seriously concerned about structural problems as well as building codes discouraged him from going forward with the building.

Left, top: Early plan. FLLW FDN # 4923.002.
Left, bottom: Later plan. FLLW FDN # 4923.039.
Right: later plan. FLLW FDN # 4923.001.

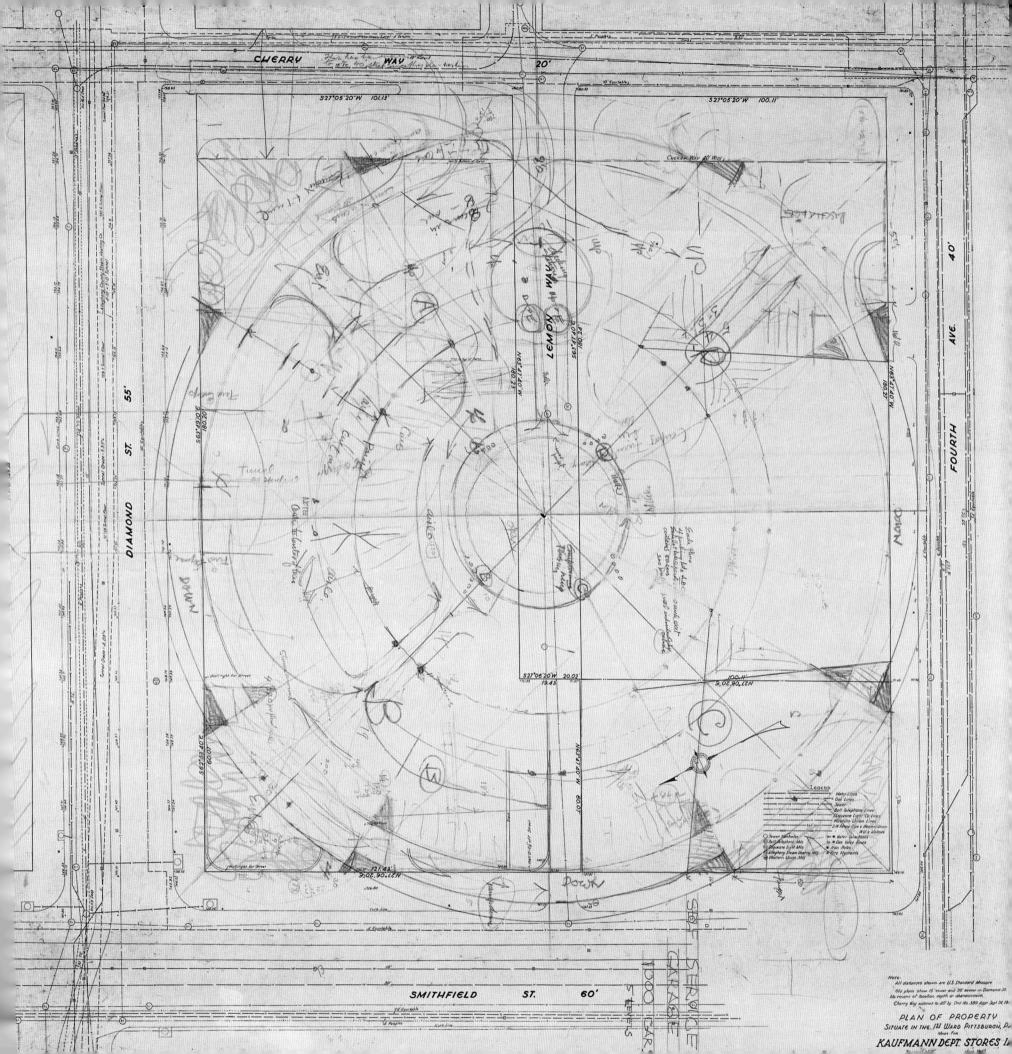

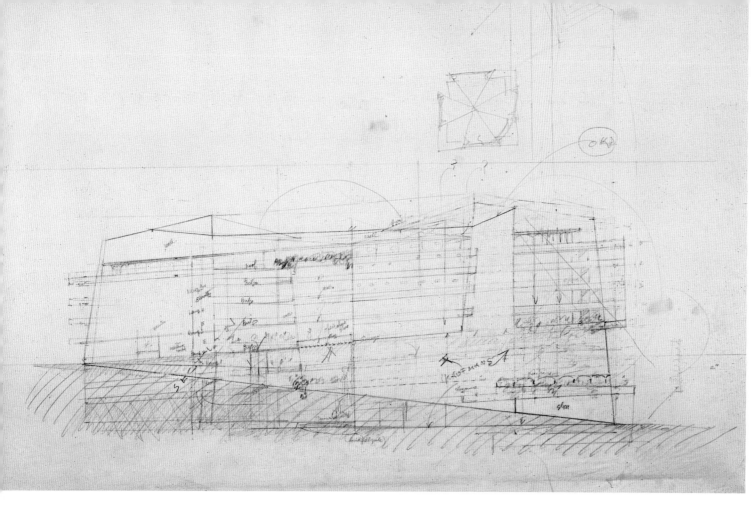

Left: Early section.
FLLW FDN # 4923.005.
Left, bottom: Later section.
FLLW FDN # 4923.047.
Right: Perspective.
FLLW FDN # 4923.053.

Following pages: Perspective.
FLLW FDN # 4923.054.

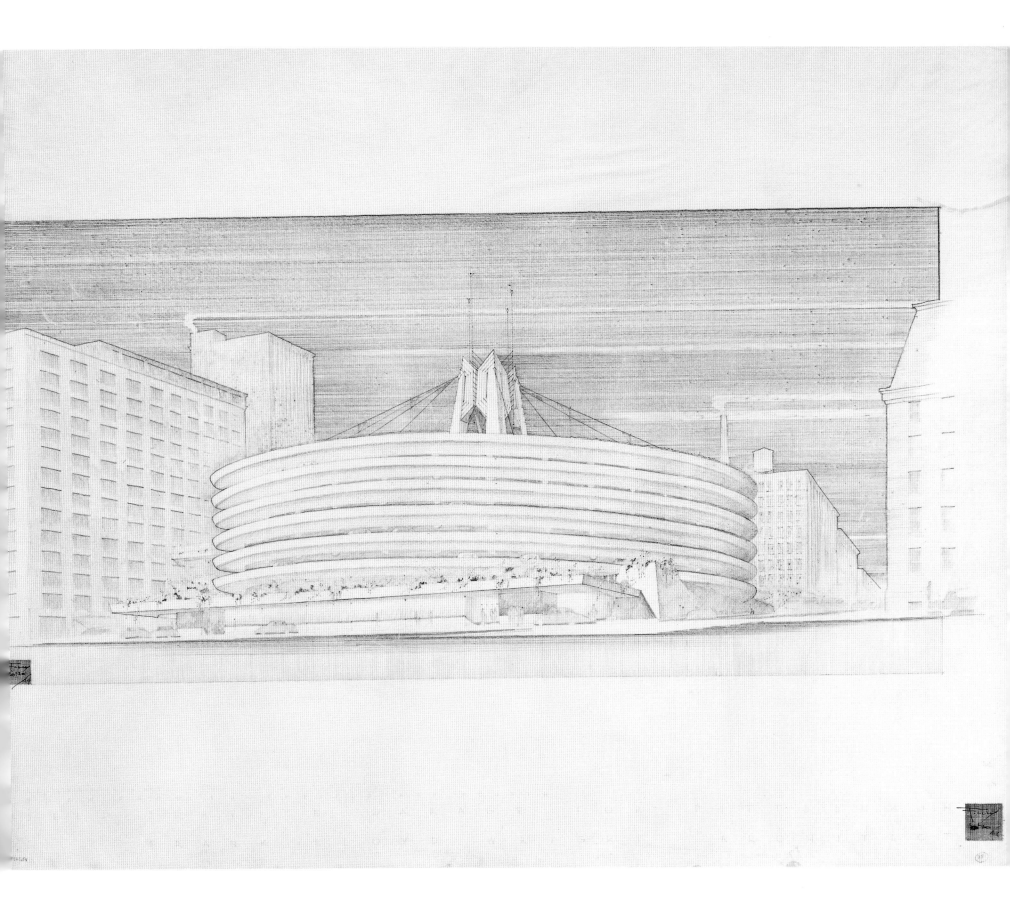

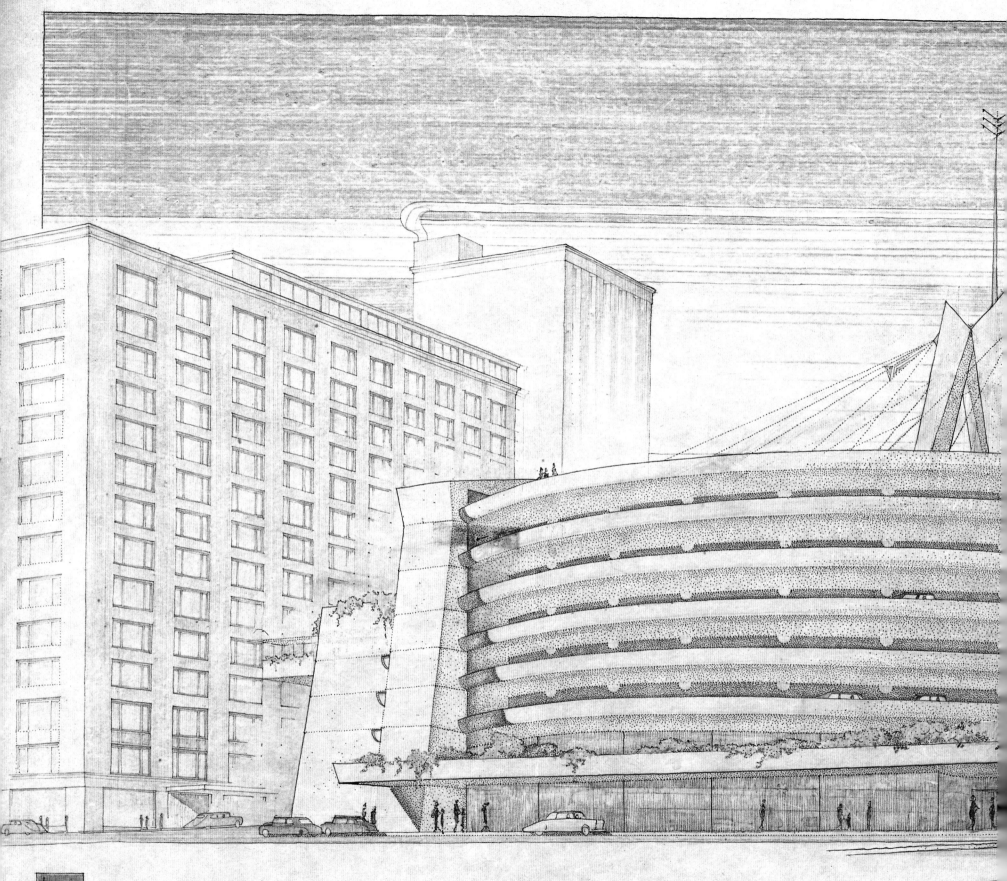

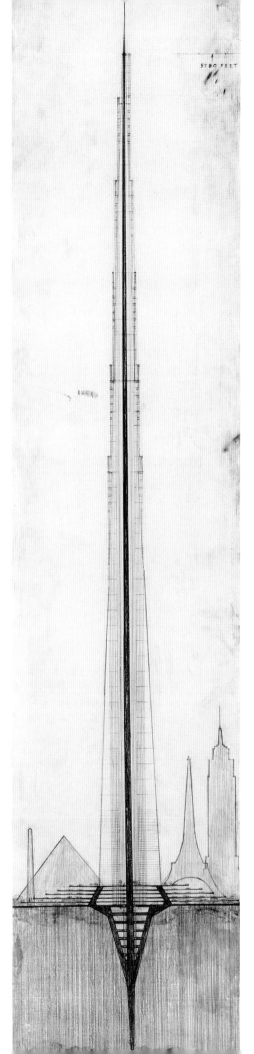

MILE HIGH SKYSCRAPER "THE ILLINOIS"

Chicago, Illinois. 1956, Project

In the summer of 1956 Wright was approached with the concept of designing a mile-high tower to serve as a broadcast antenna for television in Chicago. He felt it would be foolish to erect a tower that tall without a building beneath it. That thought gave rise to his totally unexpected concept for a skyscraper one mile high, or 528 stories. The site he envisioned was in a park on Chicago's lakefront. As he made his original sketch plan and elevation, he referred to the building as "The Illinois." It has also come to be known as "The Mile High."

His sketch (opposite page) represents a rapier-like building growing narrower as it rises from a tripod base. To explain the reason for the taper and the tripod, he said "Does a church steeple sway in the wind? No, because the wind has no pressure on the top. That is why I made it the shape that it is. It is really a steeple and no wind pressure at the top, and as it comes down, even the shape of it defies wind pressure because you notice that it is a tetrahedron in form. It is really a tripod. Now the tripod is the surest form of resistance against outside pressure from the side because every pressure on every side is felt by the other sides and resisted by them altogether as a ring. From whichever direction the wind comes, the two other sides stand braced against it . . . . Towers have always been erected by humankind—it seems to gratify humanity's ambition somehow and they are beautiful and picturesque."[21]

To place the tower in context with some other famous structures, he has sketched, from right to left, the Great Pyramid of Cheops, the Golden Beacon,[22] the Prudential Building, the Empire State Building, and the Eiffel Tower. On the same drawing he inscribed the following:

"First 20 floors, 18' high, others, 10'. Total rentable area 6,000,000 square feet; deduct 2,000,000 sq. ft. for high rooms, studios, court rooms, audience halls, etc. Probable cost $60,000,000. Net 4,000,000 sq. ft. @$10 per sq.ft. Occupancy @100 sq. ft. per person: 45,000 persons; transient occupancy in audience halls, etc. = 67,000 (approx.); total about 100,000 people. Parking 15,000 cars; 100 helicopters."

As the drawings were further developed, details were carefully considered, such as the foundation taproot that plunges into bedrock like the handle of a sword. The floors are cantilevered from a central core, as with other towers of Wright's design, but in this case for further stability cables stretch down to the outer edges of the floors, as in suspension bridges. The exterior wall surfaces are set well back beneath overhanging visors for protection against the sun and the elements. The elevators are vertical "trains" five cars tall, run on ratchets like a cog railway, and are atomic-powered. Since the building rises from five broad terraces at the base, the elevators correspond to the levels of the terraces. Although the basic building grows slenderer as it rises, the elevator shafts do not, and can be seen as they rise out of the building with corridors that connect to the various floor levels.

The floors are formed by special high-tension steel, diamond-mesh reinforced, and cast into light concrete slabs. Instead of heavy glass walls set in steel, he specified a light-weight plastic and aluminum.

The presentation perspective (opposite page, left) is an eight foot drawing, in ink, pencil, and color pencil. A companion drawing shows the section of the tower, with its taproot foundation plunged into bedrock (opposite page, right). On this drawing he has again dramatized the height of the building by placing other structures alongside which include the Great Pyramid of Cheops, the Golden Beacon, the Prudential Building, and Empire State Building.

Above the section drawing, a legend reads:

"Memorial to: Louis H. Sullivan son of Chicago, first made the tall building tall; Elisha Otis, inventor of the upended street; John Roe-

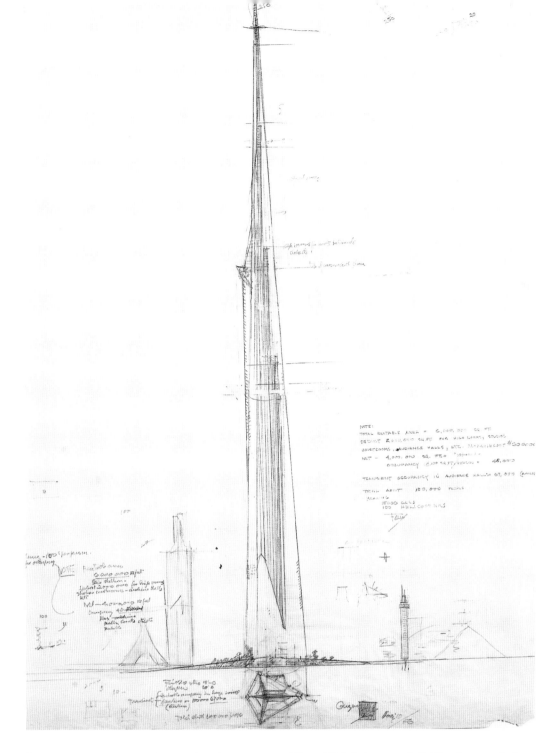

bling, first steel in tension on the grand scale, the Brooklyn Bridge; Lidgerwood, Naval architect, First ocean liner keel. Makes what it is today; Coignet & Monier, of France, reinforced concrete, the body of our modern world."

That is followed by:

"Salutations:

"Eduardo Torreja, engineer, Spain; Professors Beggs-Cross, science of continuity; Professor Pier Luigi Nervi, engineer, Italy; Dr. J. J. Polivka, engineer, University of California; Maillart, engineer, Switzerland."

Given Wright's general dislike for crowded cities and his desire for decentralization, why would he design an office building one mile high in Chicago? By placing the building in a green park, he explained, "The Mile High would absorb, justify and legitimatize the gregarious instinct of humanity, and the necessity for getting together . . . and would mop up what now remains of urbanism, and leave us free to do Broadacre City . . . the Mile High is a necessary step in the direction of Broadacre City."[23]

THE LIVING CITY

Location unspecified. 1958, Project

Up until 1929, when traveling across the nation, Chicago to New York or Wisconsin to Arizona, Wright always went by train. In 1929, however, he drove from Arizona to Wisconsin and then on to New York. Leaving the East Coast, again driving, he went through the green mountains of Appalachia and its deep dark forests, then on to the Great Plains, the Rocky Mountains with the caps of glorious white, and finally down on to the sunburnt, stark, bleak deserts of Arizona and California. To his friend Dr. Alexander Chandler, he wrote that for the first time in his life he saw the vastness of the land, the thousands upon thousands of stretches of untouched acres. It was truly a revelation to him. The automobile was now available to most American families, and it could well become the liberating element that would permit a migration out of the crowded cities and onto a variety of marvelous and rewarding landscapes.

Due to the Great Depression at this time, he had but little architectural work. Olgivanna had urged him to begin writing his autobiography, and at the same time, this recent motor trip across the United States undoubtedly prompted him to look upon the nation's cities. He saw them as medieval hangovers, dense and poisonous to those living and working within the confines of their crowded and dark canyons. These observations he began to put down on paper, and the result was the book *The Disappearing City*, which was published in 1932. In the frontispiece of the book, he chose a photograph showing New York from the air enveloped in smoke and smog, its taller buildings emerging from the morass, others swamped and suffocating. He titled the photograph, appropriately, "The Disappearing City." Further in the book another photograph, also taken from the air, shows the same view, with stark fingers of skyscrapers looming on the horizon and smaller dwelling places submerged in the foreground, with the caption "Find the

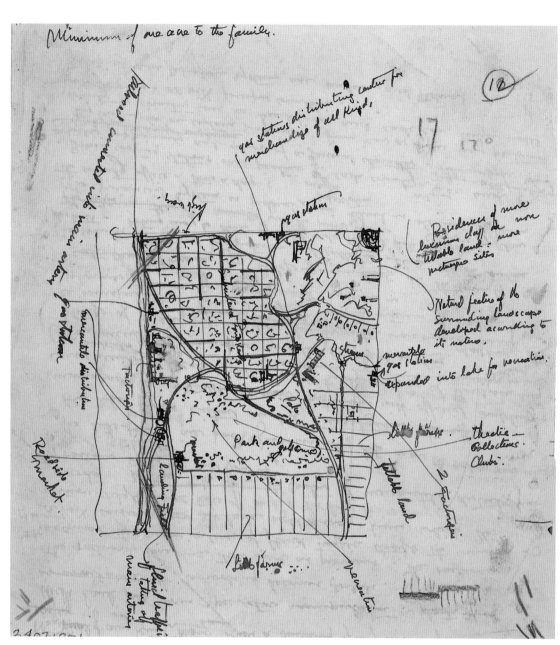

Above: Broadacre City Plan. FLLW FDN # 3402.001.
Right: Broadacre City Plan. FLLW FDN # 5825.001.

Citizen." Here, then, is truly the city disappearing with no consideration for mankind. Wright opened his book thus:

"The value of this earth, as man's heritage, is pretty far gone from him now in the cities centralization has built. And centralization has overbuilt them all. Such urban happiness as the properly citified citizen knows consists in the warmth and pressure or the approbation of the crowd. Grown Argus-eyed and enamored of 'whirl' as a dervish, the surge and mechanical

roar of the big city turns his head, fills his ears as the song of birds, the wind in the trees, animal cries and the voices and songs of his loved ones once filled his heart.

"The citizen, properly citified, is a slave to herd instinct and vicarious power as the medieval laborer, not so long before him, was a slave to his pot of 'heavy wet.' A cultural weed of another kind.

"The weed goes to seed. Children grow up, herded by thousands in schools built like factories,

SECTION C   SECTION B

SECTION D   SECTION A

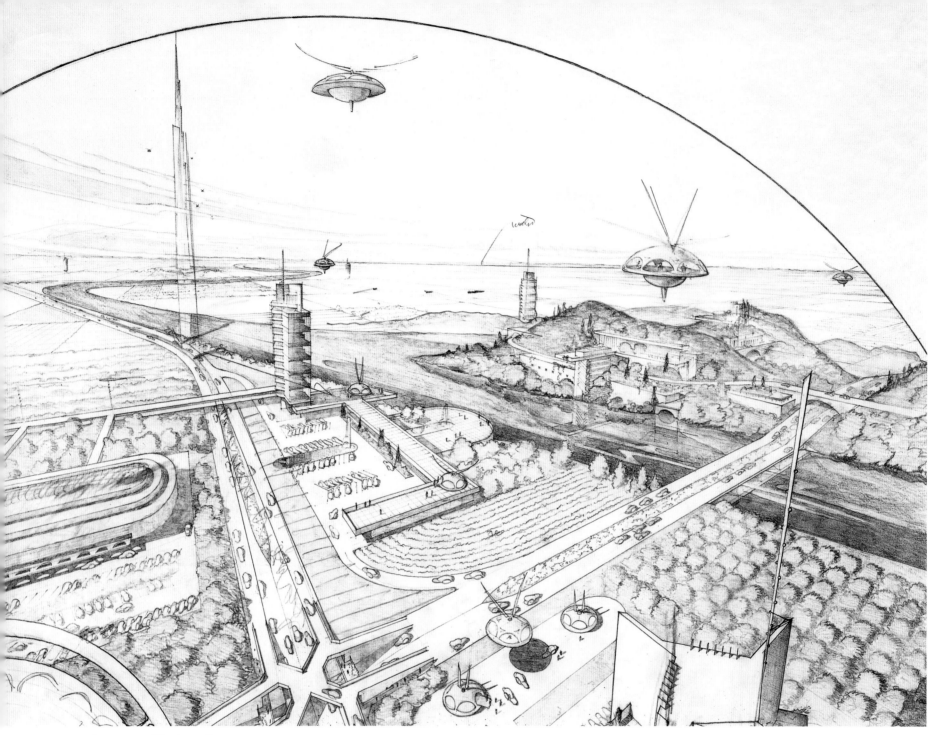

Perspective of The Living City. FLLW FDN # 5825.005.

run like factories, systematically turning out herd-struck morons as machinery turns out shoes."[24]

Concerning an antidote to the current city and its prevailing ills, he wrote:

"We are concerned here in the consideration of the future city as a future for individuality in this organic sense: individuality being a fine integrity of the human race. Without such integrity there can be no real culture; whatever what we call civilization may be. We are going to call this city for

the individual the Broadacre City because it is based upon a minimum of an acre to the family."[25]

Two years later, Wright and his apprentices began working, first in Wisconsin, and then later after a migration to Arizona, on the model of Broadacre City. The model closely followed his concept plan drawn in ink on a sheet of eight-by-ten-inch paper, with notes and inscriptions (p. 402). The model measured twelve-by-twelve feet and presented a revolutionary plan wherein all

the needed elements of living and working—education, manufacture, culture, entertainment, et al—were arranged within a landscape of trees and meadows, lakes and streams, and each of the moderate-cost homes on its own acre, the more affluent homes on larger acreage. The model, along with ancillary models such as a highway interchange, gas station, farm unit, apartment tower (St. Mark's tower) and motor hotel traveled extensively across the nation in 1935, shown in

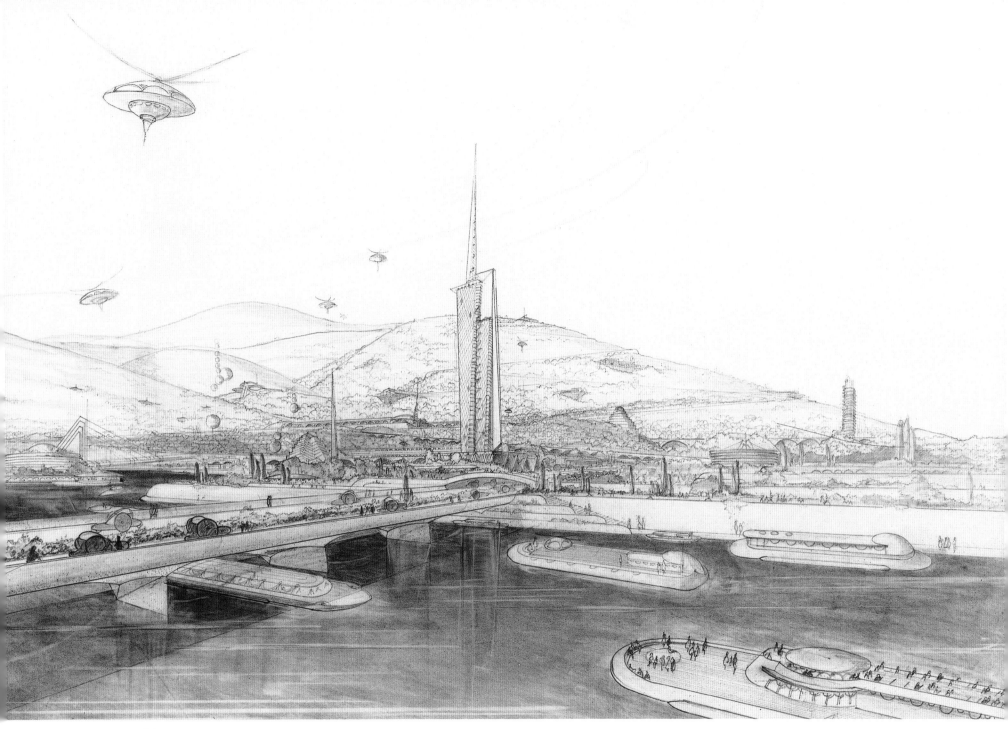

Perspective of The Living City. FLLW FDN # 5825.006.

such major cities as Pittsburgh, New York, Milwaukee, and Washington, D.C.

When the book *The Disappearing City* ran out of print, the publisher elected not to reprint it. In 1945, however, the University of Chicago Press approached Wright with the idea of putting the book back into print. Wright had a better idea: he decided to revise it, and publish it under the title *When Democracy Builds*. This time he was able to illustrate it with photographs of

the Broadacre City model, as well as other models, mainly for homes, that had been made by the Taliesin Fellowship for Wright's exhibit in the Museum of Modern Art in 1940. In his revised introduction, he wrote:

"Once upon a time conquering of physical or territorial realm was The New Frontier. But to conquer sordid, ugly commercialism in this Machine Age: this bony fiber of the dry tree; this conquest is now 'the New Frontier.' Only by giv-

ing a healthy Aesthetic in the Soul of our polyglot people can we win this victory: the greatest of all victories. So this book is on the firing line of this new, most important frontier of all frontiers: the fight for Faith, faith in democracy, faith in the gospel of individuality, and faith in Beauty that is the efflorescence of the Living Tree. Faith in Man: his faith in himself as Himself."[26]

The concept of Broadacre City never left Wright, since its inception in 1932 right up to the end of his life. As the cities increased in density and congestion, they also increased in poverty, enslavement, and crime. In opposition to this growing cancer in the cities of the United States, in 1958, he again took up the pen, this time revising *When Democracy Builds*, calling this new revision *The Living City*. At the front of the book there is a foldout illustraion, in full color, of the original Broadacre City plan, with a keyed list of the various buildings and components conveniently numbered across the drawing (p. 403). Strangely, the next inset, and this is printed in red, is a text from Paracelsus about nature, a text which expresses so clearly and succinctly the very thoughts about nature in such terms as one might believe that Wright wrote them himself.

Special drawings were prepared by the apprentices to illustrate this concept of the Living City (below and previous pages). No longer confined to a model of evleven-by-eleven feet the drawings show the same elements of the original Broadacre City but in a more expansive landscape. Soaring over the city are helicopters of Wright's design, along with taxicabs also of his design. On a river, a barge has been labeled "atomic barge." The illustrations glorify and extol the interaction of architecture and nature, all for the benefit of human life.

In the final pages of the text, he explains:

"'The Living City' then is nothing less than inspiration, or better, than restraint upon the effects of ill planning by the trustees whose responsibility it is—our young architects.

"I hope this architect's book is at least an exhortation for them, a warning for the farmer, a caution and encouragement for the small manufacturer and for national colleges of architecture and agriculture, or such cultural nurseries in this nation as the machine age has raised or razed or carelessly left standing. We cannot achieve our democratic destiny by mere industrialism, however great. We are by nature gifted as a vast agronomy. In the humane proportion of those two—industrialism and agronomy—we will produce the culture that belongs to Democracy organic. And in the word 'organic' lies the meaning of this discourse. So this book is all the more for that great invisible but potent 'in-between'—that new reality we call, here, his majesty the American citizen."[27]

The book ends with an appendix, also printed in red, "From Ralph Waldo Emerson's Essay on Farming." Wright was, lifelong profound admirer of Emerson. Again, as with Paracelsus, the emphasis is on nature, and one can easily imagine Frank Lloyd Wright himself writing this text as well.

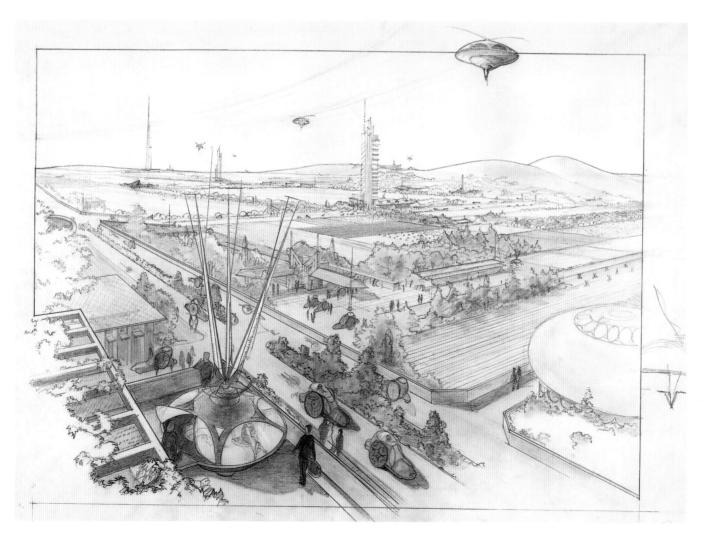

Left: Perspective of The Living City. FLLW FDN # 5825.004.

Facing page:
Left: Road machine sketch. FLLW FDN # 5826.008.
Middle: Helicopter sketch. FLLW FDN # 5827.001.
Right: Train sketch. FLLW FDN # 5828.001.

ROAD MACHINE

1958, Project

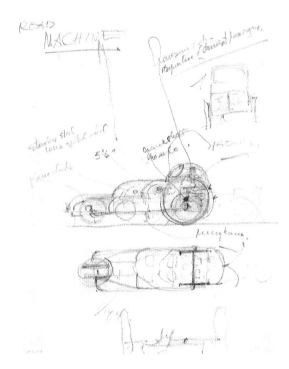

HELICOPTER

1958, Project

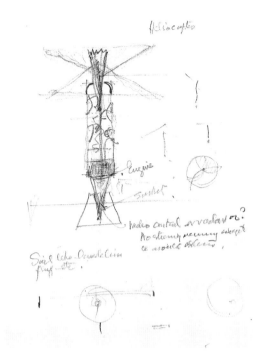

TRAIN AND RIGHT OF WAY

1958, Project

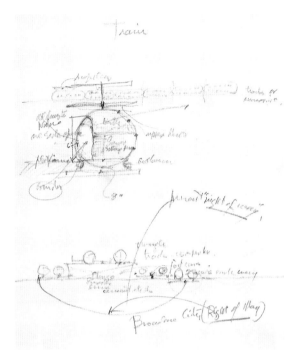

Once, when Wright saw a film on the work of Leonardo da Vinci, he remarked that Leonardo was a most inspired and creative artist, but when it came to his myriad designs for flying machines, Wright felt that he was less creative with this type of "boondoggling," as he called it.

Despite his derogatory remark about Leonardo, Wright designed a futuristic automobile, helicopter, and train.

At the same that he produced the drawings for the Living City, Wright made this design for an car which he named the "Road Machine," based on the International Harvester "M" Tractor that he had on his farm at Taliesin. Certain features of the tractor are applied to the design here: the driving force goes directly from the motor to two large wheels at the rear; the front wheel is placed in the center. In this case, designed as a taxicab, the driver sits behind and above the passengers in his own compartment. The aim of the design was to produce a vehicle with greater flexibility in traffic. He maintained that most American cars at that time, 1958, were like shoe boxes going down the highway, when they should have been like fish, with sleek lines, swimming in a school.

Wright's first sketch for a helicopter in connection with the Living City showed the machine as a vertical stack, engine at the bottom, passengers above in a spiral configuration. He inscribed on this drawing "Radio control or radar?" and "no steering necessary except to avoid obstacles." On the lower left he has inscribed "Sail like dandelion fluff, etc." He explained that the machine would travel automatically from socket or landing pad to socket, guided by some sort of electronic or radio beams. He modified it for the Living City drawings where it becomes more saucer-like. Here the vehicle is shown on its rooftop landing pad with four doors, seating two persons to each door. The machine rests in a socket device with its entrance doors level with the station platform. When all four doors are closed securely, the helicopter automatically rises and goes on its way to the next socket landing either on ground level or on a roof deck. He often referred to this vehicle as "Taxi-Copter." The aerial-view perspective shown on page 404 is drawn to represent the view from inside the taxi-copter onto the landscape below.

The train was to be a series of cylinders for the passenger cars, air-driven by a propeller above the engine car, riding on a monorail or on ball bearings. On the elevation he has inscribed "track or monorail." He proposed using ball bearings to diminish the noise generated by train wheels. In the section the corridor or aisle is on one side, sitting room and upper berth on the other.

The sketch on the lower portion of the drawing is entitled "Broadacre City—Right of Way." It is his design for a highway. He has specified how a highway should be segregated: a fast zone (on this drawing labeled as "Fast cars—150 per hr") another lane for trucks and semis, and another for slower passenger cars.

Placed above a concrete structure are the tracks or monorails for the trains. The concrete structure represents the warehouses that would be constructed at strategic locations along the way providing storage directly accessible to transportation either by truck or train.

PART SEVEN

INTEGRAL ORNAMENT:

DESIGNS FOR
A BOOK,
A MAGAZINE,
A MURAL, AND
A THEATER CURTAIN

Wright's design for what he called "integral ornament" began at the very start of his career. The frieze of the William Winslow House is an early example of this, albeit the work is strongly in the character of Louis Sullivan. The house was designed directly following Wright's departure from the Adler and Sullivan firm. Three years later, and also in connection with William Winslow, he produced a design for a book, this too in much of the same idiom as the decorative designs by Sullivan.

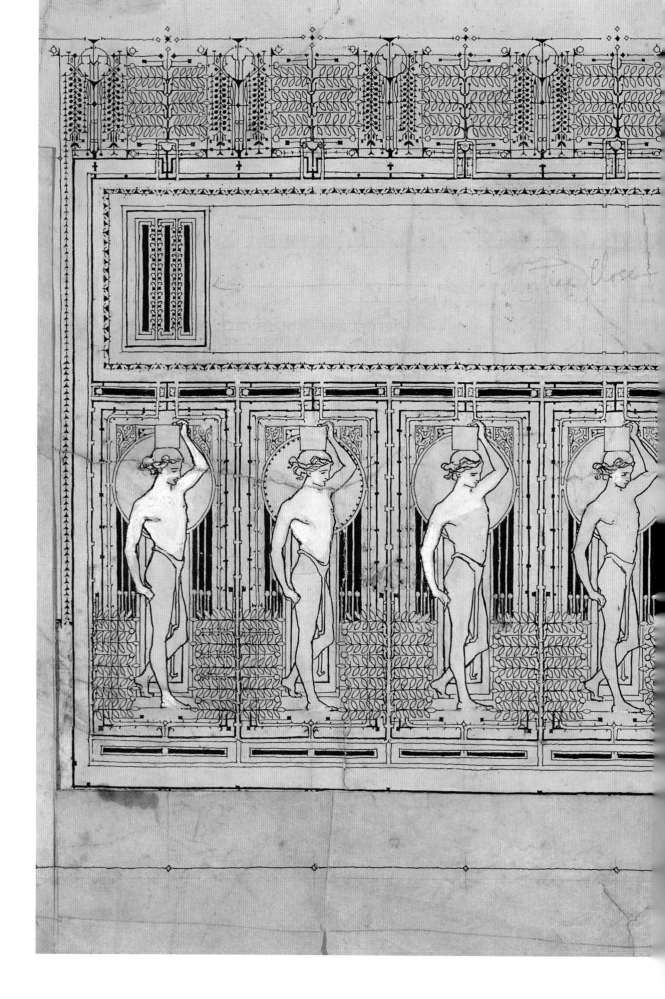

Title page for *The House Beautiful*. (See following page.)
FLLW FDN # 9609.001.

408

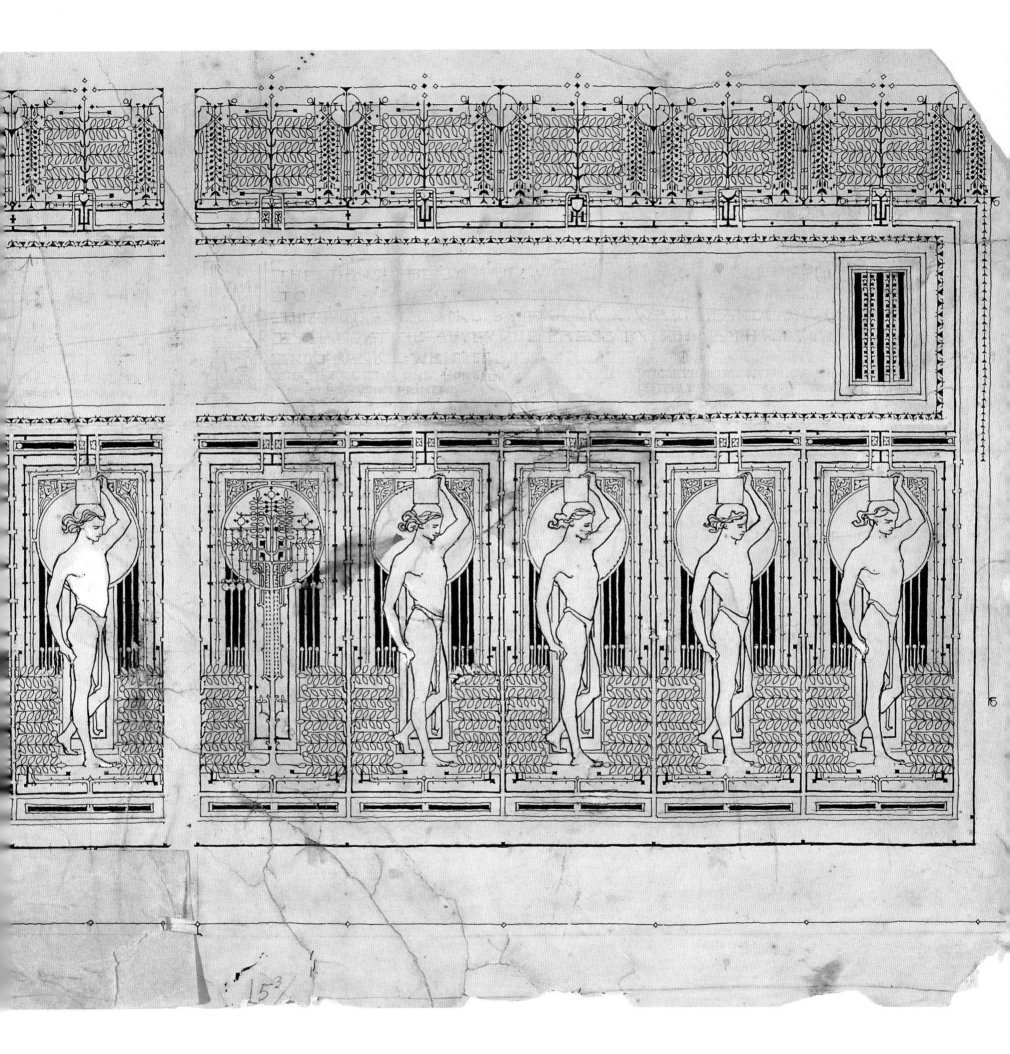

THE HOUSE BEAUTIFUL

Auvergne Press
River Forest, Illinois. 1896–7

The Unitarian minister William C. Gannett wrote a popular and widely circulated essay on "The House Beautiful." He was educated in Harvard Divinity School from which he graduated in 1868. After moving to the Midwest, he became a close friend to Wright's uncle Jenkin Lloyd Jones, a fiercely librated Unitarian minister at All Souls Church in Chicago. Undoubtedly, Wright came to know Gannett through this relationship between Gannett and his uncle. In fact, when Wright first left home and arrived in Chicago in the spring of 1887, his aunt Ellen Lloyd Jones of the Hillside Home School, wrote to him on March 9: "How near to Uncle Jenk [Jenkin Lloyd Jones] are you? I hope near enough to get the benefit of his church and his club. Do you ever see Mr. Gannett?"

In the winter of 1896, Wright and his first client William H. Winslow began a collaboration to illustrate and privately print Gannett's essay which had appeared a year earlier but in a rather inexpensive pamphlet. Winslow had established a press of his own, the Auvergne Press, named after the street on which his house was located. Wright described their process of printing the book:

"I was about 27 and I had built the Winslow House in River Forest. In the basement of the house Mr. Winslow, who was fond of avocations, set up a printing press. It was a big rotary press that you had to run by hand and by foot. We conceived the idea of printing a little book and I brought out William C. Gannett's "The House Beautiful," an essay which had been delivered at All Souls Church and which I admired very much. It was a charming thing and it charmed me. I suggested we print it. So we printed it working evenings and Sundays. Finally it was bound with large green board covers. I went out and gathered seed pods and deduced from them certain ornaments with which I embellished the volume and bound some photographs which I myself made of the weeds in the beginning of the book, with a little cover and a quotation in gold letters from Shakespeare."[1]

Right: Drawing for *The House Beautiful.*
FLLW FDN # 9609.005.
Far right: Cover design for *Liberty,* "April Showers."
(See following page.)
FLLW FDN # 2604.009

Wright's drawings for the book (above), which miraculously have survived, demonstrate a most remarkable skill in freehand drawing with ink and quill pen. The designs evoke a certain Sullivanesque character, as did the frieze of the Winslow House done at about the same time. The blank area in the two drawings represents where printed text is to be inserted. Throughout the book, each printed page has its decorative border around the text. On the title page (previous page), above the drawings of the male figures, in a special box and printed in red is the following: "The House Beautiful by William C. Gannett. The House Beautiful in a setting designed by Frank Lloyd Wright and printed by hand at the Auvergne Press in River Forest by William Herman Winslow and Frank Lloyd Wright during the winter months of the year eighteen hundred ninety six and seven."

Ninety copies were printed, each one numbered and signed by Winslow and Wright.

Soon, however, Wright grew away from the influence of Sullivan and began producing abstract designs of a totally different character.

He explained this:

"What they now call non-objective art can be seen in the patterns we designed for the Midway Gardens in 1912. Such as in the mural 'City by the Sea.' But I had been making such abstract designs for fifteen years. This principle of design was natural, inevitable for me. Whether in glass or textile or whatever, it is based on the straight-line technique of the T square and the triangle. It was inherent in the Froebel system of kindergarten training given to me by my mother—for I built many designs and buildings on the kitchen table out of the geometric forms of those playthings. Out of this came the straight-line patterns that are used today in textiles, linoleums, and so on. It grew out of my own limitations, by way of the T square and the triangle and the compass."[2]

Most of Wright's abstract designs were made with color pencils. "Colors—in paste or crayon—or pencils—always a thrill! To this day I love to hold a handful of many-colored pencils and open my hand to see them lying loose upon my palm, in the light."[3]

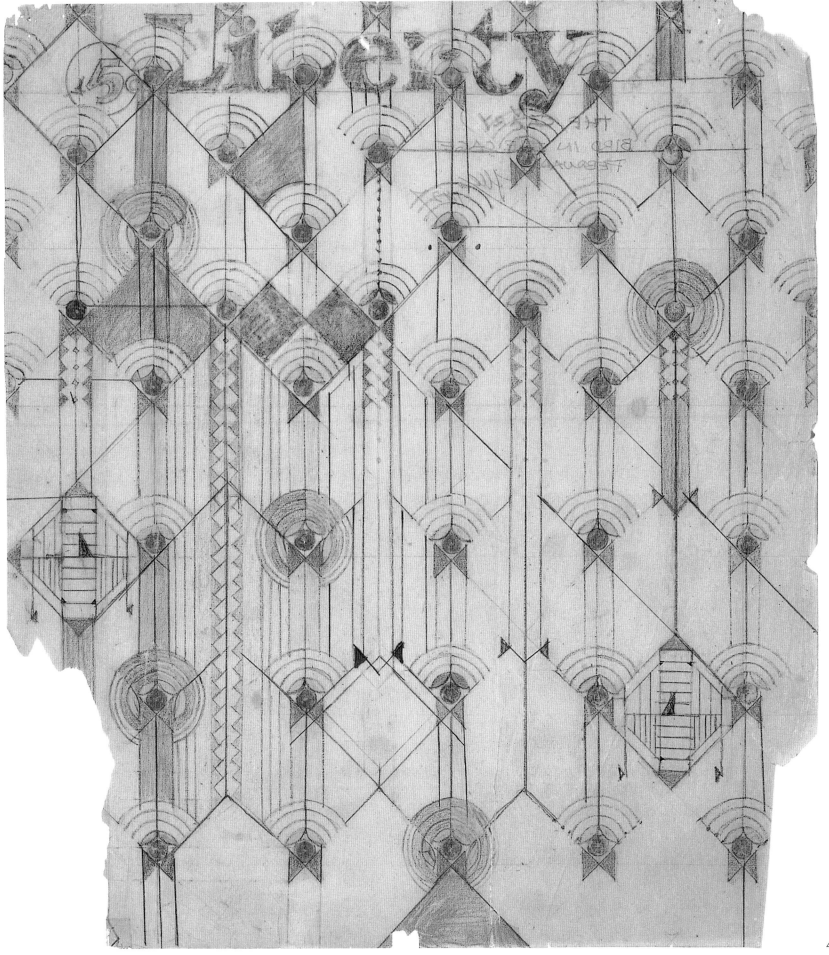

411

MAGAZINE COVERS

For *Liberty* Magazine
New York. 1926–7, Project

1926 was a difficult year for Frank Lloyd Wright. The year before, the living quarters of Taliesin had again burned to the ground as a result of a lightning strike during a fierce storm. The rebuilding drained his finances. Unable to pay the mortgage, the bank took over Taliesin. Wright and his family were forced to leave, traveling to Minnesota for a while, and then to New York where his sister Maginela Wright Barney, who was traveling in Europe at the time, graciously offered her apartment for them. Without work, without draftsmen, he still undertook to create designs. It was at this time that he drew the Oak Park Playhouses and the Skyscraper Regulation.

As well as those designs, he started to write. While in Minnesota, he began to write his autobiography, under the suggestion of Olgivanna. At first he seemed reluctant about doing this, but she reminded him that if he didn't write the story of his life and his work, someone else would, and he wouldn't like it. That sold him on the idea. This would be an ongoing task for several years until its publication in 1932.

But now, in 1926, during this trying time of his life, anxious to raise funds in any way he could, he proposed to the magazine *Liberty* that he write some articles about his work. *Liberty*, a newly formed weekly, was founded by Robert McCormick and Joseph Patterson, both men associated with the McCormick Reaper Company in Chicago. Wright was certainly aware of both McCormick and Patterson from his own connection with Harold McCormick, for whom he had designed a luxurious home in 1907. Planned for Lake Forest, if it had been built it would have been the largest home of his entire career. Unfortunately, McCormick's wife, a Rockefeller, was strongly opposed to the design, as being "perfectly lovely for the mountains but hardly the thing for Lake Forest."

Liberty did eventually publish his article

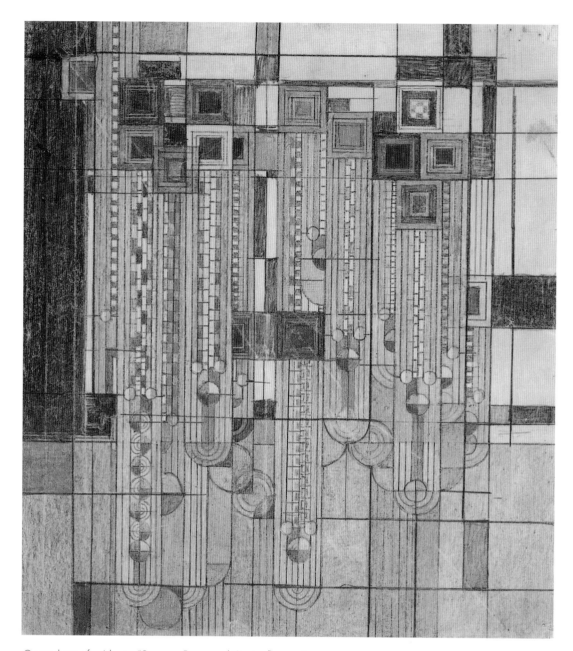

Cover design for *Liberty*, "Saguaro Forms and Cactus flowers."
FLLW FDN # 2604.010.

"Why the Japanese Earthquake Did Not Destroy the Hotel Imperial," on December 3, 1927. Wright was paid a handsome fee of $1,000.

But during that time in New York, he also proposed to the magazine that he design some colorful covers for the issues, at first suggesting twelve for the twelve months of the year, and then going even further, suggesting fifty-two for the weeks of the year. He made some preliminary designs for the months, but these seemed too radical to the publisher and were rejected. Of those designs, four survive by his own hand, in the Frank Lloyd Wright Archives. Others are housed in private collections.

The design "Jewelry Shop Window" (opposite page, left) was proposed for February,

Cover design for Liberty, "Jewelry Shop Window."
FLLW FDN # 2709.001

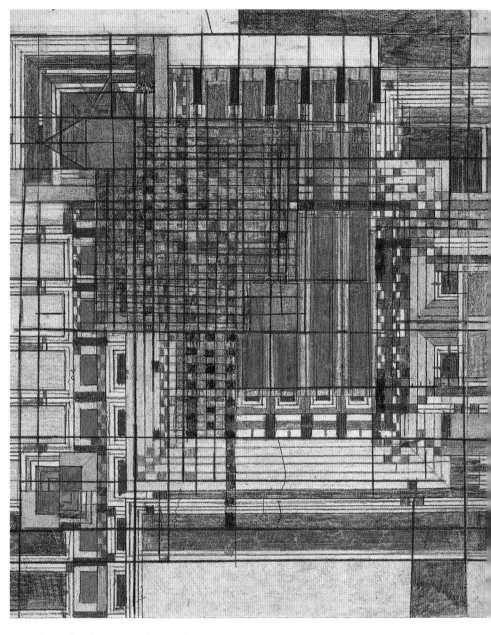

Cover design for Liberty, "Garden Window."
FLLW FDN # 2604.011.

to represent something special for St. Valentine's Day. The design "April Showers" (p. 411) was for April, and sometimes Wright called it "The Bird in the Cage." Later, he wrote on the back of an enlarged revision of this, "Scherzo." One drawing (above, right) represented the "Garden Window" or, as sometimes labeled, "The Old Fashioned Window," for the month of June. Later, he called

this design "Fugue." Finally, for November, and representing the cactus of the Arizona desert, he drew what he called "Saguaro Forms and Cactus Flowers" (opposite page). A version of this particular design was used for the cover of his Princeton lectures in 1931.

In 1955 Wright proposed these designs, and others, for carpets and textiles. For the presenta-

tion of these designs, apprentice Ling Po produced these images in a larger format. The design for July, an abstraction of the American Flag, had earlier been published on the cover of *Town and Country*, July 1937. His design for "March Balloons" was also produced in larger format by Ling Po, and Wright produced an adaptation of this for the David Wright rug in 1951.

MURAL, "CITY BY THE SEA"

Music Pavilion, Taliesin West
Scottsdale, Arizona. 1956

The mural called "City by the Sea" was explained by Wright to be "Chicago, at night, on Lake Michigan." The portion of a circle on the upper right represents the full moon, its completed circle was painted on the upper part of the niche in which it was placed. Wright once said of these geometric designs, especially in the stained glass, that he was designing these long before Mondrian came along.

The mural had its origin in an earlier application in Midway Gardens (p. 260; earlier mural not shown). In 1956, however, Wright modified the design as shown here, and it was replicated full scale by apprentice Ling Po as a special feature in the music pavilion at Taliesin West. On the back of the mural Wright wrote, "To hell with the rectilinear frame of reference" referring to a more reflex application. The design is not bound by the frame, but elements are shown as if they are going beyond the frame. In fact, the frame seems not to exist at all. This was a design detail that Wright so admired in many of the vertical prints "Views of Mount Fuji" by Hiroshige.

The mural was incorporated in a niche at right angles to the stage at the end overlooking the orchestra pit, the area under the arch left open for unusual occasions. One of those occasions was the time when the playwright Clare Boothe Luce presented a reading of the performance of her play "Love is a Verb," with a cast composed of apprentices in the Taliesin Fellowship. She directed the action on the stage while seated behind the "City by the Sea" opening, similar to what one would expect in a puppet theatre. There she read stage instructions while the apprentices were seated in a half circle onstage with their backs to the viewers. When it came time for each person to deliver his lines (reading from the script), Clare summoned the performer to turn and face the audience, the lines finished, to turn again facing back.

In 1964 the music pavilion burned, and lost with the building was the mural as well. However, when the building was reconstructed, using this drawing as he had before, Ling Po again produced the mural and it was installed in the special niche which was also reconstructed for it.

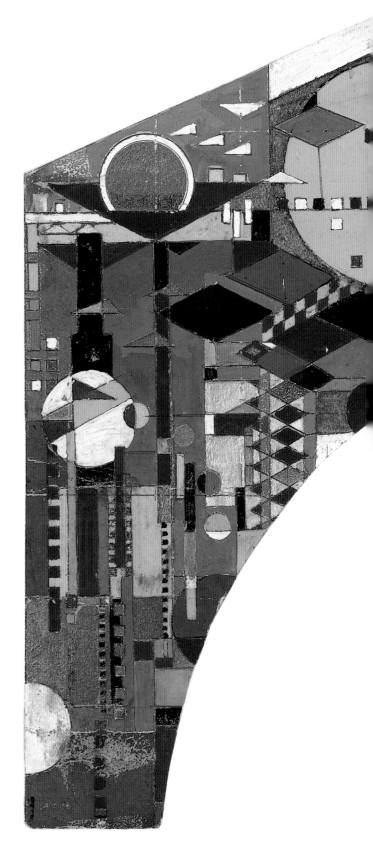

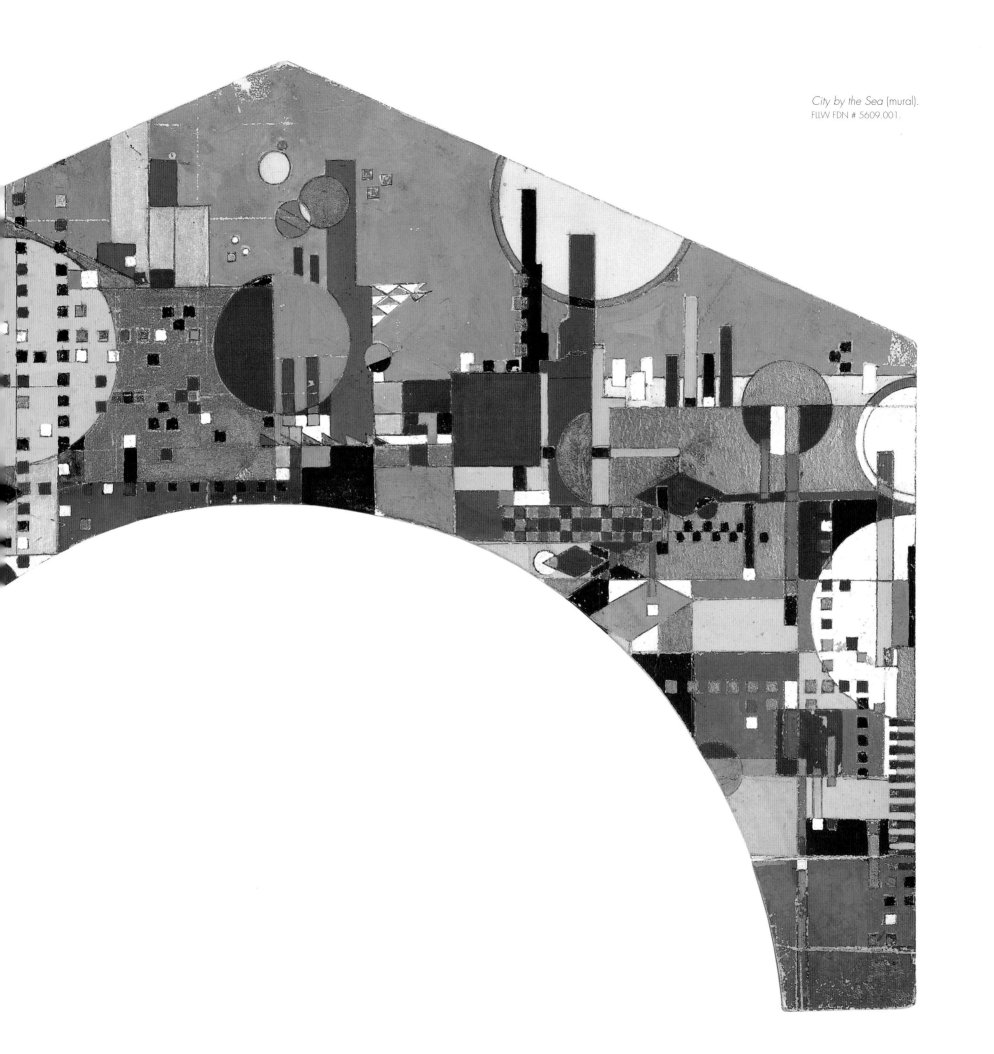

City by the Sea (mural).
FLLW FDN # 5609.001.

THEATER CURTAIN

Hillside Theater, Taliesin
Spring Green, Wisconsin. 1952

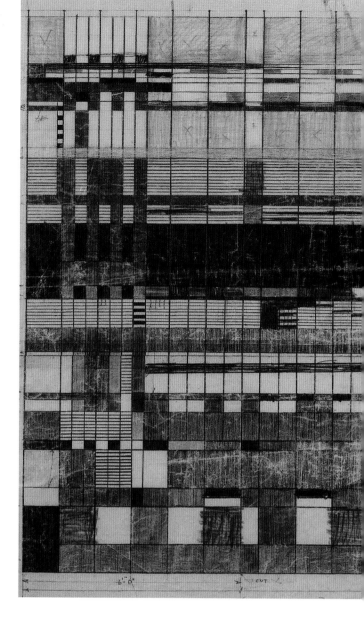

Richard Lloyd Jones, an impassioned Unitarian pastor in his native land of Wales, was Frank Lloyd Wright's maternal grandfather. His brother Jenkin had migrated to America, where he worked in the lead mines in Mineral Point, Wisconsin. It had been a difficult journey for Jenkin, arriving in a new land and speaking only Welsh. But he sought refuge in the mainly Welsh community in Mineral Point and gradually conquered the new language. He came to love America, its vastness, the pastoral beauty of Wisconsin, the deep forests and green meadows. He wrote often to his brother Richard of this land and all its new possibilities, new adventures, and most of all its new freedom. This appealed to Richard, and in 1844 he decided to migrate to the United States with his wife Mary, called Mallie, and their children. The land that they founded, farmed, and developed beside the mighty Wisconsin River became the ancestral valley of the Lloyd Joneses. To them it was lovingly called "The Valley."

Although the grandfather, his wife, and six of his children spoke only Welsh, when they arrived in America, it was not long before they, too, mastered the English language. They avidly read Ralph Waldo Emerson and Henry David Thoreau, as well as the articles written by Harriet Beecher Stowe and Margaret Fuller, a diet of strong libertarian thought indeed way ahead of its time here in the mid-nineteenth century. Transcendental ideas were a major element in their lives, with a love for the beauty and sanctity of nature. Four more children were born to this Lloyd Jones clan. His sons grew to become ministers and farmers, his daughters, educators. Education was indeed a passion for the Lloyd Jones family. Therefore it seemed only natural, if not expected, that Frank Lloyd Wright's maternal aunts Jane and Ellen Lloyd Jones in 1886 established a school in the same valley. It was called the Hillside Home School, and it took in

boys and girls from five years old to eighteen to live and study with a curriculum far ahead of its time. Although it was a nondenominational school, it fostered a strong diet of Unitarian and transcendental thought that was an underlying force in the Lloyd Jones family.

Richard Wright came to know "The Valley" intimately. His boyhood summers were spent working on the farm of his Uncle James, a hard and painful experience. Yet this rigorous life on the farm instilled in him an abiding love and faith in the agrarian way of life. This love, combined with the transcendentalism of his mother, aunts, and uncles would prove to be a source from which he would draw strength and inspiration all throughout his life.

In 1887, shortly after Wright had arrived in Chicago, the aunts wrote to their nephew about their need for a new building for their school and suggested some details about the design they wished he would develop for them. Called the "Home Building," it was a simple three-story shingle structure, without any of the "styles" prevalent at this time, in the Victorian Era. Ten years later, the aunts asked him to design for a new windmill tower on a high hill above the school. He named the tower "Romeo and Juliet," Romeo being the part that held the mechanisms for the windmill and the pump, while Juliet, snuggled beside him, rose to hold a glassed-in observation platform from which the entire Lloyd Jones valley could be seen. Still needing further facilities for their expanding school, the aunts, in 1902, requested a larger school building for more classrooms, an assembly hall, woodworking shop, and gymnasium. This building, of stone and oak (in deference to the Lloyd Jones druid heritage where oak trees and stones were sacred), became the main structure of the Hillside Home School, and stands to this day.

By 1915, age and infirmity compelled the aunts to close the school. They conveyed the

buildings and property over to Wright, and the Hillside buildings were shut down and deserted. Before they died, they exacted a promise from him that someday he would occupy those buildings in a venture of education. In 1932, when Wright and Olgivanna opened the Taliesin Fellowship, the venture of education that was promised became education in the cause of architecture. The first order of work for the newly arrived apprentices was the rehabilitation of the Hillside Home building. A drafting room was added to the north, joined to the original structure, and the gymnasium was converted into a theater-playhouse. The theater was a most magical space, with a high ceiling, balconies, and a stage consisting of three levels: one for piano and soloists, another for a string quartet, and the third, a large stage itself for dramatis productions

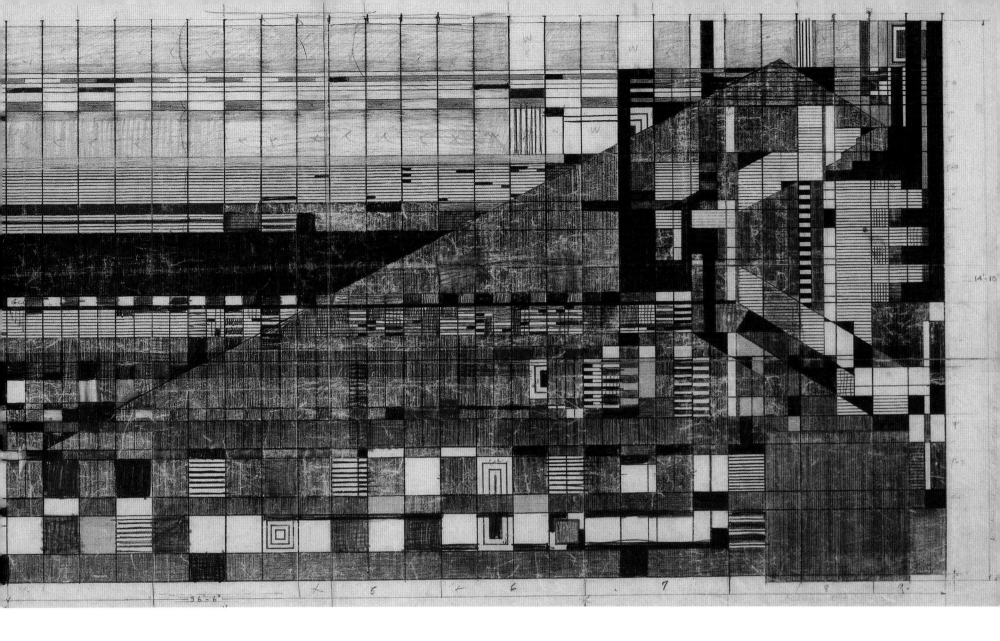

as well as cinema. He then designed a special curtain for the stage. Olgivanna and a group of women from the neighboring towns gathered together and produced the curtain by stitching geometric appliqués of various colored felts and long strings of colored yarn onto a background of strong canvas.

The theater was used for many years on Saturday evenings when Wright, Olgivanna, their guests, and the apprentices would gather there for dinner followed by a musical concert or cinema. However, on April 16, 1952, along with some apprentices, Wright was raking and burning dead leaves around the outside of the theater. Suddenly a gust of wind swept the flames up onto the building, and the theater caught fire. It had been a dry spring, and the stream south of the building did not yield enough water to douse the flames. The fire raged on and consumed the theater, several apprentice rooms, a long gallery for weaving, and the dining room. The rest of the building, especially the drafting room and two galleries that contained not only Wright's ongoing work but all his drawings dating back to 1887, were spared.

Wright set immediately to design a structure to replace the one that was lost. The stone walls had survived, and they were incorporated in the new construction. At the same time, he produced a design for a new theater curtain fifteen feet high and thirty feet wide—much larger and more resplendent than its predecessor. The design was an abstraction of the Wisconsin landscape, fields of crops, red barns, flocks of blackbirds, green meadows, and a large green hill rising at the right-hand portion of the design. It was far more complex than the first one, and Wright wondered how it could ever be produced. Again Olgivanna undertook the project, this time with the apprentices, and in secret. Working in a neighboring barn that Wright's son-in-law and apprentice Wes Peters had purchased, they set up tables, and, on large stretches of heavy canvas, they attached felt patches of red, blue, black, and green, along with cords of red, black, and gold. Two years later, when the new theater was complete and opened on Wright's birthday, June 8, the curtain (above) was hung there as a special, and totally unexpected, surprise for him.

The design of the new stage is such that the curtain hangs at the rear, becoming a glorious colorful tapestry backdrop to whatever is going on in front. For the showing of motion pictures, the curtain is drawn to reveal a screen.

ENDNOTES

INTRODUCTION

1 *Frank Lloyd Wright Collected Writings Volume 3*. B. B. Pfeiffer, ed. (New York: Rizzoli, 1993) p.331.
2 *Frank Lloyd Wright Drawings*. GA Gallery. B. B. Pfeiffer, ed. (Tokyo: 1984.)
3 Frank Lloyd Wright to his apprentices, November 28, 1954. Frank Lloyd Wright Foundation Archives: AV#1014.113, p.10.
4. Wright to Jones, June 9, 1958. Frank Lloyd Wright Foundation Archives.

PART ONE: THE DWELLING PLACE

1 Frank Lloyd Wright. *An Autobiography* (Petaluma: Pomegranate, 2005) p.125.
2 Frank Lloyd Wright. *An Autobiography*, p.128.
3 Ibid., p.138-9.
4 Frank Lloyd Wright. *An Autobiography*, p.140.
5 Frank Lloyd Wright to his apprentices, August 13, 1952, AV#1014.044, p.2.
6 The word "project" denotes that the work was not built.
7 Frank Lloyd Wright to his apprentices, March 7, 1954. AV#1014.093, p.2-3.
8 Ibid., p.4.
9 Frank Lloyd Wright. *An Autobiography* p.139.
10 Ibid., p.140.
11 Ibid., p.142.
12 Wright to Sullivan, February 5, 1923.
13 Frank Lloyd Wright. *An Autobiography*, p.241-242.
14 Wright to Guthrie October 20, 1927.
15 Wright to Guthrie March 4, 1929.
16 Wright to Guthrie March 28, 1931.
17 Wright to Kaufmann, December 26, 1934.
18 Frank Lloyd Wright. *An Autobiography*, p.448-9.
19 Wright to Mosher August 21, 1936.
20 Edgar Kaufmann jr. *Fallingwater: A Frank Lloyd Wright Country House* (New York: Abbeville Press, 1986) p.183.
21 Frank Lloyd Wright. *An Autobiography*, p.477-8.
22 Wright to Jester, August 6, 1938.
23 Wright to Pauson, April 19, 1943.
24 Frank Lloyd Wright, interview with his publisher Ben Raeburn, 1956.
25 *The Architectural Forum*, January 1948, p.97.
26 *The Architectural Forum*, January 1938, p.91.
27 *The Architectural Forum*, January 1938, p.98.
28 Frank Lloyd Wright to his apprentices February 3, 1957. AV#1014.181 p.17.
29 Wright coined the phrase "Usonia" as a contraction of United States of America.
30 Frank Lloyd Wright. *The Architectural Forum*, January 1938, p.78.
31 Wright to Bailleres May 31, 1952.
32 Wright to Liliane Kaufmann, January 15, 1951.
33 Wright to Kaufmann, July 11, 1953.

PART TWO: BUILDINGS FOR WORSHIP

1 Frank Lloyd Wright. *An Autobiography*, pp.159-160.
2 Wright to Guthrie, October 26, 1927.
3 Frank Lloyd Wright to his apprentices May 8, 1955 AV#1014.289 p.11.
4 Kaufmann jr to Wright September 2, 1951.
5 Cohen to Wright, March 19, 1954.

PART THREE: BUILDINGS FOR CULTURE AND EDUCATION

1 Frank Lloyd Wright. *An Autobiography*, p.224.
2 Ibid., p.227.
3 John Lloyd Wright. *My Father Who Is on Earth*, p.29.
4 Ibid., p.29.

5 Frank Lloyd Wright. *An Autobiography*, p.227.
6 Frank Lloyd Wright. *The Architectural Forum*, September 1952.
7 Wright to Leavenworth November 21, 1940.
8 Leavenworth to Wright, June 20, 1941.
9 Russell E. Leavenworth. *The Wright House for Chi of Sigma Chi*. AV#1026.135.
10 Ibid.
11 Frank Lloyd Wright to his apprentices, January 7, 1951 AV#1014.013, p.6.
12 Wright to Rebay, December 19, 1943. The Guggenheim Correspondence, p.22.
13 Wright to Rebay, January 20, 1944. Ibid., p.40.
14 Ibid., p.41.
15 Wright to Harry Guggenheim, July 15, 1958. Ibid., p.270.
16 Wright to Kaufmann, February 2, 1947.
17 Frank Lloyd Wright. *For the Allegheny Conference* May 5, 1947. AV2401.534.
18 Ibid.
19 Wright to Martin June 15, 1947.
20 Frank Lloyd Wright to his apprentices July 8, 1951. AV#1013.019.
21 Giuseppe Samona, Carlo Scarpa, Bruno Zevi.
22 Wright to Masieri February 19, 1953.
23 March 24, 1954. AV#2401.561.
24 Frank Lloyd Wright. Mss. AV#2401.377, June 1957.
25 Frank Lloyd Wright. Mss. AV#2401.377-379, June 1957.
26 Ibid.
27 Wright is referring to the traffic congestion in Cairo, as an example.
28 Frank Lloyd Wright. Mss. #AV2401.379.

PART FOUR: BUILDINGS FOR TRAVEL AND ENTERTAINMENT

1 Frank Lloyd Wright. *An Autobiography*, p.126.
2 Ibid.
3 Frank Lloyd Wright. *An Autobiography*, p.175-6.
4 Ibid., p.179.
5 Ibid., p.181.
6 Ibid., p.108.
7 Ibid., p.181.
8 Ibid., p.192.
9 See drawing FLLW FDN # 2205.003.
10 Wright to Barnsdall, December 13, 1933.
11 Frank Lloyd Wright. *An Autobiography*, p.306-7.
12 Ibid., p.307.
13 The contractor for the Imperial Hotel.
14 Ibid., p.315.
15 *The Architectural Forum*, January 1938, p.64.
16 *Collected Writings*, Volume 5, p.297.
17 Hood to Wright, February 16, 1931.
18 *Frank Lloyd Wright and Lewis Mumford*, p.98.
19 *An Autobiography*, p.352-355.
20 Ibid., p.355.
21 *An Autobiography*, p.356-357.
22 Eugene Masselink *Letters to Jack: Frank Lloyd Wright's Taliesin in Wartime Years*. March 11, 1945.
23 Ibid.
24 Ibid.
25 Ibid.
26 Ibid.
27 Wright to Hartford, November 8, 1947.
28 Wright to the Tremaines April 27, 1949.
29 Frank Lloyd Wright. AV#1014, p.218.
30 Frank Lloyd Wright. *A Testament* (New York: Horizon Press, 1957), p.214.

PART FIVE: BUILDINGS FOR COMMERCE AND WORK

1 Frank Lloyd Wright. *An Autobiography*. p.472.
2 Another draftsman of that time.
3 Klumb to Hoffmann September 5, 1960.
4 Frank Lloyd Wright *The Village Bank* Brickbuilder X, 1901.
5 Jonathan Lipman. *Frank Lloyd Wright and the Johnson Wax Buildings* (New York: Rizzoli, 1986) p.7.
6 Ibid., p.13.
7 Frank Lloyd Wright. *An Autobiography*, p.472.
8 Johnson to Wright, October 4, 1943. *Letters to Clients—Frank Lloyd Wright*. B. B. Pfeiffer, ed. (Fresno, California: The Press at California State University, Fresno, 1986) p.232.
9 Wright to Johnson, December 14, 1943. Ibid., p.234.
10 Wright to Johnson, December 6, 1943. Ibid., p.234.
11 *The Architectural Forum*. January 1948, p.120.
12 Frank Lloyd Wright to the apprentices, February 10, 1957. AV#1014.182.
13 AV# 1014.252.

PART SIX: BUILDINGS FOR THE CITY

1 John Lloyd Wright. *My Father Who Is on Earth* (New York: Putnam's Sons, 1946) p.63.
2 Alofsin dissertation (per Peter Reed, May 14, 1993) p.212.
3 Gookin to Wright, October 16, 1911.
4. Wright to Martin, June 1913, 1911.
5 Frank Lloyd Wright. *An Autobiography*, p.217-218.
6 Frank Lloyd Wright. *An Autobiography*, p.220-221.
7 Ibid., p.222.
8 Ibid., p.222-223.
9 *Frank Lloyd Wright Collected Writings Volume 5* (New York: Rizzoli, 1995) p.124-5.
10 Frank Lloyd Wright. *An Autobiography*, p.254-5.
11 *Frank Lloyd Wright Letters to Architects*. B. B. Pfeiffer, ed. (Fresno: The Press at California State University, Fresno, 1984), p.58.
12 Frank Lloyd Wright. *An Autobiography*, p.258.
13 Ibid., p.259.
14 Ibid., p.255.
15 Wright to Thurman, August 27, 1940.
16 *The Architectural Forum*, January 1948, p.116.
17 Ibid.
18 Curtis Besinger. *Working With Mr. Wright* (Cambridge University Press, 1995) p.156.
19 *The Architectural Forum*, January 1938, p.123.
20 Frank Lloyd Wright. Mss. #AV2401.621 copy D, p.1.
21 Frank Lloyd Wright to the Taliesin Fellowship August 19, 1956. AV#1014.167 pp.10-11.
22 A design in 1956 for a 50-story apartment tower on Lake Shore Drive, not built.
23 Frank Lloyd Wright to the Taliesin Fellowship, December 30, 1956. AV#1014.178, pp.6-8.
24 Frank Lloyd Wright. *The Disappearing City* (New York: William Farquhar Payson, 1932) p.3.
25 Ibid., p.17.
26 Frank Lloyd Wright *When Democracy Builds* (Chicago: University of Chicago Press, 1945, 1947) introduction, vi.
27 Frank Lloyd Wright. *The Living City* (New York: Horizon Press, 1958) p.222.

PART SEVEN: INTEGRAL ORNAMENT: DESIGNS FOR A BOOK, A MAGAZINE, A MURAL, AND A THEATER CURTAIN

1. Frank Lloyd Wright: talk to the Taliesin Fellowship October 23, 1955. AV#1014.145.
2. *An American Architecture Frank Lloyd Wright*. Edgar Kaufmann, ed., p.223.
3. Frank Lloyd Wright Collected Writings Volume 1, p.269.

INDEX *Numbers in italics indicate illustrations.*

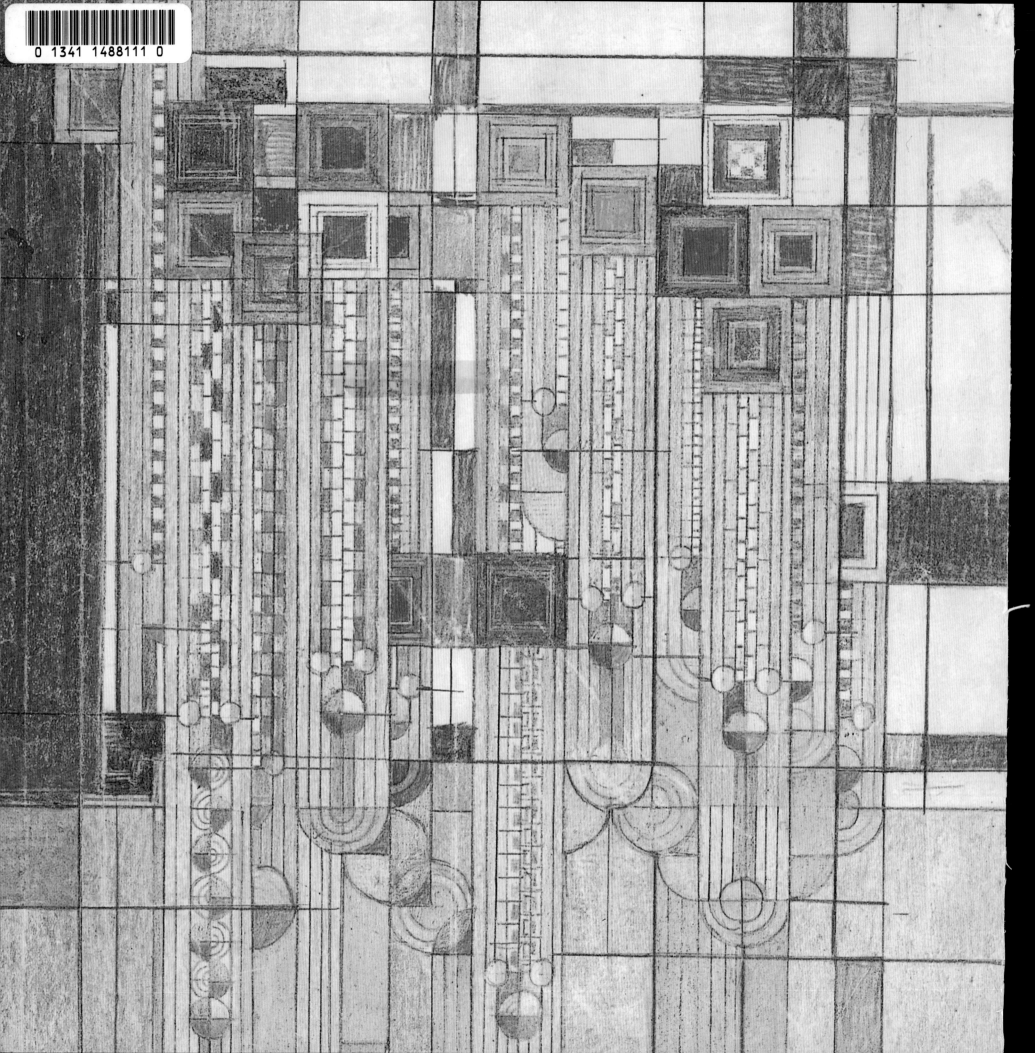